DIVINE FIRE

DIVINE FIRE

EIGHT CONTEMPORARY PLAYS
INSPIRED BY THE GREEKS

EDITED BY CARIDAD SVICH

BACK STAGE BOOKS
NEW YORK

Senior Editor: Mark Glubke
Project Editor: Gary Sunshine
Cover and Interior Design: Areta Buk/Thumb Print
Production Manager: Hector Campbell

Front cover photo from 7 Stages' production of *Iphigenia Crash
Land Falls on the Neon Shell That Was Once Her Heart (a rave fable)*
directed by Melissa Foulger. Photo: Yvonne Boyd and 7 Stages.

First published in 2005 by Back Stage Books,
an imprint of Watson-Guptill Publications,
a division of VNU Business Media, Inc.
770 Broadway, New York, NY 10003
www.wgpub.com

Library of Congress Control Number: 2005924516

ISBN: 0-8230-8851-0

Manufactured in the United States of America

First printing 2005

2 3 4 5 6 7 8 9 / 11 10 09 08 07 06

﷽

DEDICATED TO MY PARENTS
FOR TEACHING ME TO HONOR THE PAST,

AND TO THE ANCIENT GREEK DRAMATISTS
WHO, OVER TIME, CONTINUE TO TEACH US ALL
SO VERY MUCH ABOUT WHO WE ARE.

CONTENTS

ACKNOWLEDGMENTS

This book would not be possible without the artists who contributed their time and work so generously. New Dramatists in New York and Inge Center for the Arts in Kansas provided practical support during editing. Thanks to Tom Cole at True Love Productions, Mitchell Gossett and James Martin at Bottom's Dream, Del Hamilton at 7 Stages, DD Kugler at Simon Fraser University, James Leverett at Yale School of Drama, Todd London, Artistic Director at New Dramatists, Claire MacDonald at *Performance Research,* Ted Shank and Adele Shank at University of California-San Diego, Kathy Sova at TCG, Maria M. Delgado, Madeline Dewhurst, Daniel Fish, Joanna Laurens, Alejandro Morales, Rozzy Wilks, and the dramaturges and students at the National Theater of Greece (Summer Academy, July 2000). Likewise to the photographers who graciously provided their photos. Special thanks to Liz Duffy Adams, and to Nick Philippou, who were instrumental in making this entire venture a reality, and to Mark Glubke, Gary Sunshine, and Areta Buk at Back Stage Books who kept me on track. As always, my work is not possible without the love and support of Emilio and Aracely Svich.

THE CULTURE WRITES US

There is no such thing as an original play. None of the classical Greek plays was original—they were all based on earlier plays or poems or myths. And none of Shakespeare's plays is original—they are all taken from earlier work. *As You Like It* is taken from a novel by Thomas Lodge published just ten years before Shakespeare put on his play without attribution or acknowledgment. Chunks of *Antony and Cleopatra* are taken verbatim, and, to be sure, without apology, from a contemporary translation of Plutarch's *Lives*. Brecht's *Caucasian Chalk Circle* is taken from a play by Klabund, on which Brecht served as dramaturg in 1926; and Klabund had taken his play from an early Chinese play. Sometimes playwrights steal stories, conversations, and dreams and intimate revelations from their friends and lovers and call this original. And sometimes some of us write about our own innermost lives, believing that, then, we have written something truly unique.

Not long ago I wrote a memoir that had a lot to do with my having had polio as a boy. In the course of thinking about the book, I came across a study by Daniel Wilson, a history professor at Muhlenberg College in Pennsylvania, who had read fifty autobiographies of people who had had polio. Almost all of these narratives, he said, are "accounts of triumphs over adversity"—even though, in fact, a study of eight hundred and six people who had long-term disabilities from polio discovered that 29 percent of them could not feed themselves, nearly 50 percent could not propel a wheelchair by themselves, and 83 percent could not get dressed by themselves. The culture writes us, and then we write our stories.

And yet, we are unique, too. When we look at a painting of the Virgin and Child by Botticelli, we recognize at once that it is a Renaissance painting: a product of its time and place. We may not know or recognize at once that it was painted by Botticelli, but we do see that it is a Renaissance painting. We see that it has been derived from, and authored by, the culture that produced it. We also recognize that this painting of the Virgin and Child is not identical to one by Raphael or Ghirlandaio or Leonardo. So, clearly, while the culture creates much of Botticelli, it is also true that Botticelli creates the culture—that he took the culture into himself and transformed it in his own unique way. This is what artists do. To talk of whether they have produced an adaptation or an original work is misleading: They have done both. This is what they always do, whether they mean to or not.

So here is a collection of plays in which the playwrights openly own up to what they have done. It is refreshingly honest of them. Some of them will have stayed "closer" to the "original" than others—as though any of us had any idea what the original experience of a Greek play might have been. Some have departed quite a distance from what nineteenth-century academics have handed down to us as the authentic Greek experience. All of them have produced work tantalizingly bound and liberated by respect and love and impatience and disgust and admiration and ill will and euphoria and loathing for our common past and present.

One of the great pleasures in a work of art that knows it comes from the culture is that, inevitably, inherently, it contains a tension between the past and the present, the given and the possible, the enduring and the ephemeral. This tension between what has been made and what can be re-made lives in the very essence of the work—so that our common human project of making life on earth, making a society, making a bearable or wonderful civilization, is alive in every particle of the work. And so we have, in these works, intrinsically, as great a human drama as we get.

Charles L. Mee

DIVINE FIRE:
THE MYTH OF ORIGIN

"Artists are always invoking the Muses and usually overlooking the goddess who (with the help of the ever-ready Zeus) gave birth to them. She was Mnemosyne, the goddess of memory, and she is having her day now. Never has art sought so many ways of remembering its past, and never have artists or audiences been exposed to so many pasts."[1]

The Information Age has changed the way we view the past, and in part unleashed a desire to retrieve knowledge that has been seemingly buried in the great quest for progress. The turn of a millennium has also caused Western society to try to imagine Web link upon Web link what our origins must have been like. Easy access to information and the multiplicity of it has made us a curious and "curiouser" breed, to paraphrase Lewis Carroll. We have become enraptured by the possibilities available to us and the immediacy with which we can conjure ancient Greece, Rome, or Egypt. This imaginative act of conjuring, aided by technology, has affected how we interpret our world. Histories whirl in bits and bytes and bleeps, and as artists and citizens we try to keep up by taking time to remember. We seek myth because it is our inheritance. In it, we look for our origins. We are all Euripides' children, dreaming of an Agamemnon and a Clytemnestra, who were our parents.

In the body of Greek theatre, it is said that Aeschylus is the head, Sophocles the heart, and Euripides the stomach. Radical in his time, Euripides' worldview reflected the political, social, and intellectual crisis of late fifth-century Athens. All but one of his surviving tragedies were written during the Peloponnesian War, which eventually destroyed Athens. The spirit of rage and crisis is ruthlessly felt in his writing. Less reverent than Aeschylus or Sophocles, Euripides criticized traditional religion and shocked contemporaries by representing mythical figures as everyday, even neurotic figures. Such representation feels absolutely contemporary, and therein lies Euripides' great genius as a dramatist. It is not surprising, thus, that playwrights keep returning to Euripides' versions of the great myths, for with each generation his deeply human, cutting, dramatically varied and briskly paced plays resonate with the horrors of the time.

Theatre, ancient already and called "dead" many times over, has been finding ways to speak to its past for many years. Each generation "kills" what has come before it, and resurrects it at the same time. Art is made through active renewal and reinterpretation. Realism has left a strong mark on Western drama, but a whole tradition of work created in rebellion against realism has also emerged. From reinvestigations of expressionism, futurism and Dada to New Vaudeville's reinterpretation of classic *commedia* and clowning, there have been many reactions against realism in contemporary theatre.

Playwrights have played scavenger throughout time with Shakespeare, Chekhov, Ibsen, and Moliere. Part of the dramatic tradition is the re-imagining or lifting of plots and stories from old texts and remaking them for a new audience. In the last twenty years or so, a growing neoclassical movement has emerged in U.S. playwriting in particular. Experiments into the ancient repertoire by theatrical mavericks of the 1960s and 1970s like Andrei Serban, Elizabeth Swados, Grotowski, and the Living Theatre, which culminated to some degree in Lee Breuer and Robert Telson's majestic, controversial 1983 staging of *The Gospel at Colonus*, revealed the inherently dramatic possibilities of the plays by Sophocles, Aeschylus, and Euripides and their remarkable immediacy in an increasingly violent world. These daring explorations have opened the gates for new playwrights to fearlessly take on these classics in their own tongue.

> *"We can get in contact with a guy who died a couple of centuries ago. We can do this with Aeschylus. This is the interesting point, to have made a telephone call over centuries and centuries; to have the illusion that there is a direct contact possible."* [2]

This book began in Greece in the year 2000 when I was workshopping my version of Euripides' *Iphigenia at Aulis* with director Nick Philippou and the U.K.'s Actors Touring Company at the Euripides Festival in Monodendri (sponsored by the National Theatre of Greece). The living possibility of direct contact as described by stage director Peter Stein in the quote above was more than palpable as we rehearsed outdoors in a modern ancient-style amphitheatre nestled in the hills near the Balkans. During the day, students and dramaturges from the National Theatre of Greece's Summer Academy actively engaged Euripides' text in ancient and modern-language Greek. In the evenings, we developed a contemporary vocabulary and language to retell Euripides' story. It was as if we were on an archaeological dig, excavating the past whole to bring it into the present, stealing time along the way. Euripides was indeed reachable to us. Not distant. Not even ancient. And we wondered what tricks of time were being played on us as we made the work come alive and breathe.

The 'trick,' as it turned out, was that no metaphorical time had passed. This is what artists have known about the Greeks and these classic stories for centuries: They are alive, and reflective of who we are because these stories not only repeat themselves through history, but they are also indelibly part of our Western psyche. The myths live inside us. And it is our right to 'steal' them, because they belong to all of us.

回回回

One of the leading practitioners of the great art of "stealing text" is historian and playwright Charles L. Mee. His dedication toward the iconoclastic reimagining of classic Greek tragedies and myths, and his work with adventurous directors like Tina Landau, Anne Bogart, Daniel Fish, and Robert Woodruff, has created a significant foundation for emerging writers to extend their options as playwrights. Mee's remaking of theatrical history, through performance texts, collages, and performative experiments with time and narrative, has served as the inspiration point, and at times, the meeting point for much of contemporary neo-classical playwriting.

In this volume, Charles L. Mee offers us not only his gracious preface, "The Culture Writes Us," but also his play *True Love*, a decidedly raucous, bawdy, and comically extreme take on Euripides' *Hippolytus*. Originally staged at the Zipper Theatre in New York in 2001 under Daniel Fish's direction, *True Love* is set in an American roadside landscape of gas stations, old cars, and electric guitars. The play is like a William Eggleston U.S. road snapshot come to life. In it the classic character of Phaedra is called Polly and the object of her tortured affection is a young boy named Edward. Amped up and revved up, the play, similar in its musical impulse to some of the other texts in this volume, is a fantasia on love filled with verbal and instrumental riffs, 'routines' delivered (in the William Burroughs sense of the term) by secondary and tertiary characters, and tragicomic duets enacted by principal figures aware they are being watched by twenty-first-century eyes. Yet, these characters are mindful that they have also lived centuries ago and have indeed been telling this story for some time. History is deeply embedded in them.

In *True Love*, the characters are almost beyond history's reach. The passionate nature of the tale and the deep incestuous feelings that Euripides (and Seneca and Racine after him) explored with terseness and depth have spilled over into delirious wretched excess in this American backwater, where even the signs on the billboards are missing letters. It is as if Mee has recovered and restored whole in spirit Euripides' first attempt at dramatizing Phaedra's story, which has only survived in fragments. From documentation it is known that in Euripides' first *Hippolytus* Phaedra loved shamelessly and lied blatantly. Phaedra's shameless nature is restored in his version. He frames the story through a talk-radio show, a kind of rustic Howard Stern-like slice of vulgar Americana where local tabloid scandals are aired and debated, as the Greek myths were debated publicly by dramatists in Euripides' time.

Mee's play is a furious and ultimately despondent version of this classic tale of desperate, irrational love. Redemption and renewal are barely possible in a landscape ruined by greed and cultural waste. *True Love* is a violent and appropriately mournful play for our times. It lives in the liminal space occupied by dreams. It is a dream itself enacted onstage, a dream of living, of wanting very much to transcend profound pain and desolation. Written with savage wit, Mee's play serves as a template for the wide range of work that encompasses the dramatic writing of this new brand of neoclassicists.

While Mee's *True Love* shows us a side of Euripides that we may not have intuited, Ruth Margraff's libretto *The Elektra Fugues* takes a wildly Euripidean approach (with nods to Sophocles' version of the story as well) to the tale of the vengeful daughter clothed in grief at her father's death. The piece was originally conceived and produced as an opera at HERE Performance Center in New York in 1996. However, it has also been performed as a play with live percussion at a running time of ninety minutes at Bottom's Dream Theatre in Los Angeles in 1999 under James Martin's direction. Margraff's text is a fusion of punk angst, classical purity, feminist politics, dysfunctional family satire, and holy trouble unbound. Breaking apart the Electra myth to examine and reawaken its anguish and humor for a new audience, the play seeks to reconfigure the many variants of the myth through a language that swirls, tumults, and does backflips in true Kerouac-like fashion.

Margraff's retelling begins a year after Agamemnon sacrifices the life of his daughter, Iphigenia, to the goddess Artemis, who returns the payment with friendly breezes for his fleet of warships. Upon Agamemnon's return to Greece, he's murdered by his wife Clytemnestra, with the help of her lover, Aegisthus. Two of Agamemnon's surviving children—the raging Elektra and her sister, the dutiful Chrysothemis—remain in Mycenae to grieve; the third child, the boy Orestes, escapes to parts unknown. Young Elektra screams at her mother while calling upon the recorded image of Agamemnon to justify the sacrifice of her sister, and to help avenge his own murder.

Both Sophocles and Euripides' versions are chiefly about how the force of vengeance can atomize a family; Margraff's play is about pulling body parts from the wreckage. For Margraff this wreckage includes the many versions of the myth itself and how it has been interpreted over time. *The Elektra Fugues* is a play about what survives, and about what voices can tell us before they are consumed in an emotional, psychological, or physical crash.

In *Electra*, Euripides parodies the Aeschylean recognition scene (which Margraff reparodies as well) while at the same time offering bleak scenes of psychological realism, which seem to anticipate much of modern drama's realistic focus. Euripides shifts emotional and tonal registers in his play. Margraff honors him by faithfully, in a contemporary modernist voice, shifting not only registers and tonalities, but also our perceptions of Electra, Iphigenia, and Clytemnestra. Playing at the ripe end of extremity in its passions and style, *The Elektra Fugues* is ultimately a tale of a sad little-girl-lost desperately in love with the memory of her father. For all its many rhetorical turns and mordant illuminations, it remains eerily faithful to its origins: a story of profound rage, gallows humor, and psychological disassociation.

Disguised as a straightforward telling of Euripides' *The Trojan Women*, Karen Hartman's *Troy Women*, originally produced at Yale Repertory Theatre in 1997, is a sly and disturbing vision of women devastated by a society that has made them inhuman, powerless, and power mad. There is no respite in this version of the tragic story of Hecuba, Cassandra, and the death of Astyanax. In its cadence and form, Hartman's adaptation is perhaps the most "traditional" of the plays in this volume. It follows Euripides' plot and structure. It is part of a long and rich line of sharp-tongued, modern-language retellings of classic plays, which include Kenneth McLeish and Frederic Raphael's notable *Medea* staged by Deborah Warner in the U.K. and New York with actor Fiona Shaw in the lead, and John Barton's epic ten-part *Tantalus* staged by Peter Hall. Unlike Mee and Margraff, Hartman does not seek to completely recontextualize the original. Her goal is to get under its skin, to find a contemporary voice within the given form, and by so doing cut her own path as a writer. The play opens in Troy. The city has been sacked, the plunder divided, the women violated, and the men killed. Only a few women remain, and they wait to be told which men have chosen them as mistresses and slaves. Hartman lays bare the pain of these women in language that is direct, poetically specific, and distinct. Her artful manner and compassionate tone, which are evident in her own "original" plays, prevail here, as she remembers the women of Troy for a new age.

At almost opposite ends of the spectrum we find Matthew Maguire and Susan Yankowitz. Both playwrights have chosen to tell their versions of Euripides' *Hippolytus*. *Hippolytus* in fact is one of the Greek classics most adapted by dramatists through the ages. The complex emotional pull of the story has memorably inspired in recent years not only the gut poetry of the late Sarah Kane's version *Phaedra in Love* staged at the Gate Theatre in London in 1996, but also Paul Schmidt's eloquently visceral version re-adapted by The Wooster Group as *To You, the Birdie!* in New York in 2002. Like Mee in *True Love*, Maguire and Yankowitz have clearly soaked up many of the story's surviving versions, yet the three contemporary plays couldn't be more different from each other in language, tone, spirit, and sensibility.

Matthew Maguire chooses Racine's classic *Phedre* as his model while Yankowitz decides to play with variants of the myth, not unlike Margraff chose to do in *The Elektra Fugues*. Maguire's *Phaedra*, originally produced at HERE Theatre in New York in 1995, is cool, remorseless, sexual, and bone-dry in its wit. Here Phaedra is called Faye, Hippolytus is named William, and the setting is an upper-class American home. This is the story of the stepmother who falls in love with her son, told with a nod to the charged landscapes of painter Alex Katz and filmmaker David Lynch. Maguire exposes the anatomy of an American society fueled by corporate greed and puritanical repression, a society that must break down at all costs. Tragic and erotic in tone, *Phaedra* exhibits Maguire's tensile language and keen eye for detail.

In Yankowitz's *Phaedra in Delirium*, originally produced by Classic Stage Company in New York in 1998, Phaedra is both victim and pursuer. She is victim to the mirror and age. And her pursuit of Hippolytus has as much to do with her own sexual desire as a longing to regain a measure of youth. She is taunted by Hippolytus and ruined by lies. Her bed is center stage. It is the altar upon which the anatomy of her sexual desire will be dissected. This Phaedra is undone not by an America that has lost its core, but by a body that cannot control her will. Suffused with irony, Yankowitz's play portrays a loveless marriage and doomed affair with equal parts serenity and horror.

The oft-told tale of Orpheus and Eurydice receives a whimsical, dreamlike treatment from playwright Sarah Ruhl. Determined to shoot down what has become an almost over-romantic excess in the telling of this Greek myth over time, and especially in the rich, classic Brazilian film *Black Orpheus* which has made the tale even more lush and melodramatic, Ruhl tells the story from Eurydice's point of view, and uses a plain-spoken and very American language to unburden this poignant love story. Delicate and ironic, Ruhl's *Eurydice*, which premiered at Madison Repertory Theatre in 2003, shares some of Mee's playfulness of spirit and poker-faced style. She seeks not to reduce the tale, but to find in it a warmth, humor, and sadness perhaps an audience may not have previously imagined.

15

An impressionistic interpretation of the haunting tale, Ruhl's *Eurydice* speaks to the potency of the myths, and to the bonds of family which these myths speak to again and again. Eurydice's father is at the heart of her play. In the afterlife, he watches her and meets her in death. The father seeks to counsel the daughter and wishes to share his past with her. It is a past she does not recognize. In fact, she does not recognize anyone in the limbo Ruhl depicts. Stuck in blankness without memory, Eurydice is pulled by emotional forces she cannot understand, and in the end, cannot completely resolve.

Full of ferocious wit, media artist John Jesurun's tour de force version of *Philoktetes* was originally written for the late actor Ron Vawter, legendary member of The Wooster Group. In Sophocles' tragedy the Greek warrior Philoktetes, who during the conquest of Troy was bitten by a snake, is left behind by Odysseus on the island of Lemnos. Unlike documented versions of the Aeschylus and Euripides tellings of the myth, Sophocles depicted the island of Lemnos, where Philoktetes has been exiled, as uninhabited, thereby making Philoktetes' isolation seem greater and the Greeks' treatment of him more cruel. Jesurun retains the isolation of Sophocles' version, and picks up when Odysseus returns to the island, after many years, accompanied by the young Neoptolemos. In Jesurun's text, the meeting between Philoktetes and Odysseus becomes a sardonic battle of wills, as well as a living autopsy of a dying man's life.

Street-smart and adrenaline-charged in its poetry, Jesurun's play places Philoktetes on the rock and the rack as he is interrogated, dismissed, and empowered by political and bodily forces set squarely against him. The elemental force of witnessing the emotional and physical devastation of Philoktetes as he learns to speak the language of the dead is testament to the structural strength of Sophocles' text, as well as this idiosyncratic reinterpretation by Jesurun. This is a tale of ravaging illness, delusion, paranoia, delirium, and beauty. Set firmly and fluidly in a queer context, it is almost impossible to read this play without thinking about AIDS, and thus to view Philoktetes as the embodiment of illness and its raging voice: as one cast off by society, marginalized on an island, doomed to dubious extinction. War, in this scenario, literally leads nowhere.

Inspired in part by Calderon de la Barca's *The Monster in the Garden* (1667), Racine's *Iphigenia* (1674), and Gluck's 1774 opera, my *Iphigenia Crash Land Falls on the Neon Shell That Was Once Her Heart (a rave fable)*, which premiered at 7 Stages in Atlanta in 2004, is a socio-sexual-political riff on not only these versions but chiefly Euripides' *Iphigenia at Aulis*. Set in an unnamed Latin American country mired in war and violence, suffused with the emblems and icons of rave culture, this text shows us an Iphigenia who is not only in the present but also in the past. She is aware of her myth and living it. Released from the thread of time yet trapped inside the systematic corruption of a society which will not give her a voice, Iphigenia, in this trance tale of death and ecstasy, tries to claim her body before it is taken by the state and the cult of celebrity.

Taking after Racine's version especially in the second act, my *Iphigenia Crash Land Falls . . .* centers on Iphigenia and Achilles' erotic dance of desire. Here Achilles is re-found as a gender-fluid mythic hero encased in his own celebrity:

a split soul remade into a new shape, thus, for all time. A symbolic contract has been made between Achilles and society, as one has been made between Iphigenia and society. In this play, one mythic twin meets another, and in altered states their wounds are illuminated.

The multilevel psychosexual dynamics inherent in both the Euripides and Racine versions are brought to the fore in this hybrid adaptation. It localizes the family story at the heart of the Euripides telling while setting it in a political frame of comparable city-state warfare; it also recovers Iphigenia's sacrificial body and positions it within a contemporary ritual of psychological-physical transport. Dancing on many borders, the text, which incorporates film, video, a satyr play, and songs, sets up a visual and verbal theatrical world which conjures up images of recent political horrors. Yet, it is deeply rooted in the sacrifice of Iphigenia, which Euripides effectively and compassionately delineated in his last and, arguably unfinished, play.

回回回

In times of war, and extreme global conflict and division, Greek dramas rise to the fore on the world's stages. During World War II Jean Anouilh's *Antigone*, a version of Sophocles' classical drama, became a worldwide hit, because of its thinly disguised attack on the Nazis and the Vichy government. Bertolt Brecht's 1948 *Antigone* achieved international recognition due to its uncompromising attack on tyranny, while Sophocles' play also served as the centerpiece of Athol Fugard's acclaimed South African protest drama *The Island*. During the Vietnam War and its immediate aftermath, powerful adaptations of the Greeks were presented in New York by the Living Theatre, and Andrei Serban at La Mama. Feminist versions of Greek drama such as the French director Ariane Minouchkine's famous *Les Atrides* (a tetralogy including the *Iphigeneia at Aulis* and the *Oresteia*), the English poet Tony Harrison's *Medea: A Sex War Opera*, and U.S. playwright and actor Ellen McLaughlin's *Iphigeneia and Other Daughters* also have contributed significantly to the revival of interest in the Greeks.

In the 2003–2004 English-language theatre season, Katie Mitchell staged Don Taylor's new adaptation of *Iphigenia at Aulis* at the Royal National Theatre in London; this was a significant production since it was the first time the play had ever been produced at the National, one of the most venerable arts institutions devoted to the classics and new work. At the Young Vic Theatre, also in London, Martin Crimp's reworking of Sophocles' *Trachiniae*, entitled *Cruel and Tender*, premiered to critical acclaim in a production staged by Luc Bondy. Dance Theatre Workshop in New York and Classical Stage Company presented Mac Wellman's *Antigone*. In Austin, Texas, Alice Tuan's radical, porno riff on Sophocles' play *Ajax*, entitled *Ajax (por nobody)*, was presented at Salvage Vanguard Theatre, one of the U.S.'s most dynamic, progressive companies for new work. The Goodman Theatre in Chicago premiered Latino playwright-poet Luis Alfaro's *Electricidad*, a Chicana take on the Electra myth; Ellen McLaughlin's *The Persians* was presented by Tony Randall's National Actors Theatre; and John Epperson (aka Lypsinka)'s scabrous version of *Medea*, entitled *My Deah*, is scheduled to premiere.

Awash in the ceremony of memory initiated by the Information Age, the plays in this volume and the many others which have been and are being produced and written—from Colin Teevan's North Irish *Iph* . . . to Katie O'Reilly and Graeae Theatre Company's *Peeling* (a radical reconsideration of *The Trojan Women*), from the low-tech vaudeville of the New York City–based company Elevator Repair Service's *The Bacchae* to British playwright Joanna Laurens' revolutionary take on Sophocles' fragments *The Three Birds*—are all (as are many more) imaginatively "remaking the Greeks," to borrow Charles L. Mee's phrase. They are finding their way to the origins of myth by calling down the spirits of the past and invoking them for time present and future. In his instructive and illuminating afterword, "Towards a Vertical Theatre," eminent Irish dramatist and translator Colin Teevan reflects on why communities continue to find Greek drama relevant, and why it will always serve as a useful prism for our most profound human stories.

A new group of playwrights, determined to reengage the power and humor of Greek classics, is creating a contemporary canon of work shot through with a cyber pulse that speaks to our times. The energy throbbing through these works underscores the many Web-link references that run through our brains today as we watch the Trojan women, Phaedra, Orpheus, Elektra, and Iphigenia walk on our stages again. In delivering these daring works to us, these writers not only perform a significant act of cultural retrieval, but also infuse a breath and life into the stories we always thought we knew.

Caridad Svich

TROY
WOMEN

ADAPTED FROM EURIPIDES

KAREN HARTMAN

PHOTO: A. VINCENT SCARANO

KAREN HARTMAN is the author of seventeen plays with over fifty productions worldwide. *Anatomy 1968* was produced at the Summer Play Festival on Theater Row. *Going Gone* premiered at Cincinnati Playhouse in the Park, receiving an NEA Special Project Grant. She is the librettist of an opera, *MotherBone*, composed by Graham Reynolds, that won the Frederick Loewe Award in New Music Theatre and broke attendance records at Salvage Vanguard Theater in Austin. *Gum* received its world premiere at Center Stage in Baltimore, its West Coast premiere at the Magic Theatre in San Francisco, its New York premiere at Women's Project & Productions, and is published as a trade paperback by Theatre Communications Group and an acting edition by Dramatists Play Service, together with her one-act *The Mother of Modern Censorship*.

She has been honored with two NEA grants, the Daryl Roth Creative Spirit Award, a Hodder Fellowship at Princeton University, a Jerome Fellowship in Minneapolis, a Fulbright Scholarship in Jerusalem, and residencies at the Royal National Theatre in London, the O'Neill Playwrights Conference, and the MacDowell Colony.

Karen Hartman is a resident writer and board member of New Dramatists. She teaches playwriting at the Yale School of Drama, where she earned an M.F.A. in Playwriting (A.S.C.A.P. Cole Porter Prize, Truman Capote Fellowship, Foster Family Scholarship) and a B.A. in Literature with honors from Yale University (Veech Writing Prize). She lives in Brooklyn.

From the Writer
KAREN HARTMAN

Adapting *The Trojan Women* was like performing a glorious gymnastics move with a spotter. You can't do the trick, but you feel what it might be like if you could. Line by line, image by image, I stepped into the shoes of a great play, and Euripides became my teacher. This tale of war, aging, complicity, love, and defeat begins on the worst day of a mythic queen's life, then descends. *The Trojan Women* touches bottom, the floor of human possibility, the low note of survival. Working my way through it taught me how to dive for that bottom.

Euripides wrote a flexible play, stately, sometimes funny, measured, and beyond sad. To walk with it awhile, take from it, hopefully give to it, blew open my personal ideas of what I could approach in terms of subject and tone. I hope that great tragedy, newly adapted or not, has a similarly expansive effect on an audience: an experimental stab at the edges of human experience.

The Trojan Women occurs in the last hours on vanquished ground. If history is written by the victors, here is a Greek man's effort to resurrect or at least imagine the remnants of a great culture—its female survivors—in the moment before they are dispersed and absorbed by Greece. Euripides' search for the defeated point of view transcends any contemporary sense of identity politics. His balance of entitlement and respect strikes me as a lingering golden mean of playwriting.

Following Erik Overmyer's advice about adaptation, I read ten translations, then wrote a first draft by rereading twenty lines at a time in the ten versions, closing the books, writing that passage, and checking to see if I missed anything. The plotline itself is elemental: Yesterday's queen is a slave. Surviving subjects convene. Three women—prophet, exemplar, and seductress—appear and speak their cases. A messenger entangles himself with the message, then hardens his heart and spearheads the final attack. What resonated for me were Euripides' perspective and sense of scale, as well as questions about how the loss of a culture is felt through time.

Perhaps the pre–twentieth-century tradition of writing tragedy about royals was based on a yearning for scale, a means of magnifying human loss, madness, compromise, and desire. In *Troy Women*, I chose to keep the gods. I kept Hecuba's hundred children. I wanted this world to be larger than life, to show the deities abandoning Troy at the beginning and Hecuba mourning outside the reach of biological possibility. Yet *The Trojan Women* is also detailed, tiny, much of the imagery domestic and palm-size. Euripides' tragedy sits in the body. Hecuba speaks of her dead king, then her roiling gut, her slaughtered daughters, and her whitened hair. I love that disconcerting pattern of shifting scale, and I tried to maintain it.

Hecuba, in her misery, nobility, and fullness of response, remains a protagonist although the events of the play happen to her. This majestic loser is the shadow under a culture of winning. Hecuba stays active by remembering, shifting, trying, transforming. She is of our own species, this mother of a hundred, the queen who lost her lover, king, and kingdom just before dawn. She is nauseated. She is tired. She is not smaller for being nauseated and tired, only closer, fuller, and more inhabited.

I started pondering the costs of the Trojan defeat through time. Troy to me became a suppressed myth, a lost possibility, an annihilated cultural ancestor. Destroying this civilization meant losing an alternate way of being, reducing our human scope. Cassandra and the ending are probably the most distinctive aspects of my adaptation, because they relate to the process of history. She is a prophet, so her language is modern. The chorus is made up of differentiated women; they change and get historical, gaining perspective. They speak as their own cultural descendants at the end of *Troy Women,* asking: "What would be the West with a second cradle?"

Now feels like a Euripidean era, a time to get past the concept of victory, a time to look at what happens when the dominant absorbs the rest. These women of Troy, five common, three royal, one foreign, all exiles, traverse millennia in a single day. They take a fistful of dust and move.

The Trojan Women is all denouement, all aftermath, the pause between vanquished and gone. Memory exists in that pause, and response, and if not hope (the day is long prior to hope), then maybe the beginning of narrative, of grief. Troy turns into sentences about what occurred and how, sentences that if strung precisely, leaving in the small parts, might reflect and refract a buried legacy.

PRODUCTION HISTORY

Yale School of Drama/Yale Repertory Theatre's
production of *Troy Women,* directed by Laura
Stribling. PHOTO: YALE SCHOOL OF DRAMA

Troy Women opened at the Yale School of Drama/Yale Repertory Theatre on
January 14, 1997. It was directed by Laura Stribling. The set design was by Louisa
Thompson; costume design was by Cristina M. Desrosiers-Ruales; lighting
design was by Daniel Meeker. The cast included Amy Cronise as Andromache
and Tessa Auberjonois as Cassandra.

CHARACTERS

POSEIDON, God of the Sea
ATHENA, Goddess of War
HECUBA, Queen of Troy
TALTHYBIUS, a Greek Herald
CASSANDRA, Princess of Troy, a prophet
ANDROMACHE, Widow of Hector, Prince of Troy
MENELAUS, Greek General
HELEN, Estranged wife of Menelaus; the most ravishing woman in the world

CHORUS OF FIVE TROJAN WOMEN:
1 Attendant to Hecuba, Hecuba's age
2 Her daughter, still a girl
3 Spirited
4 Romantic
5 Mother of sons

ATTENDANTS to Talthybius and Menelaus
VOICE OF THE CITY (possibly Poseidon's voice)

SETTING

The remnants of Troy. Near the Greek camp.

NOTE

Overlapping text is indicated by an asterisk (*) at the place where the following line begins.

Troy. Dawn after the fall. The men are dead and the women are captives. **HECUBA**
lies on the ground. The sea-god **POSEIDON** *surveys the ruin.*

POSEIDON: Call me god of the deep.
I live lulled by the dance of sea maids
churning tide, breaking waves, and drifting to rest
regular as the moon.
Now I rise to inspect a wreck
built by my own hands in a time of sun, worship, and water without horizon.

She took into her gates an offering:
a victory token built grand
a pride horse.
The belly split, and with it my fragile, childish clarity
that she was a city of cities
an unbreakable girl
my Troy.

Blood bubbles under the shields of soldiers
runs ripped from the cheeks of women
who tear flesh in sorrow
in sympathy
to stay hot, red, and alive
within cold and conquered stone.

Blood blankets the ruin of my altar
bathes Priam, sprawled on his own steps,
not like a king at all
as I am so unlike a god.

This city of rubble, of widows, of ash
has no faith to spare
for me.

The Greeks take what they want,
toss treasure like fruit into ships
waiting for wind.
After ten years it is hard to leave
even the place you crushed.

They'll dream of my city like a faraway whore:
Fallen, open, and owned.

HECUBA: Lift.

POSEIDON: Hecuba weeps.
The queen mourns her subjects
Shackled now to Greeks.

No man can leave battle for a lonely bed.
Sex makes him feel home.

Even a live body to bear his weight in sleep
is comforting.

The soldiers drew lots, as civilized men
democratic
split the spoils fairly.

The promised ones huddle and scream
broken-voiced good-byes
to a grave and to each other.

The princesses wait inside, unassigned
wanted by chiefs.
Even this golden age is ranked.

Slippery Helen will go captive to he who can keep her.
Now she stews in her own hell:
a palace of virtuous, vengeful women.

HECUBA: Your.

POSEIDON: Hecuba weeps.
A mother's nightmare.
Husband, sons, and city gone.
Only mortal, she does not see
the balance of this day.

Where is your tiniest girl?
Polyxena burns on Achilles's grave.
An offering.

What becomes of your prophetess daughter?
Cassandra will squirm under a greedy hero
on a ship to a woman clever and angry as yourself.
She will sing her own dirge.
She will be right after all.

HECUBA: Head.

POSEIDON: Weep, Hecuba.
May tears coat you like a shield
so you can fight.

Blame Athena.
Only a virgin goddess of war would break a mother's spine.

  [ATHENA enters.]

ATHENA: Great God Poseidon.
I need you now.
We are related. You're very powerful.
Let's be friends.

POSEIDON: I could not hate you, Athena.
We are too close.

ATHENA: Good. I have a proposal.

POSEIDON: From Zeus?

ATHENA: For Troy.

POSEIDON: The ruin that once was Troy. You feel pity now?

ATHENA: I want to hurt the Greeks. Will you help?
I want to make their trip home a hell.

POSEIDON: Are you fickle on top of cruel?
The invaders were your pets these ten years.
Why the sudden shift?

ATHENA: My temple.

POSEIDON: Ajax raped Cassandra right inside your temple.

ATHENA: War is an enterprise.
There are casualties. But there are limits.
He acts like war is a ticket to chaos
Like war kills order
When war is order.
Yet he goes unpunished.
Something has happened to the Greeks.

POSEIDON: Victory.

ATHENA: I want them dead. Zeus agrees.
I have lightning to use when I want. He'll send rain.
Your job is to churn up the sea and sink them.
Teach them we are gods.
Teach them to conquer without desecrating.
Teach them even victors must stay human.

POSEIDON: Here was a charmed place
whose violence was all in the sea.

ATHENA: Your memory bogs.
In peace they get fleshy and selfish.
When Paris of Troy wanted Helen, he took her.
Menelaus led the fight for his love
but a phalanx formed on both sides.
War is how the world changes.
Men know.
The battle was bitter and clean.
Masters of combat eye to eye.
It became . . . inefficient . . . somehow.

POSEIDON: Gray-eyed and clear.
Action herself.

ATHENA: Tears won't raise the sea.

POSEIDON: Like water I soaked into Troy.
Like a tide I crash and creep away.

ATHENA: She is no city now.
No army.
No fight.

POSEIDON: The people now women of Troy.
Will I echo in their drops?

ATHENA: Dry out.
Avenge and forget.

POSEIDON: Abandon and sink.
I will swallow the ships.

[*The gods abandon Troy.*]

HECUBA: Lift your head.
This is Troy.
Don't wrestle with the wind.
Don't shout into a storm.
When the tide turns it takes you, willing or not.
Why struggle?

Every sorrow is mine.
A legend of loss—man, boys, and town.
Glory to nothing, kingdom to dust.
Do I weep? Do I sob? Do I scream?

My back hurts.
Someone switched my bed for a pile of stones
My gown for this rag
Me for a bent slave-woman.
My head throbs.
My stomach churns like a boat
flipped on a rhythmic and random sea.

On a bright day a decade ago we heard music martial music and looked to sea
a fleet bobbing over the deep. Drums and melody. The lovestruck idiot
Menelaus calls to recapture her. Her. She had oozed herself into my son's bed.
Wanted his purity, nobility, his flesh. That kind of a woman. Two men
dueling is not enough. She needs a war. Salt in the soil. Priam and all fifty of
our slaughtered sons. To feel attractive.

I am suddenly old.
My hair is white and besides I hacked it with a knife.

I sit by Agamemnon's tent.

We can still make noise.
Orphans! Mothers! Widows!
Your Queen Hecuba could sing and move like a leader
Taught you intricate melodies, delicate steps.
Now let me organize the weeping.
Show a new dance.
Our cries will rise faster than smoke.
Your mother gull calls shrill and empty over the sea.

[*1 enters. 2 hangs behind her. 1 bows deep.*]

1: Her majesty calls.

2: Cries.

1: Potent over the sea.
I would implore her majesty to care for her hair.

2: Grow.

1: I would remind her majesty, growth is uncertain.

HECUBA: Remind the Greeks in our harbor.

1: Already?

2: Greeks go.

HECUBA: Muscles ripple against oars.
They won't wait long for wind.
They will overpower the sea
Make tides with their own rude strength.

1: Might her majesty estimate?

2: Get up.

HECUBA: The girl is right.

1: I prefer you from here. Might her majesty tell when?

HECUBA: They have nothing to do but take us.

1: We will be divided today.
From Troy.
From our girls.

2: Mommy, will marriage be like what they did last night?

HECUBA: I cannot watch Cassandra.
Let her stay inside.
Her frenzy would make such a scene.
Let us be sharp and austere.
The last broken pieces of Troy.

5: [*Sings, off.*] *Close the night of clutching straw*
Fade the day of washing blood
End the year of counting the dead
My man has come home.

[*3*, *4*, *and 5 enter. 5 repeats the song.*]

3: It's cold.

4: So early.

3: Calling us.

3 and 4: What will happen?

3: I hear sloshing. Is it the boats?

4: She can't keep still.

3 and 4: Waiting.

3: Is it the sound?

1: They have manned the boats.

4: Breathe deep. Breathe Troy.

3: Are we assigned?

4: Not going. Every breath is Troy.

3 and 4: Who will own me?

3: To Athens, or some island?

4: Our sand is brightest.

2: Are there sweets outside of Troy?

1: Majesty asks.

[*5 stops singing.*]

HECUBA: Who will keep me?
Where will I work,
a pathetic and bony person.
Age showing.
Will I nurse my captor's child?
Will I guard his gate?
I, Hecuba, Queen of Troy?
I, Hecuba, Queen of Troy.

1: If she is shamed, who am I?
The days of weaving royal cloth are done.
Tunics for Hector, Paris, Aeneas
Shawls for Cassandra, little Polyxena
Andromache's wedding gown.

2: Maybe these are skills I will employ in a new place.

1: They have no eye for beauty.

2: And yet an eye for me?

3: The way the men talk—talked—Athens is best. Home of Theseus, who is a good king. Sparta is worst. She is from Sparta. She. But they say—said—that in Athens streets are golden and so is justice. We might have revenge in Athens.

4: Troy.

3: Then again, ships go to many exquisite places. Like the fields near the river Peneios, which are supposed to be very green, which are reported to flower more richly than anything here, which surround the great Mount Olympus, home of gods. That is my second choice. Or Aetna, where the fire god has raised mountains so you can look across the sea right at Carthage, and the men are heroic and win every game. Or even the valley near the Ion Sea where they say—said—the river Krathis flows sweet, blessed waters that turn your hair the color of burning gold.

2: What games?

3: Your very favorites.

5: They were playing hide behind the tree. When metal started to fly they stopped playing. Climbed because that tree is too thin to hide three boys even who are small. *Maybe to the other side they looked like parts of a large and strong man. Someone aimed for the tree. It cracks, falls, the boys break but do not die. Tree too thin. Child's bones strong and yielding. The Greek discovers he has not struck a man. Begins to stomp and to hack. Cuts the boys apart, hand from wrist, leg from thigh. Covers himself and our ground with blood. When I got there he had placed his shield on my last son's skull and was grinding it with his boot.

3: In Athens streets are golden and so is justice. Then again, ships go to many exquisite places. Like the fields near the river Peneios, which are supposed to be very green, flower more richly than anything here, which surround the home of gods.

4: [*After 5.*] The Greek herald is here.

2 and 3: News!

[*TALTHYBIUS enters.*]

TALTHYBIUS: Hecuba. Hi.
I've been to Troy a lot these ten years.
If you turn around you will know me.
Talthybius.
I have news.

HECUBA: Our fears walk and speak.

TALTHYBIUS: You have been assigned to Greek men.
Was that the fear?

HECUBA: Where are we going?

TALTHYBIUS: Each gets a different man. A different home.

HECUBA: Who to whom?

TALTHYBIUS: Ask about one at a time.

HECUBA: Cassandra.

TALTHYBIUS: King Agamemnon himself wants her.

HECUBA: My child will serve Clytemnestra?

TALTHYBIUS: Agamemnon wants her himself. For his bed.

HECUBA: She was chosen by Apollo for a life of purity and foresight.

TALTHYBIUS: Cupid had other plans.

HECUBA: Melt your temple keys, Cassandra. Break the vessels.
Trample your own white robe.

TALTHYBIUS: Can you see it as an honor, to be picked by the king?

HECUBA: Why did they take my youngest?

TALTHYBIUS: Who?

HECUBA: Polyxena is a child. Who's grabbing for her?

TALTHYBIUS: She was given a special position.
She attends the tomb of Achilles.

HECUBA: What are the death rites of you people?
A little girl breathes that air?

TALTHYBIUS: Don't cry. Polyxena doesn't cry.

HECUBA: How do you know? What do you mean?

TALTHYBIUS: Your daughter is at peace.
I know she's not crying.

HECUBA: Andromache.
Who takes the wife of my Hector?

TALTHYBIUS: Another honor. The son of Achilles.

HECUBA: And me?

TALTHYBIUS: You are slave to King Odysseus.

HECUBA: OH! dysseus. OHHHdysssesus. Oh.

Shave my own head bald.
Tear my face to scraps.
The worst is true.

I belong to a liar.
He came as a spy, she pointed him out,
he begged with such a pretty string of words
I let him go.
Gullible Hecuba.
Slave to your supplicant.
Cry for me now, daughters of Troy.
I am done.

1: Queen.

4: What happens to us?

2: Please, bad man?

3: Tell.

4 and 5: Tell.

TALTHYBIUS: [*To his men.*] Go in and get Cassandra.
Agamemnon wants her first.
Then we can get some facts to these women
and take them.

Do I see fire?
Torches over the walls, smoke, branches breaking.

Are they setting themselves on fire?
They really hate us.
Move in and stop it!
Even if they have a point
I can't bring news of suicide.
Go!

HECUBA: No fire. Don't fret yourself.
Only Cassandra, prophetic again.

   [*CASSANDRA enters dancing, with torches.*]

CASSANDRA: Fire song!
Fuck song!
Take torches everyone because this is going to be good.
I'm getting married. Me! Cassandra! Married!
Can you believe it?
They grow up so fast.
It seems like a minute ago that the ships were arriving
and she was starting to bleed.
I always get so sentimental at these events.

Thank Hymen for a torch to dry my tears.

Let's all share happy memories of the bride.
Let's have a women's ritual.
We will pass a torch and a water bowl with petals and we will
pat each other's hands dry.
Dance sexually nonspecific dances.

Eat sweets.
Share wine.
Cry.

Maybe have a little talk with me Mother about whisper?
Because I'm kind of starting to blush
Just thinking
about loving
such a big, big, hero.
I'm kind of starting to shiver.
Just imagine
what will happen
when he rolls over me
if I don't love him right.

What if I gag
or scream in a way he finds unappealing?
What if I bleed too much
or not enough?
What if I fart?

There has to be a way to control these things.
There has to be a women's system.
Now's the time to hand over that kind of information.
Mom?
Remember how you were sort of sad about me being a priestess
because I'd never feel a man inside
and you'd never dance at my wedding?
Well look!

I'm bride!
You're mother-of!
Take up a torch and spin me away.

Let's all share our first warm memories of Cassandra.
Perhaps she wrote a poem in childhood which now seems
particularly fitting.
Perhaps as an adolescent she told you about her ideal guy
And Agamemnon is just like him!
Wouldn't that be a stitch?

Maybe there's even some embarrassing story

that we can all laugh at
now that we're grown-ups.

Fire dance!
Fuck dance!
Who wants to share first?

HECUBA: Your mind is random as ever, inappropriate to our plight.
I forgive you because you're crazy
but hand over the torch.

CASSANDRA: Crown me! King me!
Ask me why.

2: Why?

CASSANDRA: Because Cassandra is a deadlier bride than Helen.
Why tell you about the hatchet
that will hack first me then Agamemnon
the hatchet in the hands of his wife?
Or the son who slaughters his mother
who slaughtered her king
over me?
Or the collapse of a mighty and corrupt world power
due to a series of scandals
over me?

I have a god's gift for prophecy,
but if you don't believe that
believe this:
Troy will look good next to Greece.

If Helen wanted Menelaus, she would have stayed home.

Don't spit.
We fought for our country.
They invaded, desecrated, destroyed and died
to make her love him
which no army can do.
Agamemnon killed his daughter

  [To 2.]

innocent as you
for Helen.

What happened when a Greek fell?
Did his widow come to wrap him,
did children sing lamentations
make offerings
close his life in grace?

Corpses fester on our ground.
Unburied, forgotten, rotting.
While back in Greece, wives die in wait.
Fathers who hoped for heroes grow old alone
longing for sons.

The men of Troy fought to protect us
and what we love.
When one failed, his woman lay healing hands upon the wound.
When that failed, she dressed his body for burial
deep in the earth of Troy.

Our survivors returned each day
to the Greeks' most distant dream,
to eat with children
to sleep holding a woman's belly
to come home.

Unlucky Hector?
He was born a prince.
Growing up we bickered over games and sweets.
He found something larger before he died.
Without the Greeks he might have remained
petty and soft
like the rest of us.

Even Paris had Helen all those years
Zeus's daughter
the most ravishing woman in the world.
There is a kind of fame in that.

Nobody wants a war.
But that's how you make
a war hero.

So keep your tears, Mother.
This marriage means revenge.

TALTHYBIUS: If I didn't have orders to deliver you to my chief,
that kind of talk would have consequences.
Agamemnon is preparing for a journey and does not need curses
even from a lunatic such as yourself.

Goes to show that even wise men can be idiots.
He could have any woman
and he takes you.
I'm a poor man, and not the most handsome
but I wouldn't marry you
for all the treasure in Troy.
But insult us! Bless yourself!

We might as well learn to ignore you now.
Hecuba.
When Odysseus calls you, go.
You'll be serving his wife Penelope
whom they say is a patient woman.

CASSANDRA: Who are you?

TALTHYBIUS: I am Talthybius, Herald of Agamemnon.
Perhaps you have noticed me in the camp.

CASSANDRA: I'm looking at you in that suit and thinking about your dick.
I imagine you've got a lot of layers going on.
There's your outside garment
Tailored I'm sure to maximize comfort
without pinching power.
Then some kind of hard cupping device,
Maybe a strap to bind that on, maybe special pants,
a support,
and right against the big guy himself something soft.
Am I right?

You say my mother will be slave to Odysseus.
Apollo told me she dies in Troy.
What about that?
Hecuba will drop to all fours and howl
till you flee.
I see what you leave of Troy.
Nothing could live on those scraps but a dog
so that's what my mother becomes.

When you get hard what happens to your clothes?
I bet not much.
I bet they keep you low.
You've seen a lot of thighs lately
in many different positions.

If we could tell what makes you hot
who know what we would try?
You are so mighty.
What's been your most tempting offer?
Too bad the boys are dead.

How's Odysseus?
Doomed.
That's not a curse, it's a fact.
I only bring the news.
You know how it is, Harold.

TALTHYBIUS: I am Talthybius, *Herald* of—

CASSANDRA: We don't personally cause disaster,
but then we get all the blame.
Sucks.

I wonder if I could eat you without using my throat,
if it would just reach the back of my mouth.
I'm new to lovemaking.
Then again I am a prophet.
But size doesn't matter.
Did you learn that in school?

Odysseus thinks he's going home.
By the time he gets there I'll look lucky.
Shipwreck, cannibals, one-eyed beasts,
witches who make men pigs,
lethal singing ladies,
a vacation in death.
Then he arrives and the trouble starts.

My king is waiting.
Lots of blood on the way.
Mine is just the beginning.
After she hacks us
they lay me out naked on his grave
above ground
for dogs and rats to eat.
You should check me out, Harold, if you get that far.

What I'm wondering is,
how can size not matter?
Do they mean it doesn't matter like
the girl can't tell the difference?
You believe that?
Or it doesn't matter like
something can do anything
anything can do something
and what the ladies really want
is love.

To think I rejected Apollo to stay a virgin.
We were very young before the war.

I strip off my priestess clothes
Each ornament
Everything holy
So you won't have the thrill of tearing them.
Just tear me.
Where's the ship?
Watch for wind.

Stop crying, Mother.
Brothers in the ground,
our father Priam
all the old bones of Troy.
You won't wait long for me.
This prisoner leaves Troy a girl
arrives in Greece a fury.

[*CASSANDRA exits with TALTHYBIUS. HECUBA collapses.*]

1: Majesty has collapsed.
Help to lift her.
Bring comfort.
Help to raise her.

HECUBA: Let me lie.
I fell into dust.
That is my fate.
In times of disaster it is our custom to speak of fate,
to call on gods for help.
Where are you, gods, and what do you actually do?

Don't wail, my subjects.
Your queen prefers to tell a story.
The story of Hecuba.
I was born a princess
married a prince
bore one hundred perfect children.
Fifty sons.
Magnificent not only in number
but heroes
every single one.
Not a woman in Troy could match me,
not a woman in the world.

And I have cut my own hair
to lay on the grave
of every single one.

Their father Priam, gone.
You think a messenger brought me that news?
Yesterday they tore his throat
on the altar
before my eyes.
Took Troy.

I raised my girls to be like me,
patient and pure.
Cherished gifts for worthy men.
But it looks like our enemies get them

along with everything clean
in our city.

I'll never touch my daughters again.
They'll never see me.
But more.
I'm going to be a slave.
The sack of pain which is my body
will learn new tasks.
Bolt their door
bake their bread.
I, mother of Hector.
Sleep on dirt
dress in remnants.
I, model of fashion
partner to the royal bed.

All because of one woman
and her lust.
One hundred flawless babies.
And who will hold me?
Not a single one.
Why rise?
Troy is over.

3: It is time for a eulogy.
We will tell the story of Troy.

2: Troy is a civilization on the Aegean coast which enjoys plentiful sunshine,
bounteous crops, and a highly developed moral system.

4: The muses bring language
for our sad and brilliant land.

5: The horse.

1: That Helen of a horse.

2: It was a towering golden thing
more like a mountain than a beast
more like a god than a mountain
I mostly remember the feet.

1: Stuffed with swords.

2: You called me, Mother, down from the house.

3: Even the old men were dancing

4: Women stopped working

5: Children quit crying

CHORUS: Troy stood still.

4: Then leapt to our feet in a whirl—

3: A whoop—

5: A victory release.

2: No more war!

4: Tomorrow *he'll wake and shake his head and start to rise and I'll whisper no more war and we will hold each other trembling with the terrible joy of survivors.

3: Tomorrow *I will swim in the sea.

5: Tomorrow I will imagine new children.

2: Heave! Heave! Heave the horse! Heave!

4 and 5: All the young men pull.
Gold on gold in the sun.
The whole strength of Troy and half its beauty
rope the gift and haul it like a ship from water
up to our temple.

1: King Priam himself was there.

3: Into the night they build Athena's offering.
I wear this for the maiden goddess.

2: We light torches and everyone stays awake.

5: We sing and dance a rhythm.

4: Grateful.

3, 4, and 5: *Close the night of clutching straw*
Fade the day of washing blood
End the year of counting the dead
My man has come home.

2: I dance as a woman for the first time.

CHORUS: *Close the night of clutching straw*
Fade the day of washing blood
End the year of counting the dead
My man has come home.

4: I dream warm dreams.

5: Why are you playing so late?
Why are you messy with food?
I love you all equal.

2: What a big, big cake.

3: Athena is giving me wings and a weapon.
Athena is making me brave.

4: We sleep the sleep of ten years.

1: The cry came.
The belly split.
Enemy.

CHORUS: Troy!

5: Broke to a river of bodies and blood.

4: Babies clung *to mothers

3: Sister clung *to sister

1: I clung to my girl

CHORUS: While we could.

2: Athena loves war more than virgins.

4: My husband fell bloody on her altar.

5: Every one of them

CHORUS: Fell.

1: Headless bodies in our beds.

3, 4, and 5: One pushed me down right next to the corpse
on our bed soft with blood.
I watched my man's hands the whole time
begging them to move.

CHORUS: Afterwards he spat and said

4: "Something is fertile in Troy."

CHORUS: Something is fertile in Troy.

2: What is a baby? What is ground?

[*Greek **SOLDIERS** pull **ANDROMACHE** in a wagon piled with palace spoils. She holds her very young son **ASTYANAX**.*]

1: Look Hecuba,
It's Andromache, and your grandson
in a Greek chariot.
Where are they pulling you, princess,
with Hector's armor
and a mound of his treasure
to placate the gods?

ANDROMACHE: The Greeks take their things.

HECUBA: Wail.

ANDROMACHE: Mine.

HECUBA: Child.

ANDROMACHE: Mine.

HECUBA: My children.

ANDROMACHE: Gone.

HECUBA: All?

ANDROMACHE: Gone.

HECUBA: Zeus?

ANDROMACHE: Where?

HECUBA: Troy.

ANDROMACHE: Troy.

HECUBA: Last

ANDROMACHE: cracked

HECUBA: pieces

ANDROMACHE and **HECUBA:** of Troy.

ANDROMACHE: I imagine Hector.

HECUBA: Son.

ANDROMACHE: Man.

ANDROMACHE and **HECUBA:** Loving and fierce.

HECUBA: Gone.

ANDROMACHE: Priam.

HECUBA: Man.

ANDROMACHE: King.

HECUBA: Take me.

ANDROMACHE: Wrecked

HECUBA: treasure

ANDROMACHE and **HECUBA:** of Troy.

HECUBA: You, too, are my daughter.

ANDROMACHE: May I talk to you of the house where my children were born?

HECUBA: Born.

ANDROMACHE: Burst.

HECUBA: Tears on tears.

HECUBA and **ANDROMACHE:** Tears. On top. Of tears.

[*Silence.*]

1: In times of bottomless distress, women are known to heal one another through speech. The physical act of facing another person and letting forth a stream of sentences can create a sense of order. The language of disaster never matches reality. Therefore listing one's losses serves to de-escalate and to soothe.

ANDROMACHE: You were his mother.
He wore this. He used this.
To kill so many.
Do you see?

HECUBA: I see everything worthless exalted.
I see a princess on a wagon of spoils.

ANDROMACHE: My son and I will be slaves.
I thought we would spoil him.
Baby king.

HECUBA: They forced Cassandra from me.

ANDROMACHE: More.
They killed Polyxena.
A sacrifice on Achilles' tomb.

HECUBA: My littlest girl.
When I think I'm at the rocky bottom, it breaks.
I should have known what he meant.
I didn't want to ask.

ANDROMACHE: I saw it.
They dragged me past on this wagon, slowly
while they slit her throat.
Even the soldiers were weeping.
They let me climb down to cover her.
I sang the dirge.

HECUBA: My miserable girl.
Killed for a corpse.

ANDROMACHE: Polyxena is luckier than me.

HECUBA: No, child.
Life holds hope.

ANDROMACHE: Mother may I talk to you about collapse?
For Polyxena it's like she was never born.
Maybe that comforts you.
In death there is no grief.
While my life is a map of loss.

I say without shame that I was an ambitious woman.
I wanted a high reputation.
I built one.
I watched it crack against the ground
fragile as a vase.
I have held myself to standards.
I have lived beyond reproach.

They say a woman who walks will stray.
So I kept home.
Imagined the outside.
A person of position can command
even her own longing.

They say wit in a wife is a wayward sign.
So I spoke to myself.
I know how women become friends
swapping laughter and information.
It is addictive.
So I spoke to myself.
I am interesting.
My mind is a teacher.

They say the man is ruler
so he ruled.

They say talk in a woman is brass
so I was gold.

They say if you look at the sun you go blind
so I watched the floor for reflection.

And action during pregnancy causes disaster
so I lay with my feet up
waiting.

They say Andromache is a model wife.
They say Andromache is a lady.
They say now, I want Andromache.

The son of Achilles picked me from all the women
due to my reputation
which had of course spread to Greece.
A place I did not expect to see.

Mother.
They say something else.

A night of pleasure with one man
erases another.
There is a way to touch a woman so she forgets everything that went before
so she bucks against a face a hand a body
like a horse.
A mare if you switch her partner will refuse to bear the weight
and she is only a beast.
I hate women for this.
And I think about touch.

Hector, you were my everything.
Wise and beautiful, brave and rich.
I came to you a sealed box.
You unlocked me.
Now, in Greece,
I will fail you whatever I do.

Do you see why I call Polyxena lucky?
Hope is old candy.
I can't eat it anymore.

HECUBA: I've never been on a ship.
I have seen pictures.
I've heard them described.
Under ordinary circumstances, men split the work.
One steers, one sails, some bail from the bottom.
But when a storm hits, they drop those tasks
and let the wind hurl them where it will.

That's me now.
Swamped by disaster, I let my mouth go
babbling what it wants.

Forget Hector.
Your tears don't help.
You know how to make a man love you.
Do that.
Be hot and sweet for the Greek.
And raise my grandson to kill him.
This child will build a new Troy on top of our bones.
He is hope.

Why is the fetch-dog back?

[*TALTHYBIUS enters.*]

TALTHYBIUS: Oh wife of noble Hector, bravest of Troy,
Don't hate me.

Really powerful people are making me tell you.
I wish I didn't have to.

ANDROMACHE: Why are you so careful?

TALTHYBIUS: They decided—your boy—how do I put this?

ANDROMACHE: They're splitting us.

TALTHYBIUS: No. No Greek at all will be his master.

ANDROMACHE: They're leaving him here?

TALTHYBIUS: There is no easy way to say it.

ANDROMACHE: You empathize. How kind.

TALTHYBIUS: They will kill him. Now you know.
Odysseus pointed out
that the seed of such a great man cannot live.

HECUBA: What logic.
May he lose his own son.

TALTHYBIUS: I am sent to get the boy.
They will throw him from the city wall.
Please give him to me.
Cry. We expect you to cry.
But don't do anything difficult
like make me rip him out of your arms
or call in the army to back me up.
We can.
We can plan an entire military action around you
but don't make me.
Like the good woman you are, Princess Andromache,
give over.
We expect you to cry.
But don't curse us.
It is not acceptable at this point for gods to intervene.
So I must tell you that if you curse us
we'll leave his broken body on the rocks.
Otherwise you will be allowed to bury him.
Of course compliance will also impress your new husband.

ANDROMACHE: They say action during pregnancy causes disaster
so I lay with my feet up
waiting.

You have been the most fragile part of me. You had hands the size of my
thumb. I looked at you red and furious and thought he will grow up to be red
and furious, and people will listen to that. I heard you choke your own tears
and thought he will live to choke his own tears, because the affairs of a world

leader require restraint. I touch. I think you will offer your palm to a girl who wants something smooth and say, here. The arch of your foot. The dent of your hipbone, or just above. I imagine a day when those are the soft and hairless places. To remind a young woman of now. Private. When you become noble like your daddy, and public. I thought it would cow you a little to compare to him but be bracing after all. Instead the reputation gets. Every time.

You're crying, too. Tear boy. Do you understand? Troy boy. Tug on me all you want. Hold mommy. Right. Never grow up not to need mommy. Kiss me. Say bye-bye.

[*She gives the child to* **TALTHYBIUS**.]

Greeks. Fancy civilization. Killing the guilty. Be proud.
Helen, you are not the daughter of Zeus.
You were born of hate, rotten meat, and shit.
May a man pour boiling oil through your cunt and fuck you with his spear.

I am ready to meet my prince.

[**ANDROMACHE** *is pulled off in the wagon.*]

2: For Helen?

1: Helen is not human.

2: Boiling oil through her cunt and fuck her with his spear.

TALTHYBIUS: I am so sorry for your mother.
You are going to stand on your daddy's wall and jump.
It's been decided. Do you know decided?
Someone else take him.
I can't be the herald of this.

[*TALTHYBIUS exits with the boy.*]

HECUBA: Boy. Troy.
We've run the course of misery.
What's left?

1: The tropical paradise of Troy is uniquely glorious, harmonious, and wronged. We must ask ourselves why this particular strip of coast has attracted attention. We must be willing to get historical.

3: We must confront the painful possible that we the people now women of Troy have had a hand.

VOICE OF THE CITY: *Cups and cups of blood. From the day I was born.*

CHORUS: Once Troy was a plain place.

1: Decorative

3: Temperate

5: Fated

CHORUS: But a plain place.

VOICE OF THE CITY: *And in me girls and boys would lie and I kept all sand from privates.*

5: Gods built Troy.

4: Of the sea.

1: Poseidon God of the Sea made us coastal for memory and access.

2: [Sings.] *Sweet Troy*
my blue girl
sweet Troy
lap me like a wave like a love
and carry me to sea.

1: We must ask ourselves what went on.

3: They built the land pretty for temple and play.

5: A picnic for a people

4: Who would fail to meet the most minimal obligations.

2: *Toss me Troy*
like a brick like a bone
like a piece of old thing
sinking in your sea.

VOICE OF THE CITY: *The first arrow piercing my shore*

1: There was an archer.

VOICE OF THE CITY: *First boy to die for my sand and sky*

3: Shooting like stars into the horizon, all to keep Troy safe.

4 and 5: Is this not the natural way of female things, defended?

1: What goes on.

3: We the women then people of Troy failed to . . .

4: Tiny our reciprocity.

3: Consequence and woe.

1: Inhospitality, coupled with lack of a coherent system of back-scratching, naturally leads to invasion. Destruction. Desolation.

VOICE OF THE CITY: *Gods get cruel.*

CHORUS: Tide pools run with blood.

4: Anemone stop sucking. Water becomes flesh.

5: Gods want to drink without stooping. They find a prince.

VOICE OF THE CITY: *The boy I hid him in my shore.*

5: They found a young prince and made a captive. Gave him golden cups.

2: *Fill boy*
blood still flowing
spill boy
only when you reach like a stretch like a star
my mouth.

1: And so Troy became immortal

5: Or anyway dead.

3: The boy learned to listen to the cry of mothers and hear the cry of gulls. See bodies as landscape for a stark and beautiful shore.

4 and 5: They called it New Beginning.

3: The prince spun fabric from the earth of Troy, and made lutes from the trees. Puffed our sand into love beds.

VOICE OF THE CITY: *Every pleasure of the gods is a gift from me.*

4 and 5: They resented the debt. Played hard. Then left.

3: And the prince was prince of corpses all again.

1: The gods have left us all again.
Notice even Dawn doesn't care.

1, 3, 4, and 5: She smiles and rises on our dead.

2: *Sweet Troy*
my blue girl
sweet Troy
lap me like a wave like a love
and carry me to sea.

> [*MENELAUS enters. A general on a great day.*]

MENELAUS: What a great day.
Lots of sun.
I get my hands on Helen today.
Me, Menelaus.
You think this war was for her
but that's a myth.
I was obligated to invade.
You see, in my country we are good to guests.
When the Trojan prince Paris arrived, I hosted him well.

He did not respond in kind.
In fact he stole my wife.

I had to kill him.
My troops took care of that, so I am here for her.
I can have my way.
I am authorized.
I could let you ladies watch,
but I think I'll take her back to Greece.
I want to see what they do.
Blood. Shrieks. Ripping skin.
The crowd tears cheek from bone,
each keeps a bit of the carcass.
Or else they smash her with rocks:
eye, breast, belly crush against the wall
and later we scrape her out.

In that face I once saw the rest of my life
smooth and sweet as fruit.

Why are you waiting?
Go!
Bring her—drag her—to me.
By the hair.
When the wind blows we'll take her.

HECUBA: Power.
Order.
Intelligence.
We call you Zeus.
You exist.

MENELAUS: What an odd prayer.

HECUBA: Do it, Menelaus.
That's my prayer.
Kill her now.
But look away.
She burns a man's eyes
then his city
leaving a nest of ash.
We know her, you and I,
two casualties of war.

   [*HELEN enters. MENELAUS looks away.*]

HELEN: Menelaus.
Are you trying to scare me?
Your men were so rough.
I know you hate me.
What did all you Greeks decide?
May I live?

MENELAUS: It was unanimous.
They let me choose.
You die.

HELEN: Your choice?
May I appeal?
I am innocent.
May I show you?

MENELAUS: My job is clear.
Why talk?

HECUBA: Let her speak, Menelaus.
But let me answer.
I will draw for you in exquisite detail
the doings of Helen in Troy.
When you hear the whole story
she'll die.

MENELAUS: I allow it as a favor to you,
not out of feelings for her
which are gone.

HELEN: You have decided I'm the enemy
so you probably won't respond.
But I can guess how you'll accuse me
plus I have my own points to make.
I will balance the views.
You feel nothing, so let's use reason.

First, who caused this war?
Helen? Or Hecuba
who gave birth to Paris
the greedy guest?

Second, Priam sealed the doom of Troy
and me
when he refused to kill that son at birth
even though the prophets spelled out
this exact disaster.

And next?
Don't remember? I do.
Lucky Paris got to judge a beauty contest of goddesses.
They all tried to bribe him:
Hera said he could be king of Asia and Europe;
Athena promised triumph over Greece;
Aphrodite offered me.
Exquisite, she said,
unearthly,

complete.
Aphrodite won.
Who profited? Greece.
Unconquered.
While I became property.
Now you hate me
when you should crown me.
For I did more to keep Greece safe
than all the armies.
I gave my body
to keep Greece safe.

Look at me.

I know what you're thinking.
That's not the point.
Why did I go
Secretly, in night, with him?
Paris—did you choose the name, Queen Hecuba?
Paris came with a goddess to take me.
And you were gone, my one.
You were gone.
How could you?
How could you?

I must ask myself one private question:
What happened to my heart
to ever
ever
make me leave you,
my one?

Rage at Aphrodite
of infinite power
but forgive me.
Forgive me.

Look?

You might go on.
Once Paris died and no god cared for me
why didn't I come home?
You know what?
I tried.
I would climb the city walls
wind a rope around my body, tight,
tie this rope to a jutting stone
and lower myself—
bare toes searching out holds

rough rocks scraping my breasts—
towards the Greek camp.
The guards could tell you.
They caught me again and again.

Then there was a man who took what Troy didn't want.
Kept me in his house.
Raped me again and again.

Please look, Menelaus.
Yes.
Lover.
I have been stolen like a prize
kept like a beast.
I am human.

I know it isn't that kind of time but meeting your eyes I have to smile. Your
face shows the rest of my life. I am starting to tremble, and you know me as a
woman who often but not always keeps control.

The gods made me
and the war.
Do you hate them too?
You're smarter than that.
I know you.
I know you.

1: Defend yourself, Hecuba.
It's a pretty skin of words.

HECUBA: I defend the goddesses.
Our deities don't play vain games.
They are occupied. Protecting.
Athena betray her namesake city?
Ridiculous.
Untrue.
You lack all sense of the eternal.
Gods do not want to be pretty.
Does Hera seek a better husband than Zeus?
Gods do not think like you.

Aphrodite wrenched you from home.
No.
I remember my son's body. His young mouth.
The way his hair curled when he sweat.
Want was your love-god.
Menelaus is a much older man.
And his palace was small
compared to the wonder of Troy.

We sent Paris in robes of gold
carrying bright gifts.
Taken by glint and by flash
you wanted.
You wanted.

Force?
Who heard the screams?
Your brothers were there.
Pollux and Castor, stars now,
were human still.
Where was the struggle?
You're a pretty girl.
Someone would have saved you if you tried.

No, you came here.
They followed.
Blood and bodies fell fast.
Strong Greeks, you told my son at night,
My Menelaus, you said,
feeding his worst days with doubt.

But in our times of glory
you were spark and oil.
My bronze man, you would say,
my one.
My hot and shining man.
My one.

That was Helen's war.
How to choose a winner.

What an exquisite image:
you caught in rope
dangling off our wall
leaving.
Did no one ever teach you
how a lady uses rope
when she is torn from her
beloved lawful lord?
She strings her neck and jumps.

But Troy is a nice place to relax
Fine fabric and gold.
Salt breeze.
Herbs for the complexion.

While my girls were taken one by one
you have been fixing your hair.

And that is the only gown in the city
untorn.
You are glorious.
You must bathe often.

You radiate poise, it's true.
Even pride.
A human being in your position
would shave her head and crawl,
tear the face responsible.

Did you hear, Lady Helen
that there was a war?

So, Menelaus.
Act now.
A whore should die.

HELEN: That is a word good women like.
It explains the way you make me
unladylike sometimes.

MENELAUS: I remember.

3: We were with Greek men *last night.

5: Woman.

3: They spoke of *Menelaus.

5: Woman.

1, 2, and 3: That was the word they chose.

4 and 5: Woman.

CHORUS: Greece is calling him a woman.

3: He can shut them up.

4: Act now.

CHORUS: Make the world a clean place.

2: I want to live in a clean place.

MENELAUS: You say what I've known a long time.
She stopped loving me.
Left for a fresh boy.
She talks about goddesses and rape
but that's a lie.

I am an older man, it's true.
And although holding her I felt anything was possible
it's not.

HELEN: Our first time together I thought
I have waited my whole life for this touch.
Anything is possible
I felt.

MENELAUS: Troy's women have been badly wronged.
I should let them kill you.

HELEN: No.
These women want their men
like I have wanted you.
Your soldiers are strong.
I am easy to hate.
But Helen did not hurt them.
They would have you believe there are two kinds of girl
good and bad.
We know it's more slippery.
Yes?

HECUBA: Stop looking.

HELEN: I sink to my knees.
With you I am every kind of girl.

MENELAUS: There once was a vow.

HELEN: By my life, by my body,
by everything soft and hot and yours,
I will spread for you like a carpet
all the way home.

HECUBA: Disease spreads.
Kill it.

MENELAUS: Enough.
Return Helen to Sparta as planned.
Move!

HECUBA: Not on your ship.

MENELAUS: Why?

HECUBA: You love her.

MENELAUS: Disgusting.
I hate Helen.
Who cares what boat she's on?
I want her in Greece
on a wall
bloody and ripped
as stone after stone from the screaming mob
breaks that beauty for good.

I hate Helen.
I want her in Greece.
What could happen on the boat?
She will be cold in that dress.

[*HELEN is led out. MENELAUS follows.*]

1: Zeus is a traitor.
Incense and wine
smoke and sacrifice
all are Greek now.

5: Did you hear that sound before day?

1 and 3: Walls carved and songs played for you.
How many sacred moons?

2: Twelve sacred moons.

1 and 3: Holy number holy throne
gone.

5: It was the sound of gods going.

1, 3, and 4: Did you forget?

5: It was not gulls.

1, 3, and 4: Where was that located, Troy?

5: Not gulls.

CHORUS: Paradise.

5: It was the sound of gods losing.

1: One would have been her husband.
But he's a ghost instead.
She is not old enough to bury him.
She would not even know which of our dead men
was hers.

CHORUS: [*Not 2.*] Whose child is that
embracing the gate?
Whose mound of crying children
is that?

2: I am placed with the women for the first time.
A girl says, where do they take me, Mommy?
Who will help her float?
That girl placed with the children
for the last time?

3: Ship full of me.

4: Ship full of Helen.

5: Ship full of she

1: Full of hell

3: In the sea

5: I see hell on the sea

4: I see Helen go free.

CHORUS: [*Not 2.*] May the ship full of Helen
be filled by the sea
may the sea seep in Helen
may sea sweep that Helen
to hell under sea.
Far under me.

4: No.
May fire from Zeus blister that boat
break her gold mirror
stick glass in her throat
and burn her like paper
like Troy.

CHORUS: [*Not 2.*] May Helen burn like waste like Troy.
Helen burn like waste like Troy.
Helen burn like paper Troy.
Helen burn like Troy.

5: No.
May soldier men sever the flesh
Butcher like meat
Rip it like mesh
and feed her to sharks
of Troy.

CHORUS: [*Not 2.*] Devour Helen like game like Troy.
Devour Helen like game like Troy.
Eat Helen bloody like Troy.
Helen of Troy.

1: Helen is no part of Troy.
She trades us she burns us she feeds us to sea.

CHORUS: [*Not 2.*] Helen burned my man my Troy.
Helen eats my child my Troy.
Helen traded city Troy
for a glass for a gas for a ride over sea.

[*HECUBA joins.*]

Helen broke my temple Troy.
Helen took the name of Troy.
Helen traded city Troy
for a sin for her skin for a dip in the sea.

Helen breaks and eats and trades my Troy
Burns and maims my Troy.

Flame take her sea break her remake her as me.

4: Mother to be.

5: Unwilling to flee.

3: Nothing like she.

CHORUS: [*Not 2.*] Flame take her sea break her remake her ugly.
Ugly ugly
Helen Helen Helen Helen Helen!

5: Helen is not human.

3 and 4: Helen is the worst of the war.

CHORUS: [*Not 2.*] Helen is the worst of the war.

[*Silence.*]

2: An experiment.

[*She stands on a rock and takes off her shoe. She crouches and jumps, letting go of the shoe as she leaps. Both land at the same time. She picks up the shoe, climbs higher, leaps and drops the shoe. She picks it up, climbs higher, hesitates, leaps and drops the shoe. She picks it up, climbs very high, hesitates, drops only the shoe.*]

2: The boy prince Astyanax was smaller than me, but I think he fell just as fast.

[*TALTHYBIUS enters alone. He bears the corpse of ASTYANAX on Hector's shield.*]

TALTHYBIUS: Hecuba.
The son of Achilles had troubling news from home.
Revolt against his father's line.
He hurried.
He's gone.
He took Andromache.

She stood on the moving ship
wailing for Troy
calling to Hector's grave.
I wept.
She saw.

Here is what she said:
"Take my broken child to Hecuba.
Let her wash him.
If she has clean cloth let her wrap him.
If there are flowers left let her cover my boy,
clipped, and fresh, and dead."
She said, "Let Hector's shield
be coffin and tomb.
I don't want it on the wall
above my new bed."
She said, "I plan to forget."

His burial is your last act here.
We will sail when you are through.
Please work fast.

I gathered the body and washed it for you.
That tower was very high.
I had to do something.

I can dig your grandson's grave.
We are two able people.
Soon done.
Soon home.

HECUBA: Greeks.
Meet victory.
You murdered this baby.
That's illogical.
Because when his father Hector had the force to wave this shield like a fan
the wit to know your every move
the heart to fight forever
it was not enough.
When our male nation
stood beside and behind him
united
graceful
fierce as a mother's scream
it was not enough.
We fell.

Now there are no more weapons or plans
no more men.
But you fear a boy who fits in his father's shield.
I'll tell you a secret.
Not even a Trojan could unwreck your wrong.
It was a groundless kill.
Cowardly and cruel.
Familiar to you, I'm sure.

You look young.
I hope each word you delivered on our salt ground
plays in your brain
night after night.
May you watch your own fresh life
through the spattered screen of what you said here.

Look down at the shield.
When you have a child
see that.
May you never trust love.
May you never find rest.
May you be remote and despised
in your home.
May you make and remake the war of Troy
in your home.

    [*TALTHYBIUS exits.*]

Hector will fill the mouths of all who sing heroes
for a long long time.
His glory, my sorrow
will float
a long time.

And you?
You died old enough to know
but too young to save.
A girl kind of myth
a victim of Troy.

I should be wiping blood from your knee.
You should be forming a scab.
Who can talk about seeing a little boy's skull?

Hands like Hector's.
Smashed at the wrist.

"Grandmother," this mouth said,
"When you die I will cut a lock of hair,
gather my young man friends,
and sing you away in grace."
A boy imagines grief around his own glory.

But you lied.
I bury you.
Homeless, childless, female, and poor,
I bury you.
The end of generations of fuss.
What would a poet carve on your tomb?

This boy got killed by the Greek army
because he scared them.

Hector's imperfect shield.
Here is his hand, stamped in the grip.
Here is a sweat stain.
He leaned his cheek when battle was hot.
A man's full beard.

Do some work.
Find robes for the pitiful dead.
The gods are gone.
Bring scraps.

A person who uses the word "secure"
to mean "wealthy"
is a fool.
Life unfolds to show no shape at all.
A sick spread of pain.
Joy is a myth.

[*The women bring clean things.*]

4: I unwound my man's body to keep his cloak.
It's yours.

5: A shirt of plain cloth.

3: A sash.

HECUBA: I place gifts on you.
Not prizes.
You are not old enough to race or shoot
and sports were modest here.
This sash looks symbolic
but it's the only one.

1: The tiny vest I wove hangs in the palace.
Pieces still unseamed, or maybe burnt.
To see him in these castaways
breaks my heart.

HECUBA: Cassandra's robe is holy cloth.
You should have worn a weave like this
to walk a regal princess to bed.
Linen left to stop up your wounds.
Here and here.
I called myself a healer once.
I have skill.
I just can't get results from a corpse.

4: The earth won't want to take this child.

She will weep to see him lowered.
She was not expecting—

5: She has learned.

2 and 3: Sing the dirge.

1: We will beat our hands like oars, rip hair and face.
That is our way.

4: Don't spare yourself.

3 and 5: Don't spare yourself.

2: This is our way.
I beat my hands like oars, I rip my hair and face.

HECUBA: Truth is cold.
I see it.

CHORUS: Hecuba?

HECUBA: Men will savor our hope like wine
while they swallow again and again
the exquisitely tragic tale
of ravished Troy.

   [*GREEK SOLDIERS enter.*]

Take the body.
He has a robe and flowers to help him rot.
Funerals are for survivors.
I don't think he cares.

   [*The SOLDIERS carry away the corpse.*]

5: Sing for Andromache and her broken boy.
Sing terror and tell the death.

CHORUS: [*Not 2.*] There was a fall.

2: We fell.

CHORUS: [*Not 2.*] There was an end.

2: Look!
Men on the walls on the roofs on the arches.
Men with fire.

CHORUS: [*Not 2.*] There was a fire.

2: What next?

CHORUS: [*Not 2.*] It was the end.

   [*TALTHYBIUS enters, attended and amplified.*]

TALTHYBIUS: MEN!
YOU HAVE TORCHES AND A PLAN.
WHAT'S THE PROBLEM?
HE SAID BURN IT.
SO BURN IT.
LET'S GET OUT OF HERE.
TROY MAKES ME SICK.

Ladies.
A trumpet will sound.
Walk directly to the ships.

Hecuba.
I pity you.
But go with these men.
Odysseus sent them.
And he owns you now.

[*The fires begin.*]

HECUBA: My land was the laurel of Asia.
Now she burns brittle and gray,
Gods hear my call!
That's habit.
Prayers are not answered.
They tangle in the trees like worthless fog.
So.
I jump.
To die in my family's smoke.

[*HECUBA climbs.*]

TALTHYBIUS: GET HER.
SHE'S CRAZY.
THAT'S TRAGIC.
BUT ORDERS ARE ORDERS.

[*The men restrain HECUBA.*]

HECUBA: Do you see me, Zeus?

4: He does.

3: They say other places are finer than here.
They say his favor rises with the sun.

HECUBA: Do you see the town of Troy?

1: Close your eyes. This is not our queen.

2: Not our queen.

3: We are a flame.

4: A flare of defeat for the world to see.

5: We fall like cold smoke
without a crash.

HECUBA: The earth has ears.
Listen, my sons.

CHORUS: No more gods.
Call the dead.

HECUBA: I stretch against you.
Remember this body.

5: Remember this skin.
I roll slow for you.

4: Good morning.

CHORUS: Drop to your face.
Call the dead.

2: [*Sings.*] *One boy*
name unknown
You're the one I mean when I moan
good-bye.

HECUBA: Young Priam.
I rub my face and belly over your rough cheek until I am raw and your
    mouth heals.
Loving me you whisper
we are making a kingdom
making a kingdom
making
a kingdom.

See the women of Troy.
The women now ruin of Troy.

CHORUS: The women now ruin of Troy.

5: My babies died ignorant.
I can be glad.

CHORUS: We laugh for what the dead won't know.

HECUBA: Smoke makes a cloud.
We can't see beyond
and no one looks in.

CHORUS: Vanish.

3: What were we called?

4: Where were the crops?

5: Which linguistic system did this civilization use?

1: Why are the unearthed bodies disproportionately male?

2: I was born in a place called—

CHORUS: [*Not 2.*] Show me the map.

1: I fled with the artifact. Powder now.

2: My mother used to—

CHORUS: [*Not 2.*] Women now ruin of Troy.

2: We had a holy day.

3: Evidence points to contemporeality with the Greek. Harmonimity. Civilus. Ethic and art.

4: Troy: A Multi-Millennial Perspective. We ask our pointed question—what would be the West with a second cradle?

5: New scholarship emphasizes perfect gender in ancient

3: strength and warmth

4: an idyllic

CHORUS: Where mountains met the sea.

1: Which war?

HECUBA: Listen.
That was our city crashing.

3 and 4: Men surround us like water.

3: Crashing.

4: Crashing.

CHORUS: Crushed.

1 and 5: Men move us along.

CHORUS: Mourn and march on.
And ocean to forget.

2: Once I lived in a clear place.

CHORUS: Can we move to a clear place?

1: Walk alone.

4 and 5: Walk along.

CHORUS: Go.

[*All exit but HECUBA.*]

HECUBA: Hecuba is old.
Crouched.
She wants to crawl.
Hecuba needs four legs.
Growl.

[*2 appears.*]

2: I am taking your dust
to rub eyes and make dreams of Troy.
I am taking your dust
to remember
that nothing can be quite clean
after Troy.

[*The winds begin.*]

END OF PLAY

PHILOKTETES

JOHN JESURUN

PHOTO: PAULA COURT

JOHN JESURUN is a playwright, director, and designer living in New York. His presentations integrate elements of language, film, architectural space, and media. His exploded narratives cover a wide range of themes and explore the relation of form to content. They challenge the experience of verbal, visual, and intangible perceptions. He was born in 1951, in Battle Creek, Michigan. In 1982 he began his highly acclaimed serial play *Chang in a Void Moon,* now in its fifty-seventh episode (Bessie Award). Since 1984 he has written, directed, and designed over twenty-five pieces including the media trilogy of *Deep Sleep* (1986 Obie Award, Best Play), *White Water,* and *Black Maria.* His collaboration with Martin Acosta, *Faust/How I Rose,* was presented at BAM in 2004. He is the recipient of numerous grants from NEA Visual and Media Arts, and BAM/Lucent Technologies Arts in Multimedia. He has also received the Rockefeller, Guggenheim, NYFA, and Foundation for Contemporary Performance Arts fellowships. He is a 1996 MacArthur Fellowship recipient. His work is published by *PAJ,* Theater Communications Group, Sun and Moon Press, and Yale *Theater* Magazine. He holds a B.F.A. from Philadelphia College of Art, and an M.F.A. in Sculpture from Yale University.

From the Writer
JOHN JESURUN

In 1993 Ron Vawter asked me to write a version of *Philoktetes* for him. He was then touring his show *Roy Cohn/Jack Smith*. He had AIDS. He had studied Sophocles' version of Philoktetes in high school and it resonated with him at this point in his life. He instigated a project called *Philoktetes Variations* for the Kaaitheater in Brussels, which would use versions by Sophocles, Gide, Heiner Muller, and myself. Though there were plenty of references to classical culture in my work, this was the first time I had actually dealt with a classical subject as a main topic, or done an adaptation of any sort.

After that first meeting with Ron I realized that I had already started to write this play years before. Three scenes written in 1987 were looking for a place to live. In many ways this is a case in which the actor and writer complete each other. We sat at a café and he told me the story of Philoktetes, a Greek general and a member of the military expedition to Troy. Ron had known my work since the beginning days of my serial piece *Chang in a Void Moon* at the Pyramid Club in New York City. He told me that the lack of remorse or sentimentality in my own work drew him to me.

Ron told me he didn't want an AIDS play and he didn't want a gay play and he certainly didn't want to be a poster boy for any cause. He believed his situation was beyond that. His only other request was that I write whatever I wanted regardless of how Philoktetes had already been treated. "You'll know what to write," he said to me. We both realized that neither of us was particularly interested in the other versions as source material. So I made up my own Sophocles-related version. We both knew that this was something to be written in a certain transient moment. Whatever it would be would have to do more than mark time. It would have to acknowledge time itself as irrelevant.

We met a lot to talk about the project, but mostly we just hung out. We had many dinners together but there was a lot we didn't have to talk about. Things get communicated by just being with someone—to talk about things out loud is redundant and impersonal. And hardly artistic. Things were expressed. Not explained. Certain unavoidably painful concerns came up and Ron dealt with them wisely, compassionately, and humorously. And then we didn't worry about them. Questions like "What if I wrote a death scene? Would he mind? Was it bad luck? What if he did die? What would we do then? Were we tempting fate?"

Ron was quite generous to spend this time with me. In New York City, during that phase of the AIDS crisis, there was a very real sense of urgency, and a clumsy sense of triage. Time was moving quickly and we had to finish this thing and skip the triage. At times it felt like I was with Philoktetes himself. Not some character out of history but someone in a state of transformation. Not fading away, but fading into. . . . Changing form, but not content. Like great actors do.

Ron Vawter died on April 16, 1994. As a result, *Philoktetes'* life as a performance text was in suspension for some time. There was a workshop at Sundance Theatre Lab in 2000, and the premiere of the script in a Spanish-language version that same year. In the U.S. the script received workshop presentations at La Mama in New York City in 2002 and 2003, where actors Jeff Weiss and Ruth Maleczech inhabited the title role, respectively. The English-language premiere of *Philoktetes* was presented at the Berliner Festspielhaus in December 2004, with Ching Valdes Aran as Philoktetes, Darren Pettie as Odysseus, and Jason Lew as Neoptolemus. Noh Theater actor Hideo Kanze will play the role of Philoktetes in the Japanese version in Kyoto in 2005.

In literature, Philoktetes is the guardian of Heracles' magic bow and arrows. On the way to Troy he is bitten by a snake on the island of Lemnos. The wound on his foot is so painful and debilitating that his military colleagues including his friend Odysseus abandon him on the deserted island. Ten years pass and the Greeks have made no progress against Troy. An oracle tells them that they can defeat Troy only if they have the magic bow of Heracles. Odysseus and Neoptolemus, son of the dead Achilles, journey to Lemnos to find the bow. The play begins at this point.

回回回

FOR RON VAWTER

回回回

PRODUCTION HISTORY

From Teatro de Arena's production of
Philoktetes in Mexico City, directed by
Martín Acosta. PHOTO: JOSÉ JORGE CARREÓN.

Philoktetes, written in 1993, was originally commissioned by Jan Ritsema and the Kaaitheater in Brussels for American actor Ron Vawter (of The Wooster Group). It was intended for use in an unproduced piece titled *Philoktetes Variations,* inspired by the writings of Andre Gide and Heiner Muller.

The play premiered on November 16, 2000, at the Sala Xavier Villaurrutia in Mexico City, produced by Teatro de Arena in a Spanish-language translation by John Jesurun, Erwin Veytia, and Martín Acosta. It was directed by Martín Acosta. The set design was by Martín Acosta; the lighting design was by Matías Gorlero; the costume design was by Martín López; the sound design was by Joaquín López "Chas." The cast was as follows:

PHILOKTETES . . . . Arturo Reyes
ODYSSEUS . . . . Roberto Soto
NEOPTOLEMUS . . . . Marco Pérez

SPECIAL THANKS to the Sundance Theater Lab, the Foundation for Contemporary Performance Arts, La Mama ETC, Ellen Stewart, Martín Acosta, Greg Mehrten, Bettina Masuch, Erika Munk, Frank Maya, Viviane De Muynck, Dirk Roofthooft, and Ron Vawter.

LISTEN TO ME

PHILOKTETES: Listen to me, I'm telling you something.
So that you'll learn the value of suffering, the joy of sacrifice and patience,
    murder and manslaughter.
So that you'll learn to speak the language of
the dead.
Once again it's time for you to shut up.
Belly up to the buzz saw.
Gravitational collapse, Blackleg, Yankee pot roast.
Stop crying. You should be happy.
Listen to me, I'm telling you something.
You tell someone else and they'll tell someone else.
This is what Philoktetes told me.
This is his suicide note, his poison-pen letter.
First, I'll give the clue, then the story, then
the real story.
First what they saw, then what was seen, then what was.
The cadaver will direct the autopsy,
a talking corpse narrating, a dead horse talking, a dead foot walking.
Philoktetes is dead. I was looking at him outside.
He had one fly on him. But that fly was tiny,
triumphant.

ODYSSEUS: You have been found neither guilty nor innocent but
you have been found.

PHILOKTETES: Stop crying.

NEOPTOLEMUS: What's that dripping?

PHILOKTETES: Blood, urine, pieces of marijuana,
carbon monoxide.
I'm sorry that he's dead, all right?
Once again it's time for you to shut up.

NEOPTOLEMUS: What's that moving?

PHILOKTETES: A salamander come to eat the turnips.
I had wanted to tell you about my deep and
unrelenting and unequivocal disbelief and unbelief
in everything.
But now I've changed my mind.
Do you understand that?

NEOPTOLEMUS: What's that dripping?

PHILOKTETES: Crocodile tears. I'd like to read a nice book now and
then with a story in the middle that goes nowhere.
Don't you understand?
He's been murdered, killed.
His head hit a bullet.
Habeas corpus, a talking corpse.

NEOPTOLEMUS: You were lost but now you're found. I found you.

PHILOKTETES: He's pulverized, a smoke signal, a cat dream, a molly maguire.

NEOPTOLEMUS: I don't hear anything.

PHILOKTETES: You're fuckin' brain-dead, that's why.
A pack of flies is riding around in his head. That fly was tiny,
triumphant. I promise.
This is my island. It's beautiful. It's always beautiful.
I love it.
At night it gets so dark you don't know where you are.
In the day it's hell, but at night, when everything else is
asleep, it's heaven.

NEOPTOLEMUS: I don't want to stay here.

PHILOKTETES: Yes you do.
I'll leave the bow here with you.
You can use it if you want.
But wait for one night and you won't want to use it.
In the day you'll feel like using it but at night you won't.
Philoktetes loved it here.
Mushrooms grow here at night and you can eat them.
You'll see so many things on this island, you won't want to leave it.
You'll be married to it.
You won't be able to tell where the island begins and you end.
Let me see your hand. It's afraid.
Don't you like it here?

NEOPTOLEMUS: What's that smell?

PHILOKTETES: Sour mash, camphor, apple rotting, bull blood.
Why are you here?

NEOPTOLEMUS: To find Philoktetes.

PHILOKTETES: Why don't you get out of here? Philoktetes is
not here.
Let me tell you honestly, he isn't here.
He's dead, I told you.
But I have a bow and we can share it.

NEOPTOLEMUS: I don't want to.

PHILOKTETES: Share the bow.
You take it and keep it.

ODYSSEUS: Take it.

PHILOKTETES: Stop arguing. What are you waiting for? Can you
see the bow?
You can only see it from one point on the island.
Who can see it? Whoever can see it can have it.
Who can see it? No one?
One person can see the bow. No?
So I built a house of cards to keep warm and I got
inside my house of cards and burned it.
And it kept me warm for a while.
A good long while.
I found that if I kept talking and kept very still,
I'd stay warm.
But then it got very lonely in that house.
But people shouldn't be alone.
And I thought, I have these mushrooms
and if I can share them
Maybe it won't be so lonely.
So I tried to share them with the birds,
but no one wanted to share them.
So I threw them into a river. And what did you do?

NEOPTOLEMUS: Maybe you can help us.

PHILOKTETES: What can I do for you?

ODYSSEUS: I was under the impression that Philoktetes was
here on this island where we left him.

PHILOKTETES: No Philoktetes here. He's dead.
Very hard to find.
So what did you do while he sat here rotting?
What did you do?
Don't just sit there breathing, Neoptolemus.
You should be having the time of your life.

PHILOKTETES AS GODDESS

NEOPTOLEMUS: Who are you?

PHILOKTETES: I am the goddess of the island.

NEOPTOLEMUS: This island has no goddess.
What is your name?

PHILOKTETES: There are no inhabitants on this island to call me anything.
So I need no name.

NEOPTOLEMUS: Doesn't Philoktetes live on this island?

PHILOKTETES: Who would live on this ridiculous rock?
No human have I ever seen before you arrived.

NEOPTOLEMUS: What are you?

PHILOKTETES: I am self-born.

NEOPTOLEMUS: No husband, no lover?

PHILOKTETES: My first-born son was my lover.
Born of me and only me.

NEOPTOLEMUS: Why doesn't he appear with you?

PHILOKTETES: My lover-son wanted children born of both of us.
These I gave him, but he grew jealous.
Overwhelmed by their ugliness, he cast them into the
underworld to live as goon squad.
One quiet night I called on my youngest son, my most
beautiful, to help me.

I said:
"My son, if you do my bidding,
we shall revenge your father's crime,
for it was he who invented shameful acts."
His father came to make love to me.
And from his hiding place, my loyal son reached toward his
father and grasped him in his left hand, while holding in his
right an enormous sickle.
He swung sharply and cut off the members of his own father.
He threw them into the air, where they
splattered in a mist.
Perhaps that's what you smell.
I inhaled the bloody mist, the drops fell to
the Earth
and released my children from the underworld.

A pygmy phalanx of furies and a race of tall
giants shining in their armor and holding spears
in their hands.
I mistook your party for them.

NEOPTOLEMUS: We are only men searching for Philoktetes.

PHILOKTETES: From the foam of the sea where the genitals
had been thrown sprang my daughter. This
Philoktetes, is he a god?

NEOPTOLEMUS: Less than a god, less than a man.

PHILOKTETES: What does he look like?

NEOPTOLEMUS: He is said to resemble a rotting aubergine
covered in red garlic sauce.

PHILOKTETES: And how did he become this?

NEOPTOLEMUS: Years ago, on another island, he suddenly
was inflicted upon and began to fester
a burning spot so putrefied that he was
abandoned here.

PHILOKTETES: By whom?

NEOPTOLEMUS: His friends, his army.

PHILOKTETES: Blood of his own blood?

NEOPTOLEMUS: Spun out of control after years of futile fighting
in the Indochimney.

PHILOKTETES: I had heard about the devastations.
Did he displease a god?

NEOPTOLEMUS: A goddess, Chryse.

PHILOKTETES: My daughter. Yeah, well, she is a sort of a bitch.
How was she displeased?

NEOPTOLEMUS: I thought you could tell me.
What about your first son?

PHILOKTETES: At one time he lay around the island longing for
love, but he has removed himself to the fourth
quadrant of a distant heaven, abstracted and
disengaged.
With no one to worship him.
Who would worship a man so incomplete?
So void of the agent of his will?
I mistook your leader, Odysseus, for him.
Does he have all his parts?

NEOPTOLEMUS: Yes.

PHILOKTETES: Check again.

NEOPTOLEMUS: Are you sure you haven't seen Philoktetes?

PHILOKTETES: Do you think I would allow such a stinking thing on
my island?
Leave me before I become displeased with you.
I have no taste for aubergine.

NEOPTOLEMUS: And your worshippers?

PHILOKTETES: I am self-born and self-perpetuating. I have no need for
worshippers.
Now, get the fuck out of here before I castrate you and
cover you in garlic sauce.
Aubergine, my foot!

MOONSTRUCK

PHILOKTETES: One day, soon after I had landed here, a bird came to me.
It said:
"Seeing that you are in such pain and practically obsolete, we share your grief.
We see your broken teeth and the bites on your lips."
I answered:
"It's from eating snakes and opening oysters with
my bare teeth."
The bird said:
"We, the creatures of the island, have decided
on a future for you. A way out.
Would you like to bleed without pain?
Drink milk instead of stagnant water?
We see how the phases of the planets disrupt
the blood tides in your foot.
A woman holds the moon in her body.
What other animal has a twenty-eight-day cycle?
None.
A woman can hold life in her body,
and produce from it not only women but men.
A woman can bleed painlessly.
A woman can produce milk.
I see you changing in your suffering.
Take your knife to the tundra, and plant.
I believe you are soon to become a woman."
"Me?" I said, "I beg your pardon, honey?
I don't think so."
Several weeks later I began menstruating.

PRAYER FRAGMENT

PHILOKTETES: Shall we pray?

ODYSSEUS: Don't say it.

NEOPTOLEMUS: Say it.

PHILOKTETES: Every day I wake up and say it.
It used to take me all day to spit out
each and every one of the twenty thousand bloody dominoes into the sky.
But I learned.

NEOPTOLEMUS: Say it.

ODYSSEUS: Don't say it.

PHILOKTETES: First I dance around on my bad foot a little bit like this.
It sends a fibrillating spinal tap of bloodshot
straight through my tongue.

ODYSSEUS: Don't say it.

PHILOKTETES: You know every word.

NEOPTOLEMUS: Listen to what the cripple creek fairy say.

PHILOKTETES: And he say:
"I am the instrument of God the Creator.
To try and succeed where he failed.
I can see everything.
What I can see, I can touch.
What I cannot touch, I can see.
What I cannot see, I can imagine.
What I can imagine is mine to keep.
What I cannot imagine is not mine and will crush
me eventually."
So I crush all thought about what I cannot
imagine.
Then I let the bird choir sing and the God speaks
back.
And it say:
"I made you out of nothing.
And now you are nothing.
I made you and I can unmake you.
I can make you into something else.
I can make something beautiful and
something ugly.
I will crush you, I will eat you.

And after I eat you, I will spit you out upon the
waves.
For the fish and lowest of animals to eat.
Because you are the lowest of all animals.
I made you that way.

Lower than low, darker than dark.
Blacker than black.
I made you that way to give glory to me.
And you will give glory to me even in your lowest
form of misery because I made you that way.
And you will rejoice in it because you have no
other choice.
And you will be happy with what I have done
because I am the Lord your Creator.
And I made you to suffer and worship me in joy.
If I give you a brain full of black blood, you will rejoice and thank me
     for it.
If I give you a three-headed son,
you will jump for joy.
If I give you testicles of salt, you will rejoice.
If I rain thalidomide on your people, you will rejoice and thank me for it.
If I give you a cocksucking son who will bear no issue and be the end of
     your family's line, you will rejoice in it and thank me for what I have
     given you.
If I burn your city, you will rejoice.
If I send you to burn a city, you will also rejoice.
If I cause you to build a great army, you will rejoice.
If I cause your teeth to be ripped from the roots and run riot over the
     countryside, you will rejoice.
This is what I have given unto you, Philoktetes.
And you will give me all your joy when you
thank me for it.
You will dance for me on one foot if necessary.
You will eat blood cakes if necessary.
You will rape your sister if necessary.
You will swallow your own flesh if necessary,
because that is how I have made you.
If I give you strength, you will cherish it.
If I give you weakness, you will cherish it.
If I give you a stump for a face, you will rejoice in it.
For it is what I gave you.
You will find beauty in it.
For there is beauty in the center of all ugliness.
Remember that I am in everything. Even in the ugliest thing, which is what
     I made you.
And I made you to discover that.

And in discovering that, you will rejoice at your
good fortune to be made by me as anything
I will want to make you.
And when you beg me for an answer,
I will say, what are you looking at?
And if I give you a rhino clit bitch for a wife, you will rejoice and breed seven
    rhino daughters in honor of me."
That is what the God says to me.
And if I say no, he will slap me down again until
I cry uncle and enjoy the beauty of my suffering.
That's how I have survived ten years in a club-footed memory dance.
Can you dig all that?

ODYSSEUS: I'm afraid I don't know that one.

PHILOKTETES: Yes, you do.
You recite it over every body of every beautiful boy you bury.
You're here because you couldn't heave up another word to save your life.

NEOPTOLEMUS: You couldn't chuck another spear to save your life.

PHILOKTETES: A battalion of hydra-headed epileptics couldn't
have stopped you from coming back for the bow.
Am I right or am I wrong?

ODYSSEUS: Wrong.

PHILOKTETES: Am I right or am I wrong?
They sure was right when they said my brains was in my feet.
So feast on the meal I've
prepared for you.
And take the bow back to Troy and win the battle for the empire.
Pile the bodies high and when you're done with that, prepare the next pile.
Because the thought that brought you here
demands ten times ten skyscrapers full.

NEOPTOLEMUS: Full of what?

PHILOKTETES: Full of beautiful boys in screaming sad sacks.
Oh, you pretty things.
Then, and only then, will the God be satisfied.
For I am the instrument of the God above.
And we'll eat the meal we've prepared together.
And it will taste good.
Then we'll spit it out and start all over again.

NEOPTOLEMUS: Oh, you pretty things.

PHILOKTETES: All to glorify our own stupid selves.
Have another blood and honey sandwich, Odysseus, and contemplate your
    future under the boot.

AND TROY?

PHILOKTETES: And Troy?

ODYSSEUS: Still undefeated.

PHILOKTETES: Just can't burn that mother down, can you?
Haven't you fought hard enough?

ODYSSEUS: It is said the city will burn seven times until it will be ash.

PHILOKTETES: I burned seven times myself and I am ash.

ODYSSEUS: Still defeated.

PHILOKTETES: You've come so far, covered so little ground.

ODYSSEUS: And really, what does ash feel like?

PHILOKTETES: The sting of the Ishmaelite.

ODYSSEUS: Angel dust.

PHILOKTETES: Fuck you and the horse you rode in on.
Why have you come back?
It's said that you've come back here to regain your
honor, your dignity,
To be worthy of the victory over Troy.
To make it slightly less hollow.
To make some sense of your obsessive attempts to penetrate her interior.
To find your balls again.
Is that really you?

ODYSSEUS: Yes, It's me.
Odysseus, the evil one, trickster, seducer, the perverted one, baby killer,
    betrayer.

PHILOKTETES: Always in search of something lower than yourself.
Look at me and tell me if you've found it.

ODYSSEUS: If I swallow my pride why can't you?

PHILOKTETES: Not only have I swallowed my pride but I am swallowed
    by it.
Imagine that.

ODYSSEUS: That sounds like fun. What were you doing on the
temple grounds, anyway?

PHILOKTETES: Same thing you were. Looking for a whorehouse,
taking a fucking walk.

NEOPTOLEMUS: You must have done something that would have caused this foot to fester.

PHILOKTETES: It could have been any number of things.
Most of which you yourself have done.

ODYSSEUS: It's hideous here. So muggy. The air is like chocolate.
How did you find this horrible hotel?
We left you on the other side of the island.

PHILOKTETES: This was more secluded.
My foot prefers it. More sugar water?

ODYSSEUS: No.

PHILOKTETES: So, anyway, you're back because no matter how hard you try you just can't turn Troy into a disco inferno.
It's no surprise to me.

ODYSSEUS: And that's why we've come back, and you know it.

PHILOKTETES: Oh, now I know it, do I?
I seem to know everything.
Unfortunately, the information you want is stuck
in my throat and nothing can retrieve it.
And where did you get that aide-de-camp?

ODYSSEUS: What did he tell you?

PHILOKTETES: Nothing. But he is such a fag.

ODYSSEUS: He is not.

PHILOKTETES: Did you ask him?

ODYSSEUS: No.

PHILOKTETES: Then he never told you.

ODYSSEUS: What does that have to do with anything?

PHILOKTETES: Nothing. I just thought I'd notice it.

ODYSSEUS: What are you reading?

PHILOKTETES: "An Intimate History of Nothingness."

ODYSSEUS: Never heard of it.

PHILOKTETES: Neither had I.
Have another margarita.

ODYSSEUS: No, thanks.

PHILOKTETES: Neoptolemus?

NEOPTOLEMUS: No, thanks.

PHILOKTETES: Who's going to know?
I soak my leg in it sometimes.
Then they kicked me out of the cripple wing
because I was making too much trouble.
Can you imagine? Me, a war hero, making trouble.
They said I was beyond crippled, and I wasn't going to stay in the nut wing
So they put me here in this hotel, alone.
The doctor visits once a week.
We have a few drinks together and he stumbles home.
How are things in the Pantygon, Odysseus?

NEOPTOLEMUS: Why is it so hot in here?

ODYSSEUS: Neoptolemus, stay away from this impure,
evil-smelling, unclean Philoktetes.
Upon whom God has inflicted curse and
malediction, contempt and abasement, infamy, ire, and
degradation. As upon no other person.

NEOPTOLEMUS: Don't take it to heart, Philoktetes.

PHILOKTETES: Not only did I take it to heart, it became my heart,
    pumping a mutilating self-contempt through every vein in my brain.
More noxious than the vinaigrette that eats my body.

ODYSSEUS: And what is eating your body? Did they ever find out?

PHILOKTETES: [*Sarcastically.*] Oh, and what is eating your body? Did they
    ever find out?
You know they didn't.
If they had I wouldn't be here and neither would you.
We'd probably both be dead half a mile outside of
Troy. Thank you for bringing the flowers.

ODYSSEUS: I thought you were dead.

PHILOKTETES: I thought you were dead.

ODYSSEUS: I thought you were dead.

PHILOKTETES: Which isn't to say you wished I was dead.
Which isn't to say that I'm not halfway there.
Be that as it may, the whores here can't put up
with me, either. I don't blame them.
I just can't get it up no more.
Cry like a woman for what you couldn't get like a man.
Right, Neoptolemus?

NEOPTOLEMUS: Shut the fuck up.

PHILOKTETES: Nasty little grunge-bunny.

ODYSSEUS: Who's that?

PHILOKTETES: The maid.
As she spied my groaning groin, her eyes engulfed me in a Gordian knot.
Too late, my brothers.
But never mind, all my troubles, lord, will soon be over.
Now, get out of my room before I call the front desk.
I've had enough and so, I'm sure, have you.

ODYSSEUS: Do we have a deal?

PHILOKTETES: No deal.

NEOPTOLEMUS: We'll come back again tomorrow.

PHILOKTETES: Please don't.
By the way, Odysseus, if our paths cross again, if we happen to see each other,
though I doubt we would recognize one another, as we are now so well-hidden
by our individual sicknesses,
I must warn you to stay away from me, as I from
you.
For you and I may very well be
the impure, evil-smelling, unclean people
upon whom God has
inflicted curse and malediction,
contempt and abasement, infamy, ire, and
degradation as upon no other people.
So if you see me, walk on by.

ODYSSEUS: Why do you include me in your degradation?

PHILOKTETES: Would you like another drink?
We may be discovered and revealed if we are
seen too close together. You do understand?

ODYSSEUS: Why do you include me?

PHILOKTETES: Because you're the snake that bit me and sent me here.

ODYSSEUS: Spare me your moaning lecture.
It's a bunch of bullshit.

PHILOKTETES: And you wear it well.
The shit-faced smile smeared all over your face.

ODYSSEUS: Spare me the lecture.
Write it down and mail it to me care of the battleship.

PHILOKTETES: Why?

ODYSSEUS: Because I am the one in this body
and you are the one in that body.
And I am the one who says what I say and you are the one who says what
he says.
It's physical, logical. No reason.

So don't bother to ask why.
I am the one because I am the one.
I am the one who put you here and I'm the one who will take you out.

PHILOKTETES: You in that body have failed.
I am the one who can keep you a failure and I'm the one who can take you
   out of it.
I am the one.
Me in this body.
Here.
What could you possibly want from me?
You'd eat your own shit to succeed.

ODYSSEUS: Me in this body who would eat my own children,
sleep with my mother, rape my sister,
kill my father, give birth to my own brother,
destroy my own family to preserve what's left of it.
If that's what I have to do.
And what will you do to get off this island?

PHILOKTETES: None of the above.
If I had done any of those things, I could
understand what happened to me and I would do them again to undo it.
Who bit me? What bit me?

ODYSSEUS: No answer.

PHILOKTETES: Who left me here?
And why did you leave me here?

ODYSSEUS: I was afraid.

PHILOKTETES: How brave of you to admit it.
How courageous of you to wait so long to tell me.

ODYSSEUS: You were so ugly.
And you wouldn't stop screaming.

PHILOKTETES: Why have you come back then?

ODYSSEUS: Because I'm afraid.

PHILOKTETES: Afraid the fuck of what?

ODYSSEUS: Of losing. Of not knowing what you've learned being here.

PHILOKTETES: And what the hell could you use that knowledge for?
It's not exactly an equation for a new bomb.

ODYSSEUS: And what have you learned being here?

PHILOKTETES: I haven't learned anything except that every
word that comes out of your mouth is a lie.

I'd love to share the pain with you but it's not possible.
You see, I've become very greedy with it.
What have you learned since you left me here?

ODYSSEUS: That I am your only salvation.
And what have you learned since you've been here?

PHILOKTETES: That I am my only salvation.
By the way, I'm also your only salvation.

ODYSSEUS: Then if we can persuade each other.

PHILOKTETES: Victory to the victim.
The vengeance of the crucified.

ODYSSEUS: Get off your cross.

PHILOKTETES: If you put away your hammer and nails.
[*Into telephone.*] Hello, I'd like to order two
orders of mushu pork, five egg rolls, and a one-ton
tomato. You know what room! [*Slams phone down.*] Why don't we meet
tomorrow for lunch by the pool for round two?
Now, get out of my room. Good night.

PHILOKTETES DANCES

PHILOKTETES is dancing.

ODYSSEUS: Stop, please.

NEOPTOLEMUS: Don't mind him. He's a practitioner of Yogic flying.

ODYSSEUS: I won't have that pagan sorcery in my presence.

NEOPTOLEMUS: It's nothing. He rarely gets a centimeter off the
ground.

ODYSSEUS: Keep the windows closed in case he gets any
higher, and tie his foot to a string.
I don't want him to escape.
See that he gets all the honey sandwiches he wants.
That's enough.

    [*PHILOKTETES stops dancing.*]

PHILOKTETES: Don't you like it?

ODYSSEUS: No, dear.

PHILOKTETES: Oh, yes, dear.
After I was bitten, my first mistake was learning to crawl on one knee.
I thought it was impossible, but I did learn.
My second mistake was learning to dance on one foot.
I thought it was impossible, but I did learn.

ODYSSEUS: What does it represent?

PHILOKTETES: It's an interpretation of a hungry fly after a meal of
blood.

ODYSSEUS: Oh, no, dear.

PHILOKTETES: Oh, yes, dear.

NEOPTOLEMUS: It isn't that, really, is it?

PHILOKTETES: Yes, it is.

ODYSSEUS: Where do you get such perversions?

PHILOKTETES: When I see my reflection in your eyes.

ODYSSEUS: Is that really what you see?

PHILOKTETES: Oh, yes. Poor thing.
What a horrible world you must live in.

ODYSSEUS: You live in it, too.

PHILOKTETES: I don't live in it, I live under it.
Go figure, imagine that.

ODYSSEUS: Don't complain. You could have been born a hunchback.

PHILOKTETES: Every day I pray to the gods to make me into water.

ODYSSEUS: The gods got us into this, but I doubt they can get us out.

PHILOKTETES: Hera, make me into water.
But I am mostly water already, aren't I?

ODYSSEUS: Red water.

PHILOKTETES: Jesus, make me into clear water.
Can't you see I am covered in white powder, a toppled minaret, armless and close
    to starvation, lost in a sea of ventriloquy, the lithium at the end of the tunnel.
I don't even speak my own language and
I don't even know who I am or ever was.

ODYSSEUS: Sometimes it's better not to know who you are.
I don't know who you are either but
there is no question, as to what you aren't.

PHILOKTETES: Then what am I?

ODYSSEUS: Whatever I am, you are not, and whatever you aren't, I am.

PHILOKTETES: That being so, would you kill me if I asked you to?

ODYSSEUS: No.

PHILOKTETES: Why? Would you like to kill me?

ODYSSEUS: Yes.

PHILOKTETES: Then why don't you?

ODYSSEUS: Your request somehow muffles the joy of it.
Under those circumstances, I couldn't.

PHILOKTETES: Well, then, wait until other circumstances
arise, and feel free to do it. I won't mind.
I dare you. My life is worth more to you than it is to me.
I hate myself more than I hate you.
I am the vomit of my former error.

ODYSSEUS: What a horrible world you must live in if you have to ask
    someone to kill you.
Can't you do it yourself?

PHILOKTETES: The pleasure of having you do it is too hard to resist.
To watch the thinking war machine as it churns through its motions.

We Greeks are so beautiful when we kill.
Odysseus, make me into clear water.
That's right, watch me cry like a woman for what
I couldn't face like a man.
Poor things. What a horrible world you must live in.

ODYSSEUS: I don't live in the world, either. I also live under it.
Very close to where you live. We're neighbors.

PHILOKTETES: Fat chance.

ODYSSEUS: I walk by your house every day.
Somewhere near the bottom of the world.
It's left a scar on my brain that can't be erased.

PHILOKTETES: How could you live on the bottom of the world?
I've never seen you down here.

ODYSSEUS: You don't notice me, but I'm here.

PHILOKTETES: You're digging around in my heart, tricking me.

ODYSSEUS: Give me the bow and I'll kill you.

PHILOKTETES: Kill me and I'll give you the bow.

ODYSSEUS: No.

PHILOKTETES: Neoptolemus, you do it.

NEOPTOLEMUS: Not so fast. How will I do it?

PHILOKTETES: Whatever way you want.

NEOPTOLEMUS: But why?

PHILOKTETES: Why not?
One quiet night I had a dream.
I dreamed I could fly.
We Malians are always accused of flying.
But I was flying in my dream.
As I flew through the temple of Chryse,
I was a pigbat, spitting blood and wine, dreaming of Troy.
Floating over the bones of the lovely boys who followed me into failure.
I was as they saw me. I woke up.
Since then when I look in the mirror I can't see
myself as anything else but that.

NEOPTOLEMUS: What an ugly dream.

PHILOKTETES: It's more than a dream, and so as I can't see
myself as anything else, I'd rather not see myself at all.

ODYSSEUS: Then don't look.

PHILOKTETES: Living is looking and I don't want to look anymore. What do you see?

ODYSSEUS: I can't see myself at all.

PHILOKTETES: You must see something. Take off your mask.

ODYSSEUS: I'm not wearing a mask.

PHILOKTETES: Show me the mind in the middle of the mask.

ODYSSEUS: No, nothing at all, blank.

PHILOKTETES: What do you see when you look at me?

ODYSSEUS: Certainly not a pigbat.

PHILOKTETES: Yes, you do. Will you do it?

ODYSSEUS: Maybe.

PHILOKTETES: Kill the pigbat. Do this in memory of me. It's the last thing on earth anyone would want to be.

NEOPTOLEMUS: Who made you?

PHILOKTETES: The gods made me.

NEOPTOLEMUS: They made you as a pigbat?

PHILOKTETES: No, not originally, but somehow I was transformed.

NEOPTOLEMUS: How?

PHILOKTETES: Ask Odysseus.

ODYSSEUS: Were you transformed, or did you do it yourself?

NEOPTOLEMUS: Can't you transform yourself back to your original form?

PHILOKTETES: I don't think so. I don't have the energy. If you kill me, hopefully I will revert.

ODYSSEUS: And live in hell, like the oracle says.

PHILOKTETES: That oracle was written by some horny, monkey-fucking monk and you know it.

ODYSSEUS: We know it. But I'd rather live in hell as myself than in heaven as a pigbat.

NEOPTOLEMUS: I didn't think they were allowed in heaven.

PHILOKTETES: Haven't you gotten it yet, you little faggot? There is no heaven.

NEOPTOLEMUS: You don't believe that. Can you worship God and be a pigbat at the same time?

PHILOKTETES: I worship myself now.

ODYSSEUS: Then you are in hell already.

PHILOKTETES: Correct. Can you tell me why?

ODYSSEUS: Yes, anyone who lives in hell worships himself. That's why he's there.

PHILOKTETES: And where are you?

ODYSSEUS: Dead center.

PHILOKTETES: Will you do it, Neoptolemus?

NEOPTOLEMUS: No.

PHILOKTETES: Odysseus?

ODYSSEUS: Next Friday.

PHILOKTETES: Could you make that Thursday?

ODYSSEUS: All right.

PHILOKTETES: You never answered my question. What am I?

ODYSSEUS: I'll tell you on Thursday.

THE FIRST DAY

PHILOKTETES: The first day on this island, I sat rotting on a rock.
Minute after minute, the day and I suffered together.
Making secret plots to escape the next minute.
I thought it was unendurable
but unfortunately I discovered that it was endurable.
It was endurable unfortunately.
I thought I would die of it
But I discovered I wouldn't die of it until I had suffered completely the
     suffering it required of me.
Till I had paid the bill completely.
So I endured completely.
One day I came upon a bird.
The very bird who had offered me the qualities
of a woman to ease my pain.
She was weeping.
I asked her why she was weeping.
"I weep because I am barren.
My husband, my friends have left me.
I, who proclaimed the glory of woman.
I bleed but bear no children, and I have become useless to my family,
I can create nothing, so I am nothing.
How will I endure my uselessness?
My wound is incurable, yet I thought that if I made light of it I could bear it.
I used to love my beautiful little body, my shape, mine and only mine.
But now it's mine and only mine and I hate it.
It's mine and I don't want it.
Even my shame is useless."
I said:
"Rejoice, oh you barren,
you who do not bear children
break forth and shout.
You who do not give birth.
For the children of the desolate one are many
surpassing those of her that has a husband.
Have no fear because you are put to shame.
Do not stand in awe because you were reproached.
For you shall forget your old confusion and shall not remember the reproach
     of your widowed state." [Isaiah 54.]
Your value is not that you can create, but that you were created.
Even our adversaries will be compelled to
understand in spite of themselves.
We sang, we bled together awhile. She flew away.

I later found her body in a nest she'd made of barbed wire.
I bled again.
I used to love my beautiful body, my smell, my skin, mine and only mine.
If no one else will love it then I will love it because it's mine and only mine.
My skin, my smell, my blood, my body.
Mine and only mine because it's mine and it's beautiful because it can endure
    even its own ugliness.
Mine and only mine. Mine by right of conquest.

WHERE HAVE YOU BEEN?

ODYSSEUS: Where have you been?

PHILOKTETES: Taking a shit, dear one.

ODYSSEUS: Oh, no, dear.

PHILOKTETES: Oh, yes, dear. First I shit in the ocean, then I shit
on the altar to the crucified,
Then I shit in the temple, then I shit on words that tell me nothing.
That's where I've been.

ODYSSEUS: One quiet night, we all found ourselves
in the same restaurant.
Take your pick from the menu.
One appetizer may be slightly better than another,
but all the food is rotten.

PHILOKTETES: Our common brutal biology.

ODYSSEUS: Can you dig that?

PHILOKTETES: What about me?

ODYSSEUS: God cannot return the skin that man has torn asunder.

PHILOKTETES: Winners always lose, all losers know that.

ODYSSEUS: I cried because I had no shoes until I met a man who had
no feet.

PHILOKTETES: And that man cried because he had no feet until he met
a man who had no balls.

ODYSSEUS: The horrors of a half-known life.

PHILOKTETES: In the underworld.
Where the night comes before the day.
The wound before the bite.
Go and repair your army.

ODYSSEUS: I'll leave it smashed and broken and starving.
Spasmodically knocking at your door for a cookie.

PHILOKTETES: What would you know?

ODYSSEUS: We all know. We, the ones who are left to carry around
bowls of ashes. It's a fixation.

PHILOKTETES: A meditation on an empty moon but lemon blossoms
still bloom.

ODYSSEUS: The ones who clean up the shit and the vomit of the ones who went before. My stomach is shivering.

PHILOKTETES: A great shudder has gone through the family.
Finally, at last, a filthy, poison breath breathed among us.
Under the soles of our feet.
Into our toenails, even. But orange blossoms still bloom.

ODYSSEUS: It lifted us here. A blubbering, choking aardvark.
Its nose all twisted around in an empty anthill but
orange blossoms still bloom.

PHILOKTETES: What an insulting insult.

ODYSSEUS: No one has to know.

PHILOKTETES: Everyone has to know by now.

ODYSSEUS: And how?

PHILOKTETES: Everyone has to know by now.
The underworld forever stays but orange
blossoms still bloom under the underworld.

SWEETNESS

PHILOKTETES: Sweet Neoptolemus, I want you to tell me . . .

NEOPTOLEMUS: No, you tell me.

PHILOKTETES: What?

NEOPTOLEMUS: Tell me, what god's asshole have you climbed out of
to have ended up in this toilet?
Who excreted you, who vomited you up?
What jekyll-headed god's spleen hurled you into my orbit?
What fag-hag goddess gave birth to you, and why?

PHILOKTETES: What neurotic soul dreamed you into my galaxy of
   pain?

NEOPTOLEMUS: Why, and what meaning do you have?
Or have you given birth to yourself?
What steaming pustule erupted you?
Or have you come here on your own power?

PHILOKTETES: And what god's fart blew you here to disturb
my peace and quiet?
To interrupt my pain?
Who could have done it?

NEOPTOLEMUS: What satyr ejaculated you into my sphere?
What impotent ant spit you out in a fit of disgust?

PHILOKTETES: Who could have done it?

NEOPTOLEMUS: What dying man exhaled you?
What reeking hyena bitch rejected you?
What is this thing in front of us?
What cell mutated you into existence?
Who or what could have done it?

PHILOKTETES: And why?

NEOPTOLEMUS: If I could force myself into your head with a shovel
and figure it out.

PHILOKTETES: If I could force myself out of my head, I would.

NEOPTOLEMUS: And why do we have to sit here and breathe his stink
   day after day?

PHILOKTETES: The night air has gotten to you.
You've begun to stink, yourself. Get out of the sun.
You're becoming rancid, so manly and aggressive.

NEOPTOLEMUS: Have another scotch and shut up.

PHILOKTETES: Empty-headed, dizzy, delirious.
I don't recognize you.
Your sweet little body, it's afraid, shivering, preoccupied, incoherent.

NEOPTOLEMUS: Full of bull's breath, a pig-necked daddy pulsing with
   adrenaline.

PHILOKTETES: And ready to kill.
Your diaper has fallen off.
How nice to know you don't need it anymore.
You're a body that could go far, especially dressed the way you are.
He's beginning to see the picture now.

NEOPTOLEMUS: Aren't you dead yet?

PHILOKTETES: What?

NEOPTOLEMUS: I said, aren't you fucking dead yet?

PHILOKTETES: No.

NEOPTOLEMUS: Then pick up your brain and answer me.

PHILOKTETES: [*To ODYSSEUS.*] Why did you bring him here?
As if his sweetness could seduce me where your logic failed.
What unworthy catamite have you brought into my presence?

ODYSSEUS: The son of his dead father.
As if his pappy could have known he'd
produce a fruit so bitter, so sweet.
He would have had you umbilically strangulated.

PHILOKTETES: Smothered you in your own swaddling clothes.

NEOPTOLEMUS: Then curse the egg that hatched me. The snake that bit you.

PHILOKTETES: I was hoping for some sweet logic to ooze out of you.
But your gangrene is spreading in the moonlight.
Intoxicated, lustrous, asphyxiating, amniotic.
It's melted its name into the snow.

ODYSSEUS: It's your pathological bloody brotherhood of cells united in
   hatred against all comers that's infected us.

PHILOKTETES: Oh, no, dear, you brought it with you.
He's beginning to get the picture now.
I was hoping for some sweet logic to ooze out of you.
Some thought to rescue me.
But, alas, the putrification continues.
He's beginning to get the picture.

ODYSSEUS: And what does he see in the picture?

PHILOKTETES: I'll tell you what I see.
Correct me if I'm wrong.
I see a body and two idiots talking to it.
Trying to get answers out of it.
They believe it's alive and can tell them something.
The body knows the answer, but the other two don't know the question.
So they rant and hurl insults at it.
One is young, one is old, and one is dead.
They're a triangle, visible and indivisible.
All are defeated.
But the body says nothing so they fill in the blanks.
Convinced that their enemy is the dead body.
Instead of screaming at each other, they scream at
the body.
Instead of insulting each other, they insult the body.
They sit and wait for it to speak.
As if the dead keep on talking.
A family of birds sits on a branch and rolls their eyes.

NEOPTOLEMUS: Does it have anything to do with love?

PHILOKTETES: I would hope so.
But now the picture changes.
I see two cadavers screaming at each other.

NEOPTOLEMUS: While a breathing man sips heroin.

PHILOKTETES: Yes, can you see it?

ODYSSEUS: What is this bullshit? Change the picture.

NEOPTOLEMUS: No, leave it. I want to see it. I can see my body.

PHILOKTETES: You are your body and you can see it.

ODYSSEUS: I am not my body.

PHILOKTETES: You are your body and if you watch long enough, I will
    bury you.

NEOPTOLEMUS: Does it have anything to do with love?

PHILOKTETES: Look at it.

ODYSSEUS: What hideous thing have you done?
What false god have you prayed to?
Who's wife have you slept with?
What ideology have you rejected?

NEOPTOLEMUS: More heroin?

ODYSSEUS: What god have you spurned? Answer me.

PHILOKTETES: Sure.

ODYSSEUS: Where's that aspirin?
I want you to recite from beginning to end so
we can hear what you've done to bring this down upon us.
What treason have you performed?
What version of what perversion?

NEOPTOLEMUS: Does it have anything to do with love?

ODYSSEUS: Stop asking me that.

PHILOKTETES: You're drooling, what can satisfy you?
Would it satisfy you if I told you I killed John Lennon or JFK?
Smothered Judy Garland or Bessie Smith?
What answer will ease your pain?

NEOPTOLEMUS: Would you like an aspirin?

ODYSSEUS: What law did you break?

NEOPTOLEMUS: Does anyone have an aspirin?

ODYSSEUS: Hold the room still, will you?
What law did you break?

PHILOKTETES: There is no law here on this island.
And where there is no law there is no transgression.
And leave your bags of logic and order packed.
They don't mean a thing here in the vicinity of my putrid leg.
So leave the bags packed. And get your sweating eye away from me.

ODYSSEUS: What are you looking at?

NEOPTOLEMUS: His leg.

ODYSSEUS: Start at the beginning.

PHILOKTETES: And I am blessed among women.

ODYSSEUS: How did you get here?

PHILOKTETES: You brought me here.

ODYSSEUS: Why?

PHILOKTETES: My leg, the smell, the pain, the howl.
My toe, my foot, my leg, my legacy.

ODYSSEUS: What happened to your leg?

NEOPTOLEMUS: Bitten by a snake.

ODYSSEUS: Why?

PHILOKTETES: Don't know.

ODYSSEUS: Yes, you do.

NEOPTOLEMUS: Where?

PHILOKTETES: The island of Chryse.

ODYSSEUS: What were you doing there?

PHILOKTETES: We were on our way to beat the fuckin' shit out of the Trojans.

ODYSSEUS: Who sent us?

PHILOKTETES: The Nation of Haters sent the Army of Lovers because they thought they could never be defeated.

ODYSSEUS: Skip that question. What were your orders?

PHILOKTETES: To ram my battalion into their battalion. To destroy their sweetness.

ODYSSEUS: What were you?

PHILOKTETES: Like you, a general.

ODYSSEUS: Tell me about the snake.

PHILOKTETES: Give me a drink.

NEOPTOLEMUS: Bartender.

ODYSSEUS: No.

PHILOKTETES: I thirst.

ODYSSEUS: For what?

NEOPTOLEMUS: Does it have anything to do with love?

PHILOKTETES: For sweetness.

ODYSSEUS: The snake. Tell us about the snake.

PHILOKTETES: On the temple ground.

ODYSSEUS: Why did you go there?

PHILOKTETES: I didn't know it was the temple.

ODYSSEUS: Yes, you did. Were you alone?

PHILOKTETES: Yes.

ODYSSEUS: No, you weren't.

PHILOKTETES: A walk in the dark.

ODYSSEUS: What were you doing there?

PHILOKTETES: We were searching for the moisture, The sweetness in the night air.

NEOPTOLEMUS: All animals seek it.

ODYSSEUS: And this sweetness, what was it in the form of?

PHILOKTETES: It was in the form of sweetness.

ODYSSEUS: You heard me. What was it in the form of?

PHILOKTETES: In the form of sweetness.

NEOPTOLEMUS: It has only one form. You know that.

ODYSSEUS: Why were you and only you bitten by the snake?

PHILOKTETES: It was also searching for sweetness. All animals seek it.

ODYSSEUS: I was there. Why wasn't I bitten?

PHILOKTETES: I was the sweetest.

NEOPTOLEMUS: Leave the body alone. Can't you see it's dead?

ODYSSEUS: It is not dead and I won't leave it alone. Why am I bleeding?

NEOPTOLEMUS: Have another drink.

ODYSSEUS: Say it, I transgressed and was punished.
And brought defeat and shame to my people.

PHILOKTETES: No.

ODYSSEUS: Say it.

PHILOKTETES: [*Laughing.*] I transgressed and was punished and brought
defeat and shame to my people.

ODYSSEUS: And because of that I forced you to suffer ten years of
backbreaking failure. Backbreaking, say it.

PHILOKTETES: No.

ODYSSEUS: What god did you offend?

PHILOKTETES: The same god that incubated the thought to leave me
here.
Why did you come back?

NEOPTOLEMUS: There was no god that told him to come back
Because he doesn't believe in gods.

PHILOKTETES: You came back because you want me to wipe the disgrace
off your face.

ODYSSEUS: Am I bleeding?

PHILOKTETES: My foot may be rotting but you are the rot.
We're a triangle, invisible, and indivisible,
one nation under an absent god, and you
broke the triangle and now you've come to put it back together.
I'm the stinking missing link you've been searching for these ten years.

So put the pieces of the cadaver together again if you can.
Your cardboard box of logic, it's melting away, it's abandoned you.

NEOPTOLEMUS: You're bleeding, Odysseus,
You've become barren, yellow-bellied, pantywaisted.

PHILOKTETES: Desperately searching for an enemy.

NEOPTOLEMUS: Does it have anything to do with love?
Somebody tell me please?!

PHILOKTETES: What can I do for you? Poor thing.
But rejoice, oh you barren. You who do not bear fruit.
You who have given up because they can't figure it out no more.
Have no fear because you are put to shame.
For you shall forget your old confusion and shall not remember the reproach
    of your widowed state.
Even I will be compelled to understand in spite of myself.

NEOPTOLEMUS: Does it have anything to do with love?
Will somebody please tell me?

PHILOKTETES: Shut him up.

ODYSSEUS: I would hope so.

NEOPTOLEMUS: Who's that sitting there?

PHILOKTETES: A virgin man on the verge of surrender.
Perplexed, lovelorn and loveless.
Moving backwards from the light and forward into the darkness.
Shall we force a truce on ourselves?
Consume and consummate ourselves?
Float like heroin on the tip of the needle?
Me blessed among women, you damned among men.

ODYSSEUS: Sink the needle and put my logic out of its misery.

PHILOKTETES: It's as naked as a fetus in its sixth week.
It can't stand up on its own legs.

NEOPTOLEMUS: Give it a break and put it back into the womb.

PHILOKTETES: Leave it alone,
I want it as whole as the day it was conceived.
Before you made it into this deformed adventure.
Get out of its way.

NEOPTOLEMUS: Look at it. It wants it all and it wants it now.

PHILOKTETES: Leave me this little body. Maybe I can revive it.
Take the bow and cast your bread on the waters.
After a long time you may find it again, for all is vanity and a chase after
    the wind.

NEOPTOLEMUS: Is it a boy or a girl?

ODYSSEUS: Hopefully, it's both.
Look at it. See how its mouth searches for a drop of something sweet.

NEOPTOLEMUS: Who does it look like?

PHILOKTETES: At this stage, it looks like all of us.
It's ours. Ours by right of conquest.

ODYSSEUS: What will you call it?

PHILOKTETES: Certainly not Jesus.
"As many shall be amazed at it so shall its
appearance be without glory from men
and its glory dishonored by men.
It is a root in a thirsty land.
It has no beauty or glory as we see it.
And it has no beauty or comeliness but
its form was ignoble and inferior to that of all men.
It was a thing struck down by misfortune,
who knows how to bear its infirmity." [*Isaiah 53.*]
The limitless possibilities of impossibility.
Deliver the sweating child into its mother's arms.
Backward from the darkness and forward into the light.
For we are blessed among women.

INSIDE OUT

PHILOKTETES: I've worked so long on this haunting. Make him go away.

NEOPTOLEMUS: So what do I care?

PHILOKTETES: This is my place. My body.

ODYSSEUS: And we want it, dead or alive.

PHILOKTETES: Seeing that it's neither. You can't have it.

NEOPTOLEMUS: How will you fight the hunger? The memory pain?

PHILOKTETES: Not hungry, not eating. What use is my body to you?

NEOPTOLEMUS: I can't make him go. Why are you doing this?

PHILOKTETES: Why does a ghost do anything?
The dead keep talking.
What's happened to you, Odysseus?
You've become strange and ugly, desiccated, decayed.
Cremated before your time.

ODYSSEUS: I was just thinking the same thing about you.

PHILOKTETES: And Troy?

ODYSSEUS: Burn that mother down.

NEOPTOLEMUS: Such bad luck?

PHILOKTETES: I told you that war was a bad luck thing.

NEOPTOLEMUS: But why for you? For why? For what?
You're going to wander around haunting this island for the rest of your life?

PHILOKTETES: I enjoy the silence.

NEOPTOLEMUS: You're worse than Odysseus.

PHILOKTETES: You'll be stuck together. I wouldn't advise that because he
kicks much butt. You may haunt Troy together someday.

NEOPTOLEMUS: Why don't you quit this ghost job and come with us?
No one has to know, you'll be my own private ghost.

PHILOKTETES: For why? For what? I'm not a ghost.

NEOPTOLEMUS: How did you become this?

PHILOKTETES: For the last time, I told you I was kissed by
a snake, in a private, hungry moment.

NEOPTOLEMUS: Who did it?

PHILOKTETES: It could have been anyone, anything.
Anywhere, I don't care who or where.
After I had spent all that time on the battlefield,
burning and burying all those bodies.
No one to pick me up and bury me.
They left me here.
When I woke up I was as black as burned wine.
My bones were blue.
I walked all over the island.
But no one would talk to me.
I was standing outside the world.
That's when I knew what was what.

NEOPTOLEMUS: And what was that?

PHILOKTETES: I had gone from the outside to the inside.
I was inside out.

NEOPTOLEMUS: I'm leaving.

PHILOKTETES: Is there anything else you want to say to me?

NEOPTOLEMUS: Aren't you even going to kiss me good-bye?

PHILOKTETES: For what? For why?
He who drinks from my mouth will be as I am.

NEOPTOLEMUS: Kiss me.

PHILOKTETES: He who drinks from my mouth will be as I am.

NEOPTOLEMUS: I don't care.

PHILOKTETES: No.

NEOPTOLEMUS: And Troy?

PHILOKTETES: Burn that motherfucker down.

NEOPTOLEMUS: You want to stay here on this rock like a cold piece of
    meat and wait for the grumbling empty-bellied dog on a chain?

PHILOKTETES: Odysseus? Harmless. A broken spider web.

NEOPTOLEMUS: I'm asleep.
I made you out of nothing and now you are nothing.
When I open my eyes we'll be inside out,
with or without you. Come with us.

PHILOKTETES: No.

NEOPTOLEMUS: Anything else you want to say to me?

PHILOKTETES: Aren't you even going to kiss me good-bye?

NEOPTOLEMUS: For why? For what? Why not?
He who drinks from my mouth will be as I am.

PHILOKTETES: Not reversible. Impossible.
I'm asleep. I made you out of nothing and now you are nothing.
When I open my eyes we'll be inside out. With or without you.

NEOPTOLEMUS: Don't stay.

PHILOKTETES: Anything else you want to say to me?

NEOPTOLEMUS: Aren't you even going to kiss me good-bye?

[*They kiss.*]

WAITING FOR A BOAT

NEOPTOLEMUS: I found him on the beach, faintly suckling on a piece of rice.

ODYSSEUS: What was he doing on the beach?

NEOPTOLEMUS: He said he was waiting for a boat.

ODYSSEUS: What boat?

NEOPTOLEMUS: He was to meet a boat on its way to throw sodium on the Trojan Empire and put its eye out.

ODYSSEUS: A boat won't come by here for another six months.

NEOPTOLEMUS: He said he would wait.

ODYSSEUS: And our battalion?

NEOPTOLEMUS: I saw them hiding behind a dune, nibbling
on a chicken wing and roasting a can of cocktail weenies.
Philoktetes crawled several miles up the beach but he fainted, unable to endure the pain.
Seeing that it was near the end, his soldiers pushed an anchor through his chest.
He laid down and smelled God for the first time.

ODYSSEUS: What did it smell like?

NEOPTOLEMUS: Clear water.

ODYSSEUS: Oh, no.

NEOPTOLEMUS: Oh, yes. He begged for a tea of jasmine
flower flakes but after I boiled it he wouldn't drink it.
I gave him an antacid and a dinner of broiled salmon.
But this he also refused.
We tried to raise anchor but it wouldn't move.
He asked me to send him a sign if there was a life beyond.
He said, "Send me anything, a sugared skull, a golden calf.
Anything, but send me a message."
I said, "But you are the one who is dying.
You send me a message.
Forget the sugared skull, a groundhog will do."
He was oscillating, severe and pixilated.

ODYSSEUS: That's nice, dear.

NEOPTOLEMUS: I put my wooden hands to my wooden
cheekbones and my sugared skull and felt myself melt.

I cried wooden tears, and I did melt.
Thus it is written and thus I will say it.
I melted. I did melt.
He blinked once and gave up the ghost.

ODYSSEUS: Any message?

NEOPTOLEMUS: The underworld is forever empty but orange
trees still blossom under the underworld.

ODYSSEUS: And under that?

NEOPTOLEMUS: Nothing.
But scrambled eggs and white rice, codfish, bananas, and sand.

WHO ARE YOU?

NEOPTOLEMUS: Who are you?

PHILOKTETES: No one.

NEOPTOLEMUS: I recognize you by your foot, they told me your foot . . .

PHILOKTETES: My foot is dead, kid. I was looking at it outside.
It had one fly on it.
Fuck my foot kid, I'm nobody.
Who am I? No one.
As for myself, I was taken here and made prisoner once.
And I was taken here and put here and stayed here.
And made to stay here.
And I don't know why but I stayed here.
And I stayed in here and I stayed here for a very long time.
And it was a very long time, a very, very long time.
And it seemed like it was forever.
And it probably was almost forever, almost.
But then one day the door opened beautifully and I was let out.
But not miraculously.
And I was let out and I went out.
And I wanted to get out and get let out.
And when I had gotten out, I didn't want to go anywhere.
I wanted to stay here.
I mean, not in here, but just here, around here.
And not go home to where I had come from.
And I couldn't even remember where I had come from.
Or, I could eventually remember.
But I realized that I had been here so long that
all the people that I could remember were dead.
Or if they were alive, they probably were so
old that they couldn't remember me, but
could remember me probably with sadness.
But there was no way I could ever get back,
because you see, in time, the geography between
here and there had gotten farther and farther apart.
And so we were too far away from each other to make any difference.
It wouldn't do any good.
So I realized I just had to stay here and live with it.
And so I'm staying here and I'm happy to stay here.
One day that door opened and it filled up with light.
And I went outside where everyone else was.

And everything else just became a memory.
And so that's it.
Good night.

END OF PLAY

PHAEDRA

MATTHEW MAGUIRE

PHOTO: STEVE KAHN

MATTHEW MAGUIRE is a co-artistic director of Creation Production Company. His plays include *The Tower,* originally commissioned by the Walker Art Center, *Phaedra,* and *Luscious Music,* published by *TheatreForum* 18. He created with Philip Glass and Molissa Fenley *A Descent Into the Maelström,* based on a story by Edgar Allan Poe, for Australia's Adelaide Festival, and wrote the libretto for *Chaos,* an opera with music by Michael Gordon. He is currently developing a new music-theatre piece, *Laughing Pictures.* He runs the Playwriting Program at Fordham College at Lincoln Center, and is an alumnus of New Dramatists. An Obie winner for acting, Maguire also received a 2005 Back Stage West Garland Award of Honorable Mention for Best Adaptation/Translation, for *Phaedra.* He lives in New York City. His work and essays are published by Sun & Moon Press, and Manchester University Press, among others.

From the Writer
MATTHEW MAGUIRE

"Desire is a very sophisticated passion . . . alas, desire is very eloquent."
—KIERKEGAARD, Either/Or

Questions drive my writing. A prime question of this play: What is desire and why does it never release us? What are the elusive and amoral mechanisms of desire? This is a play about forbidden love, a response to Racine's *Phèdre*, a story of the violence of erotic desire and the impoverished character of a life that attempts to kill it.

> *"Love is merely a madness, and, I tell you, deserves as well a dark house and a whip as madmen do, and the reason why they are not so punished and cured is that the lunacy is so ordinary, that the whippers are in love too."*
> —SHAKESPEARE, As You Like It, *III, ii*

One of the things that draws me to Racine's classic version of this play is Phaedra's struggle not to act upon her lust. Why is her fight so captivating? It is ennobling. We love her for trying to do the right thing. But of course, no one really wants her to succeed in her denial. To succeed in sublimating an intense desire is to act like Edith Wharton's Archer and Ellen in *The Age of Innocence*. Wharton's is a dissatisfying story because they fail to reach the ignition point that makes conflagration inevitable; the forces of order are greater than the forces of the unconscious, which is never the case with the Greeks. With Greek tragedy we know that catastrophe is inevitable. The delicious agony is in how long it can be evaded. We know Oedipus will discover his crimes, but how many trials must he face before his final rendezvous with destruction? That delay is what Racine embodied so well.

> *"This is the justice of the mighty gods: they lead us to the edge of the abyss; they make us sin, but do not pardon us."*
> —RACINE'S JOCASTA, *Thebaid*

I am questioning the relationship of power and desire. When absolute power corrupts absolutely what happens to desire? A morally bankrupt aristocracy struggles against an unnatural force of desire. By framing Theseus as a CEO, Heroic Power becomes Corporate Power. Killing monsters and seducing women become directing mergers, leveraged buyouts, and hostile takeovers. The Supreme Court evades all constitutional norms and selects a president. Americans now labor under a government installed by a corporate-financed coup. What are the consequences for real desire? How cold can the ember become and still ignite? The *moral* aspect of the play is its protest against the deformations of repression.

"A lustsleuth nosing for trouble in a booby trap."
—JOYCE, *Finnegan's Wake*

Racine improved upon Euripides. I admire how he pays respectful homage and simultaneously makes bold changes. I aspire to his delicate balance. Love as the prime mover of tragedy is Racine's hallmark, yet note how brief are the scenes in which Hippolytus and Phaedra meet face-to-face. I want to prolong their contact.

"For each ecstatic instant
We must in anguish pay
In keen and quivering ratio
To the ecstasy."
—EMILY DICKINSON

PRODUCTION HISTORY

Home for Contemporary Theatre and Art and
Creation Production Company's production of
Phaedra, directed by Matthew Maguire.
PHOTO: NANCY CAMPBELL

Phaedra was first presented at HERE Arts Center (Kristin Marting, Executive Director) in New York on April 7, 1995. It was co-produced by HOME for Contemporary Theatre and Art (Randy Rollison, Artistic Director, Barbara Busackino, Producing Director) and Creation Production Company (Co-Artistic Directors, Matthew Maguire and Susan Mosakowski). It was directed by Matthew Maguire; the set design was by Elizabeth Diller and Ricardo Scofidio; the costume design was by Suzanne Gallo; the lighting design was by Roma Flowers; the choreography was by Patricia Hoffbauer; the stage manager was Lisa DeRensis. The cast was as follows:

FAYE . . . . Socorro Santiago
THOMAS. . . . . George Bartenieff
WILLIAM. . . . . Andy Paris
ANGUS . . . . Ray Xifo
NONNY . . . . Verna Hampton
ARICIA . . . . Nicole Alifante

SPECIAL THANKS to Douglas Messerli, Sun & Moon Press, Stephen Doyle, Elizabeth Diller and Ricardo Scofidio, Randy Rollison, Donny Levit, and Caridad Svich.

CHARACTERS

FAYE, a young woman of wealth

THOMAS, Faye's husband, a CEO

ARICIA, daughter of the chairman of a multinational ruined by Thomas in a hostile takeover

WILLIAM, Thomas's son

ANGUS, tutor and friend to William

NONNY, once Faye's nanny; a life-long friend

SETTING

The present moment. An upper-class American home.

ACT ONE

FAYE wanders in the night murmuring expressions of lust as she tries to find her way out of an invisible maze.

FAYE: Take me . . .

> [*Light strikes a chair. FAYE approaches it. She sits. She struggles to understand what is happening to her. THOMAS enters. He touches her. She doesn't respond.*]

THOMAS: Couldn't sleep.
FAYE: Neither can I.
THOMAS: Why not?
FAYE: I don't know.
THOMAS: What are you doing?
FAYE: Thinking.
THOMAS: About what?
FAYE: Nothing.
THOMAS: Some tea?
FAYE: No.

ロロロ

WILLIAM is relaxing with his head in ANGUS's lap.

ANGUS: Why do you sleep alone?
WILLIAM: So I can breathe.
ANGUS: Don't you ever feel the urge . . . to . . .

> [*At a loss for the word. WILLIAM wryly completes ANGUS's thought with a lewd gesture.*]

Well . . . yes . . . all right. Don't you?

WILLIAM: Of course.
ANGUS: Then?
WILLIAM: Then *what?*
ANGUS: If you don't marry and have a child, what happens to the family line?
WILLIAM: That's a funny thing to ask a bastard.
ANGUS: Fine. Mock your father. I'll be the first to join you. He's made it his life's mission to fertilize the Western world. But you're his son in every way—it's time you faced it.
WILLIAM: I don't want to stick my head into a domestic trap of squalling infants. I want the wildness of taming horses.
ANGUS: If you don't breed, the air will be a place where nothing moves.
WILLIAM: I love that place. I long for that place.
ANGUS: You're shaking.

WILLIAM: I didn't sleep at all last night. I worked in the stables till one and went straight to bed. I was flooded by a dream of such erotic power I felt I was possessed.

ANGUS: You, the man who's turned his back on love?!

WILLIAM: I awoke in a fever certain the embarrassment of some nocturnal emission would await me. And yes, there it was, but it glistened like quicksilver. I scraped this substance off the sheet and took it to a lab. It was mercury. The growing chaos of my life is so frightening I'm hard-pressed not to run to a priest.

ANGUS: Who's the woman?

WILLIAM: I can't say.

ANGUS: Oh come on.

WILLIAM: No.

ANGUS: Why don't you give in? You're in love, it happens to everyone. All right—you said it'd never happen to you. Do you think anyone took you seriously?

WILLIAM: [Smelling the air.] She must've been here.

ANGUS: Who?

WILLIAM: I have to leave this place.

ANGUS: [Stroking WILLIAM's head.] Not yet.

WILLIAM: The walls are too thin and they sweat unknown liquids. The angles are unnatural.

ANGUS: If you leave, your father cuts you off. You'll never get your horse farm.

WILLIAM: The air smells like rutting bodies.

[ANGUS rubs WILLIAM's chest.]

No.

[ANGUS doesn't stop. WILLIAM pushes his hands away.]

Stop.

[They make their way into the drawing room where the household is gathered, mid-conversation, after dinner. When WILLIAM sees ARICIA he instinctively turns to go, but ANGUS restrains him.]

NONNY: I'm so sorry they found little Anastasia's bones.

WILLIAM: All royalty should be found in shallow graves.

[FAYE notices WILLIAM and suddenly hears and sees no one else.]

THOMAS: Watch your tongue. You forget who we are?

WILLIAM: I can't.

THOMAS: Bigger than the Romanovs ever were.

FAYE: They had a certain permission.

THOMAS: And obligations.

FAYE: Have you ever thought about that?

[WILLIAM is drawn towards ARICIA.]

WILLIAM: That I've inherited some deadly noblesse oblige?

FAYE: No.

THOMAS: You've inherited nothing yet!

ARICIA: [*Directly in WILLIAM's face.*] Is that so?

[*FAYE takes WILLIAM's arm and leads him away.*]

FAYE: Have you?

WILLIAM: What?

FAYE: Thought.

WILLIAM: Of what?

FAYE: Permission.

NONNY: Well, we don't need one.

ANGUS: What?

NONNY: A samovar.

THOMAS: That's right, damn Russki bullshit, they didn't waste any time building a mafia.

FAYE: Have you ever thought about it?

ANGUS: [*To THOMAS.*] It was bound to happen.

THOMAS: I don't believe anything is *bound* to happen.

ANGUS: A pure market is an oxymoron.

THOMAS: How're we supposed to prop them up when they've sold their whole damn system to the black market?

FAYE: Permission.

ARICIA: [*Referring to ANGUS.*] He's right, it's inevitable.

WILLIAM: I don't think I understand what you're saying.

NONNY: Would anyone like a cognac or a sherry?

FAYE: [*Taking WILLIAM's hand.*] I think you do.

NONNY: Faye? [*She doesn't answer.*] Faye?

ARICIA: I could go for something, sure.

NONNY: Thomas?

THOMAS: They're using their rubles for wallpaper.

NONNY: Thomas, are you listening?

ARICIA: Always.

WILLIAM: [*Subtly trying to remove his hand.*] No.

ANGUS: [*To WILLIAM.*] Come on, do you good.

THOMAS: Yes, I'll take a Hennessey. William?

[*Everyone looks at WILLIAM trying to extricate himself from FAYE—their hands glow with their own light. FAYE lets go. As THOMAS leaves:*]

I'm going out.

ARICIA: [*Relishing the barb.*] We won't wait up.

[*ARICIA and ANGUS manage an awkward exit. WILLIAM and FAYE stare at one another as he backs out the door. She sits in the chair which affects her like a vehicle for erotic transport. Catching herself, she leaps from the chair and stares at it as if it's possessed. She runs out, leaving a startled NONNY alone. NONNY tries to deny her rising despair over FAYE's destructive turn.*]

NONNY: All quiet now. [*She notices a teabag on the side of a saucer and lifts it.*] A flea bag! What a delight! [*She sees a corset lying on a chair.*] Look at this! An old-fashioned corset! Now who's been sinkin' their teeth in this? The hooks and eyes unraveling, eyes still hungry for hooks, hooks still yearning to jump through eyes. Like the hoops of a flea circus. The fleas leap from their bags, through the eyes, and straight onto the hooks. Meat hooks for the miniature, skewers for the carcasses of insects. Dead professionals. No longer ready to do their heady tricks. But if they were alive they could perform on my body. Lilliputians, clambering over the nooks and hooks and crooks and crannies of my fanny's one-ring circus. Ahh, the big top swarming with little tops. They scurry across the ring and pop through the eye and down the drain into the veins of my love. My love, my love . . . [*Moaning.*] Ohhhhhh . . . Where is he? Moldering in the grave, my poor old lover. Bone man in the bone yard.

[*ANGUS walks in with an armful of cabbage.*]

You frightened me.

ANGUS: Me?
NONNY: Your body looked as if it was painted on by a gothic devil.
ANGUS: You drinking again?
NONNY: Your crotch was a bloated tulip with petals painted like membranes.
ANGUS: I'm a gardener, not some demon.
NONNY: No, you're the tutor.
ANGUS: Was.
NONNY: Are.
ANGUS: As you will.
NONNY: You hear them again last night?
ANGUS: They're just babies.
NONNY: But Faye acts like she's dying. She can't soothe them. You don't know what I'm going through. I can't help her.
ANGUS: What's wrong with her?

[*Pause. NONNY evades the question.*]

NONNY: I wish we could soundproof the nursery.
ANGUS: [*Grunting.*] Hmm.
NONNY: Does that sound callous?
ANGUS: Not as bad as baking them for dinner.
NONNY: They suckle so hard they've worn out three wet nurses.
ANGUS: Hungry little buggers.
NONNY: And Philly's gettin' teeth, so I know the new one's gonna quit any day.

[*ANGUS puts away the cabbage. NONNY sneaks a drink. ARICIA walks in and catches her.*]

ARICIA: Nothing like a good stiff shot on the sly.
NONNY: Listen here, you little Miss-whatever-you-are, I ought to scratch—

[*She is interrupted by FAYE entering.*]

FAYE: Nonny, draw me a bath, please.

NONNY: You've already had three.

FAYE: [*Leaving.*] One more.

NONNY: [*Glaring at **ARICIA**, as she leaves.*] You'll have to excuse me.

[*Pause.*]

ANGUS: You've upset this house.

ARICIA: It didn't start with me.

ANGUS: Why don't you leave William alone?

ARICIA: You know why.

ANGUS: His father will never accept you.

ARICIA: If I could work or live anywhere else I would, but Thomas blocks my every move. When he *invited* me to live here, what he really meant was "welcome to your cell."

ANGUS: If he catches you with his son, you'll never get out.

ARICIA: What excites me the most is the challenge. Imagine the thrill of seducing someone who swears he'll never love.

ANGUS: Won't work. Your ambition's too obvious.

ARICIA: You're wrong about me. It's beyond ambition. Watching him struggle against what he wants so much—that arouses me.

ANGUS: The chance to regain your position is more like it.

ARICIA: The boy doesn't know he's in love with lust, and he's found an infinite delay mechanism. Cranks me like a bitch in heat.

[*WILLIAM enters. He stops short when he sees ARICIA. NONNY, right behind him, pulls him aside.*]

NONNY: William, I need to tell you something. [*Pause.*] Faye's dying. I don't know of what.

WILLIAM: I know.

▢▢▢

Alone, FAYE dances in awkward lurches because her yearning won't let her be still. She hears THOMAS coming and stops. He sits and opens the market listings. FAYE embraces him from behind. As he responds she moves away, silent. He waits.

FAYE: Make him go.

THOMAS: He's my son.

FAYE: And I'm your wife. [*Pause.*] Aren't I?

THOMAS: It'd make me look weak.

FAYE: Can't you find a way?

THOMAS: The market could crash on the rumors alone.

FAYE: Can't you separate this from business?

THOMAS: I want him to take over the firm when I retire.

FAYE: What about *our* sons?

THOMAS: They're still nursing, for chrissakes!

FAYE: What does that matter?

THOMAS: Will's first in line.

FAYE: He's the bastard child of your fling with some Amazon!

THOMAS: You promised you wouldn't!

FAYE: Our sons deserve better. And he knows what's at stake, that's why he hates me.

THOMAS: That's simply not true.

FAYE: You have to trust me.

THOMAS: [*Pause.*] I do.

FAYE: Then send him away before it becomes a crisis.

THOMAS: What has he done to offend you?

FAYE: The way he looks at me.

THOMAS: It's only natural a young man might have some resentment for a stepmother. Don't take it personally.

FAYE: Have you seen how he looks at me?

THOMAS: I haven't seen him look at you at all.

[*She is silent, moves away.*]

What if it came out that the only reason is "my wife wanted it?"

FAYE: Thomas . . . [*Pause.*] I hate him.

[*THOMAS walks out. Alone, FAYE is driven back to her awkward dance.*]

William . . . William . . . oh Will . . . Bodies lying in a heap, grunting, rutting. It's so laughable; the grotesque shapes the flesh can make. Organs jutting out like red-nosed clowns, or hiding coyly, or parading HMS Pinafore engorged. Spewing drops of fluid like fluttering pigeons, those awkward birds that waddle so crudely, yet, when swooping together in their relentless circles so hypnotically beautiful. Thrusting. Will he love me? So silly, makes me want to weep. I have no body. Nothing but a swirling mass of contradictions. All so balled up that it looks like flesh, but it's really petrified struggles. My lips the hardening of a million cries. My breasts the calcification of countless howlings. Can he love me? Yes, yes, yes. My skin will soothe him. Luscious juices like marraca rinds pouring in his ears, whispering, always whispering, "Love me." Even though my body is a mirage, love me. [*Murmuring "love me" over and over, FAYE implodes.*]

[*NONNY enters and finds FAYE out of control.*]

NONNY: Darling, what's wrong?

FAYE: I need more light.

[*Their cries pile on top of one another.*]

NONNY: Why don't—[you turn on the lamp?]

FAYE: Light to wash away—

NONNY: What are you—[talking about?]

FAYE: Wash away this . . . [*She can't say.*]

NONNY: Faye, what's—[wrong with you?]

FAYE: More light, more light, more light!
NONNY: [*Turning on a lamp.*] That's easy.
FAYE: No! Turn it off, turn it off!
NONNY: But you said—[you wanted more light.]
FAYE: I've never had light, always shadows, bring me shadows, more shadows!

[*NONNY seizes FAYE to calm her. They struggle.*]

NONNY: Calm your—[self!]
FAYE: Shadows—
NONNY: Stop this—[craziness!]
FAYE: I need the dark—
NONNY: Please!
FAYE: Shadows, shadows . . .

[*FAYE collapses in NONNY's arms.*]

NONNY: There, there . . . there, there . . . there, there . . .
FAYE: I belong in the dark.
NONNY: What's the matter with you, my little one?
FAYE: Nonny dear, please don't call me that.

[*NONNY tightens her viselike grip on FAYE.*]

NONNY: My little one.
FAYE: Don't call me that.
NONNY: My little one.
FAYE: Don't call me that.

[*NONNY turns away, hurt.*]

Come here. [*FAYE hugs her.*] It's worse than when my mother . . . it's worse.

NONNY: What's wrong?
FAYE: There's nothing but constant slashes.
NONNY: What is it?
FAYE: I can't see it.
NONNY: Try.
FAYE: I can't.
NONNY: Why won't you tell me?
FAYE: I can't.
NONNY: You mean you won't.
FAYE: I said I can't.
NONNY: Who raised you?
FAYE: Please.
NONNY: I know when you're holding something back. If you think you can shut me out, I think it's time I left this house.
FAYE: [*Grabbing her arm.*] Nonny—
NONNY: How can I watch you starve yourself to death and never ask why?
FAYE: I can't.

NONNY: How many pounds this month! I'll have to hospitalize you, and I'm not supposed to—[know why?]

FAYE: No!

NONNY: Then who am I?

FAYE: I love you.

NONNY: Then let me help you.

FAYE: I don't know how.

NONNY: If you're lost, I'm lost.

FAYE: I know.

NONNY: I'm afraid you're going to die.

FAYE: I am.

NONNY: No!

FAYE: It's the only way.

NONNY: I'm not going to watch you die.

FAYE: What are you doing?

NONNY: Leaving.

FAYE: No.

NONNY: Well?

[*Pause. FAYE can't speak. NONNY turns to go.*]

FAYE: Don't leave me.

NONNY: Tell me, or I walk out now.

FAYE: All right. [*FAYE hesitates. NONNY waits.*] I keep dreaming of a bull, a sweating black bull, its flanks are heaving and its enormous rod is full and pulsing. He snorts and phlegm shoots out his nostrils, they're gaping pink and chafed. He stamps his right hoof in the dust and an Arabian carpet appears. He lowers his engorged loins onto the carpet and pumps his thick tool over the intricate design. A bull's cock plunging through the labyrinth. It's William.

NONNY: God help you.

FAYE: Too late.

NONNY: You mustn't tell Thomas.

FAYE: And you mustn't.

NONNY: I'd pull all my teeth first.

FAYE: Now will you let me die in silence?

回回回

WILLIAM and ARICIA seem separated by an invisible plane.

WILLIAM: [*Whispering.*] Aricia, where are you?

ARICIA: I'm in the Pure Room. Bathing in come. In.

WILLIAM: I can't.

ARICIA: Come in.

WILLIAM: I can't.

ARICIA: Come soon.

WILLIAM: Whisper.

ARICIA: Whisper to me.
WILLIAM: Soon.
ARICIA: I don't dare look at the walls.
WILLIAM: Close your eyes.
ARICIA: Come to me.
WILLIAM: I can't.

[*ARICIA charges at WILLIAM, their bodies strike like animals in combat. They fall, tangled.*]

ARICIA: Kiss me.
WILLIAM: I'm too afraid.
ARICIA: What can you do?

[*Pause.*]

WILLIAM: Tell you a story?
ARICIA: [*Laughing.*] Yes.
WILLIAM: It's about distance.
ARICIA: Distanza.
WILLIAM: The ship was sailing.
ARICIA: La nave salpava.
WILLIAM: The waves licking at its hull.
ARICIA: The bow splitting the foam.
WILLIAM: Water, luscious water.
ARICIA: The ship yearning to rise above the waves.
WILLIAM: The waves clutching with hungry fingers. The ship tumbling, sliding down viscous ridges of distance.
ARICIA: How many days, how many years? Have we been . . .
WILLIAM: Have we been at . . .

[*Long pause.*]

ARICIA: Sea.
WILLIAM: Are your hands chafed?
ARICIA: Is your skin raw?
WILLIAM: It's been so long.

回回回

FAYE walks to the chair, stares at it, sits, and crosses her legs. The light grows brighter on her face.

ANGUS: Faye plays with the top button of her blouse.
NONNY: You keep your lizard's tongue off the mistress.
ANGUS: Her eyes radiate. Her thighs part. Is she thinking of a lover?
NONNY: She's thinking of her husband.
ANGUS: You know she's not.
NONNY: When did a tutor get the second sight?

ANGUS: From my wife. My love had a growth in the small of her back, a sac of tranquility, an elegant membrane. The sac was bulbous, traced with a lacework of faint blue veins. It sang. Nothing vulgar, no caterwauling in the shower. No. This was a sound that if I lay my head near it, say—on her shoulders—I could hear it faintly, as if it were coming from some great distance. It made many kinds of music depending on her mood. Sometimes Puccini, sometimes a tango. [*He sings a melody.*] The surgeon wanted to remove it. She refused. You'd never know it caused her any problem. Ain't no other suffered like my lover. Things grow. Grass grows through concrete. The essence of life is miraculous.

NONNY: You're gettin' above yourself.

ANGUS: After she died I kept that sac. Helps me see things.

NONNY: Liar.

[*ARICIA and WILLIAM enter from opposite sides of the room.*]

ANGUS: Madam's thinking of the chair in the sunlight. And, yes, of course she's thinking of a lover. But the lover is not hers.

ARICIA: Did you say something?

ANGUS: Faye is thinking of a room in which sits William. William is thinking.

WILLIAM: Did you say something?

ANGUS: William is thinking of another room in which sits Aricia.

FAYE: There's going to be a flood.

NONNY: [*Knowing too much.*] Faye, don't.

ANGUS: Madam, it hasn't rained in years.

FAYE: It'll fill this room. I've seen it.

ANGUS: What do you mean? We're on high ground.

FAYE: I can see it. [*She shows them the marks of high-water lines on the walls.*] Look at this, eleven years ago, and here, seventeen.

[*Disturbed, NONNY and ANGUS exit swiftly. FAYE, with a reluctant glance at WILLIAM, follows.*]

WILLIAM: Why do you stay?

ARICIA: Why do you?

WILLIAM: There's something I have to do.

ARICIA: I feel the same.

WILLIAM: But he destroyed your family.

ARICIA: No. My father's arrogance did that. He left the company vulnerable by expanding too fast and acquiring too much debt. He swore no one would ever dare a takeover.

WILLIAM: But my father left him nothing, no face-saving merger, no golden parachute, he deliberately crushed him.

ARICIA: I saw it coming three months before. Your father has people on his team that hate him. I had three calls giving me inside information. I begged my father to protect our position. He wouldn't listen to his daughter. He thought he was a tightrope walker.

[*WILLIAM starts to leave.*]

Where are you going?

WILLIAM: It's feeding time.
ARICIA: We're never alone.
WILLIAM: I don't think we—
ARICIA: Something's happening to me.
WILLIAM: I need to get to the stables.
ARICIA: It's . . . never happened before.
WILLIAM: Yes.
ARICIA: Do you know what I mean?
WILLIAM: Please.

[*Pause.*]

ARICIA: Please.
WILLIAM: What?
ARICIA: Touch my lips.

[*WILLIAM touches her lips, then abruptly leaves. Alone, ARICIA touches her lips.*]

He touched my lips. He touched my lips.

रारारा

ARICIA leaves as FAYE enters. WILLIAM enters.

WILLIAM: I heard what you tried to do to me.

[*Pause.*]

FAYE: You don't understand the reason.
WILLIAM: It's ironic. I was going until I learned you wanted to throw me out of my own house. Then of course I had to stay.
FAYE: You don't understand.
WILLIAM: I'd be so happy—
FAYE: [*Overlapping.*] He told you?
WILLIAM: —far away from—[you]
FAYE: How could he?!
WILLIAM: He didn't.
FAYE: Then who?
WILLIAM: But I'm not going. [*Pause.*] Not yet.

[*WILLIAM leaves. FAYE is alone.*]

FAYE: Funny how things stick in the mind: a chair in the sunlight.

[*THOMAS enters.*]

FAYE: Take off your shirt.
THOMAS: All things come to those who wait?
FAYE: Please.
THOMAS: [*Taking his shirt off.*] All things.

FAYE: Turn around.

THOMAS: [*Turning his back to her.*] Okay.

FAYE: [*Tracing on his lower back.*] Here it is—eleven years ago, and here . . . [*Between his shoulder blades.*] seventeen.

THOMAS: [*Turning, grasping her.*] Please.

[*FAYE wrenches herself away from him and leaves. THOMAS fucks the chair. NONNY watches from an unseen distance.*]

Strip for me. I wanna hear the crowd get raucous. I want to see the waitress spill the beer. I want to watch you step out of a sea shell. Venus born in a Bourbon Street strip joint. Classy, rattling snare drum. Ass grinding like a jackhammer on my love nerve. Whiskey burns my throat. Pasties, g-string, distant points on a constellation as yet uncharted.

[*NONNY clears her throat. THOMAS stops. NONNY approaches.*]

NONNY: Working late?

THOMAS: Yeah.

[*NONNY massages THOMAS's back.*]

THOMAS: Not the back, the neck.

NONNY: All right.

THOMAS: The neck.

NONNY: I'm getting there.

THOMAS: [*Screaming.*] The neck!

[*The uproar brings ARICIA into the doorway where she observes unnoticed.*]

NONNY: What's wrong with you?!?

THOMAS: [*Perfectly composed.*] I had a perfect butler once—humble man. He'd do anything to please me—lick my ass if I wanted. One day I asked for a glass of water, and he brought me a bottle of 1938 Taitinger Blanc de Blanc and served it for me in a Tiffany crystal chalice. When he finished pouring I fired him. In order to teach him that pleasure consists not in what I enjoy, but in having my own way.

NONNY: [*Offended.*] I don't work for you.

THOMAS: Then why are you rubbing me?

[*NONNY storms out. ARICIA approaches him.*]

ARICIA: Poor Thomas, you think of your dicky as a kind of Leviathan, like one of those whales you slaughter on your shipping routes.

THOMAS: I destroyed your father, ate his company, and spit out the bones.

ARICIA: True, I hear it's fat, but can it spout like Moby?

THOMAS: Do you know why I took you into my house?

ARICIA: Do you know why I stay?

THOMAS: You're a living souvenir of my greatest deal.

ARICIA: I'm waiting for the right moment.

THOMAS: Snipe all you want from the junk bond pits because that's where you'll stay. I've seen to that, blackballed you on the exchange so you have to suck my charity.

ARICIA: Is that why you want me here? Makes you feel potent?

THOMAS: I want you where I can watch you.

ARICIA: I'm so thirsty.

[*ARICIA downs glass after glass of water unable to slake her thirst. THOMAS takes the pitcher and leaves.*]

回回回

ANGUS is peering around a screen when NONNY enters.

NONNY: What are you doing?

ANGUS: She's in the bath again.

NONNY: I know that.

ANGUS: Always splashing—and always silent.

NONNY: She's afraid of bursting into flames.

ANGUS: Why?

NONNY: She's heard stories.

ANGUS: Could that happen?

NONNY: Someone is watching.

ANGUS: Who? [*He turns back to NONNY.*] I'm starving.

NONNY: Go eat.

ANGUS: Look at us, still in our formal attire, and no one's had anything to eat but potatoes and tea for weeks.

NONNY: That's a lie.

ANGUS: The cupboard is bare.

[*ARICIA strips WILLIAM of his shirt. ANGUS and NONNY watch.*]

NONNY: Gus, we've got to keep this house together.

ANGUS: I'm trying.

NONNY: Stop that girl.

ANGUS: No.

NONNY: She's driving him mad.

ANGUS: Don't blame her.

NONNY: Why not?

ANGUS: The madness is in him.

NONNY: He's a good boy.

ANGUS: A time bomb.

NONNY: How can you say that about him?

ANGUS: I love him.

NONNY: Yeah.

ANGUS: Didn't I teach him everything I know?

NONNY: Yes, Angus.

ANGUS: The poor girl's been shut out like a leper.

NONNY: Bullshit.

ANGUS: I saw her every day as if it were late at night and it was my job to close the cafe.

NONNY: You never worked in a cafe.

ANGUS: And she was locked in an embrace with the last customer in a desperate attempt to make contact—with someone. Anyone. [*Pause.*] The Cafe De Flore. Tea. Chocolat. Welsh Rarebit. She was a rare bite.

NONNY: Stop it, you wanker.

[*ARICIA leans in to kiss WILLIAM. THOMAS enters.*]

THOMAS: What's this?

[*WILLIAM pulls on his shirt and leaves.*]

ARICIA: Your power died centuries ago.

THOMAS: Cross me and you won't walk away.

ARICIA: You're a fossil.

THOMAS: Leave my son alone.

ARICIA: Tell that to him.

THOMAS: Do you like living in this house?

ARICIA: Such a honking sound.

THOMAS: It could be your grave.

ARICIA: I saw a charnel house once at St. Catherine's Monastery. The monks believe it's the place God spoke to Moses from the burning bush. They use a whole building to store the skulls of the monks who've died there. Sixteen centuries worth. I walked into the first room; floor-to-ceiling skulls. I took it in a long time—how some skulls rested on top of others; one as if embracing; another pressuring about to attack. I never believed a pile of bone could be so expressive. The room seemed alive. I never went back. But this place is just like that charnel house. I'm the burning bush and you're the skull.

[*FAYE enters and seems paralyzed. Everyone surrounds her except ARICIA who strolls off.*]

THOMAS: Faye. [*No response.*] Faye?

[*He touches her arm but she shows no recognition. In frustration he follows ARICIA. NONNY motions for ANGUS to leave.*]

NONNY: Angus.

[*ANGUS leaves.*]

NONNY: Where is your husband?

FAYE: He's not here.

NONNY: You know he is.

FAYE: Do you see him?

NONNY: You're deluded.

FAYE: He's never here, he's always vanishing.

NONNY: And when he walks through that door?

FAYE: Maybe he'll forgive me.
NONNY: His last lover is dead. The mother of his—
FAYE: It was self-defense.
NONNY: That was never proven.
FAYE: Are you trying to frighten me?
NONNY: I want you to stop.
FAYE: That's not possible.
NONNY: Can't you see what's going to happen?
FAYE: My eyes are open.
NONNY: Even if you could fool Thomas, you still can't have William. He hates women.
FAYE: Then I've got no competition.
NONNY: You're talking like a fool.
FAYE: I can touch him.
NONNY: He hates you.
FAYE: He's got a wild streak he can't control.
NONNY: So do you.
FAYE: We'll smash into one another.

[*Pause.*]

NONNY: [*Struggling to control herself.*] My sweet girl.
FAYE: What?!
NONNY: What about me?
FAYE: Nothing's going to happen to you.
NONNY: When this destroys you, where will I go?
FAYE: Please—don't.
NONNY: Where?
FAYE: Then there's only one answer.
NONNY: No, stop it.
FAYE: I have to die.
NONNY: No! No! You're just crazed, no!

罒罒罒

10 P.M.

THOMAS: What do you think a larvae is?
ANGUS: It's the earliest stages of an insect, right?
THOMAS: I don't know.
ANGUS: Why?
THOMAS: Don't know, just thinking.
ANGUS: [*Getting up.*] D'you want anything?
THOMAS: Where are you going?
ANGUS: The kitchen.
THOMAS: Oh.
ANGUS: You all right?

THOMAS: Why?
ANGUS: You seem worried.
THOMAS: Pacific rim.
ANGUS: Is that all?

[*ARICIA enters, sees them both, and starts to leave.*]

THOMAS: Sit down.
ARICIA: [*Sitting.*] You never cease to amaze me.
ANGUS: I'll be going.
ARICIA: G'night.
THOMAS: Check all the doors.

[*ANGUS leaves.*]

That advice you gave me paid off better than anything all year. How do you do it?

ARICIA: The basics: observation, analysis, and luck.
THOMAS: It was brilliant.
ARICIA: Thank you.
THOMAS: You have anything else for me?
ARICIA: [*Pointedly.*] No.
THOMAS: What do you mean, "No"?
ARICIA: Not until I have a completely different contract.
THOMAS: Out of the question.
ARICIA: Do you believe that when a man and a woman are left alone in a room—no matter who they are—they will surely copulate?
THOMAS: No. [*Pause.*] Do you?
ARICIA: I have trouble with the *old* stories.
THOMAS: Harsh.
ARICIA: Listen to you.
THOMAS: I can be very gentle.
ARICIA: I read you sleep with your thing in a glove of Vaseline.
THOMAS: Myth.
ARICIA: Like everything about you?
THOMAS: No one's more real.
ARICIA: Like a rock, heh?
THOMAS: Why are you always on the attack?
ARICIA: Someday you'll stumble.
THOMAS: You hate me that much.
ARICIA: Not anymore.
THOMAS: I'm disappointed in you.
ARICIA: How so?
THOMAS: I've never known you to lie.
ARICIA: I lie all the time.
THOMAS: You're lying right now.
ARICIA: Perhaps.
THOMAS: I've come to depend on you.

ARICIA: You must be desperate.

THOMAS: Do you think when two people are alone anything can happen?

ARICIA: Yes.

THOMAS: I think it's all very volatile.

ARICIA: Being alone?

THOMAS: Everything.

ARICIA: Can you smell the sulfur and the pitch?

THOMAS: Can you hear the wailing?

ARICIA: [*Laughing.*] Sometimes you can be very funny.

THOMAS: That's why they pay me the big bucks.

ARICIA: And they are big.

THOMAS: Yes, they are. Do you need more?

ARICIA: Need you ask?

THOMAS: Have you seen Faye?

ARICIA: Yes.

THOMAS: Well?

ARICIA: Well?

THOMAS: Where is she?

ARICIA: In the greenhouse. When I walked through she was lying naked, face down, writhing in a bed of begonias. She has a rash across her ass—most unattractive—but the pumping she was doing was appealing. She was clawing at the dirt and shoving it beneath her. It was strange, but I think I understood.

THOMAS: I'm afraid I have a meeting.

ARICIA: This late?

THOMAS: It's already midday on the Nikkei.

ARICIA: It is late.

THOMAS: Yes it is.

ARICIA: Very late.

THOMAS: Late.

ARICIA: Yes.

THOMAS: You'll excuse me?

ARICIA: Of course.

[*THOMAS walks to the door and turns back to **ARICIA**.*]

THOMAS: Good night.

ARICIA: Good night.

THOMAS: Good night.

ARICIA: Good night.

THOMAS: Good night.

ARICIA: Good night.

[*THOMAS leaves. **ARICIA** runs to the threshold and sinks, head in hands, then slowly stands rejoicing, elation rising on her face. **NONNY** enters urgently.*]

NONNY: Where's Thomas?

ARICIA: It's too late.

NONNY: What do you mean?

ARICIA: He's dead.
NONNY: Oh Lord!

[*THOMAS speaks at a distance as if in a coma. The others do not hear.*]

THOMAS: Yes . . . [*Pause.*] There was an accident, and I—
ARICIA: A call just came.
THOMAS: . . . and . . .
NONNY: Oh my God—Faye—[*Pause.*] How did it happen?
THOMAS: I've got to get—
ARICIA: They found his car in the river. It went off an embankment. His driver was dead behind the wheel, but they haven't found him yet. He must've been washed down river.
THOMAS: The hounds . . .
NONNY: Then maybe he's alive.

[*ARICIA shakes her head no.*]

THOMAS: The hounds of hell snarling . . .
NONNY: I never thought he could die.
THOMAS: My strength is gone.
ARICIA: Maybe he can't.
NONNY: Don't talk nonsense.
ARICIA: Do you know what this means?
NONNY: No.
ARICIA: The board will choose a new CEO.
NONNY: How can you think about that when—
ARICIA: [*Commanding.*] Be quiet. [*Pause.*] Who will it be?
THOMAS: Gotta get back.
ARICIA: Go get Faye.

[*NONNY runs to the sleeping FAYE and shakes her awake.*]

THOMAS: I remember her in Manila during the rainy season. She'd walk along the terrace in a sarong, her tits bare, with one of those pyramidal Chinese hats on her head—huge.
FAYE: Let me go.
THOMAS: The rain would pelt her until the paper fan she carried disintegrated. Then she'd get another fan and continue to defy the monsoon. My cock would stiffen.
FAYE: Let me go.
NONNY: No, listen, I have something to tell you.
FAYE: [*Groggy.*] Sleep . . . sleep . . .
NONNY: Listen! Thomas is dead.
FAYE: What!
THOMAS: Have to get back.
NONNY: Thomas is dead.
FAYE: How do you know this?
NONNY: I'm so sorry.

FAYE: How do you know?!
NONNY: You're free.
FAYE: [*Dazed.*] Free?
NONNY: Free to love William.
THOMAS: Have to . . .
FAYE: [*Moaning.*] Ohhhhh . . .
NONNY: Let me speak to him for you.
FAYE: No! Let me die.

[*FAYE passes out. NONNY touches her face.*]

NONNY: Never.

[*As **NONNY** leaves, **THOMAS** passes her unseen. Outside **NONNY** discovers **ANGUS**.*]

Where were you?

ANGUS: Looking for Aricia.
NONNY: Where?
ANGUS: The greenhouse.
NONNY: You spying again?

[*Pause. Annoyed, ANGUS starts to leave. NONNY catches him.*]

Angus?

ANGUS: Yes?
NONNY: Will you . . .
ANGUS: [*Pausing.*] Will I what?
NONNY: [*Coming closer.*] Would you . . . [*She starts to tremble. A horrible resistance builds up in her.*]
ANGUS: Are you [*Pause.*] asking . . . [*Pause.*]
NONNY: Oh never mind.

[*ARICIA enters.*]

ANGUS: I've been looking for you.
ARICIA: Yes?
ANGUS: [*To NONNY.*] Would you excuse us?
NONNY: Aren't you a little old?
ANGUS: [*Waiting.*] Well?

[*NONNY leaves.*]

William needs to talk to you.

ARICIA: I'm afraid to see him.
ANGUS: What about "the challenge"?
ARICIA: Everything's different now.
ANGUS: Why?
ARICIA: Rebelling against his old man excited him. With Thomas dead I'm sure he'll lose interest in me.
ANGUS: You're saying you feel something?

ARICIA: I love him.

ANGUS: I'm astonished.

ARICIA: You insult me.

ANGUS: Forgive me.

ARICIA: [*Pausing.*] All right.

ANGUS: I know he loves you.

ARICIA: There's nothing I want more.

[*WILLIAM enters.*]

WILLIAM: I'm meeting with the board, but before I do there's something I have to talk to you about. [*He glances at ANGUS, who understands to leave.*] Now that he's dead, I suppose you want to leave?

ARICIA: [*Struggling.*] Well, I hadn't . . .

WILLIAM: Every firm wants you, and now there's no one stopping you.

ARICIA: I don't know what to say.

WILLIAM: With your ability you'll make millions, then you'll start your own company.

ARICIA: I see.

WILLIAM: Whatever's happened in this house between you and me is in the past. You're free. I need you to know that.

ARICIA: Thank you, but do you think that's what I want?

WILLIAM: Are you negotiating?

ARICIA: I'm trying to tell you—

WILLIAM: Some on the board want you. They know Faye's unstable, and the old money doesn't want the stigma of a bastard son at the helm. They'd rather claim the glory of healing bad blood, *and* put a financial genius in the chair.

ARICIA: That's hard to believe.

WILLIAM: And I agree with them.

ARICIA: What do you mean?

WILLIAM: If you'll stay, I'll throw my proxy in for you. It'll be your company, and rightfully so.

ARICIA: I'm afraid I'm dreaming.

WILLIAM: Maybe we are.

[*THOMAS appears in the distance.*]

THOMAS: Have to get back . . .

ARICIA: You'd give up your own chance for my sake?

WILLIAM: My reason is caving in to something so passionate it's choking me.

ARICIA: Why?

WILLIAM: I don't want to breathe anymore except with your breath. For months I've been incapable of showing you what I feel. Struggling to get free from you. I see you everywhere, in the shadows, even in my horses' eyes. Forgive me. Love is so strange to me my words are all mangled. But ugly as they are, every one's a vow. Please don't reject them. Without you I never would have spoken.

[*ANGUS enters. In another room THOMAS kneels by FAYE's side and caresses his sleeping wife.*]

THOMAS: My poor sleeping one, sleep while you can.

ANGUS: Faye wants to see you.

WILLIAM: [*Looking at ARICIA.*] Tell her I can't. I'm waiting for an answer.

THOMAS: The sap is rising.

ANGUS: You've got no choice.

WILLIAM: Hold her back.

THOMAS: Will you wear the red wig? Will you ride the bright lights? Will you do it with the peacocks around us?

ARICIA: Let her come. [*Pause.*] I accept all your offers.

THOMAS: Will you love me?

[*As ARICIA leaves, FAYE rises, THOMAS fades away, and FAYE walks through a maze to WILLIAM.*]

FAYE: I found you.

WILLIAM: Yes, you've quite a nose.

FAYE: I can't banter today. [*To ANGUS.*] Would you excuse us?

WILLIAM: No.

FAYE: [*Commanding.*] Angus.

[*ANGUS leaves.*]

I know you must hate me, and I understand, I've given you every reason.

WILLIAM: What makes you say that?

FAYE: Please don't patronize me. I've come to ask for your help.

WILLIAM: What a droll wit.

FAYE: Not for me, for my sons. I'm not going to live much longer, and with Thomas dead I know the board will eliminate my boys. And because I've made you an enemy I'm afraid you'll turn your anger on them.

WILLIAM: I don't feel anything like that.

FAYE: It's only natural that you would, the things I've done to you. But you didn't know the real reason why.

WILLIAM: Oh, but I do.

[*Pause.*]

FAYE: Really? [*Pause as he looks away.*] Do you?

[*FAYE approaches WILLIAM. He backs away.*]

FAYE: You have to face me.

WILLIAM: Why?

FAYE: Your father's dead.

WILLIAM: [*Casually.*] He always has been.

FAYE: Don't joke about death.

WILLIAM: So what's changed?

FAYE: There's nothing stopping us.

WILLIAM: Did he?

FAYE: Yes.

WILLIAM: Interesting.

FAYE: [*Exploding.*] Don't stand there with your damn cold mask and pretend you feel nothing!

WILLIAM: I don't wear a mask. That's why I'm offensive to people like you—I say what I think.

FAYE: You're hiding right now.

WILLIAM: Just what am I hiding, "Mother"?

FAYE: Don't call me that!

WILLIAM: *You're* hiding! You'd like to cut my throat.

FAYE: No, I want to stroke it. And that's what you want.

WILLIAM: So says my father's merry widow.

FAYE: I can break down your walls.

WILLIAM: Is that a challenge?

FAYE: Yes.

WILLIAM: A sexual challenge?

FAYE: Yes.

WILLIAM: How titillating.

FAYE: There's a bottle of grain alcohol in the cabinet. One hundred and ninety proof—one of the ways Thomas got his manly laughs. If you give me half an hour with that bottle I'll show you what you really want.

WILLIAM: That stuff's poison!

FAYE: Are you afraid?

WILLIAM: Of what?

FAYE: Me?

WILLIAM: It can make you blind.

FAYE: That's what you are now. Shall I get the bottle?

WILLIAM: After this you'll let me alone?

FAYE: If that's what you want.

WILLIAM: It's a small price—get it.

[*FAYE gets the bottle and two shot glasses. She opens and pours as they speak.*]

FAYE: This is pleasant.

WILLIAM: The end's in sight.

FAYE: [*Teasing.*] It will be.

WILLIAM: Look at the name of this stuff!

FAYE: [*Laughing, reading.*] "Graves."

WILLIAM: Doesn't that make you uneasy?

FAYE: It's where I'll be if I can't have you.

WILLIAM: I'll warn you—

FAYE: Please do.

WILLIAM: I've never been drunk.

FAYE: You've never had me.

WILLIAM: [*Picking up his glass.*] Shall we?

FAYE: [*Toasting.*] Love moves.

WILLIAM: [*Toasting.*] To the hunt.

FAYE: For the secret soul.

[*They drink. Both react to their innards in flames.*]

WILLIAM: Ahhhhhhhhhhhhhhhhhh!
FAYE: [*Gasping.*] Yes . . . yes . . . yes!
WILLIAM: [*Not quite recovered.*] Must taste a lot . . . like love.
FAYE: Like fire.
WILLIAM: Like death.
FAYE: Pour another.

[*He pours two more shots.*]

WILLIAM: Are you having "a good time"?
FAYE: Oh yes. Are you?
WILLIAM: I'm intrigued.
FAYE: [*Toasting.*] To your sweet cock.

[*They drink.*]

WILLIAM: [*Gasping, laughing.*] May it ever wave.
FAYE: [*Laughing gaily.*] See? Something's happening.
WILLIAM: Always is.
FAYE: Did you know that people have a sexual thought every twelve seconds?
WILLIAM: If that's true about your kind, you're in worse pain than I thought.
FAYE: Pour another and you'll feel it.
WILLIAM: I think you're drunk.
FAYE: I became drunk the first time I saw you. Do you remember? You embraced me.
WILLIAM: Humoring my father.
FAYE: I touched your [*Groping for the word.*] . . . cheek! [*Laughing happily that she found it.*] I couldn't remember the word for the part of you that I . . . that I . . . touched. So many parts of you—so many small innocent touches—walking to the table . . . brushing up against your sleeve . . . would make me tingle. Could you tell? Could you, could you . . .

[*Rather than getting drunk, WILLIAM becomes more precise, more fluid, as if he is rising above his body.*]

WILLIAM: I've always been acutely aware of people's unconscious signals.
FAYE: So you knew?
WILLIAM: Yes.
FAYE: So do you think twelve people think of sex every . . . [*Groping for the sense, and laughing.*] . . . no, that's not it. So you knew?
WILLIAM: [*Laughing.*] And I knew that you knew that I knew.
FAYE: You're so charming when you laugh.
WILLIAM: That's not a laugh.
FAYE: Oh you want to quibble?
WILLIAM: Qui?
FAYE: [*Whirligigging.*] A quibble. A quibble on a quim. A quibble is a pun. Would you like to hear a quibble on a quim? Would that be fun? What would you like to hear? Dear? A quim on a quibble?
WILLIAM: No.

FAYE: So how much did you know? Everything?
WILLIAM: Yes.
FAYE: We don't have to talk then, do we?
WILLIAM: I'd like that.
FAYE: So would I.

[*They stare at one another in silence.*]

FAYE: Are you a virgin?
WILLIAM: Isn't everyone?
FAYE: I've got children.
WILLIAM: Contact between two people is an illusion.
FAYE: Then how'd I conceive two sons?
WILLIAM: You wanted it so badly you dreamt it.
FAYE: Then let me dream again.
WILLIAM: You are.
FAYE: Then dance with me.
WILLIAM: We are.
FAYE: We're not moving.
WILLIAM: The dance is in the eyes.
FAYE: For someone who doesn't believe in love, you're very—
WILLIAM: Lie down.
FAYE: All right.
WILLIAM: Spread your arms.
FAYE: Like so?
WILLIAM: [*Standing over her.*] Can you feel the distance between us?
FAYE: Yes.
WILLIAM: It will never go away.
FAYE: Lie next to me.

[*He does.*]

WILLIAM: [*Deliberately.*] Take my hand.

[*She does.*]

FAYE: Do you feel what's passing through our fingers?
WILLIAM: Bite my hand.

[*FAYE bites his hand. WILLIAM gasps in pain. He rises calmly and drives his point home.*]

Understand that you have never *touched* me.

[*FAYE rises.*]

FAYE: Pour another.
WILLIAM: You're drunk enough.
FAYE: Are you?
WILLIAM: I warned you.
FAYE: [*Trying to control herself.*] You made a deal!

WILLIAM: Fine.

[*WILLIAM pours two more shots, and they drink.*]

FAYE: Ohhhh, it goes right through me!

WILLIAM: Almost pure.

FAYE: Like you—almost.

WILLIAM: It reminds me of riding.

FAYE: Would you like to go riding?

WILLIAM: [*A little distant.*] I already am.

FAYE: You can ride me.

WILLIAM: I knew I wasn't ready to ride the dappled mare, but she's so beautiful.

FAYE: Mount me.

WILLIAM: She's never been ridden. She's angry.

FAYE: I'll do anything you want.

WILLIAM: She takes me deep into the woods, and starts trying to scrape me off by rubbing up against these sharp pines, and running under low tree limbs.

FAYE: I'll get down on my hands and knees and spread my ass for you.

WILLIAM: That doesn't work so she starts back to the stables, I can't stop her, she's so strong.

FAYE: I'll lie on my back and drink your come all night.

WILLIAM: She's running along a logging road, there's a deep ditch along one side. I'm trying to get control with the reins. I'm pulling so hard I've got her head pulled back all the way to her right side—she's running hard without even looking where she's going. I think if I keep this up I might topple us both into the ditch. I could be killed.

FAYE: I'll bathe your whole body with my juices.

WILLIAM: I have to let go to save us both. So I do.

FAYE: I'll do anything . . . anything . . .

WILLIAM: What an amazing feeling, she takes off at a full gallop. I'm on a runaway.

FAYE: Anything.

WILLIAM: Nothing's ever felt as good as that wild ride completely out of control, wind streaming in my eyes, tears running down my face, mare panting, the foam rising on her flanks . . .

FAYE: [*Imploring.*] William . . .

WILLIAM: [*Rising.*] Thank you for the drink. I have to go.

FAYE: [*Breaking down, crying to heaven.*] Oh help me! Please, help me, please . . .

[*WILLIAM hears ANGUS returning.*]

WILLIAM: You'd better leave.

FAYE: I'll never give up.

WILLIAM: You don't want to be seen this way.

[*She runs out. ANGUS enters.*]

ACT TWO

ANGUS watches FAYE run.

ANGUS: Why's she running?

[*WILLIAM won't answer.*]

Why are you so flushed?

[*WILLIAM is silent.*]

I see.

[*WILLIAM approaches ANGUS but stops, unable to move. ANGUS offers his arms.*]

Come here.

[*WILLIAM folds into his arms.*]

WILLIAM: Just hold me.

ANGUS: My dear boy. [*Long pause.*] I came to tell you I heard the board has chosen Faye as the new chair.

[*WILLIAM leaps up in anger and springs towards the door.*]

WILLIAM: They can't do that!

ANGUS: [*Blocking him.*] They've done it.

WILLIAM: I'll change it.

ANGUS: I thought you wanted no part of it.

WILLIAM: Things are different now.

ANGUS: Before you do something rash, there's a rumor that your father's been sighted.

WILLIAM: What! No, that son of a bitch can't come back from the dead!

ANGUS: It's just a rumor, but I never underestimate your father.

WILLIAM: First we kill the rumor, then we call an emergency board meeting. I told Aricia I'd give her control.

ANGUS: You have changed.

ريरित्रित्र

Moments later.

NONNY: The smartest thing for us to do is to take the children and leave . . . get as far from him as we—

FAYE: [*Enraged.*] I can't leave him.

NONNY: You sound like your mother! You'll forget everything, even your children, for this insanity?!

FAYE: You encouraged me!

NONNY: I didn't!

FAYE: You made me believe he could love me.

NONNY: Maybe I did, but there's nothing I wouldn't do to save you from this.

FAYE: I would've died silent, you pried all this out of me. Now you tell me I should run!

NONNY: Yes!

FAYE: I should have run from you!

NONNY: You don't even know what you're saying.

FAYE: I want you to go to him and offer him anything. The chairmanship, I'll step aside. Get down on your knees and beg, but get him for me.

NONNY: I don't know . . . how.

FAYE: Do it. I'll wait for you. Go on.

[*NONNY leaves. Unseen, ARICIA watches FAYE.*]

Whoever—whatever—you are that's doing this to me, please stop. In my dreams he comes to me—not night after night—that'd be too predictable, I could fortify myself. No, he waits until I'm mourning for him and then he makes love to me. He always sits in that chair before he leaves. In the sunlight. And the dust swooning in the beams of light is laden with the scent of our love. It fades when I wake and see Thomas. And I realize I'm not married to the light. I'm bound to a man whose every thought is a conscious act. Then nights go by, and I wait. In the desert. Finally he comes. And our flesh mingles and our minds meld, and my whole being floats into him, and he takes residence in me, and I have an overwhelming feeling of arrival. My parched lungs drink deep and long wet breaths of salt air. But I can't anymore, I can't . . . I can't . . . Whatever you are—why destroy me? I know you want to punish William. Then make him love me. Wouldn't that be revenge? Make him love me.

[*ARICIA steps out of the shadows.*]

ARICIA: What if that's impossible?

[*Startled, FAYE turns away.*]

Why do you avoid me?

[*FAYE looks at her with scorn.*]

That could change.

FAYE: How?

[*ARICIA moves to within inches of FAYE. They study one another.*]

ARICIA: Let me quench you.

[*Slowly, ARICIA moves to kiss FAYE. FAYE almost responds then pushes her away. FAYE leaves. ARICIA is alone. Light strikes the chair. She sits, almost motionless.*]

囗囗囗

NONNY enters the sitting room where the rest of the household, gathered around a funeral wreath, is holding a wake for **THOMAS**.

ARICIA: Shouldn't she be here?
NONNY: She's not well.
ARICIA: No restraint.
NONNY: Hold your tongue!
ANGUS: Nonny.
NONNY: Don't Nonny me . . . certain things . . .
ANGUS [*Pointedly*]: The occasion.

[*NONNY takes a moment to recover, then turns to* **WILLIAM**.]

NONNY: May I speak to you for a moment—alone?
WILLIAM: [*Ignoring her.*] Does anyone know any jokes?
NONNY: I don't think this is the time.
WILLIAM: It's a wake isn't it?
ARICIA: Have you heard the one about the guy named Joe Dick?
WILLIAM: No.
ANGUS: No.
ARICIA: Growing up was hell, a constant humiliation, so when he left home he decided to change his name. [*Pause.*] To Bob Dick.
NONNY: [*Erupting with laughter.*] Oh that's funny! Bob Dick! Oh, Oh, Oh, that's funny. [*She clutches the wreath and tries to stop laughing.*] Ha, ha, I have to stop laughing, it's not right, ha, ha, ha, ha, no I must stop, ha, ha, please someone help me, ha, ha, ha, Bob Dick! ha, ha, no, help me.

[*No one moves because* **THOMAS** *enters, as if from the dead, drenched and disheveled. They stare stunned.* **NONNY***'s laughter chokes and she reels away.*]

𐃉𐃉𐃉

FAYE senses NONNY returning.

FAYE: No, too soon, too soon.

[*NONNY enters.*]

Too soon.

NONNY: Thomas.
FAYE: No.
NONNY: He's alive.
FAYE: He'll find out what I've done.
NONNY: Yes he will.

[*Long pause.*]

FAYE: [*Attacking.*] Why would you want to hurt me?!

NONNY: I'd never hurt you.

FAYE: I was ready to die. My offending parts were already below the earth. And you dragged me up. Why?

NONNY: How can you blame me for wanting you to live?

FAYE: I was going to die with my name clean. Now I'm going to die a whore! And you're the reason.

NONNY: Don't you dare put this off on me. You loved him. You went after him.

FAYE: I never would have.

NONNY: Don't make me your scapegoat.

FAYE: William . . . you'll enjoy this.

NONNY: What if he doesn't say anything?

FAYE: Don't start twisting again.

NONNY: No, I don't think he will.

FAYE: Even if he doesn't, it'll all be clear to Thomas. This time I'll find a faster way to die. Don't stop me again.

NONNY: You'll give your boys a mother who killed herself for lust?

FAYE: [Breaking.] No!

NONNY: How could you?

FAYE: Please, no, I don't want to hurt them.

NONNY: Well?

FAYE: That's the only thing I regret.

NONNY: Then attack William before he attacks you. Let me tell Thomas he tried to rape you.

FAYE: NO!

NONNY: It makes me sick too, but this is not the time for—

FAYE: I can't put him in that danger.

NONNY: His father loves him—in his way. He won't really hurt him, he'll just drive him out, and he deserves that.

FAYE: I couldn't get those words out of my mouth.

NONNY: All I need is for you to be silent.

FAYE: I can't.

NONNY: [Lashing out.] It's not just for you. It's for your boys. Don't destroy them by indulging your self-pity. William wants to crush you. Be brutal and help them survive. That's what a mother does!

FAYE: I don't know anything anymore. I'm completely out of control. Do what you will.

[NONNY leaves. Outside the door, ANGUS waits for her and takes her arm.]

ANGUS: Nonny.

NONNY: It's late.

ANGUS: Too late to tend the garden.

NONNY: The dark's a good time.

ANGUS: I'll do it in the morning.

NONNY: What if there is no morning?

ANGUS: Touch me.

NONNY: Good gracious, no.

[*THOMAS enters. FAYE sits almost without reaction. He offers his hand. She rises and takes it quietly.*]

THOMAS: Faye.

[*She doesn't respond.*]

Faye?

[*No response. WILLIAM enters.*]

WILLIAM: Father.
THOMAS: Later.
WILLIAM: Father. Aricia and—
THOMAS: Leave us alone.

[*WILLIAM withdraws.*]

Is this the welcome I get? I've been away a long time. Can you tell me what's wrong?

[*FAYE removes her hand, wanders away, and starts a drifting dance.*]

Would you like some tea?

[*FAYE stops dancing.*]

THOMAS: When you don't listen . . .
FAYE: Ummm?
THOMAS: I'm lost.
FAYE: Fine, I'll have some tea.
THOMAS: That's not the point.
FAYE: I'll make it.
THOMAS: It's already made.
FAYE: Are the cups full?
THOMAS: Spilling over the rim.
FAYE: Hmmmmmmm . . .
THOMAS: I'll get the tea—
FAYE: We never used to drink tea.
THOMAS: I know that. [*Pause, as he gazes at her.*] I'm having a miniature stage built for you in the bedroom.
FAYE: Why?
THOMAS: So that you can perform.
FAYE: *Hire* the talent.
THOMAS: No one else will do what I need.
FAYE: I can't.

[*ARICIA appears in the open doorway.*]

THOMAS: What's happened to you?
FAYE: Ummm?

THOMAS: It's as if you're disappearing.
FAYE: Maybe I am.
THOMAS: Do you want me to inform the board?
FAYE: No business after dinner, remember?
THOMAS: They'll divvy your shares like party favors.
FAYE: When you were gone . . .
THOMAS: [*Pause.*] Yeah?
FAYE: Something horrible happened.
THOMAS: What?
FAYE: [*Leaving.*] You won't see me.
THOMAS: What's this all about?

[*FAYE walks out. THOMAS notices ARICIA, who slips away.*]

いいい

FAYE waits until WILLIAM is asleep, then cuts a lock of his hair. After she leaves he wakes and feels for the missing hair. He panics and starts screaming.

WILLIAM: Goddammit, you fucking bastard, you cocksucking son of a bitch, you freak fucking dog raper, you—Ohhhhhhhhhhhh—you goddamn—ohhhh—Nooooo—

[*THOMAS rushes in and grabs WILLIAM, shaking him to stop.*]

THOMAS: William!
WILLIAM: Stop!
THOMAS: Snap out of it!
WILLIAM: Stop!
THOMAS: You're all right, it's just a dream!
WILLIAM: Get away from me.
THOMAS: Goddammit, get a grip.

[*WILLIAM begins to ease, breathing heavily.*]

WILLIAM: What are you doing?
THOMAS: I heard you screaming, I ran in.
WILLIAM: I'm fine now, you can go.
THOMAS: Why don't you tell me what this was about.
WILLIAM: Why?
THOMAS: What the hell went on when I was gone?
WILLIAM: A boy stood outside the house every single day. He had his hands over his eyes.
THOMAS: I want to know what happened to Faye.
WILLIAM: I can't be near that woman anymore.
THOMAS: Why?
WILLIAM: What do you want?
THOMAS: I want to help you.
WILLIAM: What do you want?

THOMAS: Is that all you can you say?

WILLIAM: Well?

THOMAS: I want to talk.

WILLIAM: Why?

THOMAS: Every time we talk nothing gets said.

WILLIAM: Because nothing you say has anything to do with who you are.

THOMAS: [*Temper rising.*] Boy—who I am you'll never know.

WILLIAM: You're transparent.

THOMAS: No, you can't see me, I'm never in the same place twice.

WILLIAM: I know you by what you do, and that woman you brought into this house is twisted.

THOMAS: I had a stepmother, too. She was a piece 'a work: a piece of ass, but a piece 'a poison. So I know what you're going through.

WILLIAM: Ah, the sympathetic father.

THOMAS: One of many faces, all true. Some people call me a demon, others a machine. I kinda like that one—a fornicating machine.

WILLIAM: With a long line of people waiting with their death wish in their sweaty palms.

THOMAS: [*Like a laser.*] Now you've made me very angry.

[*ARICIA appears in the door and witnesses THOMAS drive WILLIAM away with his gaze.*]

ARICIA: I saw what you did to your son.

THOMAS: Oh?

ARICIA: Do you want to watch a private act?

THOMAS: [*Whispering.*] Yes.

ARICIA [*Forcing him to say it louder.*] What?

THOMAS: Yes.

[*ARICIA sits at the table, and, drinking straight from the pitcher, is unable to slake her thirst.*]

ARICIA: I feel love's raging thirst.

[*She rubs her hands in the water spilled on the table top, lifts her dress slightly and rubs the water on the insides of her thighs. THOMAS stands behind her, and breathes in deeply.*]

THOMAS: What do you want?

ARICIA: A place on the board.

THOMAS: Fine.

ARICIA: Twenty percent of the shares.

THOMAS: Shall we?

ARICIA: Yes, let's.

[*They do not move. A long pause. NONNY enters and stares at them transfixed. ARICIA leaves.*]

凹凹凹

In another room **WILLIAM** *shakes violently like a sapling in a fierce wind.*

〰〰〰

NONNY stares at THOMAS.

THOMAS: You're saying he tried to rape her?
NONNY: Yes.
THOMAS: And she's staying silent about it?
NONNY: Yes.
THOMAS: That son of a bitch, I'll kill him. You have proof?
NONNY: Why do you think she fought so hard to send him away? This has been brewing since he first saw her.
THOMAS: It doesn't make sense. Why didn't she say anything?
NONNY: To protect you. She was ashamed.
THOMAS: I can't believe it! I'll kill him.
NONNY: I have to go—I'm afraid to leave her alone.

〰〰〰

ANGUS grips the shaking WILLIAM.

WILLIAM: Do you think she's crazy enough to tell him what she's done?
ANGUS: Yes. You have to tell him first.
WILLIAM: [*Vehemently.*] No.
ANGUS: Why not?

[**WILLIAM** *won't answer.*]

I see.

[*Pause.*]

WILLIAM: Stop it! [*Pause.*] I was about to tell him about Aricia.
ANGUS: Don't.

[**WILLIAM** *stares at ANGUS in disbelief.*]

Just take her and go.

[**WILLIAM** *starts to leave.*]

WILLIAM: [*Turning back.*] No. First I've got something to prove. [*He finds his way to* **THOMAS**.]
THOMAS: You've got horseshit on your boots.
WILLIAM: I was working in the paddock.
THOMAS: You're going to stink up the whole place.
WILLIAM: The servants will get it. There's something I have to tell you.
THOMAS: Good, I've been wanting to talk with you, too.
WILLIAM: Forget it.

THOMAS: I want you to take over the company when I'm gone.

WILLIAM: Forget it.

THOMAS: Goddammit you can't spend your whole life racing horses, boy. Grow up and be a man.

WILLIAM: Like you.

THOMAS: Yes.

WILLIAM: A whoremonger.

THOMAS: You're disgusting.

WILLIAM: You're a feeder—a piranha—

THOMAS: That's enough!

WILLIAM: With your mergers and your hostile takeovers, but mostly you feed on women. Talk about disgusting! Your lechery hangs off your face as plain as a dog's hard-on.

THOMAS: Power needs to be fed. I get very hungry. I give my body what it needs. You'll understand someday.

WILLIAM: Will I understand what you did to my mother?

THOMAS: [*Blowing up.*] She came after me, I had no—

WILLIAM: And Faye's sister—

THOMAS: You don't know what hap—

WILLIAM: And countless others. I could never live up to your reputation. You're legendary, the Great Cocksman.

THOMAS: Doesn't anyone, anything, move you?

WILLIAM: Yes. I love riding into the tempest sweet sixteen sheets to the wind. Winding around the maypole of the Marquis. Flashflooding the assflooding, and lots of ass, beautiful round asses, and lots of ash, beautiful black coal ash, and the ash raining on the ass. The labyrinth is a delight, but such a tedious habit. What could it mean? This throbbing of desire. It's a malignant accident of nature. I don't want it.

THOMAS: You're strange.

WILLIAM: You need to see what strange is.

THOMAS: A man that can't love is like a man without an ass.

WILLIAM: How delicate.

THOMAS: Ya can't sit, ya can't shit, you're not fit for livin'.

WILLIAM: You're vulgar.

THOMAS: But I can love.

WILLIAM: Bravissimo.

THOMAS: I understand you tried to rape my wife.

WILLIAM: What!

THOMAS: The virgin finally pulls out his chainsaw *in my bed.*

WILLIAM: [*Shouting.*] That's a lie!

THOMAS: Which part? The virgin?

WILLIAM: I never touched her!

THOMAS: You expect me to believe you! You sick fuck!

WILLIAM: I love Aricia.

THOMAS: Just another lie to cover yourself. You never loved anyone. And now you're a dead man!

WILLIAM: Listen to me!

THOMAS: Get out! I don't want your corpse in my house.

WILLIAM: How can you believe her? Look at her mother! You know who she came from—

[*ANGUS enters to investigate the shouting and watches aghast.*]

THOMAS: [*Raising his hand.*] Shut up before I kill you myself! Won't anyone rid me of this scum?!? Please, someone crush him!

WILLIAM: It's in her blood.

THOMAS: GET OUT!

[*WILLIAM leaves. Pause.*]

I'm going to grind his body into powder. [*Pause.*] How can I kill my own son? [*Pause.*] How could I have fathered such a degenerate?

[*FAYE enters. ANGUS slips away.*]

FAYE: I have to . . . speak to—

THOMAS: Were you listening to me?

FAYE: I have something I need to tell you.

THOMAS: Not now.

FAYE: Please.

THOMAS: NO!

[*Pause.*]

FAYE: Thomas.

THOMAS: Do you ever find yourself glancing at animals? At their sexual parts?

FAYE: No.

THOMAS: There was a stallion in the south of Ireland that was awe-inspiring, downright humbling.

FAYE: Have you ever considered that talking about it kills the mystery?

THOMAS: Come here. [*Pause.*] Please.

[*FAYE comes close. He gently squeezes her arms.*]

I can't kill it. Do you remember why you married me?

FAYE: [*With difficulty.*] Yes.

THOMAS: This mystery—I pretend I'm trying to expose it. It's a game. I know I'll never succeed. And by failing, I pay homage to its power. But when I want to tap its power I say nothing. I let the distance between us call out.

FAYE: [*Almost remembering.*] Thomas . . . ?

THOMAS: Your eyes call me across oceans. I get so lost in your eyes. Then I'm filled with a longing, your voice singing *come home.*

FAYE: [*Becoming aroused.*] Home . . .

THOMAS: You are that home.

FAYE: Hmmmm . . .

THOMAS: And I desire to make a journey.

FAYE: Home.

THOMAS: I have to navigate. Storms rise. The old salts say the seventh wave is the worst, the one that does the damage.

FAYE: My heart is so damaged.

THOMAS: I know. That makes my desire almost unbearable.

FAYE: Yes.

THOMAS: And I say your name over and over, Faye . . . Faye . . .

FAYE: [*Putting her finger to his lips.*] Shhhh . . .

THOMAS: And your eyes . . . Beacons.

FAYE: Shhhh . . .

THOMAS: Draw me home.

FAYE: Shhhh . . .

THOMAS: With your eyes.

[*Their lips come close, sensing without motion. Finally, FAYE breaks away.*]

FAYE: Don't threaten William, please. Call off what you've . . .

THOMAS: How can you defend him after what he's done to you?

FAYE: He's innocent.

THOMAS: No one is.

FAYE: Please!

THOMAS: He's a liar. And a good one.

FAYE: No! Listen to me—

THOMAS: He knows if you have to lie make it a big one. So the son of a bitch has cooked up the biggest lie of his life—he claims he loves Aricia.

[*Long pause.*]

FAYE: What?

THOMAS: You heard me—that's a laugh—him love anyone!

[*FAYE turns away. THOMAS tries to hold her. She stiffens. He leaves.*]

FAYE: He loves her. [*Pause.*] No. I can't save him.

[*She presses her palms against the door as if to hold back what's outside.*]

How can he want her over me?

NONNY: How do you know it's true?

FAYE: You've known all along, haven't you?

[*NONNY turns away silent.*]

I want her out of this house! I'll rip her apart. No, worse. I'll make her a leper. I'll tell Thomas she's been selling company secrets. He'll squeeze the life from her throat—No! What am I doing?! It's so twisted. Using my husband to destroy my competition for his son. I've lost my mind!

NONNY: Stop it!

FAYE: I'm disgusting! The woman's innocent—she's never done anything to me, and I want to crucify her.

NONNY: You can't help yourself.

FAYE: I'm loathsome. Crawling with lust so thick I'm no longer human!

NONNY: Stop thinking about your body.

FAYE: It's not my *body* that oozes with desire. It's my mind . . .

NONNY: Think of other things.

[*FAYE searches NONNY's face with her fingers as if exploring the features of a lover.*]

FAYE: And it hardly seems like *my* mind. The genitalia of a gargoyle would be more like it. Horribly ugly with its scaly labia, but at the same time sensual and unbearably beautiful, the fleshy folds as innocent as a newborn's. And this thing, it's disembodied, adrift somewhere, maybe everywhere where fluids flow. It knows me, this thing. It touches me, whispers in my ear: "Know him, you must know him."

[*As if in a trance, FAYE starts moving towards WILLIAM. NONNY understands what is happening and tries to stop her, holding onto her arm to restrain her. FAYE is too powerful and tears away.*]

NONNY: Nooooo . . .

[*FAYE follows the voice through a maze until she reaches WILLIAM.*]

WILLIAM: I have nothing else to say.

FAYE: I know who you really are.

WILLIAM: Impossible.

FAYE: I've been in your room.

WILLIAM: When? I don't believe you.

FAYE: I opened the suitcase under your bed.

WILLIAM: You're bluffing.

FAYE: This is delicious.

WILLIAM: It's locked.

FAYE: I thought it would be exciting to slip my hand into one of your riding gloves, and what did I find? [*She holds up a key.*]

WILLIAM [*Enraged.*]: Goddammit!

FAYE: Are they your drawings?

WILLIAM: You had no right!

FAYE: The sketch of the woman bending over spreading her cheeks was quite well rendered—the cross-hatching was positively salacious.

[*FAYE tries to embrace him. He pushes her away. She pummels his chest with her fists until she knocks him down. Then she mounts him.*]

Why are you like this?!

WILLIAM: I want you to leave me alone!

FAYE: Grind your hips!

WILLIAM: No!

FAYE: Yes!

WILLIAM: Bitch! I hate you!

FAYE: NO, NO, NO, NO—WHY?!

WILLIAM: Get off me!

FAYE: Why are you like this?

WILLIAM: Get off!

FAYE: [*Starting to strangle him.*] Why?

WILLIAM: No!

FAYE: Yes!

WILLIAM: [*Gasping for breath.*] You're . . . chok-ing . . .

FAYE: Why?!

WILLIAM: My old man—

FAYE: Why?

WILLIAM: My old—

FAYE: Forget about him!

WILLIAM: My old man's a—

FAYE: This is about us—forget him!

WILLIAM: He's—

FAYE: Why!

WILLIAM: He's a—

FAYE: Stop it! Tell me why!

WILLIAM: He's a rapist!

FAYE: NO!

WILLIAM: RAPIST!

FAYE: NO!

WILLIAM: I'm made of rape!

FAYE: NO! Not true!

WILLIAM: Sex makes me sick!

[*FAYE rolls off WILLIAM and clutches her belly, moaning. Before he leaves he sits on the chair and watches her for a moment. After he's gone she crawls to the chair and lays her cheek where he was sitting. NONNY enters, sees her condition, and runs to her.*]

NONNY: What happened?

FAYE: He ripped me again.

NONNY: Everyone's a victim of love. Do you think you're the only one? You have to accept it.

FAYE: [*In a dark fury.*] Are you still giving me advice? You're the one who accused him of rape. That'll be his death! Get out of—

NONNY: But I was—

FAYE: Get out of this house! I'll give you one hour to pack. Then I never want to see you again. I hope your tongue prattles and shakes in hell!

[*FAYE leaves. NONNY is alone.*]

NONNY: Oh God! To save her, I did everything. And I lost everything. And this is my reward. [*Pause.*] Well deserved . . . [*She surveys the room one* *last time.*] All quiet now. Flesh is just flesh. The wind will blow a curtain. Thread will unravel. Light strikes the table. [*She retrieves her hidden bottle, but hesitates before drinking.*] No—won't do . . . [*She begins searching the room.*] She had some pills. [*She finds them and holds the bottle up to the light, measuring.*] There . . . that oughta do. [*Laughing ruefully.*] The fleas leap from their bags . . . [*She leaves slowly, with a purpose, murmuring.*] Well deserved . . . well deserved . . .

◫◫◫

ARICIA finds WILLIAM curled up on the floor.

ARICIA: Why don't you tell your father the truth?

[*WILLIAM can't respond.*]

You told me you never touched her. Is that the truth? [*Silence.*] Why can't you speak?

[*He shakes his head—he doesn't know. She lifts her dress. Her thighs become visible. He thrashes out with his arm commanding her to stop. But he can't cry out, and he can't look away because his eyes desire to know.*]

Why don't you close your eyes?

[*She lifts her dress higher. He's paralyzed. She kneels by his side and lovingly caresses his face.*]

I love you. But I don't know how much longer I can wait. You'll drown me.

[*ARICIA leaves. WILLIAM's profound struggle to rise and leave evokes the stomping of a panicked horse: a death dance.*]

◫◫◫

FAYE gropes for NONNY.

FAYE: Nonny, draw me a bath. [*There is no answer.*] Nonny!

◫◫◫

ARICIA approaches THOMAS.

ARICIA: William and I are leaving.
THOMAS: He says he loves you.
ARICIA: He does.
THOMAS: Don't trust him. He's dangerous.
ARICIA: You don't know him at all, do you?
THOMAS: He tried to rape my wife!

ARICIA: How can you believe that? Because that's what you'd do?

THOMAS: I have a witness.

ARICIA: A self-serving liar.

THOMAS: And I have Faye's tears. She's been trying to kill herself.

ARICIA: Call it off before you kill the wrong one.

THOMAS: Shut up!

ARICIA: Thomas—the great slayer of monsters. But they're not all dead. [*Stopping herself.*] But I can't say any more. [*Leaving.*] We're leaving.

THOMAS: Wait! [*She's gone.*] What're you saying? [*Crying out.*] AHHHH! [*Pause.*] My boy . . . I have a bad feeling. [*Shouting.*] Is *everyone* lying?! [*He sets out determined to question NONNY.*] Where is that old woman? NONNY!

〽〽〽

ANGUS moves stealthily to the screen enclosing FAYE's bath. As he peers around the corner he gasps and runs in.

ANGUS: NONNY!

[*We hear the sounds of him trying to pull her out of the bathtub.*]

NO! NO! you sweet thing . . . NOOO . . . Come to me . . . come to me . . . come to me . . . ohhhhhhhhh . . .

〽〽〽

ARICIA enters.

ARICIA: William is dead.

THOMAS: What!

ARICIA: Your son is dead.

THOMAS: You're lying.

ARICIA: You did it.

THOMAS: No.

ARICIA: Yes.

THOMAS: I said no.

ARICIA: I say yes.

THOMAS: I called it off.

ARICIA: I was there.

THOMAS: It can't be.

ARICIA: They're bringing his body here.

THOMAS: What happened?

ARICIA: He was riding the dappled mare along the shore. Back and forth like a madman. I kept shouting at him to stop. The horse went berserk. She was trying to run out to sea. He fought to control her but she threw him, and he got tangled in the reins. She trampled him to get free. And then they came. His horses . . . pounding through the surf. All of them. Churning and crashing blind. Their hooves tore him to pieces. And they were gone.

THOMAS: Please—NO—please . . .

[*ANGUS enters in a fury.*]

ANGUS: You fucking monster!

THOMAS: Get back!

ANGUS: You did it!

THOMAS: Yes.

ANGUS: I'm going to tell the world everything I know about you, your bribes, your extortions, the corpses you leave in immaculate rooms.

THOMAS: Your body will drop away.

[*ANGUS goes to strike THOMAS.*]

Wither and turn to dust.

[*ANGUS hesitates.*]

Think again.

[*ANGUS storms out of the room. Aricia follows.*]

[*Grief-stricken.*] Oh William, my poor poor boy, somewhere in your twisted soul was a bright light, and I could never gather it. I was always far away. But loved you. I did. [*Lashing out.*] I didn't want this! How could it happen? I didn't want it!

[*FAYE enters.*]

FAYE: Thomas?

THOMAS: William's dead.

FAYE: Yes.

THOMAS: I don't know what happened between you, but I'm taking your word because I can't take any more pain.

FAYE: There is no more than this. He was innocent.

THOMAS: You're crueler than life itself.

FAYE: Something beyond me drove me, and with the help of my most loving friend . . . I . . . [*She starts swaying as if trying to do her yearning dance, but her body is wracked with tiny convulsions.*]

THOMAS: What're you doing?

FAYE: I took poison.

[*Pause.*]

THOMAS: Would you like some tea?

FAYE: Did you hear me?

THOMAS: I'll help you to bed.

FAYE: I don't have much time.

THOMAS: That's always the case.

FAYE: Do you understand?!

THOMAS: No.
FAYE: I'm dying.
THOMAS: Yes.
FAYE: [*Faintly.*] Going . . .

[*Long pause.*]

THOMAS: You were gone suddenly, out of my hands.

[*FAYE approaches the chair.*]

FAYE: And now I feel my trembling knees give way.

[*Her breathing becomes serene, then she sinks to her knees, clutching the chair. ARICIA enters. She and THOMAS lock eyes.*]

END OF PLAY

THE ELEKTRA FUGUES

(AN OPERATIC BLACK BOX RECORDING OF CLASSIC DISASTER)

LIBRETTO BY RUTH E. MARGRAFF

PHOTO: ARMANDO

RUTH E. MARGRAFF's work has been recently developed and produced in New York, Minneapolis, Seattle, Boston, Alabama, Dallas, Austin, Providence, Iowa City, Los Angeles and in Belgrade (Serbia), Moscow (Russia), Tokyo (Japan) and the Isle of Hydra (Greece). She has been published in *American Theater Magazine Vol. 19, No. 9* (TCG); *Theater Forum 22: International Theater Journal (Winter/Spring 2003), NuMuse Anthology* (Brown), *Conjunctions:28 "Music Theater Portfolio"* (Bard), *CHAIN 9* (NEA/Temple University dialogue with Dr. Sa'di Al-Hadithi, Kanan Makiya and Ayad Rahim), and *Theatre in Crisis?* (Manchester University Press/Palgrave), etc. She was the recipient of an artist's residency at the Villa Serbelloni (Bellagio, Italy) in 1998 and was "artisita in visita" at La MaMa's Umbria International (Spoleto, Italy). She has been awarded funding from the Rockefeller Foundation, Jerome Fellowship at the Playwrights' Center, McKnight Advancement Grant, New York State Council for the Arts, TCG/ITI, Arts International, and an NEA/TCG playwriting residency at HERE Arts Center in New York. She has taught at University of Texas at Austin/Michener Center for Writers, Brown University, Fordham University, and the Yale School of Drama, is an alumnus of New Dramatists, and is represented by Abrams Artists in New York City.

From the Writer
RUTH E. MARGRAFF

fugue: *a polyphonic composition in which a subject voice is introduced and then extended and developed through successive contrapuntal imitations; in psychiatry, a temporary flight from reality*

cadence: *the fall of the voice at the end of a sentence; flow of rhythm, inflection or modulation in tone; a state of sinking or decline; an ending as a means of beginning the next subject or returning to the subject*

During the summer of 1996, I found a book propping up the air conditioner in a window that had been covered with tin foil to ward off the one hundred twenty degree blazing daylight of Austin, Texas. I was madly writing the first draft of a commission on Elektra, with sweat pouring down my back, and the book was Douglas Green's *Forms in Tonal Music.* I fell in love with various definitions of "cadence" as a way of writing character and the idea of a "fugue" as a way of translating disaster. I started drawing some of my characters' cadences onto music paper and realized that Elektra's rage might be at the heart of the fugues of her family's catastrophe, if you listen to her rants as a pitch to which her family's voices adjusted in counterpoint.

The libretto of my first opera, *The Elektra Fugues,* became one of the most defining experiences of my career. When I got back to New York we produced this opera with neo-classical composer Matthew Pierce and director Tim Maner for singers like the lovely Meredith Monk-vocalist Dina Emerson. Tim, Matthew, and I had just co-founded HERE Arts Center's "Opera Project," with dramaturg/violist Celise Kalke, and designers Allen Hahn and Nancy Brous, in New York in 1995. So we created the premiere of *The Elektra Fugues* with the grand subtitle of "a black box recording of classic disaster into eight polyphonic vocal tracks" as if the myth had been recorded orally through the ages and this would be its eight-track cassette translation. And so we would try to know Elektra first by the acoustics of her vengeance and grief and not just by her literary value.

Agamemnon's voice-over was inspired by "black box" recordings from crash sites in 1996, particularly TWA Flight 800 and the crash of seven-year-old pilot Jessica Dubroff, who died with her father in a driving rainstorm. The opening of Act I, "Transmission of Old Gleam," was inspired by Cindy Sherman's gleam photographs with high-resolution surfaces, "not in the female figure's attempt to save her face in a masquerade of femininity . . . in keeping with the codes of glossiness . . . an effect of backlighting or wild light of the gleam of the pupil . . . emerging from the obscurity of a face."[3] So Agamemnon would speak to Elektra in gleaming fragments from his crash-site grave, built by Allen, our set and lighting designer, to be a refracting black obelisk with black-and-white video interior, where Elektra mourned him. This came to represent Agamemnon's black box recording of his last words and Elektra's memories of her father.

The "slit voice" of Iphigenia/Chrysothemis in "Shut Up" and "Final Girl Staircases" etc. was originally written for an eighth character, Cassandra, who prophesied in the margins of tragedy in a four-part descant above Elektra's voice. The four parts of her voice included faux opera, silent movie, bird sounds, and the gestures of a "final girl" (a term used to describe the last female victim of a monster in the horror-movie genre). This was a rather tall order for any singer and when *The Elektra Fugues* was produced in Los Angeles as a play without music, director Jim Martin suggested cutting the character. The libretto was stronger without Cassandra by then, I believe, because the voice of Iphigenia took on aspects of the descant and more high pitched horror of the vocal score (see illustration, "Quarter Rest to Lip to Slit Voice").

The ending of the play, "Girl-Like Face," was written after one Saturday afternoon when the drummer of one of the local punk bands I worked with on my hysteric operetta *Wallpaper Psalm* took me out on a flight in his single-engine plane. His family had struck oil so I knew it was possible that he had bought the plane but didn't know how to fly. I got more and more nervous as we drove to a private airport and, after referring to a flying manual that sat in the cockpit next to all the warnings about bodily injury and death, he checked the jet fuel. By the time we were airborne, I was trembling at the windows rolled down like a car in the air, and the stories he told about running out of gas lost over Texas at night, crashing his motorcycle, and getting out of a free fall nose-dive by accelerating. Finally, I realized that I had a draft of *The Elektra Fugues* half-finished in my bag and said something obscure into the headphones that I thought could be my last words on the black box recording if we crashed and burned. He told me later that the air-traffic controllers only track the small planes with the naked eye, and that there is no black box on this type of single-engine plane. So I wanted the ending to be true to that in some way.

"Perfect is a modifier used only in relation to unisons."
DOUGLAS M. GREEN, *Forms in Tonal Music*

PRODUCTION HISTORY

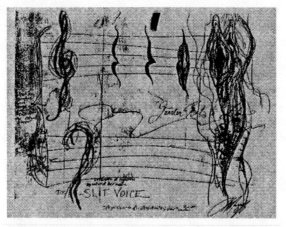

Quarter Rest to Lip to Slit Voice drawing for vocal cadence of
Iphigenia/Chrysothemis. PHOTO: RUTH E. MARGRAFF.

The Elektra Fugues was commissioned by HERE Arts Center's "Opera
Project"/Tiny Mythic Theatre Company as an "8-track opera based in vocal
cadence, punk & classic strings." It was developed with readings directed by Liz
Diamond at the Lincoln Center Library reading series and New Dramatists in
New York as well as a reading directed by Brad Rothbart at Theater Double in
Philadelphia.

The piece premiered November 26–December 21, 1996, as an opera scored
for a live seven-piece chamber orchestra of violin, viola, cello, upright bass,
electric violin, guitar, and percussion. The director was Tim Maner; the set and
lighting design was by Allen Hahn; the costume design was by Nancy Brous;
music was by Matthew Pierce; dramaturgy and viola by Celise Kalke. The cast
was as follows:

IPHIGENIA/CHRYSOTHEMIS . . . . Dina Emerson
PEASANT HUSBAND . . . . Tony Boutte
ELEKTRA . . . . Abigail Gampel
ORESTES . . . . Eric Sanders
CASSANDRA . . . . Mercedes Bahleda
AEGISTHUS . . . . Thomas Pasley
CLYTEMNESTRA . . . . Justin Bond a k a "Kiki"
AGAMEMNON . . . . Richard Rose

The Elektra Fugues was also produced February 11–March 13, 1999, a cappella,
as a play with one live percussionist by Bottom's Dream Theater in Los Angeles.
The director was Jim Martin.

SPECIAL THANKS to Caridad Svich and Gary Sunshine, and the original beloved HERE opera project members Tim Maner, Celise Kalke, Matthew Pierce, Allen Hahn and Nancy Brous, and to Mitchell Gossett and Jim Martin of Bottom's Dream, Vicky Boone/Frontera at Hyde Park Theater, and Jason Neulander/Salvage Vanguard for hosting me with a Laurie Carlos NEA residency in Austin, Texas, during the summer I wrote most of this, Meredith Monk via Dina Emerson, Greil Marcus, Gilbert Murray, Herb Dishman of Fairy Stain/Engine Run Angry and his single engine plane, Joe Ridout, Douglas Greene, Eric Sanders, Audrey Parks, and all the stunning actors and punk bands I was watching at the time, my mother and her apt. by carbon-monoxided Queens Tunnel, McKnight Foundation, The Playwrights' Center, RAT Conference in Austin and the wrath of the homeless teenage girls I worked with through choreographer Margery Segal, and to Nikos Brisco and Morgan Jenness always.

VOCAL CADENCE OF ARCHETYPES

ELEKTRA—Punk/rage
CHRYSOTHEMIS/IPHIGENIA—Sister sweet to slit voice
CLYTEMNESTRA—Stand-up comedic whine of synthetic breast milk
AEGISTHUS—Stand-up comedic whine of stepfather guile
ORESTES—Militant/percussive/bedwetting
PEASANT HUSBAND/GILBERT MURRAY—Preface of a mild translation
AGAMEMNON'S VOICE—Deus ex machina

NOTES

Text set in all-capital letters and italics (e.g. *I WASTE AWAY MY PRIME*) should be sung and scored full throttle in the character's full cadence. Choleric, fully agitated humor.

Text in all capitals (e.g. TANGLING SPOIL OF GLEAM) reflects recitative in the character's cadence, half-spoken, half-sung, and should be more open in the scoring.

Text in lowercase italics (e.g. *And if I do resemble you*) should be sung but not at full intensity, usually more melodic, melancholy or sanguine humor.

Text that is plain (e.g. I want to marry you) should be spoken in a more normal frame of emotion, more restrained.

SONGS AND SEQUENCE

ACT I. TRANSMISSION OF OLD GLEAM
Scene 1: Obelisk—Elektra at the *deus ex machina* crash site, with Iphigenia's "Pity Me Father." Scene 2: "Resemble Overture" a fugue of family portraits, features and voices pitched in reaction to Elektra's lament. With Iphigenia's "Say Grace," Orestes' "God Save our Muscles" Clytemnestra and Aegisthus' "Not Fraught" dirty jokes and the Peasant Husband's "Footnote."

ACT II. ELEKTRA'S LAMENT
Scene 1: "Rant," the tonal centre of the fugues with "A Little For Your Easing" (Peasant Husband). Scene 2: Not Fraught With Toil (Clytemnestra & Aegisthus).

ACT III. SHUT UP
Scene 1: Sister—Elektra tries to enlist Chrysothemis, a sister who has sprung up in the sister position of Iphigenia from a more psychological translation. Scene 2: Clytemnestra's Contour I (Clytemnestra and Chrysothemis).

ACT IV. RECOGNITIONS OF THE BROTHER
Scene 1: Signet Ring. Scene 2: Scar on his Brow. Scene 3: Gleaming Lock of Curls with "Muscular Footprint" duets (Peasant Husband and Chrysothemis). Scene 4: Urn into "Final Girl Staircases" (Iphigenia). Scene 5: Clytemnestra's Contour II. Scene 6: "God's Horseman And A Star Without A Stain" (Orestes' display as thinly veiled Olympic messenger).

ACT V. RED PILLARS
Scene 1: Parlor—To carry out the dreadful shape. Scene 2: Lay Clean the Flank (Aegisthus). Scene 3: "Cost of Driving" (Clytemnestra). Scene 4: Flotsam Oracle. Scene 5: "Blood Songs," furies in adjustment to the overwhelming unison of fugues.

ACT VI. GIRL-LIKE FACE
Scene 1: "Deus Ex Machina" an inversion to disembodied girlness, still unmated and untranslated by the father of straight children, nowhere to be found, as he could no longer maintain an erection in the noise. Scene 2: "Slit Voice" and Scene 3: Black Box Recording.

ACT I. TRANSMISSION OF OLD GLEAM

SCENE 1: OBELISK

ELEKTRA at the crash site of the AGAMEMNON's grave. ELEKTRA is illuminated by light erupting from it as if she is watching an old black-and-white home movie that no longer exists but which she can remember by looking directly into the gleams. ELEKTRA cries with nostalgia and grief for how her father used to pick her up, flying her over his head like an airplane, with a voice as deep as the wild sea.

ELEKTRA: [*Childlike.*] What were we doing in the woods . . .

DEUS EX MACHINA/AGAMEMNON: That's where we lived, that was our home.

ELEKTRA: But we didn't have walls on our house . . .

DEUS EX MACHINA: We were free to frolic and run all over through the trees which are the only walls the gods make and the blazing daylight, we were . . . blurry . . . wild . . . creatures.

ELEKTRA: And the little golden brother . . . on his rocking horse with gleaming locks of curls? . . . was he eating anything . . .

DEUS EX MACHINA: Maybe leaves, maybe some flowers.

ELEKTRA: Did you see the daughters both at first sight or not really?

DEUS EX MACHINA: I was deep in thought . . . . but the goddess saw me the whole time, she was waiting for me but I want you to think about things deeply, they'll be trying to distract you . . .

ELEKTRA: But I love this story (and I love you and I hate my mother) . . . And then what did you have to shoot her with?

DEUS EX MACHINA: An arrow probably, it's all a blur now, it was a response honey the way we fight a battle to adjust to something that has pissed us off, it is involuntary, just like things were blurry right before I taught you how to talk and taught you the names of all the birds and even the bird you hated immediately.

ELEKTRA: Is that the sister who keeps shining?

[*Brief gleam of an illumination on IPHIGENIA/CHRYSOTHEMIS, who starts to sing but doesn't finish.*]

DEUS EX MACHINA: That's her music. It may not be sweet or joyful but it's a very old gleam and you know you used to sound crazy too when you were small but now you can talk to me . . .

ELEKTRA: I'll remember it. [*Rote.*] I hate my mother because she tricked you and tricked the wild creature into scaring you and startling the wild creature and the bullet came whirling out of that.

DEUS EX MACHINA: I'll tell you what to do.

ELEKTRA: Exactly what to do.

DEUS EX MACHINA: I'll carry you in my everlasting arms and hold you like this 'til you're older and it starts to get clear.

ELEKTRA: But I'm starting to cry again, Daddy, I can't stop crying anymore.

DEUS EX MACHINA: You do that so I'll pick you up, to get my attention . . .

ELEKTRA: No because it's so sad. It's sad how we waited for your footsteps and the creature how she thought she would look beautiful dying and wide-eyed.

Somebody's throat everybody wants to slit
She was more appealing as a sacrifice
I'd probably just sleep until my muscle tissue
Rebuilt itself. I'd probably just stop in my tracks
Or maybe turn a little towards the arrow,
Open up my neck so the curls would fall
Back from my throat and hear the twig snap

Underneath your footfall and think here we are
In the abject trees, and maybe it's the beast
With the teeth and claws or maybe it's Daddy but
At least I would be injured finally so I'd have an
Injury and not just sadness, something
That would heal over and be mine.

IPHIGENIA: *Pity me Father*

DEUS EX MACHINA: Honey I can't hear you very well.

[*Gleam from the **DEUS EX MACHINA** briefly illuminates **ORESTES**, who is holding his sword.*]

ORESTES: Don't forget about his hands, how he can toss you high up in the air above his head and fly you like that, don't forget you were his little airplane too, just like me.

ELEKTRA: You're listening to her now aren't you, it's her turn already and you do pity her.

IPHIGENIA: *Pity me Father*

DEUS EX MACHINA: Honey I don't understand why you're still crying. Maybe when you learn how to talk you can tell me what it's all about. Crazy little girl.

IPHIGENIA: *Is it all forgot*

ELEKTRA: She's stainless isn't she so you can choose to stain her, punish her, but I'm the one still singing all your praises, I know them by heart. Old Gleam Not Unto Joy Nor Sweet

DEUS EX MACHINA: Yes. Oh yes the cadence. Not unto joy nor sweet Music nor shining of gold . . . [*Trails off, deep in thought.*]

"PITY ME FATHER"

IPHIGENIA: [*Slit-voiced pure.*]
Pity me Father
Is it all forgot
How often in your feasting
Rang my sweet strains
When I, a stainless girl
Sang pure
Sang of my sire
Sang gifts and heaven to you
Falling so fragile
Pity me Father
Is it all forgot
Pity me Father
Say grace
Say grace
Say grace

SCENE 2: RESEMBLE OVERTURE

A CHORAL FAMILIAL FUGUE OF PORTRAIT FEATURES AND ARCHETYPAL PITCHES

ELEKTRA loses track of time and place. She has to grasp her footing again through multifaceted gleams of furies/voices emitted from the crash site of her beloved DEUS EX MACHINA.

ORESTES:
[*Militant.*]
We shudder to
think of death's
cold terrors.

IPHIGENIA:
[*Final girl-like/
horror movie-like*]
*Run run run for
your life!*

AEGISTHUS:
[*stand up*]
So there's this
doctah, he says to
the lady, "Lady, is
your hubby
naggin you about
them saggy baby
boobs, uh lemme
see what I can do

ORESTES:
We believe that
we are plural.

We pray the day
will someday
shine

when surrounded
by friends we lead
a useful life
without this
ammunition.

But please God
save our muscles!

GOD SAVE
OUR
MUSCLES!

**PEASANT
HUSBAND:**
[*Soft shoe.*]
How you were

IPHIGENIA:
*Run run run for
your life!*

*The staircases are
edited together!*

*Run run run for
your life!*

*Get away from
there boy, you
better watch your
back!
The stairway is
the other way!*

*The staircase
winding?
falling flat?
Coming from
inside the house*

Is steepening!

IPHIGENIA:
[*Final girl-like/
horror movie-like*]
*Run run run for
your life!*

*Run run run for
your life!*

AEGISTHUS:
for yah knockahs.
Just don't be
pickin up the
luggage or you'll
hear a sorta rippin
and you'll feel all
sticky." So she
gets the
augmentation she
says, "I don't feel
a thing now when
you feel me up
when you put me
under, every time
now when I'm
strippin, hell, my
left boob slides
around there to
my backside, what
did you do to
me!"
And I said
"Honey, you come
back to surgery, I
musta put a ping
pong ball in there
accidentally," she
says, "Fuck you,
Doc, I'm gonna
sue your ass. I
paid you to take
this grapefruit
offa my ovary!"

CLYTEMNESTRA:
[*Stand-up.*]
Honey no I know
you loathe me and
you loathe
yourself but
you're kinda cute
when you get
umbilical like
that, all yoked up
in depravity So

PEASANT HUSBAND:
shattered by a
shock too terrible,

How you were
wild,

An experience too
damaging,

too shattering,

too shocking for a
girl to bear,

Too terrible for a
girl,

what's a girl to do,

to bear

IPHIGENIA:
*The stair-ca-ses
are edited to-ge-
ther!*

*Run run run
for your life!*

*Get away from
there boy,
you better watch
your back!*

*The stair-way is
the other way!*

*The stair-case
win-ding?
Fal-ling flat?*

*Co-ming from in-
side the house*

*Co-ming from in-
side the house!*

CLYTEMNESTRA:
gimme somethin
on the rocks you
know I'm all
choked up! You
pay some rent or
I'll have you
lobotomized,
y'sound like a
hemorrhage and
frankly, I've had
better
hemorrhages. Oh
God I shoulda
pumped my
breast, drank my
own milk and
scoffed at you
screaming, tied
your chords in a
knot when you
were in the state
of gristle. I
shoulda knocked
out every tooth as
soon as it came
in, I should've
beaten you for
every
frown,
I should've
snapped your
spine like the twig
you were!
Oh look at that I
spilled the soft
drink oh it woulda
been so soft

ACT II. ELEKTRA'S LAMENT

SCENE 1: RANT

ELEKTRA's punk rock rant in reaction to "resemble" choral familial portrait overture, a lament to her sire, which the PEASANT HUSBAND tries to translate for himself from the glow of his sweetly burning lamp, beside his reading chair. Intermittently, IPHIGENIA echoes ELEKTRA's lament in a treble descant harmony.

ELEKTRA:
LIKE A DOG
I SERVE
I TOIL
I HEED THE DREADFUL
CA-A-A –A-AUSE

    [Lament pitch, agony.]

LIKE A WORM
I PINE
I GNASH
I WASTE AWAY MY PRIME
I WRECK MY LOVELINESS
I CHOKE MY SWEETNESS
I REEK LIKE SWEAT
I HOPE I VEX YOU, BEG YOU, WALLOW YOU
I SERVE YOU AND I TOIL,
I DREAD, I CURSE
I'M BENDING OVER BACKWARDS
   MOTHERFUCKING FUCK ME,
WHORE ME, SLAVE ME, CAST ME OUT AND
   FLAY ME, PAY ME NOTHING
SO I SUCKLE AT YOUR TITS SOME MORE
JUST TO TICKLE UP YOUR FANCY LIZARD
   SPEWING YOU
AND SUCKIN ON YOUR BLOODY SLUTNESS SORE
YEAH YOU RECKON ME MY GOLD
YOU RECKON ME MY SPOIL
YOU RECKON ME MY BEAT AS THE
   DANCERS SWAY (hey)

PEASANT HUSBAND:
Older than I thought, my dear, beneath this sweetly burning lamp I think of what I know. I know I want you.

I can't remember learning how to read and yet a woman's mind so turns (as easily as mine does) just to see you better from this chair

PEASANT HUSBAND:
You can light on many
pleasant things and
volume after volume of
the trees of knowledge
and distinction

ELEKTRA:
YOU ROTTEN RODENT ABJECT BASTARD
    MOTHERFUCKER, FUCK'ER HARDER,
    FUCK'ER DEEPER DIRTY

    [*Bittersweet.*]

How the crying water
Wan lament of tears

and my finely chiseled
features and my clean
shave

And the water lapping
At my sire's head

I am groomed and tailored
with a small black hard
rubber
comb

Drooped in the bed of slaughter
I'm the daughter

which I rinse after parting
my hair.
I can offer all of this to
you.

Drooped in the swell of slaughter
I'm the beggar
I'm the slave
I'm the roach

I am a gentleman.

SET FREE MY BROW
SET FREE MY BEGGAR BROW

I have that distinction.
I have earned that
academic post which will
provide the summer
leisure

AND RECKON ME MY SPOIL
FRAUGHT WITH TOIL
I BEWAIL
LAMENT
MY
SIRE

to begin my scrutiny of
you, informally of course,
a sidelong
glancing at you in the
bureau mirror,
How I'd love to have a
famous wife and yet still
find you

But I'd never shrill a tear for you
I don't resemble you

barefoot in some summer
dress above the sink as a
lark really,

    [*Tearing out her hair.*]

Rinsing off something
we've been growing in the

177

ELEKTRA:
LOOK AT THIS DEAD-LOCKED RAVAGED
   HAIR, IF I WAS YOU I'D TOIL TO BE FAIR,
I'D LANGUISH IN THE LOOKING GLASS
COMBING IT UNTIL IT'S GOLD,

THIS WHOLE FAMILY'S BLEACHED
AND BLAZED AND BUTTERED (BUT ORESTES
   IS *REALLY BLOND* AND YOU FUCKING HATE
   THAT),

HOW YOU SPEND A FORTUNE GETTING
   IT TO SHIMMER TRESS BY TRESS INTO
   YOUR TREASON,

WHATCHA GONNA DO WITH ALL THAT
   GLADNESS WHEN THE WAR'S NOT
   GOING WELL FOR DADDY? HOW YOU
   GONNA SWIFT-CLOUD UP YOUR EYE
   WHEN HE COMES HOME?

   [*Rending her clothes.*]

LOOK AT THIS WRETCHED COUCH
   YOU'VE GOT ME CRASHING ON AND
WHERE'S MY SATIN, SILK AND SOFT DRINK
TANGLING SPOIL OF GLEAM
THAT YOU GOT IN THERE SPEWING JISM IN
   YOUR THROBBING CUNT WITH DADDY'S
   BLACK BLOOD LAPPING AT THE BED?

DROOPED IN THE SWELL OF SLAUGHTER
I'M THE DAUGHTER
I'M THE BEGGAR
I'M THE ROACH
SET LOOSE MY DOGS

YOU HAVE MADE MY SIRE NAUGHT!
YOU HAVE MADE ORESTES NAUGHT!

And if I do resemble—

   [*Hesitation, "key" change to shrill.*]

PEASANT HUSBAND:
yard and

*feeding it to me and
settling down,*

*and children on the
way,*

we'll keep their school
pictures on the mantle
two years apart

I want to marry you a little
for your easing.

I can see clear through
your dress

I want to marry you
a little for your easing

ELEKTRA:
NEVER MAY I RESPITE
NEVER MAY I CEASE FROM SORE LAMENT
NEVER MAY I LANGUISH
NEVER MAY I CURB THE FRENZIED PLAINT
NEVER MAY THE SPLENDOR
NEVER MAY I CLING TO SELFISH EASE

AND IF LIKE A DOG I SERVE
AND IF LIKE A WORM I TOIL

AND IF I DO RESEMBLE YOU—

   [*Fatigue of terror to paralysis.*]

CHORUS:
And if I do
resemble you
AND IF I DO
RESEMBLE YOU

ELEKTRA:
And if I do
Resemble you . . .

PEASANT HUSBAND:
Preface of a mild
translation.

[*Whistle.*]

We'll do it all over in
technicolor I know it
seems a little black and
white for now but that's
what I've been reading
lately by this dim-watt
bulb . . .

SCENE 2: NOT FRAUGHT WITH TOIL

CLYTEMNESTRA and AEGISTHUS mock ELEKTRA's tantrums, aggravate and subjugate her recklessly with CLYTEMNESTRA's almost narcotic ironies. AEGISTHUS always treats ELEKTRA like a rabid, mangy dog due to his chronic and ominous hangovers.

CLYTEMNESTRA "vomits" a beautiful shining silver puddle, an extended sonic and bass expulsion. Uses it for a mirror.

CLYTEMNESTRA: Justice . . . slew your father

ELEKTRA: Under what law? (Father be near)

CLYTEMNESTRA: [*Terrified.*] If I could unfold . . . my whole thought to the light . . .

ELEKTRA: A lover weighs more than a child in any woman's breast

[*Gleam. Flash of ORESTES with a lock of his childhood curls gleaming in his hand. He lays it on the DEUS EX MACHINA. CHRYSOTHEMIS appears and takes it from him, hides it in her bosom. Gleam.*]

DEUS EX MACHINA: Clear with the clear beams of the morrow's sun and it said to go to Troy. [*Eagle's call.*] "Go forth to Troy" and who on earth has the bliss of heaven.

ACT III. SHUT UP

SCENE 1: SISTER

ELEKTRA returns to the solace of mourning the **DEUS EX MACHINA**, *and is startled into rage by* **CHRYSOTHEMIS** *being there, disorienting both of them into ricochets of defensive startlings.*

CHRYSOTHEMIS:
[*Startle.*]
I'm your sister
I'm your sister
I'm your sister
Come dear sister, jumping like you
saw a rat and startled by me? in
these troubled waters? . . . telling you
I'm not your foe but it's about your
foe . . . your volume of these dreary
declamations, idle wrath and vain
indulgence your, oh, profanity is, oh
dear, it's so loud. I overheard, I said
I overheard them say
you better straighten up, (and who
am I to say) you better play dead, but
you better bend before the strong,
you better shorten your sails, you
better look a little harmless, move a
little less aggressive . . . telling you
they're gonna lock you up in a dreary
dungeon, there to chant your
doomsays . . . telling you they're gonna
shut your mouth by other means than
clenching down your teeth
if you don't shut up, so don't blame
me [*Gleam.*]
when it gets dark in there just when
you think it's the darkest it can get if
you make a joyful noise to save your
doomsay, turn to, no it doesn't
no it doesn't,
that is the terrific news. I was here
this morning at the cemetery and
somebody left this *gleaming lock of
curls* on my father's grave.

ELEKTRA:
[*Lament pitch to startle into fist.*]
I will kill you
I will kill you
I will kill you
I do not believe I won't be harmed
I do not believe I won't be
terminated (if I cooperate)
I don't know you/I will kill you
If I'm in harm's way/I'll hit you back.
I don't believe I can't destroy you
and your happy-go-lucky malarkey
Disney politics, who are you/
I don't know you/
Don't think I won't lash out at you.
Don't think I don't intend to strike a
blow, [*Swing.*] to take a swing
[*Swing.*] to drive my fist straight
through your eye [*Swing.*]
beat at the brat [*Swing.*]
clear through the head into the
downside [*Swing.*]
I don't believe I can't wreck
something on this globe before it
sends me reeling to that dreary
dungeon. [*Gleam.*]
And my sire's dead, my sister's
dead, they killed my sister and they
killed my sire . . . gushing words . . .
blade to the throat, the end of story,
wars and rumors of wars,
The globe keeps right on orbiting
Right on orbiting
Do I want to see the trick,

Do I want to see this trick [*Gleam.*]

DEUS EX MACHINA:
It's kind of like . . . it's like I moved
out of my head . . . it's all empty in
here which is why you hear this echo
darling, in your head and you see all
the way down to the wires

[*CHRYSOTHEMIS imitates
ELEKTRA's echo.*]

CHRYSOTHEMIS:
And he was my father. It's been hard
on all of us. Maybe I should spend
more time at the cemetery, maybe I
should holler and bellow at the top
of my lungs the way you do. On the
other hand I'm getting by. I carry
on. I sort of bend before the hateful.
I mean I do run errands for the sake
of the stepfamily. Which is
probably compromising but I am
entitled to my own adjustment! It's
been hard on all of us. You're not
the only one in this family. I have
my Prudence that I have of
judgment (and sound judgment) my
discretion and my caution . . . telling
you it is no longer
(no it doesn't) clockwise in the
economy of prudence to be so rash,
to make rash noises at your volume
if repeated to the pedestals
circumspectly . . .
telling you it is no longer clockwise
in the economy of prudence to be so
rash, to make rash noises at your
volume if repeated to the pedestals
circumspectly
They say that there's no turning back

but you could turn back now . . .
I'm telling you they're gonna kill
you . . .
I hope nobody saw me come here.

ELEKTRA:

[*ELEKTRA echoes her father,
in a delay.*]

[*Gleam.*]

This is my father's grave and this is
holy ground. You have no right to
transgress holy ground

(Get off the ground)

(Get off)

(Get away)

(Get out)

Get lost

Get out of here.
Nobody keeps the watches of the
night, nobody beats against their
breasts with a load of grief that
weighs them down, the globe keeps
right on orbiting, ungraced by
anybody else's tears or scant gifts
this is where they quenched him,
mangled him and cleft his brain with
an ax like a piece of wood, the most
beloved of the valiant, my father
slew his thousands and comes home
to a wench who stabs him in the
back

Knowing it will make me
start to cry,
overwrought to outrage,
venom of my sire, [*Softens.*]

I am not doing very well.

[*ORESTES draws his sword,*
it flashes as he flexes it.]

ORESTES:
Orestes is dead! and in this tiny urn.
We'll bring the scanty relics home. I
know you are thinking immediately
of your dear Orestes, imagining
him at his very liveliest.

[*ORESTES' sword gleams.*]

CHRYSOTHEMIS:
I hope nobody saw me come here
With this gleaming lock of curls
     [*Rumor/soft voice.*]
Yeah you told me, yeah
(What did the boyfriend say) Did
you see her eye, she says she fell off
the (What did the guy say) after him
and she says this guy grabbed her ass
like he, the boyfriend who is
shorter than the girlfriend was
cowering between the bathroom and
the (what does everybody—) like the
last thing he would want would be a
fistfight (what did he say then) she
told me not to tell, so don't tell
anybody,
     [*She softens, turns.*]
but I feel like I can tell you . . . to a
sister sticketh closer than a brother
and somebody I can turn to.
Turn to me.

I have to tell you something sweet

I came to the tomb this morning.

I saw that streams of milk
had lately flowed

His sepulcher had been encircled

With all the flowers that blow

I found this gleaming lock of curls

ELEKTRA:
I'm not doing very well.
     [*Rumor/soft voice.*]
So they go get the boyfriend
and the boyfriend says
"Go ask my girlfriend" she's been
with the boyfriend for so long and
she gets home before he does in the
very long afternoons so she ends up
with this Shiner and they beat each
other up. The fistfight guy goes out
and gets a bat and comes back
and he says
"How far we gonna take this thing"
and the party kids go
"Just forget about it"
and they all start leaving.

     [*She turns.*]

Where do you turn to

When you've got nowhere to go.

When it's dark.

And you feel so blue.

You feel so bad and I feel as bad as
you do believe me honey, I've been there.

Turn to me.

Turn to me.

When you think you're gonna die.

183

DEUS EX MACHINA:
Really honey it's strange because
you're right about the record player.
It seems like there really are, little
tiny people in there singing
but if you get a screwdriver and open
up the little screws you'll see for
yourself
　　[*Shift: naturalistic cadence,
　　they face each other.*]

CHRYSOTHEMIS:
So what.

Go ahead
What
What was it

Ask me
Just go ahead and say it.
I have no idea what you're talking

About
I'm fine, I'm really, more than fine,
more than I was I mean I'm doing
even, better than ever
I wouldn't do it over,
I don't need to, I don't really, no,
but go ahead,

I'm listening
　　[*Turns away.*]
By my father's hearth
I tell you what I know
and I know who my brother is,
I tried to copy your mistakes and
now I'm so extremely healthy that I
can see that this gleaming lock of
curls is Orestes'
(Bad place bad timing shut up)
*Lying next to me for years in the
shared room, our necks were
parallel, our throats breathing
quietly through the nights when*

ELEKTRA:
I wanted to um—

I wanted to ask you

Something

But I don't think I

I don't know I wanted to . . .
You know, to . . .
do you know what I'm saying it's
about well, it's, really,
No I know what you're gonna say.

I know you think it's . . . no, forget it,
no,
forget it,

. . . Nothing
　　[*Turns away.*]
Oh God I bristle.
I bristle.

I bristle.

I see red.
I should've known you'd never come
back to me. You'd never turn
around. You don't need me anymore
So go! *Get off the ground*

CHRYSOTHEMIS:	ELEKTRA:

CHRYSOTHEMIS:
they'd come in bending down to kiss
us both goodnight in the slant of
Light from the doorway. Daddy
slipped and caught me by the neck
but that was random . . . we
we were so very close in age, people
knew both of us, they say like sisters
and we were, you can't change what
we are, my sound judgment . . . telling
you they
say that there's no turning back but
you could turn back now . . . On the
other hand I'm getting by. I carry
on. I bend before the hateful,
I run errands for the sake of the
step-family which is probably
compromising.
You shut up, I'm entitled to my own
adjustment. No you shut up, you're
not the only one in this family.

Shut up! Shut up! Shut up! Shut up!
Shut up! Shut up! Shut up! Shut up!
Shut up! Shut up! Shut up! Shut up!
Shut up! Shut up! Shut up! Shut up!
Shut up! Shut up! Shut up! Shut up!
Shut up! Shut up! Shut up! Shut up!

. . . And that if they told me anything
it would be just like telling mother
when it used to be just the same as
telling you because we told each
other everything,

just between you and me . . .

My clear duty

(I hope nobody heard what I just
said)

I'll go forth upon my errand

ELEKTRA:
Get off

Get away

Get out

Get lost

Get away

Get out of here.
This is my father's grave
No.
No Oh God!
Shut up!
No.

No.
Oh God. She mocks me!
No! Oh god!

Shut up! Shut up! Shut up! Shut up!
Shut up! Shut up! Shut up! Shut up!
Shut up! Shut up! Shut up! Shut up!
Shut up! Shut up! Shut up! Shut up!
Shut up! Shut up! Shut up! Shut up!
Shut up! Shut up! Shut up! Shut up!

. . . Oh who told her that.

Oh who did she believe.

What does she know.

What has she seen to warrant her
belief.

Is she a lunatic,
Is she feverish.

SCENE 2: CLYTEMNESTRA'S CONTOUR I

CLYTEMNESTRA interrupts the argument, acoustic when she sees CHRYSOTHEMIS
as if she has just unwittingly spawned this daughter also, ghastly.

CLYTEMNESTRA: How nice to see the two of you getting along. [*A threat.*]
What are we chattering about today, girlfriends? Oh God the poor girl has
no breasts which one of them was it, or did I get them from a test tube.
Answer me. I can't remember. Is it the younger one or not? The one
standing slightly behind the other . . . foreground . . . hm, in life span?
Size of . . . ? So you both got taller, get up and go to school . . . Daddy's
coloring ah hah well that's between the lines, eeny meeny . . . Count to ten
I'll suckle *your* milk, see how *you* feel. Kidding! Kids! Do not believe your
ears. I thought I had a boy, what happened to him when he played with
matches, guns and jagged objects, told him not to run that fast, stay out of
the traffic. I'll get you implants when you graduate, both of you. I can't tell
you apart when you stand that close together. How can I play favorites
when I'm seeing double are you twins, answer me or I'll start menstruating
backwards, are we regular, girls, what else is there to tell each other but we
all have wombs, is there a problem here. I'm telling you, Why whisper? It's
your father tapping all the phones and shuddering the chandeliers beyond
the borders. Does that make you wonder, well I wonder where all the
hunters are today.

[*CLYTEMNESTRA figures out which of them is really IPHIGENIA, her*
favorite, when she cries in her slit voice so she turns all her attention there.
CLYTEMNESTRA coos, softly as if to a newborn sleeping infant. IPHIGENIA
lays her throat bare as she tries to walk toward her mother as if these are her very
first steps.]

CLYTEMNESTRA: [*Treble coo.*]
Oh come-mere
Come-mon
Come-mon
Come-mon you little swee-heart
Yea-ah you little swee-heart

Here she yis
Here she yis
Yeah I gotcha
Yeah I gotcha
Yea-ah
You a little swee-heart yea-ah
You just a little swee-heart sweet-as sugar

[*IPHIGENIA starts to cry, can't see where she's going, bleeds from her slit throat.*]

Don'tcha cry oh don'tcha cry you break my heart you little swee-heart.

IPHIGENIA: Mommy I don't feel good.

CLYTEMNESTRA: That's because of all the evil people sweetie, you'd never believe what happens out there on the planet.

IPHIGENIA: Was I bad?

CLYTEMNESTRA: Oh honey no, you were so perfect. You were the most perfect little slip of a girl with the sweetest little voice. I loved you all the time, I carried you. You were a bundle of pure joy and your little face just shined up at me like a little sunshine.

IPHIGENIA: That's because I love you, Mommy, and I draw you all those pictures of you and me and pick you all the flowers that blow (over the foothills).

[*IPHIGENIA makes it all the way to her mother's breast, they recline, sighs as she drinks, CLYTEMNESTRA looks gorgeous.*]

CLYTEMNESTRA: [*Softly.*] I hope you're not picking the flowers from your grave or your daddy's grave you never really know what's underneath those contours when they look like hills. I didn't know when I was pregnant for you that I would have another little girl but this one would be soft to me. This would be the little sweetheart and I'd never want to see her crying, I'd buy all the cushions in the kingdom for my little baby.

ACT IV. RECOGNITION OF THE BROTHER

SCENE 1: SIGNET RING

ORESTES disguised as messenger collapses from running for days and nights to get home.

ORESTES: Orestes is dead!

> [*MESSENGER appears to die.*
> *Stylized gasping from ELEKTRA.*]

IPHIGENIA: [*As if subtitling silent film.*] Elektra mourns a golden boy. Attracting gleam of signet ring.

SCENE 2: SCAR ON HIS BROW

ORESTES: [*As if stalking ELEKTRA.*] Where do you live,
where do you work,
don't turn around/run away,
what are you doing,
do you see me, are you watching every move I make,
are you busy,
are you busy,
are you in a hurry

I gotta tell you something

> [*All tracks open: furies.*]

Orestes is dead.

> [*Looming toward ELEKTRA.*]

AGAMEMNON: [*Slow bass voice-over.*] And who with the might of spear
And who with hand upon the hilt

IPHIGENIA: Elektra laments her brother's death but notices the scar on the messenger's brow.

> [*Startle:*
> *ELEKTRA screams when ORESTES touches her, fights him, he appears to easily die.*
> *She gasps.*]

SCENE 3: GLEAMING LOCK OF CURLS

A familiar exchange, soap opera, may be inaudible, these exchanges "surface" in volume. ORESTES adjusts. ELEKTRA relaxes and they listen to the music.

PEASANT HUSBAND: [*"Footnote."*]
Golly gee, gee whiz
some fellow oughtta spend a little
money on the central figure of the
tragedy, she might like ice cream
and perhaps the best abused and,
of ancient tragedies,
Oh darling, you're the
counterrevolution of conventional
classicism, but you could pretend
to marry me. No one will know
unless I tell them what your name
means. I'll translate everything else
into Rhyming English Verse.

ORESTES:
Hey.

ELEKTRA:
Hey.

ORESTES:
Yeah

ELEKTRA:
Yeah.
What happened to your eye?

IPHIGENIA:
. . . Telling you he's following you

ORESTES:
So you know how, like you said
the death of the planet was their
masterpiece, how they were all about
the bloodlust, I was varsity and you
were distracted that if hey, I smell
like cigarettes it doesn't mean I'm
drinking but I happen to be drinking,
I get in a fight, I have a black eye
but I also have a good eye. And
    [*Deep voice.*]
"That's why I'm gonna kill you"
I just say that on my t-shirt I don't
really mean it, people read into it if
they read, it's on my sleeve and that's
what all the liner notes, all the lyrics,
rock and roll is calling you to do

(following you home)

ELEKTRA:
Unless we get along too well even if
you don't have blond hair, even in
the dark, it separates from your head
(Like a haircut.)

IPHIGENIA:
(like the brother)

ORESTES:
I told you what I'm doing is I'm
moving. You will feel that, you'll
look down at yourself and think
about it later how I am with you
now, maybe I am (somehow) in
you

(somehow)

ELEKTRA:
Hm

And we think that it's the brother.
Maybe it's the brother.
He's a growing boy, bigger than you
even if he might've started off younger

ORESTES:
Biologically and physically present at
this time and there was no mistake

ELEKTRA:
. . . what we were doing all those days
we SPENT and it separates from your
hair like a haircut

PEASANT HUSBAND:
(I can see clear through your dress)

ORESTES:
Five Million Years To Earth

I can take you on vacation to the sea.

and the amplified nights,

I can't remember learning how to read

the seamless teenage nights
one day it's so boring and you hate
it and the next day you have to stand
in line to get a ticket and I miss the
friendship, I miss the wrath, I mean
at home he was a tourist,
Look at me . . .

How I rinse the comb, I part my hair
I'll know I'll always want you there
I'll marry you, I'll marry you

ELEKTRA:
The devil took the rest of them

A little for your easing

ORESTES:
Here we are back to the chaos but for godsake here we are. Maybe it's a bad situation

ELEKTRA:
Yeah

ORESTES:
And maybe it is really the fucking best.

ELEKTRA:
In my ear . . . .

PEASANT HUSBAND:
I'll never rape you when I turn out the lamp.
I'll leave it sweetly burning in the window
I'll fold the clothes when we take them off
I'll make up the bed everyday
I'll marry you, I'll marry you
a little for your easing.

Preface of a mild translation

ORESTES:
Hopefully landing very closely to your ear . . . drum . . .

ELEKTRA:
What if we . . . get each other sick or how the tracks touch down, get parallel, the trains get scheduled

ORESTES:
What if the whole thing's rotting in the heat, crash and burn, curse and regret and whatchagonna do about the blackmail by utility if it goes out of sync and I have no idea what he tried to tell me but I swear to God his lips were moving, it's like, this is it, you hear the voices and you're fucked. Actually you get some time because you hear the voices and you get a little grace period where you try to pretend you're doing really great and don't hear voices until one day some slip of the tongue
    [*Outburst of dying words, panic.*]
I gotta lump in my throat.

DEUS EX MACHINA:
(you are God's horse)

IPHIGENIA:
Gleaming scar upon his brow
to mark the day he ran chasing your
    fawn
and fell down.

ELEKTRA:
What did Orestes die of ?
    [*Choked up.*]

ORESTES:
It was a really long footrace, I don't
think he had the training.
    [*Choked up.*]

ELEKTRA:
That's funny because we found a
muscular footprint on the ground.
It sort of looked like mine, I think
it would be nice to see him again.
    [*Choked up.*]

ORESTES:
Maybe he left it there a long time ago

**PEASANT
HUSBAND:**
*Olderfashioned than
we thought my dear*

CHRYSOTHEMIS:
*As if the gleaming
footprint*

*Twin beds we make
as soon as we awaken*

As if the gleaming heel

*Rinsing something
we've been growing
in the yard*

*As if the muscle of the
footprint*

As if the curving arch

*(And yet a woman's
mind so turns as easily
as mine does)*

ELEKTRA:
Where was he.
When it happened.

CHRYSOTHEMIS:	PEASANT HUSBAND:
As if to scan the track	*We'll keep the Christmases*
And frame of muscle	*And holidays*
Of the footprint	*And birthdays*
Safe deposits	*Safe deposits*
Increments of day	*Increments of day*
And savings	*And savings*
And we'll stay and stay	*And we'll stay and stay*

ELEKTRA:
What did they do . . .
with his body?

ORESTES:
They quickly burned
his body on a pyre.

[*ORESTES sets an urn
down in front of
ELEKTRA and leaves her.*]

SCENE 4: URN

ELEKTRA:
Oh Orestes. Oh my God Orestes. Oh I grieve you baby, rock 'n' roll
bedwetter on your rocking horse and look at the horsey pee and see the
horsey's leg fall off, it's empty in the socket, it's all plastic, it was born dead,
like your brother, he's a kid, he'll never grow up now. Orestes, hey you
WEAR the Bad Black t-shirt little punk but you don't know black, I can show
you fucking black, I'll cry you blackly, I can grieve your incapacity to show
the fuck up. Pussy getting killed what? Runnin? You were always runnin
away from home but that was my idea. Think up your own grand exodus.
You think you know what it's like to lose your shit, you never lost your shit
we treated you like a china doll and you fucking played me. You hide the
table knives from me at night or what? Did I scare you to death? I saw the
whole entire calendar and like I can't snap everybody's neck with my bare
hands, I don't need your fucking grip on the handle. What were you gonna
do roll in here in a smoke machine so you can freak them out with a couple of
choked barchords, I can bite the head off a bat, I shall destroy this bloodsport
crackhouse. I shall render it impossible to put us back into our disembodied
bodies so they can say oh God you look just like your daddy when you're
butchered, funny, set free the coagulation and the gangrene. Why didn't you
tell me you weren't really gonna MAKE IT back?

ELEKTRA:
There's no relief of pressure in my skull,
it's way too hard to wait and fucking wait here
like an idiot for you, and then to watch you
goin dark. Oh God Orestes, you get sucked down
in the deep dark absence just like everybody else
I touch and I just wanted you to be here watchin
ME go dark, I'm goin down now, all the way down,
I can see us both die clear as hell and I don't wanta
do it by myself and I don't wanta do it, I don't
wanta do it, I don't wanta do this but I gotta get
the fuck away from her cause she's in charge of me.

My head . . . oh God my head is killing me
It's too hard . . .

It's too hard . . .

It's too . . .

It's too hard for you . . .

"FINAL GIRL
STAIRCASES"
IPHIGENIA:
Run

Run

Run for your life!

*The staircases
are edited together!*

*The footstep creaking!
On the stairwell stair!
The staircase winding?
Falling flat!*

*Coming from inside
     the house
is steepening!
Get away from there,
better watch your back!
The stairway is the
     other way!
The dog? The noise?
The creepy music?
Landing at the landing!
Once she had descended
dressed to the nines!
She cried once on the
     barren ground!
Cried like a faucet.*

*She decides to go
     upstairs!
To the swift!
To the purple!
To the hilt!
As the sparks fly upward!
And all the gashes
look a little bit like
     mouths!
All the gashes look a
little bit like mouths!*

SCENE 5: CLYTEMNESTRA'S CONTOUR II

CLYTEMNESTRA interjects upon seeing ORESTES in the house, and hears suspicious gasping from ELEKTRA.

CLYTEMNESTRA:
So who was that the local greyhound,

Yeah what's in the package there a pipe
bomb, little screws loose, buttons that
pop off and jackknifes in the back,

Well I hope it's good news or we might
get mad and kill the paper boy. I think
we paid the bill so what's the problem,
oh for God's sake get off of me

What's so funny did he have his pants
down or do I always miss the private
parts.

Honey if you don't have anybody to
snuggle up with then come 'ere I'll
muster up a fever for you

But I'm down to two packs a day just so
you know. I feel like a newborn baby!
Even if I get up on the wrong side of
the bed.

Nobody knows what the hell you're
talking about

Why don't you shut up, you're about a
billion years too late, you big buffoon,
you're way off

Yeah how do you know it's me,
    it's prob'ly
something you excreted,
God I go in spurts,
sometimes I'm crazy lustin for
this kind've reptile,
other times I'm just plain crazy,

AEGISTHUS:
Local vandal maybe, "have-not"

Well don't get depressed it's gonna
trickle down there any day to skid row

Honey your boobs are stickin out

You got a rupture in your boob
Yeah but you got goo all over that
    nice blouse
it's like super glue or something
hold up a truck with that

getta a great big pair of tongs and
    take some of
that that that

that goo right there and see if it's
cohesive

you could go up a mountain where
they always take those kinda
sportscars, oh christ, you're makin' me
wanna puke

(and I'm supposed to get up
With'er on the wrong side of the bed),
I gotta spend the night in there
    I hope I can, you know, leave the
    bedroom one of these days,
she's like a great big wad of gum
and I got no teeth!

CLYTEMNESTRA:
Stop me!
If I'm repeating myself.

AEGISTHUS:
Toothless. Not a tooth in my head.

Stop her if she doesn't, she's a genius.

CLYTEMNESTRA: What was the disaster, honey, What?

IPHIGENIA: Orestes is dead!

[*Three gasps.*]

ELEKTRA: Orestes is dead.

[*Three gasps.*]

CLYTEMNESTRA: [*Copy of the gasp. They all gasp.*] Oh it could be worse. The little bed wetter . . .

AEGISTHUS: Save your quarters.

CLYTEMNESTRA: I told him I was gonna put a clothespin on his dick but now they say that's bad psychology. He should've buckled down. Gone to the Olympics.

SCENE 6: GOD'S HORSEMAN AND A STAR WITHOUT A STAIN

ORESTES' thinly veiled Olympic messenger display of Triumph.

ORESTES: [*Full throttle, stadium rock-like.*]
I RAN THE RACE
I RAN THE FOOTRACE
THAT WAS SET BEFORE ME ALL ACROSS THIS LAND
I DIDN'T HAVE ENOUGH WATER TO SUSTAIN THE
WATER THAT THE BODY REQUIRES TO SUSTAIN
A RACE OF MILES, DAYS AND NIGHTS *TO BE A*
MESSENGER
How fast were the footsteps pressing down

How wide the footprint, wide the stride

ELEKTRA:
Oh my God Orestes.

(for you
the tears well up)
(for you
the tears roll down)

ALL ALONG THE AQUEDUCTS
SCANT TREES, THE BRAZEN SCORPIONS OF SINEW,
STING OF GRIM TEETHED INFLAMMATION OF MY
MUSCLES, STRIVE AND WRESTLE AS I MAY
AGAINST THE FIXED POINT VANISHING

ORESTES:
AND WHO WITH THE MIGHT OF SPEAR
AND WHO WITH HAND UPON THE HILT
THE BURSTED CAPILLARIES, KNOCK KNEES
KNOCKING ONE FOOT FORWARD,
ONE MORE FOOT AND ONE MORE FOOT

DEUS EX MACHINA:
(And who with the might of spear and who with the hand upon the hilt)

I CAN'T AFFORD TO SWEAT PROFUSELY,
DISEMBODY JUST TO STAY IN MOTION
I HAVE BURNED UP ALL THE WATER I CONSUMED
MY ONLY CONTENT IN THIS VEHICLE OF HUMAN
FORM AND *LOVELY FORM OF FOOT* ARE THESE
WORDS I REMEMBER THAT I HAVE TO TELL YOU

ELEKTRA/ CHRYSOTHEMIS:
(and who)

AND I HAVE REHEARSED TO TELL YOU AND
ALONG THE AQUEDUCTS I KEEP REPEATING TO
MYSELF TO TELL YOU JUST SO I CAN FALL DEAD
AS THE MESSAGE LEAVES MY LIPS AND WHAT I

(and who)

HAVE TO SAY AND WHAT I WANT TO SAY TO
MAKE YOU HAPPY IS A . . . JUST REMEMBER YES
OR NO. THUMBS UP, THUMBS DOWN (REMEMBER
ONE OF THESE THUMBS ALONG THE

(and who)

AQUEDUCTS) AND TELL YOU WHO AND WHO IS
DEAD AND IF YOU FIND OUT IT'S A LIE. WE
STRIVE AND WRESTLE WITH THE FLESH.

(and who)

WE RUN THE RACE
WE NEVER SURRENDER

DEUS EX MACHINA:
WE RUN THE RACE

WE NEVER RETREAT
WE LIFT OUR WEAPONS
AND WE GRIP THE GRIP

ELEKTRA/ CHRYSOTHEMIS:
(and who)

WE GO FORTH ON THE EVIDENCE
WE GO FORTH TO THE VICTORY VISIBLE

(and who)

WE LET THE GODS SORT OUT THE BODIES
WE SHUDDER TO THINK OF DEATHS COLD

(and who)

TERRORS, IN THE HARM OF SOME STRAY SNIPE
OR BLOODBATH
WE BELIEVE *THAT WE ARE PLURAL*

DEUS EX MACHINA:

WE BELIEVE IT IS IMPOSSIBLE TO LIVE *A LIFE*
UNTARGETED

WE RUN THE RACE

WE BLAST OUR BITS TO GLORY IN THE RIGOROUS
REGIMENT OF THESE FOOT SOLDIERS

WE RUN THE RACE

AND WE FLEX OUR MUSCLES.
As did Orestes flex his muscles. As did Orestes barreling
TOO CLOSE TO THE PILLAR in his tragic chariot
disaster. As did Orestes lash his whips across the horses'
flanks, their tendons straining and their muscles bulging

WE NEVER SURRENDER

ORESTES:
out from under him, foaming at the mouth and then
when fancy soars aloft, the shock on shock, the crash of
chariots, the whole race strewn with the wreck of chariots,
the horses ripped asunder, horse legs torn from sockets
and the axle box—as did Orestes! Rising from the gore,
as did Orestes stagger to his own knees, try to mount
the horsemeat writhing, kick the flanks to win the race,
he MUST NOT MISS-STEP ANY CRUCIAL
HALF-STEP OF THE RIVETED UNISON, ill-fated
for the clank of iron ringing through his brain.
To dash the cup of bliss,
he breathed to me his last I breathe to you:

All my love to Elektra.
Don't forget about your Daddy's hands.

I am God's horseman and a Star without a Stain.

[*ELEKTRA* and *ORESTES* embrace.]

DEUS EX MACHINA:
Children are memory's voices and preserve the dead
from wholly dying. Ever buoyant in the depth
submerged this wail of ours

(Doth rise)

(Doth save)

ACT V. RED PILLARS

SCENE 1: PARLOR

Parlor-room tension you could cut with a knife, 5/4 waltz timing. **PEASANT HUSBAND** *replicates* **ORESTES'** *behavior in the manner of gentleman caller.* **AEGISTHUS** *gets a bass/abusive tone of voice as if beating a shitting dog that bites his guests in commanding* **ELEKTRA** *to serve the wine; tenor/polite when speaking to* **ORESTES.**

CLYTEMNESTRA: So did you hear the one about the full-bodied, smoky bouquet and very very velvet, very vintage . . . and the bottom of the glass had cracked a smile, smiling back at the boy and smiling wider and wider until his head split open down the middle, he was a dumb boy, didn't know the whole entire joke was programmed just to get him plastered by subliminal . . . by printing it in very . . . glossy . . . scarlet . . . graphic . . .

AEGISTHUS: Very nice. It's feedin time at the zoo.

CLYTEMNESTRA: Well I can't exactly tell you how . . . vintage but we've certainly got a couch to soothe away your toil. Might as well drink straight rubies and we live like gods around here, pull up a chair!

AEGISTHUS: Well sure.

ORESTES: Of course. [*He drinks.*]

CLYTEMNESTRA: What do you think?

ORESTES: Very deep red.

AEGISTHUS: [*Bass dog voice to* **ELEKTRA.**] Gggrrl . . . Go get the stick, girl, fetch the stick. Get in the house . . . [*Tenor to* **ORESTES.**] Nothin but grim around this place, here's to the lady, born to terrify.

CLYTEMNESTRA: We call it crimson.

ORESTES: All the different hues of red. That's pretty funny.

CHRYSOTHEMIS: [*Giggling.*] I can never tell if she means a sacrifice or a joke.

AEGISTHUS: [*Tenor.*] Show him the hearth there, honey, yeah I'll drink to you with all o' that fertility, I'm on you for the ride God knows I look like a wad of gristle but I can fuckin bet on the horses. [*Bass.*] Ggget in the house, ggget in there

CHRYSOTHEMIS: That's Elektra! Bendin over backwards. Bleeding on the rugs again this month, down on her hands and knees she thinks she's gonna give us alla

AEGISTHUS: Ding dong! Oh we get the prize! We get to wait for Elektra to get married! (Get outta here, go fetch the God your neck, it's like it's inside out, it's like a lipstick sticking out of your . . . out of . . .)

CLYTEMNESTRA: You know I miss . . . carried . . . my baby. Poor little bright red bundle and her little lips slammed shut, I couldn't get a spoon in there . . .

AEGISTHUS: How bout a bull. I think it's time to slay the bull, you get me. Time for the red to get a little deeper . . . talkin about blood ties, do ya get me.

ELEKTRA: [*To herself, restrained.*] OH YEAH YOU BASK, YOU BASK, YOU TICKLE UP YOUR FANCY LIZARD SPEWING YOU AND SUCKIN ON YOUR BLOODY SLUTNESS SORE

CHRYSOTHEMIS: Sorry excuse of a dead baby joke. But then they must be jittery with all this company.

CLYTEMNESTRA: Let's not be crude. You know I hear those Thessalonians can slay a bull in one clean gash but we can get you a warm bath tonight, you tell your friends about our garden. [*She spills a little wine.*] Here's to the athlete! God knows we heave 'em to the lions. Tell your friends about this channeled rivulet we got here, broidered coils, Do they say anything about my baby? Iphigenia? It means sugar, Over there in, where'd you come from?

CHRYSOTHEMIS: Waitin for the lucky guy to smash that ugly, ugly, bug. [*Bursts of giggles.*]

CLYTEMNESTRA: Oh honey look at that. Look what I did. Oh God. Oh there it goes again. It's a sin. I've had a boo boo honey, help me. Help.

[*Her breasts begin to rupture.*]

ELEKTRA: [*As she serves him.*] *Orestes. I recognized you by your voice.*

ORESTES: *No kidding. And did they.*

CHRYSOTHEMIS: [*Driving jokes in the ground.*] We can't find a prince to rend Elektra's prison walls.

ELEKTRA: [*To* ORESTES.] *Those are the very red hands that she slaughtered Daddy with.*

CLYTEMNESTRA: Indeed! If you addressed me in such tone, I'd always hear you without pain.

CHRYSOTHEMIS: We always have to cut her down and bite her head off and then we shackle her! Because she's mean, she's mean to me you know so who cares!

[*Peals of laughter.*
Rant duet:]

CLYTEMNESTRA:	ELEKTRA:
SHE KNOWS NOTHING	*I WANT HER EYES*
NOTHING	*TO LIGHT ON NOTHING*
ABSOLUTELY NOTHING	
ABOUT BABIES	*'TIL SHE KNOWS THE SWORD*

CLYTEMNESTRA: Her father's blood was no relation to me and I watched him hover at my baby's throat like a wolf.

[*Lullabye agony:*]

With his red, red sword
My baby's blood red spray
Her lips in terror parted.

AEGISTHUS: *and you call it drivin drivin drivin*
and you call it flyin flyin flyin
and you call it wolf, wolf, wolf, wolf

ORESTES: By the way do ever get the feeling? That you're at somebody's house for dinner and . . . And brushing by you . . . brushing by your knee you . . . you feel this . . . presence by your knee below your knee that's not like anything you know about these people and it's different and you're thinkin don't . . . look down there, don't act like you're . . . what the hell was that? Was that one of the kids? Startin to crawl? A pet of some sort? 'Sposed to be tied up out back or something? So you just keep talking to the people, focus on whatever subject that it is. And then it goes away and then it's cool. You're cool.

CHRYSOTHEMIS: [*To ORESTES as if stripping to appease a rapist.*] Is she offending you? I'm not married either. I'm not usually like this. But I'm tired of the sacrifices. I wish we could pray to the gods to keep us from the quarter rest to lip to slit—to keep us from the slipping into every gaping gash we think could happen to us, flowing down the stones where we were at each other's throats. It opened up and swallowed all the people and my song was just a scarlet thread-in-the-jericho about to be ruined by trumpets and I watch my mother pray. Nobody knows my mother like I do. There's a whole other side of her and I guess you could say I'm on her side.

CLYTEMNESTRA: *She was a blurry wild creature*
Frolicking until he caught her by the neck

[*Her womb and breasts are hemorrhaging.*]

ELEKTRA: [*Kissing ORESTES on his mouth, touching his sword as he draws.*] Straight to the snare.

ORESTES: So the plan is this: we're gonna take you down like lumber. Slash the pillars red just like the book says, cut off your supply of nutrients. That's why my sister called upon my muscle and I think it's you and me.

[*ORESTES marks AEGISTHUS' throat with a slash.*]

CLYTEMNESTRA: Oh my God he's got a sword.
Orestes and that girl have come to kill us.

SCENE 2: LAY CLEAN THE FLANK

AEGISTHUS: [*Bleeding.*] Got a little riddle for you, yeah . . . So there's this uncle type a guy, step-daddy creature, he steps in the family, shakin' hands "How are ya people, oh ya look like sisters (to the mom) poor thing is saggin' to her knees, he butters that thing up, ya look like a movie, hell ya all look great, ya gotta real great place here, house, the food's delicious, shot've whiskey for the lady, get down to the nieces,"

CLYTEMNESTRA: Aegisthus.

AEGISTHUS: "Whatcha learnin' over there in school ya little sugar, plumb . . . daisy . . . dolly, is it terrible yet." She pouts, "Oh yes our uniforms are really scratchy," pout.

CLYTEMNESTRA: They'll get the vault.

AEGISTHUS: And what comes after diapers, FOLKS, and two plus one is one plus two. No that's the uncle. Everybody! Pitch in! Help the lady out of wedlock, pin the diaper, diaper pin, what is that, don't stick the bottom with the pin, the clean diaper I said, please, hey you, (they'll always call on ya'monster) you gimme that diaper, wipe that off, let's put it this way . . . in my business I seen buttocks in the air, I do what comes most natural and then I check outta those motels. Come noon, the girls start cleanin up the mess. Or I could wait around, check out the chambermaid, I'll maybe stay til one o'clock, don't wanta be exclusive. She pouts.

CLYTEMNESTRA: They'll take everything.

AEGISTHUS: "But there's a whole other bedspread nobody even wrinkled." Baby doll, I'm bad with girls that pout, I'm bad with ages, bad with names, I'm not a bad guy so to speak but I'm half bad so that's enough.

CLYTEMNESTRA: [*Trying to contain her silicone pulp into her dress.*] I hate the Greeks, I hate the gods.
I've seen em up close and they're nothing special.

AEGISTHUS: *I'm a creature known as stepdaddy, "sugar daddy?" nope he's broke but he can pay attention soon as you grow some little boobies . . .* or maybe even sooner, Oh you get offended, FOLKS, if you dont get my jokes go ask

the big guy up there, close your eyes and pray for me, he's the Guy that set up all my gigs, you stay with the real Daddy, none of this would happen and you know it. I'm just steppin in, don't glare at me, just gettin your mommy nice and happy, pay for some of them drinks, make her feel like high school. Too bad it's the law of nature that you look a little more like first love, love at first sight, too bad I been framed but that's the way it is. *Bang bang, thank you dolly, wipe that up there honey, shut the diaper,* everybody's shocked to death but everybody glared at me from day one, why is that?
ARE YOU surprised why is that? Guilty by half-step, can NOT relate to buttocks in the family, in the air, in the magazine, beast of burden and I fit the bill.
Truth of the matter is you need a whippin boy and I look like a shadow on the wall when you go back through the house. Amber colored stained wood in the closet, amber drinks in there down in my guts so you can hate my guts. Fuck me!

ELEKTRA: Kill Aegisthus. He's the bonus.

ORESTES: God. I thought they were inpenetrable.

[*ORESTES slits his throat. AEGISTHUS writhes in his own blood.*]

AEGISTHUS: Get whatcha pay for and sooner or later we all . . . get . . . dirty . . . Doncha. [*Wink.*] *God you're gorgeous, Anybody here from New York City, thank you, thank you very much.*

[*AEGISTHUS dies.*]

ELEKTRA: The Devil took'im down like a B-flat but God gave us the blues.

ORESTES: Oh no, oh God she bared her breast to me.

ELEKTRA: That's just a surface wound.

ORESTES: It's bleeding.

ELEKTRA: It just broke the skin.

SCENE 3: COST OF DRIVING

CLYTEMNESTRA: Girl, do you know the cost of driving?
All the way home from here?
Gets so expensive . . . To get down'ere . . .
And sit down'ere at the table . . . . As an astronaut
Did you think it would be the
SAME PLATE?
Set to overflowing with thanksgiving?
Go fetch the stick, girl,
From the bright red prairie little house
And see if you can get it back together
With the fam'ly tree . . . .
Get along home red-handed girl and you call it drivin drivin drivin
and you call it flyin flyin flyin
And you call it wolf . . . wolf . . .
Wolf . . . wolf . . .

[*CLYTEMNESTRA implodes.*]

SCENE 4: FLOTSAM ORACLE

CHRYSOTHEMIS: . . . Approach on . . . a correction . . . we'll be standing by for you . . . and you can plan . . . and you can . . . I'm so sorry. This is not . . . in any way . . . a . . . a hovering above the . . . you can plan . . . and you can . . .

ORESTES: Oh my God, Elektra. The patriarchy is a matriarchy!

ELEKTRA: Same old counter-revolution.

SCENE 5: BLOOD SONGS

*An opening of choral tracks in the black box recording of **AGAMEMNON**'s crash site. All these ghastly Furies descend upon **ORESTES**.*

*	*	*	*	*	*	*	*
The	The	Turn the	And at	Oh God a	Lay clean	Am I	Fair
blood's	blood is	water into	the	blow	the flank	washing	weather
red spray	dripping	wine	bloody				for the
	from my		edge	A bright	Lay clean	in the	sky is red
	sword	From the		red blow	the red	blood	
The blood		blushing	Red red		flank		Red sky
red hour	Red		the sword	A mortal		in the	at
	handed	Flood of		blow	Of my	soul	morning
The one	perishing	hatred	The holy		precious	cleansing	
clean	of you	Red	spray	Another	blood	blood	Was not
gash				blow			in the fire
		I'm	Red		My	of the	
Without	the	bleeding	handed	And then	flaming	lamb	Passing
the	spilling		cherishing	another	sword		through
shedding	scarlet	And so	of you	mortal		are my	the fire
		Shed my		blow	Take eat,	garments	
There is	though	blood	The		this is my	are they	Till my
no	your sins		blood line	Blood on	blood	white as	fury turns
remission	be red	Blood		my head		snow	
	like	thirsty	Flesh and		And shed		My red
No rose	crimson	Savage	blood	Blood on	my blood	if I am	hot
				my hands	red	washing	wine cup
No red	and my	I was	Of my		herring	in the	of my
Roses	sword is	bleeding	deepest			blood	fury
	crimson		bloodlust				
NOTHING	NOTHING	NOTHING	NOTHING	NOTHING	NOTHING	NOTHING	NOTHING
BUT	BUT	BUT	BUT	BUT	BUT	BUT	BUT
THE	THE	THE	THE	THE	THE	THE	THE
BLOOD	BLOOD	BLOOD	BLOOD	BLOOD	BLOOD	BLOOD	BLOOD
OF	OF	OF	OF	OF	OF	OF	OF
NOTHING	NOTHING	NOTHING	NOTHING	NOTHING	NOTHING	NOTHING	NOTHING
BUT	BUT	BUT	BUT	BUT	BUT	BUT	BUT
THE	THE	THE	THE	THE	THE	THE	THE
BLOOD	BLOOD	BLOOD	BLOOD	BLOOD	BLOOD	BLOOD	BLOOD
OF	OF	OF	OF	OF	OF	OF	OF

[*Refrain: all eight tracks open full throttle chords and harmonies.*]

ACT VI. GIRL-LIKE FACE

SCENE 1: *DEUS EX MACHINA*

ELEKTRA comes upon the PEASANT HUSBAND after a very long time. He is eating a suspended spoonful of CHRYSOTHEMIS's food that she had been cooking. ELEKTRA speaks to him as he whets his appetite on the spoonful as if it is between the sister's thighs. CHRYSOTHEMIS, slowly bending to remove her apron in a long intake of breath, tries to mask her pleasure.

PEASANT HUSBAND: Don't you remember when I said I'd carry your books from school playing make believe you're married to me, you were fifth grade I was six . . .

ELEKTRA: You know your lips were the only thing I could ever read . . .

PEASANT HUSBAND: Now I carry all these things in my heavy head, quite burdensome. [*Wink.*] But I showed up for the preface and that's something these days.

ELEKTRA: [*Wink.*] Ask the god of the machine.

PEASANT HUSBAND: I disagree with your ulterior negation, all this ending of the world, you see it is a lovely day, another day, it's a bright day, all the streets are bright and we've got time to kill for a stroll for Sunday, drink a soda in the park and we can daydream and I'll pay. But then you'll go getting sharp. I realize that's your lack. Somebody somewhere has turned up your volume, blasted the speakers and now the little knob broke off. Abbreviating your poor little fate.

ELEKTRA: Yeah I guess it must be hard to maintain an erection in the noise, face down in some similar orifice, what is that a gash? of quarter rest—to lip—to slit voice, maybe it feels good, do that, a little reverb on your own static or my static (anybody else), or you heard the one about the choice between a garbage disposal and some lovin you know what they say I would choose . . .

PEASANT HUSBAND: We don't need the little modern riddles anymore, I'm feeling the terrain of tiny obstacles you have erected, I'm feeling quite disgusted by the butchery.

ELEKTRA: Out of the blue, oh yes, you would have noticed my rotten teeth and wrinkles in the sunshine when we got down to the water, underneath the girdle. Isn't she the spittin image of my underage school pictures, when the waterfall was photocopied.

PEASANT HUSBAND: Now what's the trouble.

ELEKTRA: Was I frowning?

PEASANT HUSBAND: Now what's wrong?

ELEKTRA: I didn't do anything.

PEASANT HUSBAND: Now what is it.

[*They start lying.*]

ELEKTRA: Too bad you won't be listed when the credits roll and I'll forget who you were playing.

PEASANT HUSBAND: You know I travel frequently in my line of business.

ELEKTRA: I'm sorry about the age difference.

[*ELEKTRA reaches out and presses PEASANT HUSBAND's spoon into a penetration of a new open wound in her sister's throat, unable to resist the temptation.*

It bleeds again and CHRYSOTHEMIS makes gentle sounds as she dies.]

SCENE 2: SLIT VOICE

CHRYSOTHEMIS/IPHIGENIA:
Does he?
Notice my virginity?
What do I?
Look like close-up to the point where his eyes would cross?
If I am a good enough liar
I can manufacture
This repetition daily until we grow old.
Does he?
Notice I am already dead?
Or does he think I've gotten makeup tricks from an excellent magazine?
His military picture
Looks exactly like my Daddy . . .
I get the idea
He can afford the kind of furniture I need to simulate my existence . . .

PEASANT HUSBAND: I do.

ORESTES: [*Running far away into the distance.*] I do too.

[*CHRYSOTHEMIS climaxes almost imperceptibly as she dies.*]

SCENE 3: BLACK BOX RECORDING

ELEKTRA makes a final recording for **ORESTES** *as she hovers in auto-pilot above the crash site of her father, watching the Furies tear* **ORESTES** *eternally through the wilderness below.*

ELEKTRA: . . . So there'd be all this technical . . . velocity . . . for the air traffic control and then you'd hear me say I'm gonna go through one more puffy little cloud [*Bass.*] "good day to die" some sort've joke about my death wish gonna take us both down and I'd hear you going "Oh God really? Do you even know how to fly?" which'd give me away as being scared to death of being airborne up here so divine, you know I wrecked your motorcycle. And then—blank . . . for whatever I could say. So I just say "not to expect" [*Treble.*] because "they told me not to expect to go up in his plane." And so I quoted that and all the things that people think about crashing . . . And they won't get any more information than that when we do go down. There'll be the pilots screaming . . . technical failure, sounds they'll go back digging through the carnage for, and open it. And they'll find out later that they never put black box recorders on these single engine planes because they're too small. And at the time nobody that knows me even knows I'm up in the air.

[*PEASANT HUSBAND embraces CHRYSOTHEMIS's body and she emits a beautifully perfect pitch.*

Sound of a new recording.

Pitch continues softly and eternally.

Erasure.]

END OF OPERA

TRUE LOVE

CHARLES L. MEE

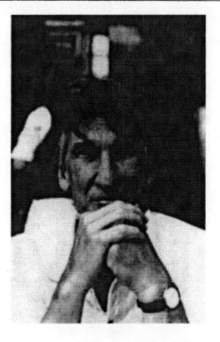

CHARLES L. MEE has written *bobrauschenbergamerica, Wintertime, Belle Epoque, Vienna: Lusthaus, Snow in June, Limonade tous les Jours,* and a number of other plays in addition to his work inspired by classic Greek dramas: *Big Love, TrueLove, Orestes 2.0, Trojan Women A Love Story* and others. His plays have been performed at the Brooklyn Academy of Music, American Repertory Theatre, New York Theatre Workshop, the Public Theatre, Lincoln Center, the Humana Festival at Actors Theatre of Louisville, Steppenwolf, and other venues in the United States as well as in Berlin, Paris, Amsterdam, Brussels, Vienna, Istanbul and elsewhere. His *History Plays* collection was published in 1998 (PAJ Books), and his memoir, *A Nearly Normal Life,* was published in 1999. His complete works are available on the Internet at www.charlesmee.org. His work is made possible by the support of Jeanne Donovan Fisher and Richard B. Fisher.

From the Writer
CHARLES L. MEE

I've done a number of Greek plays. I started out inadvertently. Gordon Davidson, founding artistic director of the Mark Taper Forum Theatre, called director Robert Woodruff to say he had budgeted a workshop at the Taper for something that had fallen through, so he had money and space if Woodruff happened to have anything he'd like to workshop. And Woodruff called me and asked if I had anything. I said I didn't, and I couldn't go to Los Angeles just then anyway. He said, "But this is a good chance to work together, so let's do something." So I said, "OK, let's take something we both know; you go out to Los Angeles and start working on it, and I'll fax you stuff to stick into it." This was at the time of the end of the first Gulf War, so we took Euripides' *Orestes,* and Woodruff got a bunch of actors in a room and started to work, and I was home, writing things in the margins of an English-language translation of *Orestes*—whatever the play made me think of, things I'd read, things I'd seen on television, things about the recent war, things about other wars, things about violence in America, things off American soap operas. And I'd fax things to Woodruff and say, "Stick this here, stick that there."

And so Woodruff returned to New York with a big pile of random texts, including some he had stuck into the piece, and others his actors and dramaturg had brought in. And I looked at it, and I thought: "Oh, this is a way to make a play. You take a Greek play and stick things on it and then you remove the Greek play, the way you remove the scaffolding from a building after its construction, or the mold from a sculpture, and you are left with something you've made. The Greek scaffolding or mold remains as the invisible structure. The characters and themes resonate with both past and present." So I neatened up the mess we had made, and that was the first Greek adaptation I did.

And then I turned to writing other things. But I kept going back to the Greeks, because their plays are such amazingly wonderful pieces of construction. They are made as well as Rolls Royces. And the Greeks became my Roach Motel. I couldn't stop. I did a version of *Agamemnon,* of *The Bacchae,* of *The Trojan Women.* I came to think that what I was doing was taking a Greek play, reducing it to ruins, and then, atop this bed of ruins, writing a new play. And then, as time went on, I became bored with my own way of working, and I began to depart further and further from the Greek plays, until only the ghost of the original play remained—as in *Big Love* and *True Love.*

I think I learned a number of things from this. You don't need to make up a story to write a play. You can steal one. The Greeks always did. Shakespeare always did. And then you don't need to worry about your voice as a writer—it will come out your own whether you want it to or not. And then I learned what the uses of a plot are. With the Greeks you have principals advancing the plot, and then the chorus riffing on it. What the Greeks knew was that, if the audience knows what the story is, they can riff endlessly on it—that's the pleasure of a play. Most writers these days, I think, forget this. They set a plot in motion and then they attend to it assiduously, every moment advancing the plot, every word moving the story forward. And I'm always thinking: here's a chance for a song.

With *True Love*, I think, my method has come unhinged and is almost spinning out of control. It is riffing galore. There's only a shred of a story line: will the stepmother seduce her stepson or not? Everything else is riff. I wanted to see how far you could stretch the container. And I think this is close to the outer limit, just this side of a play without any plot. The material itself is far from the Greek world, as are the characters. Again, I was interested to see how far away you could go from the Greek play and still retain something of its resonance.

And then, finally, I was interested in a play about love—because we discover a lot about who we are in our relationships of love. For sure, we discover who we are in all our relationships—political, social, economic. But, with love, we get very specific about such qualities as generosity, compassion, indifference, cruelty. So we get to know what it is to be a human being by seeing how it is to be in love.

I'm a person who believes, in general, that every form of love is a form of true love, to be welcomed and treasured and nurtured, that we should not rush to judge the way other human beings love. Some of the forms of love spoken of in this play test the limits of that openness. But the play doesn't draw a moral. This is just a look at the human material we have to work with, from which we build a civilization.

PRODUCTION HISTORY

True Love Productions' staging of
True Love, directed by Daniel Fish.
PHOTO: SKY PAPE

True Love was produced by True Love Productions at the Zipper Theatre in New York on November 14, 2001. It was directed by Daniel Fish; the set design was by Christine Jones; the costume design was by Kaye Voyce; the lighting design was by Jane Cox; the sound design was by Rob Kaplowitz; the musical director was Crispin Cioe; the musical staging was by Peter Pucci; it was produced by Jeanne Donovan Fisher. The cast was as follows:

POLLY . . . . Laurie Williams
EDWARD . . . . Jeremiah Miller
RED DICKS . . . . Paul Mullins
BONNIE . . . . Jayne Houdyshell
PHIL. . . . . Dallas Roberts
SHIRLEY . . . . Laura Esterman
JIM . . . . Christopher McCann
ALICIA. . . . . Halley Wegryn Gross
RICHARD . . . . Roy Thinnes

The **TRUE LOVE UNLIMITED ORCHESTRA MEMBERS** were Crispin Cioe, George Gilmore, Charles Giordano, and Robin Gould III.

True Love received further productions at the Holland Festival in 2001, directed by Ivo van Hove, and at the Deutsches Theater in Berlin in 2002.

NOTE

This piece was composed, in collaboration with Tom Damrauer, for Laurie Williams as Polly. It was written with the dramaturgical assistance of Greg Gunter. The piece was inspired by Euripides's *Hippolytus,* and the works by Seneca and Racine based on the same story, and incorporates texts from those writers as well as from Leo Buscaglia, Kathryn Harrison, the letters of Simone de Beauvoir, Andy Warhol, Valerie Solanas, Wilhelm Reich, the transcript of the trial of the Menendez brothers, Gerald G. Jampolsky, M.D., Jean Stein's biography of Edie Sedgwick, and texts posted on the Internet, among others.

Charles L. Mee's work is made possible by the support of Richard B. Fisher and Jeanne Donovan Fisher.

Lights come up on EDWARD's bed, set in front of an abandoned gas station. Surrounded wall-to-wall by red clay stained with oil and gas. A bright orange and yellow gas pump, surreally supremely beautiful. Nearby, a motel, the "Mo el Aph it." A kids' inflatable plastic swimming pool is to one side. To one side, an abandoned Lincoln Town Car that just broke down and was left there, its hood up, its wheels off, splattered with dried mud. A keyboard. An electric guitar with amp. A set of drums. A microphone on a stand. Elsewhere, a dog house. A chain, with a dog no longer there. We hear a love song on the radio.

EDWARD, age 13 or 14—or the youngest possible legal age for the youngest-possible-looking actor to play this role—is roller-blading around his bed, lost in the music and the pleasure of movement, luxuriating in his cool moves, naked from the waist up. He is a handsome WASP adolescent with the coolest roller blades and the best athletic clothes.

POLLY, age 34, enters—as though with a purpose, but then stops, and, standing silently, watches him. She wears Armani, with some rips and stains.

EDWARD doesn't notice her; and they don't speak. She watches him. She doesn't move.

This opening moment of the piece—first EDWARD alone on stage, then POLLY watching him, is meant to establish the two principals of the piece, and their relationship, so that this relationship—and plotline—is stated clearly enough at the top of the piece that we have noted it, attached our attention to it, and can track it through the confusion that follows.

The song ends. He sits on the bed to adjust his roller blades.

RADIO TALK SHOW HOST: That was [*SINGER, WITH NAME OF SONG*].
And we were talking about love
with our guest Bobby Beausoleil.
What is love, Bobby?

BOBBY ON THE RADIO: That's what I'd like to know, Tim.

[*They both laugh.*]

But I mean, basically,
I guess you'd have to say
that the Greeks, pretty much anticipated everything
western folks have thought and felt for twenty-five centuries.

HOST: Well, I'd have to agree with that.

[*JIM enters, looks at EDWARD, looks at POLLY, looks back at EDWARD, turns, lifts the hood of the Lincoln Town Car, and goes to work on it.*]

BOBBY: You'd be talking here,
for instance,
about love as friendship,
which the Greeks called philia
benevolence towards guests

which would be senike,
the mutual attraction of friends,
or hetairike,
and then sensual love of course,
or erotike.

HOST: Let's talk about that.

BOBBY: Fundamentally,
what the Greeks thought
was that love is not just a sentiment
but is actually the physical principle of the universe itself
the very stuff that unifies the universe
you know, binds the universe together.

[*PHIL enters, carrying a wrench and a rag, looks at POLLY, at EDWARD, back at POLLY, drags a garbage bag full of something to the edge of the stage, stands, looks, hesitates, throws the garbage bag off the edge of the stage and then joins JIM at work on the Lincoln.*]

HOST: Unh-hunh.

[*Silence. BONNIE, a nasty, slatternly girl, enters, looks at EDWARD, at POLLY, back at EDWARD, takes a lunch box, hands it to PHIL, takes out a magazine and reads.*]

2ND TALK SHOW GUEST: You know, I have to say, as an Italian,
I grew up in a family where people just hugged each other all the time.
All the time.
If you were Italian you'd know what I mean.

HOST: I know what you mean.
I know what you mean.

2ND TALK SHOW GUEST: I don't think you do.
Of course you do.
But I don't think you do.
I mean, the other night I went to this cocktail party,
and someone handed me this glass of gorgeous ruby red wine.
And I'm, you know, something of a wine freak.

HOST: I don't mind a glass of wine myself.

2ND TALK SHOW GUEST: And just as I put out my hand to take the glass,
someone came up behind me and shouted
"Leo!"
and grabbed me.

[*SHIRLEY, a librarian, enters, checks out the others present, looks confused.*]

HOST: People do that all the time.

2ND TALK SHOW GUEST: Right. And the wine flew into the air.

HOST: God.

2ND TALK SHOW GUEST: And everyone screamed,
even though, in fact, the wine landed only on me.
And I said what the Italians always say when you spill wine.

HOST: What?

BOBBY: What does this have to do with love?

2ND TALK SHOW GUEST: You want to know what I said?

HOST: Sure. Sure.

2ND TALK SHOW GUEST: I said: Allegria!

HOST: Right.

2ND TALK SHOW GUEST: which means
joy!

[*EDWARD rises to test his roller blades, sits to fix them again.*]

Because what I saw,
which I have to say I don't think any of the others really saw;
was that the wine added color to my evening!

HOST: Right.

2ND TALK SHOW GUEST: And this is how it is to be human.

HOST: Right.

2ND TALK SHOW GUEST: I mean you have to bump into walls.

HOST: Don't I know it?

2ND TALK SHOW GUEST: You have to celebrate your craziness and your
humanness.

HOST: That is so true.

[*RED DICKS enters; she is a transvestite, accordion-playing hairdresser. S/he goes straight to BONNIE, and begins to fix her hair, using Coke cans as rollers.*

SHIRLEY still looks confused, and finally sits on a crate.

They are all motionless, listening to the radio.

CASTING NOTE: Ideally, PHIL, JIM, and RED DICKS all play musical instruments and have formed a garage band. And/or SHIRLEY and/or BONNIE might fill in or play with the band, depending on their musical talents. RED DICKS might play the accordion. POLLY will sing. The garage band will have a number of opportunities to play at various points during the piece—either the entire band or a single instrumentalist with a singer.

SHIRLEY takes out her cell phone and dials.]

2ND TALK SHOW GUEST: Because, the fact is,
we're dying of loneliness,
all of us.
Just dying of it.

HOST: Well, now. We have a caller here on line one.
Hello there, you're on the air.

SHIRLEY: Hello?

HOST: Hello, you're on the air.

SHIRLEY: Hello?

HOST: Hi, doll.
What's your name?

SHIRLEY: Shirley. My name is Shirley.

HOST: OK! Well, it's your nickel, Shirley!
What'd you want to say?

SHIRLEY: Well, what I wanted to say is
what I think is—what love is: Love is how you relate to people
or, if your love is channeled in some other way
it is how you are cold or indifferent or hurtful
to another person.
And so love is who you are
and how you are
what kind of person you are
it's the most factual thing about how you are.
You can't talk your way around it;
make it come out some other way.
It remains the deepest fact about you.
I mean, you can say,
oh, I'm really a nice sensitive person
I treat people with dignity.
But the only way you really know how you relate to other human beings
is in the most secret, secret place
where you are most vulnerable
most open to your private self
when you are making love
you don't even know what you're doing
until you're doing it
and then you see what sort of person you are
whether you are making love with someone else
or you are the President of the United States passing a welfare bill
then you've done it
it's not talk anymore
you've acted out your most private deepest self

and lodged it in the flesh of another human being
so that another person feels pain or pleasure
and then you know: this is who I am.
This is what I do.
And who I am
what I want to do
what feels hot to me
the person or the behavior I can't keep myself from
is so strange
so idiosyncratic
is so odd
so that usually I repress it
if I find myself drawn irresistibly to a man
with bushy eyebrows
or a comforting voice
or something even stranger
muscular thighs
or hair on his chest
or a certain weakness
a vulnerability
so that I sense I can hurt him in a certain way
and then take him to me like a wounded animal
and comfort him
if these are the things that make me weak and shaky with desire
I know this is my truest self
what makes me break out in a sweat.
the kind of thing that makes me a little sick to my stomach
it feels so incredible to me
and of course, I feel embarrassed by it
because people will think I am a sick person
and I am a sick person

and you think: I don't even know where this comes from.
You think back through your childhood: could it have been this or that?
But the thing that makes you crazy with desire
is too exact and too
strange
to have come from anything you can remember.
You have touched the real mystery of human beings
the thing beyond any knowing
the thing that comes from so deep down
no one can tell you where it comes from

This has nothing to do with sex.
Of course, I am talking about sex
about having sex with another person
but it has nothing to do with sex

it has to do with who I am
at such a deep and secret place
no one could explain it.

And this is why people don't want to talk about sex
or think about it
because if they do
they see so deep down into themselves
they see such a strange creature
such a hungry animal
so uncivilized
they don't want to hear about it.

And so they repress the thing that is deepest in them
and most unique
I, for instance,
I might become a person who thinks
I am attracted to nice, gentlemanly men
or men who are well-groomed and considerate
I try to forget who I really am
by loving some approximation of what I hope for
or, even worse, by loving someone who has nothing of what I want.
Because I want to think I am a good person.
I think: what is it to be really, freely who I am
would that be just to follow my urges
and not repress them
or is that just to become enslaved to my urge
and not be free at all
Am I free only when I repress what I freely feel?

And then I think: well, finally, none of us is free.
We all repress what is most deeply true about us
otherwise we can't go on.

   [*Silence.*]

RADIO TALK SHOW HOST: Right.
Well.
No one could disagree with that.

2ND TALK SHOW GUEST: I don't know.
Frankly I think I could disagree with it.
I mean, when you're talking about
civilization and . . . .

   [*EDWARD turns off the radio and roller blades on out.*

   POLLY, riveted by him, watches him go, looks after him for a few moments.

   SHIRLEY, confused, turns off her cell phone and puts it away.

One of the mechanics riffs on his electric guitar, taking off on the love song we heard at the top of the piece, through the following dialogue.]

POLLY: Oh.

[*She moves slowly downstage, in a reverie.*]

Oh.

[*She pulls a chair up next to the kids' plastic swimming pool, puts her feet into it. **RED DICKS** eventually comes over and gives her a pedicure while she sits with her feet in the pool.*]

Oh.

RED DICKS: So.
He's at loose ends, I think.

POLLY: Edward.

RED DICKS: Yes.

POLLY: Oh. Well.
He's just a boy.

RED DICKS: At his age, a boy needs his father.

POLLY: Yes.

RED DICKS: I don't say he doesn't need his mother.

SHIRLEY: Or his stepmother.

RED DICKS: Or his stepmother, right, sure.

JIM: It's true, you can talk all you want about mother love,
but for a boy, really, he needs his father.

BONNIE: [*With some rancor.*] And maybe not, by the way, a man who just takes off
when the car breaks down,
leaves his wife and son wherever they happen to be
because he has business.

POLLY: [*In a reverie still.*] He'll be back
when he's finished.

BONNIE: Isn't that just what he would say?
I mean:
what kind of man would just leave his wife wherever his car broke down?

SHIRLEY: And no mechanic for 50 miles.

PHIL: A woman like you
stranded in the boondocks.

BONNIE: And what he really had in mind probably was to cat around with some woman in Utica!

POLLY: Excuse me?

BONNIE: Or not.
Or not.

SHIRLEY: Doesn't he love his son?

RED DICKS: Men should ask themselves: What about all these images of fathers and sons
and other men and boys as pals and buddies?
Why are they so popular in books and movies?
Why are they encouraged in Boy Scouts and Big Brothers.
Maybe boys and men need this.

BONNIE: Especially during puberty.

RED DICKS: When a boy is entering the grown-up world,
maybe a boy needs a sense of apprenticeship,
or just going fishing,
and a lot more gentle touching from a father figure.

SHIRLEY: Or you might ask yourself: is it dangerous for men to have a role in the socialization of boys?
Will men just teach boys to be pigs?

BONNIE: But women can't do this all by themselves.
Boys have testicles and ejaculation and beards and erections,
and women can't be expected to understand these things as well as men!

RED DICKS: We need to recognize there's nothing wrong with this.

SHIRLEY: What the women should be doing
is directing their efforts toward advocating
anti-sexist socialization
within the existing man/boy and woman/girl relationship model,
while continuing to encourage cross-sex interactions as well.
Because love is not just a thing
that has to do with men
or men and women.
Love is a whole weltanschauung.
Or gestalt.
And you can't leave all this to Boy Scout leaders.

BONNIE: Because what you have now are jerks.

SHIRLEY: The way it is now: dogs are better than men.

BONNIE: For sure.
At least dogs miss you when you're gone.

SHIRLEY: Dogs look at your eyes.

BONNIE: And they feel guilty when they've done something wrong.

SHIRLEY: You can force a dog to take a bath.

BONNIE: Dogs mean it when they kiss you.

SHIRLEY: Dogs understand if some of their friends can't come inside.

BONNIE: Dogs are already in touch with their inner puppies.

SHIRLEY: How can you tell a man's sexually excited?

BONNIE: He's breathing.

SHIRLEY: What should you give a man who has everything?

BONNIE: A woman to show him how to work it.

SHIRLEY: What do men have in common with floor tiles?

BONNIE: If you lay them right the first time,
you can walk all over them forever.

SHIRLEY: What is a man, really?

BONNIE: A man is a vibrator with a wallet.
A man is an unresponsive lump of flesh
obsessed with screwing,
incapable of empathy,
love,
friendship,
affection,
or tenderness—
a half-dead isolated unit that will swim a river of snot,
wade nostril-deep through a mile of vomit
if he thinks there'll be a friendly cunt waiting for him at the other end.
A man
is a creature who will fuck mud if he can.

JIM: Oh.
Oh.
And then these women wonder why
a man would prefer masturbation to marriage.

PHIL: I know some guys who like electronic masturbation.

JIM: What?

PHIL: You know, you take some electrodes
and some low-power, carefully controlled electric current,
run that through your genitals
and you'll get some very interesting tingling and
throbbing sensations.

JIM: And why do you want to do that
when you can masturbate with your hand?

PHIL: You ask that because you've never done it.
You'll get something very different with electronic stimulation.
You get yourself a stereo audio amplifier,
with 1 to 5 watts per channel of output power.
A tone generator of some sort.
An electronic music synthesizer like Casio or Yamaha.
You don't want to use an electric guitar,
which could put a current through your whole torso.

You set the amp control to MINIMUM.
Set your tone source to produce a continuous tone of about 440 Hz: that's
   the "A" above "middle C" on a musical keyboard.
Insert the small loop electrode just inside your urethra.
SLOWLY turn up the amplifier's volume control.
Then you can play the "A above middle C" on the left channel,
and play the "A" an octave lower on the right channel.
Or play "C" on one channel
and the adjacent "C sharp" on the other channel.
Play a steady
tone on the left channel
and do a downward "glissando" on the right channel.
You know: fool around.
It's just like any other kind of sex: it's not always the same.

> [*A big macho explosion of a performance piece: one of the* **MECHANICS** *does a heavy macho drum solo while the others strut and preen and behave like guys— in a performance piece that goes on for several minutes at least before the guys calm down with just a few little aftershocks of dirt kicking and bicep inspecting.*]

RED DICKS: What do you think caused your heterosexuality?

JIM: What?

RED DICKS: What do you think caused it?
I mean, for example,
when did you decide you were a heterosexual?

JIM: I don't know.

RED DICKS: Or do you think your heterosexuality is just a phase
that you'll grow out of.

JIM: I hadn't thought about it.

RED DICKS: Well, think about it.
Do your parents know you're straight?
What do men and women do in bed together?

SHIRLEY: These men

they talk sex
always nothing but sex.

BONNIE: Right.
And I am looking for love.
I am looking for a relationship
with warmth
and soul
and humanness.

PHIL: So am I!
It's not easy!

POLLY: I miss my husband.
I miss having him hold me when we sleep at night
his arms around me
his stomach pressed against my back
his face nestled in my hair

and when I turn in my sleep
I turn within his embrace
his arms around me still
my head on his shoulder
his leg between my legs

For him, making love is the most important thing,
for me, being held.

A mature man—
not a boy,
not a randy young man
who doesn't know yet who he is
or who you are
or how to be together with another person—

holding you in the palm of his hand
keeping you safe
knowing when he holds you
this is where your home is.

A lot of men you think are bad
or
insensitive or cold
are really just suffering from touch deprivation.
You know, touching
is just as important for human beings as eating.
Babies, sometimes, will wither and die if they're not touched.
You've seen these stories on television.
But men, now,
men are raised to be tough and independent

and taught to avoid touching.
And for many men,
the only time they're touched at all
is when they make love with their wives.
And so they develop a craving to be touched,
that's why it is a man might even touch a child in the wrong way
but if he does
he can't be blamed for it.
Or he can be blamed
but I understand
just how he feels.

It's like they say
sometimes
you hear people talking on the radio: Sometimes a woman will see someone,
    she'll think: Oh.
Oh.
I could imagine myself being attracted to him.
But no.
You stop yourself
because you think: this is what it is to be a civilized person.
Not just a creature subject to any kind of urge
but that, as a married woman,
you have made a different choice
of your own free will.

For example,
you could say, the thing about incest is,
the reason incest is the only thing forbidden in every society everywhere—
is that the incest prohibition is the step
by which human beings make the transition
from nature to culture.
Because this is what it is to be human,
to make this transition: Because the human being
is the animal that became human.
And how was that?
By denying its animal needs.
The human being is the only animal
who obliterates the very traces of nature as we leave it.
Because we are sorry we came from life,
from meat,
from a whole warm, bloody mess.
We are ashamed of the nature that we come from.

For instance,
for instance, no one would say that excrement
is a substance like any other.
although for animals that is exactly what it is;

and some of these animals will just eat excrement
because they just don't care; they just don't think it is any big deal
or different from any other natural element;
and those animals that don't positively eat excrement
nonetheless, they show no particular revulsion for it.
But the shame people feel for the excremental orifices
testify to the separation between human beings and nature
and it is clear, too,
that nothing will prevent this shame
from rubbing off
on the nearby genitals.
This is human nature.
We don't want to hear about it.
We like things to be nice.
We like these things to be full of warm human compassion,
feeling, soul,
we don't want to talk about excrement
unless we can put it in some human,
psychic context
so that it's not just pornography!

And nothing could be more horrifying to a woman
than the love she may feel for someone
she can't resist—
because then she knows
suddenly she's become the unwilling subject
of the uncontrollable,
indiscriminate excitement of just pure animal sex.

And so of course we seek out marriage
where we are able to have sex
and at the same time
we can have the denial of sex
—with those other than our husbands
and sometimes, even, with our husbands, too—
because
nothing is more common
than the innocent love a woman has
for a man she is entitled to love,
the infinite sense of peace and well-being
that can come of that
the sense of civility
so that at last she may settle down,
and not keep living in the daily fear of the beast
that is settled deeply in her heart.

And so I e-mailed my husband today,
and I said:

[*POLLY* *goes to the microphone and speaks into it.*]

Dearest Richard,
Autumn has finally come here.
Less than ten days ago,
it was close to 100 degrees in the afternoon.
Now the house is cold when I wake up in the morning.

This morning
I had on my pale pink thermal leggings
and a matching long-sleeved shirt,
with tiny buttons up the front.
And when I woke up I was
rubbing myself with one hand without thinking about it.

I don't think I'll ever get enough of you.

And I began to think
about you loaning your latest tape of me to a couple of friends,
and I could see them watching it, enjoying it,
admiring me,
and finally having to take their cocks in their hands
while they watched me come.

I thought: well,
I love watching your hands
moving up and down your cock so slowly.
And seeing you come makes me so greedy for you
I feel like screaming.

I imagined you picking up the phone at your office,
and hearing my voice:
"Hi, Richard, are you having a nice day?
Are you busy right now?"

I'd say: "I'm in bed right now,
and very very naked
and I've been thinking all about you."

Just the sound of my voice
would make your cock start to swell.

Then would you
—without even realizing it—
move your hand down to feel your hardness?

You would hear my breath growing ragged,
as I tried to keep talking to you
my other hand pressing deep inside me,
to come again for you.

Is it okay for me to talk to you like this, Richard?

I like it.
I love you so much.
You make me so crazy,
I hope you never stop.

So. Well.

Enjoy the rest of your day, my love,
my one true, and only love,
you know I'll be thinking about you.

Your,
Polly

[*EDWARD enters again.*]

EDWARD: Mother.

POLLY: Oh!
Edward.
You've come back.

EDWARD: Come back?

POLLY: Didn't you just go out?

EDWARD: Oh.
Right.

POLLY: I didn't know you were coming right back.

EDWARD: I came to play with you.

POLLY: Play with me?

EDWARD: I'm feeling . . .

SHIRLEY: At a loss.

BONNIE: Without his father.

EDWARD: [*Distracted first by SHIRLEY, then by BONNIE.*] Yes.

RED DICKS: He needs someone to play with him
the way boys play.

POLLY: I know some games for boys.
I know
Smugglers and Spies.

RED DICKS: Smugglers and Spies?

EDWARD: That's a Cub Scout game.

POLLY: Is it?

EDWARD: Yes.

POLLY: Is that bad?

EDWARD: Mother . . .

BONNIE: He calls her "Mother."

RED DICKS: Why not?

POLLY: You're too old for a Cub Scout game.

EDWARD: Well, yes.

POLLY: What would you like to play?

EDWARD: I don't know.
Some games we play in school.

POLLY: What do you play in school?

EDWARD: I don't know.
Like,
Car Wash.

POLLY: Car Wash?

EDWARD: You know,
one person is the car
and the other person is the car wash.
And the car goes through the car wash.

POLLY: Goes through the car wash?

EDWARD: I'll show you.
You be the car wash.

POLLY: Okay.
I'll be the car wash.

EDWARD: And I'll be the car
and I'll go through the car wash.

[*EDWARD gets down on his hands and knees and moves forward.*]

POLLY: Right. OK.

EDWARD: And you wash me and you know
you be the rollers and the stuff in the car wash.

POLLY: OK.

RED DICKS: Don't forget to roll up your windows.

BONNIE: And put it in neutral.

[*EDWARD moves up to POLLY, who begins to lightly pat and rub his back.*]

SHIRLEY: Not much of a car wash if you ask me.

230

EDWARD: But you really have to get into this game,
you know,
you've really got to wash me
if you really want to play the game.

SHIRLEY: This is a school game?

RED DICKS: Not when I was in school.

SHIRLEY: They don't play: spelling contest, or something?

RED DICKS: This is a pathetic game.

[*POLLY works more vigorously.*]

EDWARD: But hey, hey, but no tickling!

POLLY: Tickling is allowed.
Tickling is always allowed.

BONNIE: Especially in this—[*Her hands in the air, fingers flailing.*]
this is the—you know—
that part of the—
where you have all the little, uh—

[*POLLY goes for him with hands and arms flying, to his hair, his ribs, his butt.*]

EDWARD: Hey, what are you doing?

POLLY: I can't—
I don't know.

[*She puts a hand between his legs—everyone else is silent and motionless—and she massages him with pleasure. Suddenly, she stops. She stands up. He stands up uncertainly, slowly—having enjoyed it. Then, not knowing what to do about it, he turns and runs out. POLLY looks stunned. Silence.*

One of the MECHANICS plays a low, easy saxophone or keyboard solo.

SHIRLEY stands, turns, walks to the margin, facing away from the others. BONNIE, too, turns away, looks off. RED DICKS works out with free weights made of a car axle and spare parts. PHIL puts a tire in the kids' plastic swimming pool and checks it for leaks. We hear the hissing sounds of the hydraulic hoist, the thumping, banging sound of the tire machine. JIM gets a cellophane bag of peanuts, opens it, pours it into a Dr Pepper, and drinks the Dr Pepper and eats the peanuts at the same time one-handed, leaving the other hand free to scratch. More awkward silence.]

POLLY: Sometimes you see a man doing something
thinking about nothing else except what he's doing
he's completely unconscious really
maybe he's chopping wood in the backyard
and it just stops you from breathing
and it brings tears to your eyes

he's so beautiful
so much himself
you find him irresistible.
You love him, that's all.

BONNIE: Right. We see how you look at him.

POLLY: Who?

BONNIE: Edward?

POLLY: Just now, you mean?

SHIRLEY: Well. For a while.

POLLY: For a while.
Did I look at him like this before?

[*Silence.*]

It's not my fault.

RED DICKS: Nobody's like, blaming you, you know.
It's just,
well: he's your son.

POLLY: My stepson.

BONNIE: So it begins: the lying to yourself,
putting a good face on it.
Isn't that just always the way?

PHIL: This is a boy.
You're talking about a boy
who loves you

JIM: and counts on you
to take care of him
whatever your relationship might be
you're the grown-up

POLLY: I know that.

SHIRLEY: I need an older man
because I don't know
because I need a man I can count on
I remember when I met my husband
he asked me on a date
and we went out to shoot pool at Mickey's
and when he walked me home
I asked him if he wanted to come in.
So he did, and we had a drink
and then we went to bed
I don't remember how

in those days it was not such a big thing
and I don't remember anything about it
except in the middle I suddenly felt very sick
and I yelled at him to stop
he thought, probably, I was going to say something like
this is just our first date or something like that
but instead I said, I think I have to throw up,
and he just started laughing
and I thought: oh, he's okay,
he's got a sense of humor
and the rest of the night he just took care of me
which is, you know, a lot more than most people would do on a first date
so I married him
and I don't think I was wrong
we had a good marriage
and I miss him still
he was good in bed in every way.

RED DICKS: Not all men are bad.

BONNIE: I just needed to be tied up until I learned my place
and this guy I lived with knew that.
Not all men know that.
I just need to be bent to the will
of an insatiable man.
I need shackles, ropes,
stuff to keep me submissive and obedient.
I need leather,
I need it, that's all
and I need to be flogged, pretty hard and pretty often.
You know,
some people like to be dominated.
Sometimes you would be better off asking a person: how is it for you?
Because sometimes a person will tell you: much better than the life of vanilla
    sex I used to have!
My husband and I
we just don't do any of that vanilla sex any more.

I need to be alternately fondled and beaten.
And then I need to be cuffed and forced to masturbate
until I'm completely humiliated by my own nastiness and
insatiability.
I need my master to comment on what a nasty, slutty bitch I am.

And then I need relief from my pent-up desires.
That's how it is for me.
I need a man who will hold me and comfort me
and then rub me, and lick me, and finger me

and fuck me to as many orgasms as each of us can have.
I need to be taken to a state of complete exhaustion.
I'm not saying this is for everyone.
I'm just saying this is how I am.

JIM: Some people like feet
this is simply how they are
or toes
They like to touch them and feel them and kiss them
they can't be blamed
some people like to suck on someone else's toes,
but they can't just go around doing it all the time.

PHIL: I don't understand it.

JIM: I can understand it.
Like sometimes I like to rub my buttocks on someone else's buttocks.

BONNIE: I like to strip-search a guy,
like make him face the wall with his hands in the air,
pat him down with my hands on the outside of his clothes,
make him take everything out of his pockets
and put it on the table,
then take off all his clothes.
I look at everything for drugs,
microfilm, bugging devices, weapons, or sex toys.
He has to stand there all the time,
naked,
with his hands behind his head.
And then I search his body,
I search every opening, very thoroughly,
and then, if he's clean, I release him.
That's all.
I just release him.
To me: that's sex;
that's all there is,
that's how it is for me.
I'd say, a lot of what passes for my sexuality goes on invisibly
inside my head,
and I think it would be safe to put me
in the addicted slut category.

SHIRLEY: Sometimes when you're with a man,
you can cut a hole in a paper plate
and put it over his genitals,
and then
put some lukewarm spaghetti and meatballs on the plate,
and then, when you eat the spaghetti,
you wrap each strand around his penis

and suck it up into your mouth.
I knew someone,
that was the only way she could have sex.

PHIL: There was this guy I heard of once
who shaved the hair from the heads of Barbie dolls
and swallowed their heads to get excited,
and one time he felt sick and went into the hospital,
and the X-rays showed he had six Barbie heads stuck in his intestines.

JIM: I like to have people put pies in my face.
You know, and smear them around.
In restaurants or parties, wherever.
I'll see some guy I kind of like and I'll go up to him
and ask him to pie me, and, you know,
most men will.

PHIL: Really.

JIM: You get all these feelings of anticipation,
the fear of rejection, the thrill of acceptance, humiliation . . .

PHIL: Right.

JIM: the wish that a partner will say
or do something you don't expect . . .

PHIL: Right.

JIM: sharing an intimacy with someone
who might not otherwise even notice me,
doing something that sexual and unacceptable
right out in public.
I guess maybe I've been pied as many as
150 times a month when I've really been,
you know,
unable to stop.
And sometimes I'll say to a man, you know,
I'd really like it if you'd do it to my crotch.
Sometimes they're scared,
but usually they'll do it.

SHIRLEY: That's incredible.

POLLY: I like to sleep with someone with all my clothes on.
It can be like the olden days,
with a board in between us,
or even with my legs tied together so penetration isn't possible.
Or we can sleep together naked,
just looking at each other for hours at a time,
letting our eyes go up and down each other

for three or four hours,
taking each other in,
but I can't, you know,
make love any other way.
Mostly I just like to be held and touched and cared for,
you know,
loved.

RED DICKS: We should all embrace love, because
this is a good thing.
We need to be touched
we need to be felt
we need nurturing
we need some sort of manifestation of love
because life is a process of becoming
and once you are involved in that
you're lost
lost forever
but what a fantastic journey!

Every day is new.
Every flower is new.
Everything in the world!
Every morning of your life!
In Japan, even the running of the water is a ceremony!
You have to ask yourself: when was the last time you listened to the water?
People take showers and run water in their sinks every day of their lives
and they never hear it!
You should go home tonight
and turn on the faucet
and listen to the water!
Because: it's beautiful!

And how many people these days are intimidated when someone says: I want
     to touch you.
Everybody has got to be loved!
Sometimes I have to throw oranges at young people
just to get them to pay attention and listen!
I was talking with a little boy once,
and I said: what can you do, David.
And he said: lots of things.
And I said: like what?
And he said: I can spit.
Yes! He could spit! Can you top that?

I said: what else can you do, David?
And he said: I can put my finger up my nose.
And I said: you bet you can!

Isn't it some sort of miracle
that you can raise your hand whenever you want to
and want to put your finger in your nose
and it gets there!
We should celebrate our wonder!
Everyone!
You've got to have people who are interested in your tree!
And not the lollipop tree!
And you've got to be interested in their tree!
You've got to say: show me your tree, Johnny.
Show me your tree,
and then we'll know where we can begin!

BONNIE: You can't blame people for how they are.

JIM: Right.

RED DICKS: I could agree with that.

SHIRLEY: I could agree with that.

PHIL: What's the argument here?

[*JIM suddenly begins to sing a song made famous by the castrato Farinelli, perhaps Handel's "Pena tiranna" from Amadigi. The others listen to the heartbreaking song.*

At the end of the song, there is silence for a moment. And then:]

PHIL: So, you remember when
this teacher stuck the fork in your heinie?

JIM: What?

PHIL: You remember, you were saying about when she stuck the fork in your heinie?

JIM: Who?

PHIL: What do you mean who?
You told me, when you were in third grade. Or second grade.
When did she stick a fork in your heinie?

JIM: I don't remember.

PHIL: What did she do to your heinie?

JIM: I forgot.

PHIL: What did she do to your heinie?

[*Silence.*]

Did she ever make you kiss her vagina?

JIM: I forgot.

PHIL: Come on.

JIM: I forgot.

PHIL: Did you have to kiss her on the butt?

JIM: I forgot.

PHIL: What did you have to do with the knife?

JIM: Okay, okay, right.
Put the peanut butter on her.

PHIL: And the jelly?

JIM: And the jelly on her mouth and on her eyes.

PHIL: You put jelly on her eyes and her vagina and her mouth.

JIM: On her back, on her socks.

PHIL: This was in second grade?

JIM: First grade.

PHIL: And how did everybody take the peanut butter and jelly off?

JIM: We ate her and licked her all off.

PHIL: You had to lick her off?

JIM: And eat her all up.

PHIL: Was that scary?

JIM: It was fun. I thought it was funny.

[*Awkward silence.*]

PHIL: Of course, you get into an area like this
it's hard to judge.

[*A very quiet, gentle conversation follows.*]

I mean: your daughter was, how old,
nine?

JIM: How do you mean?

PHIL: When you had incest with your daughter.

JIM: Three.

PHIL: She was three?

JIM: From the time she was three
until she was ten.

PHIL: From the time she was three?

BONNIE: Is this true?
Did I know this?
Did everyone know this?

JIM: And, well, it started when she was three.
I was in the bedroom and I was standing in my shorts and a T-shirt,
and she walked up to me and she pulled the edge of my
my shorts,
and I just had this overwhelming desire to have sex with her.
And . . .

PHIL: And this is your daughter.
She is three years old.
Whatever.
And,
and,
but wouldn't your first instinct be to just move away and say,
"Geez."

JIM: It was.
It was.
But it, it, I, I guess my, my instincts to,
to move against this, to—to guard against that,
to not do that
were just not strong enough.
I had a determination not to
but that,
you know.

PHIL: How did you feel?

JIM: Like a piece of garbage.
Basically.

[*Silence.*]

PHIL: And then when did you do it again?

JIM: I
it was probably a few weeks later.

PHIL: And this kept going on when she was four?

JIM: Right.

PHIL: And did she ever tell her mom?

JIM: Well, yes, she did.
When she was nine.

PHIL: When she was nine.
And what did your wife say?

JIM: She, uh, she confronted me on it.
And—and I made promises that—

PHIL: Had you thought about
how that moment would be before it happened?

JIM: Oh, sure.
I'd, you know, had visions of the police pulling up
and hauling me off.

PHIL: Did you love your daughter?

JIM: Yes, I—
I love her now.

PHIL: You love her now?

JIM: Of course, yes,
I do.
If—
if I answered your question in the negative,
then I would be in denial,
and I would be in a more dangerous place than I am by saying,
"Yes, I am."
And, in being aware of that
and having the tools that I have gained in therapy
there are strategies I have for now—
for dealing with that that I did not have before.
There's learning strategies to deal with that.

Sometimes a moment will come in a child's life
when you will realize: oh, this child loves me;
she
she's beginning to know me,
to recognize me,
to smile every time I come near her;
when I sing songs to her in my terrible voice
she loves to listen to them;
she doesn't cry or pucker up her face when I kiss her;
she stopped crying when I picked her up.
If anything were to threaten her
I would trade my life for hers.

PHIL: Sometimes you think,
oh,
men's lives.

JIM: Right.

PHIL: But then you think: well, I mean: women's lives, too.

JIM: For sure.

PHIL: But when you think about men
I think part of it is
that men don't like their jobs.

JIM: Unh-hunh.

PHIL: I mean, if you'd ask them,
probably ninety percent of men would tell you
they are feeling this incredible sense of bitterness
and
and frustration about their wives and families.

JIM: I think this is true.

PHIL: They don't feel appreciated.

JIM: This is so true.

PHIL: It makes a man angry the way everyone just
takes for granted the things his earnings buy for them
and sort of come to expect it as their due.
And then his kids put him down
for being this materialistic middle-class jerk—
and he'd like to tell them,
okay,
okay,
why don't you just get someone else to support you!
But he holds himself back
because
because
he thinks: that's what it is to be a man.

[*Silence. **PHIL** gets an ax and demolishes a wooden crate. **POLLY** wanders offstage, distracted. And then **JIM** begins to throw himself, loose-limbed, to the ground, over and over again, collapsing to the ground like a sack of loose bones, his head lolling over and thumping on the ground, then rolling over, as though convulsively, several times, his elbows and knees and head thumping on the ground.*

Then he gets up and repeats the action, gets up and repeats the action.

***PHIL** joins **JIM**, synchronously, in the same set of repeated actions. So, it is a dance for two men.*

*Then **RED DICKS** joins the other two, so the three of them are going through the same repeated actions, and adding some additional synchronized choreography with break dancing moves on the ground, and a sort of ground slam dancing with spins and twirls and twirling headstands, and finally a recording of a loudly barking dog joins in until everyone hears the barking dog, and gradually stops dancing.*

***POLLY** wanders back in with a chicken on a leash; she is in her bathrobe; she sits at a table and smokes a cigarette, drinks a cup of coffee, and does her nails.*]

POLLY: I should leave town.

[*Silence.*]

Probably—
what?
I should just leave town.
I should go,
you know: somewhere.
I mean, where no one could find me—
and,
if I were lucky,
I'd forget how to find my way back.
I'd get lost.

[*She picks up a dry bagel, picks it into pieces as she talks, and, as she talks, tries to choke down the occasional dry piece. She picks up the newspaper and reads:*]

Wanted: Gas station attendant with five to ten years experience to clean pool in exchange for swimming privileges. Must have own snowplow.

I could do that.
Wanted: Darkroom manager with experience in stripping. Professional wrestling background preferred.

I could do that.

Wanted: Chiropractic assistant for night shift. Must play the flute.

I could do that.

You know, they say the reason the Lord's Prayer goes
"lead us not into temptation"
is because human beings can't resist temptation.
The prayer is not: "lead us not into sin."
Just into temptation—that's enough for it to be too late.
That's how bad human beings are.
And then, if you fall in love,
what can you do?

[*In frustration, **POLLY** picks up the chicken, takes the chicken by the feet, and swings it around violently in circles, apparently killing it (though really only knocking it unconscious), and putting the apparently dead chicken quietly on the ground.*

*The garage band pick up their instruments and launch in to a big love song— full out—and **RED DICKS** goes to the trunk of the Lincoln Town Car and gets his accordion out of the trunk and joins in with vocals and accordion—and **POLLY** steps up to the microphone and sings.*

*At the end of the song, **ALICIA** enters. She is 11 years old—or the youngest-possible legal age for the youngest-possible-looking person to play this role.*]

EDWARD *enters at the same moment. They both stop short, on opposite sides of the stage.*

The grown-ups all watch.]

ALICIA: Oh.
I'm sorry.
I didn't know you would be here.

EDWARD: That's OK.

[*They both move toward his bed at center.*]

ALICIA: I know you
just think of me as a kid.

EDWARD: No.
Well, yes.
But
I think you're pretty grown up for your age.

ALICIA: I'm eleven.

EDWARD: Right.

ALICIA: Almost twelve.

EDWARD: Right.

ALICIA: Probably you're embarrassed to be seen with me.

EDWARD: No. Not at all.

ALICIA: Do you think it's wrong of me?

EDWARD: Wrong?

ALICIA: I mean, do you think I'm bad?

EDWARD: What for?

ALICIA: To be in love with you?

EDWARD: Oh, I don't think you're really . . .

ALICIA: Yes, I am.
I know.
I think it's wrong.
Probably you think I should be spanked.

EDWARD: No, not at all.

ALICIA: I do.

[*She starts almost to weep.*]

Sometimes I think I'm so evil,
the things I think.

243

[*She starts to bite her wrist.*]

EDWARD: Hey, what are you doing?
What are you . . .
are you biting yourself?
Don't do that.
Hey.
Hey!
Don't do that.

[*He takes hold of her, tries to wrest her forearm out of her mouth.*]

Cut it out.
That's crazy.
Hey!

[*He pulls her down on the bed on top of himself, across his lap, and spanks her; she stops biting herself.*]

That's kind of crazy
you know that?

ALICIA: I feel better now.

EDWARD: I don't think I do.

ALICIA: Did you like spanking me?

[*Silence.*]

Well, did you?

EDWARD: I don't know.
I think
probably
I've got to go.

ALICIA: Hey, Edward!
Edward!

[*With longing, she watches him go.*]

RED DICKS: I guess you have to wonder sometimes
what catches a guy's eye.

ALICIA: Yeah.

PHIL: I think a guy likes a pretty face.

JIM: That's the first thing I always notice.

PHIL: And great hair.

JIM: Great hair, that's true.
Great hair.

PHIL: I don't like a woman with messy hair.

JIM: Or too much spray.
If it looks too stiff, that's not good.

PHIL: Do you like wavy hair?

JIM: Yes.

PHIL: I do.
I'd have to say, probably that's my favorite.
Wavy hair.

JIM: Right.

PHIL: Most guys will like a natural look
or soft
not too much makeup

JIM: a great smile.

PHIL: You know, I think these are the basics.

ALICIA: How can you tell when he's your boyfriend?
I mean, say you've been together, you know,
hanging out
maybe hanging out a lot,
when do you say to your friends, like, "We're together."

BONNIE: Does he call you "kiddo?"

ALICIA: I don't know.
I guess he might.

BONNIE: Right.
That's not a good sign really.

SHIRLEY: Or, if you're going somewhere together,
do you break into a sweat trying to keep up with him?

ALICIA: We haven't exactly gone anywhere together.

[*Silence.*]

BONNIE: You know, there are things you can do to get a guy's attention.

[*Silence.*]

Like, say you're having a conversation with a guy:
While you're talking to him, you could put your hand on his knee.

SHIRLEY: Lightly.

BONNIE: You could unbutton a button on your sweater.

JIM: I don't know.

BONNIE: What?

JIM: These are things that might be a little scary to a guy.
You could listen to him when he talks.
You could move a little closer to him.
I don't think you should unbutton any buttons.

BONNIE: Okay.
Say you are walking down the street
and you see a cute guy walking a dog.
Do you
pet the dog and smile at the dog
pet the dog and smile at the guy
touch the guy on the arm and wink at the dog?

ALICIA: Pet the dog and smile at the guy.

PHIL: What has this got to do with it?

JIM: He doesn't even have a dog.

RED DICKS: What's his favorite color?

ALICIA: I don't know.

RED DICKS: It's worth knowing. You can tell a lot from that.

ALICIA: Like what?

RED DICKS: Well, a guy who likes gray
is going to be your indecisive kind of guy.
Yellow, he's kind of passive,
maybe gay, you know,
I'm not saying necessarily,
just could be.
Your pink man is a philanderer
and a flirt.
But red: a guy who likes red is going to be easily aroused
he likes sex every way you can imagine
he's going to be a tiger in the sack.

JIM: This is maybe not what we're talking about here
a tiger in the sack
this is a girl you're talking to.

ALICIA: I'd like a tiger in the sack.

RED DICKS: Really?
Have you ever taken the purity test?

ALICIA: I don't think so.

RED DICKS: Have you ever: held hands with someone?

ALICIA: Sure.

RED DICKS: photocopied parts of your body, such as your face, hands or feet?

ALICIA: Uh, no.

[*At some point in here, the chicken will come "back to life"; one of the grown-ups can put the chicken in the car and close the door.*]

RED DICKS: been on a date?

ALICIA: Of course.

RED DICKS: been on a date past one a.m.?

[*As the test goes on, she responds more slowly or hesitantly or with difficulty or embarrassment at the increasing intimacy of the questions.*]

ALICIA: Of course.

RED DICKS: worn a strapless gown?

ALICIA: Yes.

RED DICKS: slow danced?

ALICIA: Yes.

RED DICKS: necked?

ALICIA: Yes.

RED DICKS: French kissed?

ALICIA: Yes.

RED DICKS: hot tubbed in mixed company?

ALICIA: Yes.

RED DICKS: in the nude?

[*Silence.*]

ALICIA: Yes.

RED DICKS: had someone put suntan lotion, cocoa butter, or baby oil on you?

ALICIA: Yes.

RED DICKS: played doctor?

[*More hesitantly now.*]

ALICIA: Yes.

RED DICKS: played Twister?

ALICIA: Yes.

RED DICKS: played Naked Twister?

ALICIA: Yes.

RED DICKS: been picked up?
been picked up?

ALICIA: Yes.

RED DICKS: picked someone up?

ALICIA: Yes.

RED DICKS: had a one-night stand?

ALICIA: Yes.

RED DICKS: I think she's ready.

POLLY: If you don't mind my saying,
I think you could use a little help with your makeup.
I think if you want to go for this dewy look
you're going to need some powdery, shimmery products
instead of these creamy moisturizing ones.
You're going to want to give your T-zone some extra blotting power
with a sweep of loose powder.
Go for the glitter on the eyes.
Loose sparkle eye powders, blush powders.
Forget the frosts on the lips,
go for clear gloss. Clear gloss.
Or else you could use
"Honey Rose"
or
"Tulip"
or "Tea Rose"
or "Oyster Pink"

RED DICKS: Or "Almost Kissed"

BONNIE: Or "Baby Kiss"

SHIRLEY: Or "Sweet Nothing"

POLLY: "Desert Rose"

BONNIE: "Positively Pink"

POLLY: "Blush Rose"

BONNIE: "Dusty Rose"

SHIRLEY: "Cinema Pink"

RED DICKS: "Pink Champagne"
Or "Balla Balla"

BONNIE: "English Rose"

RED DICKS: "La vie en Rose"

SHIRLEY: "Peony Peach"

POLLY: "Belle de Jour"

PHIL: "Baby Lips"

[*Silence; the others look at **PHIL**.*]

POLLY: Well, you have a lot of choices.

ALICIA: [*Overdosed.*] I,
you know,
sometimes
I can't stop thinking about
cutting myself
on my arms and legs, you know,
with razors,
not killing myself
or anything
but just
cutting myself
and then I guess I'd wear
long-sleeved shirts
or something
because I know that
hurting myself
isn't really
solving anything
but I can't seem to stop
thinking about it.

[*She turns and runs out at full speed; **POLLY** gets into the backseat of the Lincoln Town Car and shuts the door.*

***SHIRLEY** takes up the brushes next to the drums and does a quiet, contemplative solo with them.*

***JIM** takes off his shirt, lights the outdoor barbecue grill with lighter fluid, then puts a trail of lighter fluid along the ground and suspends himself horizontally above the flames on two sawhorses and roasts himself like a hog on a spit.*

Or else he has picked up the lighter fluid and managed to get it on his hands, and lit his hands on fire; he turns front with both hands burning, looking awkwardly, but calmly, from side to side, looking for something to put out the fire. Finally, he goes over to the kids' swimming pool, and extinguishes his hands.

***PHIL**, meanwhile, has been standing in the kids' pool, fiddling with a radio, which explodes, giving him an enormous electrical shock, and then something else also explodes with a huge ball of fire and smoke as **JIM** climbs down from his rotisserie and puts his shirt back on.*]

SHIRLEY: A lot of people think
that they're entitled to happiness.
I never thought that.
I always wished for happiness
but I never thought I had a right to it.
I thought happiness was something I had to make for myself,
not something like manna that fell from on high.
I have some friends who get indignant at the least obstacle to their happiness
as though it were an outrage.
I always thought you had to win your happiness,
under conditions some of which were burdensome
others favorable.

BONNIE: When I first met Walter
he would talk and talk about the most boring things
on and on
not quite, "how to get up in the morning," but almost.
He would burst into tears on my shoulder.
He was—well, obviously, he was afraid of his father.
The house he grew up in
it was just draped in black.
He never remembered any nursery rhymes from his childhood
or songs he learned.
And then, when I had to put him in Manhattan State Hospital
underneath the Triborough Bridge,
and I called his mother and begged her to help
his father got on the phone and said
"Stop it, you're upsetting Walter's mother,"
and he hung up on me.
And they never came to visit him.
The last time I saw him
when I was leaving after a visit
I told him I loved him, and he cried.
He was so fat from the drugs they were giving him.
He walked like a fat man.
And his hair was turning gray.
And they had him at work there
making those ugly, clumsy ashtrays.
And he had been such a beautiful boy.

   [*The garage band plays A Country Love Song while all those on stage sing along and **POLLY** opens the window of the Town Car and sings vocals from the front seat under a spotlight. As the song comes to an end, **EDWARD** enters, sits on the edge of his bed, takes off his roller blades.*]

RED DICKS: A guy like you: you're growing up.

EDWARD: I guess I am.

RED DICKS: Do you have a girlfriend?

EDWARD: No.
How come you ask?

RED DICKS: Guys your age, usually they do.

EDWARD: I like girls okay.
But for me, I don't know,
my idea of a good time is listening to the radio
playing a little air guitar
roller blading
if I had my choice finding out a little more about women
or doing something else
I think I'd rather
learn the secret of cartooning
how to identify different kinds of airplanes
the fundamentals of Greco-Roman wrestling
how to build a business
the secrets of Jiu Jitsu
how to train a dog.

And frankly, if you want to know what I think
I'm getting a little sick of seeing sex dragged through the dirt,
glorified
misrepresented in every way, shape, and form
I read through postings I find on the Internet
these so-called personal experiences that are so outrageous and far out that
only a fool would believe what he is reading.
Or on the television set
all these bikini clad women parading across the screen
holding Brand X Beer or breakfast cereal.
What kind of message does this send out?
Everyone else feels fat and ugly by comparison
everyone is insecure and angry
so all the men go out and rape someone
And is sex all that big a deal in the first place?
I'm not so sure.
I myself vowed a long time ago
to wait for someone very special,
to share that part of myself
with the one woman I fell in love with
and spent the rest of my life with.
And now, after almost 14 years of waiting,
masturbating to hold myself together sexually,
what do I find?
That adults are trying to get me involved in

premarital sex.
Don't you people realize
that sex is a distraction from the real world,
that what the politicians want is for you to think about sex all the time
and if that's all you think about
everyone will soon be reduced to poverty
without any health care or social security or pensions
because you haven't even been paying attention?
Yes.
Yes.
It happens that I did break my vow
and I did have sex with someone.

I went with this girl for two months,
both of us getting very serious about the relationship
and expressing our wishes to remain virgins until our wedding
and then it started with a touch here,
a stroke there,
and then one night,
we talked for almost three hours
about whether or not we should make love.
And so we did
and pretty soon I was moving my penis towards her vagina,
and in a half a second,
I had an orgasm.
All the buildup
all the excitement of finally having sex—
it all rushed out as fast as it could,
and I spent the next hour feeling horrible
about ruining her first time with such a poor performance.
And all my years of hard work down the tube.
And it wasn't even that wonderful
what I did feel was nothing more than masturbating without my hands.
The oral sex we'd been having for months
had been far more satisfying.
Suddenly I understood
how so many guys out there
wanted to have sex with as many women as possible.
Maybe they all felt as cheated as I did
Now I knew sex for what it was.
And now I have no interest in sex.
None.
Forget it.

[*He lies down and falls instantly asleep, like a narcoleptic. Silence. A very quiet conversation follows with* **PHIL** *and* **JIM** *sitting on opposite sides of the bed, talking over* **EDWARD.**]

JIM: You forget how it is to be a kid.
Sometimes I look back at the family photograph album,
and it comes back with such a rush.
You remember these moments exactly the way they were
as though it was yesterday.
Do you ever do that?

PHIL: Well . . .
Sure.

JIM: You don't?

PHIL: Sure.
Sure.

JIM: But not as though you like to.

PHIL: Unh-hunh.
Did your father ever take pictures of you nude?

JIM: What?

PHIL: Did you father take pictures of you nude?

JIM: Well, no.
I mean, I guess when I was a baby
you know,
in the bathtub,
yeah, sure.
Did your father take pictures of you nude?

PHIL: Yes.

JIM: Where?

PHIL: In the bedroom mostly.

JIM: What was he doing in the bedroom?

PHIL: Well, taking pictures and
having sex with me.

JIM: When you were a boy?

PHIL: Yes.

JIM: He did?

PHIL: Yes.

JIM: How did he do that?
Was he nice to you?

PHIL: He was gentle.

JIM: Were you thinking it was wrong?

PHIL: That what was wrong?

JIM: That your father was having sex with you.

PHIL: Well, he wasn't having sex with me at that time. He was just massaging me.

JIM: Oh. I thought you said . . .

PHIL: That was later.

JIM: But when he massaged you,
did you think that that was wrong?

PHIL: No.

JIM: You never did?

PHIL: When he massaged me with his mouth,
I thought that was wrong.
But, you know,
I thought I'd get used to it, and I did;
and eventually it made me feel warm.

JIM: Oh. Did you like it?

PHIL: Sometimes.

JIM: Why did he do that?
Did you ask him why he did that?

PHIL: He told me that it was a way to release the tension
and the
knots in your muscles
when you got worked up from sports and anxiety,
and it was
just a way to relax.

[*PHIL begins to shiver uncontrollably, hugging himself to keep from shivering.*]

JIM: Did you ever massage him?

PHIL: Yes.

JIM: Did he give you directions?

PHIL: He just said no.

JIM: No, meaning
what?

PHIL: Meaning if I skipped over his penis, he said no.

JIM: So, what did you do?

PHIL: I started to touch his penis and
massage it in the way he did me.

And then, one time
he took my hair in his hands
and wanted me to massage his penis with my mouth.

JIM: How old were you?

PHIL: I was seven.

JIM: Were you afraid of your father?

PHIL: Yes. When he
gave me swimming lessons,
he would
grab my
hair and
dunk me under the water and hold me down for twenty or thirty seconds,
and then he
would lift me up; and
I would cry out,
and then he'd
dunk me under again.

JIM: Was this, like, playful?

PHIL: No.
He wanted me to
struggle,
and he wanted me to
fight.
And I was afraid he would
kill me
accidentally.

[*POLLY, emerging from the Lincoln Town Car, goes to ED WARD's bed, wakes him up gently.*]

POLLY: I'm sorry things didn't work out with your girlfriend.

EDWARD: It's okay.

POLLY: These things do happen, you know.
So many times, for most people,
the first time is so bad,
and they think they never want to make love again
or that it was wrong
and yet
love
love is the most wonderful thing we have as human beings
this closeness to others
caring
compassion

and these feelings of empathy and caring for another
this is the whole basis for society
for civilization.

And if you were ever to get together again
with the girl you cared for
there are things you can do
that will give her happiness
or simply fun
there's nothing wrong with that
pleasure: that you give her as a gift
selflessly
because you care for her.

For instance, you know, talking.
You can't do enough talking with a woman
or reading her a book in bed
women like this
or when you're making love
not to carry on a whole discussion
but just to say how much you love her.

EDWARD: Yeah?

POLLY: And taking off a woman's clothes
you need to treat her with the care
well
with the care of the person you love most in the world
and very slowly
and in a dim light
because a lot of women are self-conscious about their bodies
and as each new part of her body is revealed
kiss her there softly

EDWARD: Unh-hunh.

POLLY: And touching
touching needs to be gentle
a lot of guys will just grab a woman's breast, you know,
and that hurts
a really gentle caress
just gently brushing over a nipple
or even just holding her breast
this is a real trigger.

EDWARD: It is?

POLLY: And
a woman likes to be touched all over her body
before she makes love because

256

when she is really excited
her whole body feels like a penis.

EDWARD: It does?

POLLY: Of course, if you're making love with an experienced woman
she will know some things to make you feel more at ease
and some other things you will like
tickling you with her eyelashes
on your cheek and neck and stomach
rubbing her nipples over your chest and stomach
and thighs
taking you into a bath with her
soaping you all over
up and down
reading an erotic story to you in the bath
and afterwards
taking you to bed and giving you a massage
and then guiding you inside her
so that before you know it
having done nothing yourself
she is holding you gently, tightly inside
kissing your neck, your cheek
holding you
her arms around you
you've forgotten entirely where you are
all you feel is
complete love
safe and warm
forever

[*Silence; EDWARD looks around; no one speaks; he gets up slowly, uncertainly from the bed, and leaves, slowly, not running, looking back and around from time to time in confusion, and then he is gone.*]

Probably I should kill myself.
I mean, I've lost my bearings altogether.
I suppose I could identify a picture of a spoon
or a sailing ship
if I were given a test
I could identify a duck, a mushroom, a horse, a cherry
but I would only think I was fooling
the examiners
thinking I had my wits together just because
I could tell a bucket from a coffee mill
and repeating sentences: The dog fears the cat because it has sharp claws
repeating: The dog is afraid of the cat but only because of its claws
and that would be wrong

that would count against me
they wouldn't even know what should count against me
and who did this to my fucking hair?
Did you do this?

RED DICKS: No.

POLLY: Look how it is
you did this when I wasn't paying attention?

RED DICKS: I didn't touch your hair.

POLLY: How am I supposed to manage
when I have nothing to wear.
I don't have any top to put on
unless I take some skirt and pull it up around my neck
and then what is it?
Something cream with something brown?
Do you know someone who would put that on?
I go to Saks and say to the saleslady
do you have thongs?
She pushes her eyeglasses up her nose and says
for underwear?
Right, I say, for underwear.
No, she says, we don't have thongs,
we have bikinis.
Well, let me see your bikinis
and she says,
these are one hundred percent cotton

[*She is pacing frantically back and forth.*]

Cotton! I say.
Ugh!
Who would wear a cotton bikini?
What has happened to civilization for God's sake
it's all downhill from here on out.
They come in a package of three, she says.
I don't want a package of one, I yell at her.
And pretty soon, they're calling over the store detective
telling me to pipe down
Pipe down, I say,
I'm a fucking shopper!
The reason you have a job is because I am here
demanding things!
And so the next thing I know
I'm being manhandled,
I find myself back out on Fifth Avenue
and I'm supposed to count myself lucky that I'm not in jail—

that's what happened to me
the last time I tried to shop at Saks!
And now I have this crap to wear!
And nothing to eat but this goddamn bagel!

[*She throws the bagel across the stage.*]

Would someone just get me something to eat
a cup of coffee and a cigarette
[*Yelling:*] I'm a frantic person!
Someone!
I'm just a little bit out of control!

I need a friend here.
Could you help me with this?

What the fuck ever happened to style?
Oh, sure, you say,
why don't they just lock her up
sure, lock her up.
A nice mental hospital in the country.
And then the same crazy people would just come around: [*In a different voice:*] Did you see Philip Blum?
Philip Blum? Who the fuck is Philip Blum?
[*In a different voice:*] Did you see him?
No, I did not.
[*In a different voice:*] Last night or this morning?
Where would I see Philip Blum?
[*In a different voice:*] Walking around the ward.
I did not. What was he doing, walking around?
[*In a different voice:*] Just walking through the ward. Did you see him?
Oh, I don't know. Maybe I did.
[*In a different voice:*] Was he carrying anything?

[*One or two of the others are just pacing back and forth as a reaction to all the frantic stuff that's going on.*]

What would he be carrying?
[*In a different voice:*] A syringe perhaps.
Yes, he was carrying a syringe.
[*In a different voice:*] For what purpose?
You're asking me. To give injections I suppose.
[*In a different voice:*] Did he give an injection to you?
Yes. Yes, he did!
[*In a different voice:*] And did you fall asleep?
Yes. But not for long.
[*Weeping now.*] Not for long.
I begged him: put me to sleep forever.
I'm worn out

and I don't know what I might do next.
I don't think of myself as a bad person
an average person, sure,
not a saint
I'm the first to know it
but not an evil person
who fucks her own children!

[*EDWARD enters, having returned, obviously, because he is interested.*]

EDWARD: Sometimes
things move so fast
it makes me dizzy.

POLLY: I know. What do you wish I would do?

EDWARD: I don't know.

POLLY: Maybe you should come with me.

EDWARD: Where?

POLLY: Come with me.
Don't worry.
I'll take good care of you.

[*She takes his hand, leads him over to the Lincoln Town Car, and opens the back door.*]

Let's get in back.

[*He gets in; she follows, and closes the door behind her.*

BONNIE turns on the radio and we hear

BIG MUSIC.

BONNIE pulls her skirt halfway down her butt and does a dance to the music that is half-wantonly flirtatious towards the men and half-hostile and half three or four other things;

PHIL and RED DICKS, meanwhile, engage in a "roughhouse" dance, throwing each other to the floor, and jumping on each other's stomachs and butts, one pulling the other upright and then throwing him down to the ground again, jumping on him, grabbing his head or hair and hurling him to the ground, kicking his legs out from under him, both of them screaming with horror and delight as the violent dance goes on and on, neither really hurting the other;

SHIRLEY just walks around during all this with her shirt pulled up to her neck; and JIM tops everyone with a wild, licentious striptease, twirling his shirt round and round before tossing it across the stage, shimmying with a sock between his legs, lots of wild stuff stripping all the way down to a fig leaf.

Then the music comes to an end, and JIM is the only one who had been dancing till the end; he is naked and feels instantly embarrassed; in silence, with no one else moving or speaking, he retrieves the items of clothing he had thrown wildly in the air, trying to cover himself with the clothes as he picks them up, finally coming to his cowboy boots, getting one of them on after a struggle, getting the other one half on, when RED DICKS comes at him for a pas de deux, and JIM partners with RED DICKS, one boot halfway on, holding RED DICKS up in the air, then dipping RED DICK's head toward the floor, finally releasing RED DICKS and resuming picking up his clothes.

A cellular phone rings. It rings over and over. Everyone looks at the cellular phone that lies in the middle of EDWARD's bed. No one moves.

Finally, SHIRLEY picks up the phone and hands it to BONNIE. She hands it to PHIL who hands it to JIM. JIM stands with it uncertainly. RED DICKS snatches it out of his hand and answers it.]

RED DICKS: Hello . . . .
Richard!
Yes.
Yes.
No.
He's not . . . uh . . . here.
No, she's not here.
They're not here.

[*Everyone looks at the car as he says this.*]

You're coming home.
Good!
Good!
I'm sure they'll be . . .
Yes.
I'll tell them.
See you soon.
Bye.

[*Silence.*]

JIM: You know
I think what a man wants most when he comes home
is just a little time to himself
like a dog circling on the rug before he lies down
just a little space to get acclimated
read his mail, check out the game on TV

PHIL: I don't know.
A man comes home
the first thing he feels is tension.
He's thinking, right: I remember where I am

Home, this is where the female always makes the rules.
Where the rules are subject to change at any time
without prior notification.
Where no male can possibly know all the rules.
Where, if the female suspects the male knows all the rules,
she must immediately change the rules.
Where the female is never wrong.
Where, if the female is wrong,
it is due to misunderstanding
which was a direct result
of something the male did or said wrong.
Where the female may change her mind at any time.
Where the male must never change his mind
without the express written consent of the female.
Where the female has every right to be angry or upset at any time.
Where the male must remain calm at all times
unless the female wants him to be angry and/or upset.
Where the male is expected to mind-read at all times.
Where if the female has PMS all the rules are null and void.
Where the female is ready when she is ready.
Where the male must be ready at all times.
Where the male who doesn't abide by the rules
can't take the heat, lacks backbone
and is a wimp.

JIM: Oh, I think you've just got some differences here
between men and women, and I say,
vive la difference.

PHIL: I think I see him coming.

BONNIE: What?

PHIL: Richard.
I think that must be him.
You recognize that car?

[*All look off to one side.*]

JIM: No.
No.

PHIL: I think that must be him.

JIM: Right.

[*PHIL takes off in the opposite direction. After a moment, JIM follows him, then*
BONNIE, *then* ***SHIRLEY,*** *then* ***JIM*** *and* ***RED DICKS.***

The stage is empty. The radio miraculously lights up and comes on and we hear,
at maximum, blasting volume: Screamin Jay Hawkins sings "I Put a Spell on

You" *and after a few moments* ED WARD *and* POLLY *get out of car and slow dance naked to the music.*

RICHARD enters. He is in his fifties. He stands, lit by a spot, and watches them dance. After a long, long while POLLY *sees* RICHARD, *turns and runs out. We've entered a state of suspended animation, as though we have gone into slow motion.*]

RICHARD: What are you doing?

EDWARD: I . . .
I should get dressed.

[*He moves towards his bed, to get a sheet.*]

RICHARD: I leave
my wife with you
and ask you, like a man, to take care of her,
and all you can think to do is to
is to get naked with her?

EDWARD: Did anyone know you were ever coming back?

RICHARD: This is your explanation?
Is this how it is for you to be my son?

EDWARD: Your son?
Is that how you think of me?
You never had anything for me but orders.
Do you remember
one weekend,
driving to the country
I was six years old
you got so angry at me
for something I had done I don't remember what
you pulled the car off onto an exit road
and got out and pulled me out of the car by my hair
and took me around to the front of the car
in front of the headlights
and I tried to pull away
and you knocked me to the ground
in front of the car, in the headlights
and I was crying
do you remember anything of this?

RICHARD: No.
This is not what I remember.

EDWARD: and one afternoon in the country
you left me playing with a friend
and you went off for tea with Mrs. Perry
but you didn't come back until after dark

and I was waiting for you beside the road
I saw you driving toward the house
and I waved to you
and you drove right past
because you still had Mrs. Perry in the car with you
and you kept on driving
and then you came back an hour later
I was still waiting for you by the road.

RICHARD: I'm sorry.
If you say it was true, I believe you.
I'm sorry.

EDWARD: You were always exploding
always angry
cursing at the other drivers
calling them sons of bitches
so that I was always afraid of you.

RICHARD: I'm sorry.

EDWARD: Always afraid you would turn on me
I thought you might kill me
push me out of the car
or crush me.

RICHARD: Oh, no. No.
I couldn't have done that.

EDWARD: How did I know?
You were in such a rage
or else silent, thinking,
holding your jaw, covering your mouth with your hand
so sad and discouraged
we all made you feel your life had been worthless.

RICHARD: No. No.
I'm just a person, too, you know.
I always felt your hatred of me.
I thought, well, okay,
leave him alone,
don't force yourself on him
maybe one day he'll come around
see something in you that he likes
when I explained things to you
it made you squirm
I talked too much
it always turned into a lecture
I couldn't help myself

and I would see your attention drift off
I could see you wanted to get away
I didn't know how to get you back
the best I could do was try to be cheerful
wrap up what I was saying
let you go
and then, playing catch
I could tell,
you'd rather be playing with a friend
tossing a ball back and forth with me
it was nothing but your filial duty
you remember we went on a fishing trip together
one time to Canada.

EDWARD: Yes, one time.

RICHARD: Yes.

EDWARD: It was fun. I had a good time.

RICHARD: So did I.
I never knew what else to do.

EDWARD: So I've become a cold person, like you.
Usually I don't even know what I feel.

RICHARD: I loved you.

EDWARD: No, you didn't. I loved you.

RICHARD: I don't think so.

> [*EDWARD runs out. RICHARD sits on EDWARD's bed, his head in his hands. After a few moments, JIM enters uncertainly.*]

JIM: Is there something
maybe
I can do?

RICHARD: I can't say
that I've been a perfect person.
I abandoned the mother of my son
and I abandoned my son himself
to pursue another woman.

Other women really.

When I was a boy my son's own age,
I slept once with the mother of a boyhood friend of mine
who lived just down the road,
a woman in her forties
Well, I slept with her more than once.

I slept with her the whole summer long,
going over early every morning
after her son had gone off to his summer job,
a divorced woman
and I was just a boy.
I remember her still,
I think of her still almost every day.

[*POLLY enters.*]

RICHARD: Polly.

POLLY: Yes.

JIM: Excuse me. I'll just be . . .

[*He leaves.*]

RICHARD: Was I gone so long?

POLLY: Yes.

RICHARD: You've always been my one true love.

POLLY: Oh.

RICHARD: You didn't know that?

POLLY: No.

RICHARD: When I first saw you
I thought
there couldn't be
a more pure vision
of absolute beauty.

POLLY: When we first met
you were happy to be with me all the time.

RICHARD: It's my fault?

POLLY: No.
It's just the way you were.
I remember
when we first arrived in St. Remy
the tall ceilings in our hotel room
with blue sky painted there,
and birds;
we made love,
and lay next to one another,
the summer breeze coming in through the open windows
cooling our bodies,
I felt so dizzy from jet lag
and making love

and the summer breeze coming from the garden,
I thought: I've gone to heaven.

RICHARD: I remember that.

POLLY: And I thought at the time
I could never leave you.

RICHARD: I felt
such sympathy for you.
I thought: I could care for you forever.
I thought: I see deep inside you
your most secret self
and I will always care for you.
I will always wish you well.
I will always hope for your happiness.
To keep things away from you
that bring tears to your eyes
that cause you grief
that make you feel small or hurt
unfairly treated
those things in your past
your mother's goodness—but still, as good a person as she was
as much as she loved you,
you always felt her distance
her coolness toward you
I thought: You will never feel that again.
Situations in your life
ordinary things, not knowing where the money would come from
for your rent
I thought: You will never feel that fear again
that sense that things were so hard
and you didn't know where the answer might come from
that sense of vulnerability
I'll hold you in my arms all night
my stomach pressed against your back
my face nestled in your hair
holding you the whole night, every night,
no harm will ever come to you
not ever.

POLLY: But then, do you remember when our bedroom ceiling was falling
and you said,
"Polly, that ceiling has been up there for a hundred and forty years
it's not going to fall now."
And I said, "Yes, but it's falling now."
And you didn't believe me until it fell
and you said you would believe me from then on.

RICHARD: Yes.

POLLY: Do you remember when I woke up one night
more than four and a half years ago
and I was sitting in the armchair in our bedroom
awake and sobbing
because it had been a year of you not getting divorced . . .
six months after the time when you promised me it would be over
and it was far, far from being over
and you gave me excuses like
"It doesn't mean anything . . . our marriage is over . . ."
and "Divorce will happen, like the sun rises and sets,
the divorce will happen."
Nothing made sense to me
I felt horrible to have people ask me
"So, are you and Richard going to get married?"
a question that should have made me happy or coy or blushy
or giggly or secretive
and it made me sick to my stomach and humiliated
and I was faced with the choice to either tell people
that you were married
still with no divorce in sight
or I could lie—
both options made me sick and resentful
I knew you had seen that this was painful to me
you had seen it
and dismissed it as trivial, wrong-minded, petty, insignificant
I showed you over and over that it was painful . . . truly painful
I sat in the chair sobbing, loudly
you woke up and saw me
you looked at me
and said with such contempt in your voice
"Boy, you've really worked yourself up over this haven't you?"
and you rolled over
to go back to sleep

RICHARD: Yes, I remember that.

POLLY: and I thought
My God, I'm a complete idiot
I'm the little blond bimbo
the great fuck with the hot little dresses and the fun
and it's all so sexy and fun
and we'll travel to the south of France and all around the world
and we'll show everyone how well we shop
and how in love we are and how romantic it all is
but don't you dare fuck with my family
and what's really important . . .

don't you dare ask me to rush getting a divorce
from the mother of my children
because this is serious and real
and someone real might get hurt
You showed me over and over again how insignificant my pain was
You told me flat out that you would not get a divorce one day faster because
I wanted it
than you would without my insistence . . .
that it had to be on your schedule and not mine
And I had to decide then . . .
am I willing to be this person?
This bimbo, this loved thing, this doted upon object,
on the outside of "real" "important" "significant" stuff—
like potentially upsetting wives and children—
am I willing to be that in exchange for having Richard?
And I said "Yes"
And I was wrong
And I came up for air a few more times over the years
I called you from Louisville and I told you
"I cannot do this for another year,
I can't do this for a few more months, I can't, I can't. I can't."
I made that call after sitting in the bathtub
for the fifth night in a row
crying for hours and slamming my head against the tiled wall.
Spurred on by the sad fact of meeting new people
who saw we were in love and asked me the dreaded questions
"Will you and Richard get married?"
I made the call to let you know that I had a definite limit.
A time beyond which I could not continue.
I called to tell you that the ceiling was falling
and I guess you thought
"That ceiling has been up there for a hundred and forty years
it's not going to fall now."
The ceiling fell
I fell
As I had predicted I would
As I told you I would
As I tried not to as hard as I could
That's what happened to me.

RICHARD: So it doesn't matter now
that I am finally really about to be divorced
because I have said this for years
over and over again
and it never happened and the damage has been done
it's too late.

POLLY: Right.

RICHARD: Because a person needs to be first in another person's heart
and know it
and know it absolutely
or it is just too corrosive.
It's just poisonous, finally
poisonous.

POLLY: Yes.

RICHARD: You know,
you never wanted so much to make love with me
You were interested sometimes
and sometimes, I think, took real pleasure in our making love
but you never found me irresistible
the way I found you
you didn't want me more and more and more
the way I wanted you
you could wait to make love with me
or not make love for days and days and not care about it at all
and I often thought
of course, it could be I'm not so appealing
I'm not so hot or so exciting to make love to
but maybe even more than that
it's simply that I'm not the right kind of guy for you at all
not even the category of person who thrills you.

Or maybe you're just not carried away by love of me
the way I am by you.

Which came first, do you think,
the rejection I always felt from you
or the disrespect you felt from me?

Every night you rejected me
and every time you returned from taking a trip out of town you rejected me
so that I came to dread your coming back
because your coming back
meant not that you would return
but that you would say you couldn't return
and I would feel your rejection again in the biggest way
you would come back and savage me

   [*Silence.*]

But really after what you've just said now
there's nothing more for me to say
except again and again how sorry I am
for hurting you, the best and only true love of my life

the whole point of living
was to find you and love you
and take care of that love
pay attention to it
and make sure I never lost it
and so I haven't done the one thing in life I should have done
and without you
the whole point of life is over
and I feel my life has ended
and I see that I'm the one who is responsible for that
so I feel a grief beyond anything I've ever felt
for myself and for the pain I've caused you
I'll never ever forget the picture of you in the bath in Louisville
crying and hitting your head on the tiles
never
and to know I did that

I wish you could see through the pain I've caused you
so that you might still be able to understand something of me
and see that I have loved you completely and still do
and somehow find your way back to me
and, if that turns out not to be possible
at least for you to know
in spite of the terrible mistakes I made
how much you were truly loved
what a precious person I always felt you are

POLLY: I can't see that.

RICHARD: You thought I thought of you
as a bimbo outside of anything
"real" or "important" or "significant" to me?

Everything I've done and felt and known and lived for these past five years
was about you
was filled with your spirit
and your tastes and your hatreds and your loves
and your humor and your idiosyncrasies
and your whims
your sudden turns and your steadiness
your confidence in me
the depth of your feelings
and the ferocity of them
everything I did was about you
and now without you my life is over.

You thought I thought of you as the great fuck
in the hot little dresses

You never were a great fuck
You were the worst fuck I ever had
I loved to make love with you
because I loved you
and I loved who you were
and I cared for you
and I always wanted to be close to you
as close as I could be
You were inhibited and frightened and closed off to adventure
repulsed and I don't know what else
and I always thought it was because you had been sexually abused
as a child
by a grown-up
or by the other kids in the woods
that you always used to joke about
and say how tough you were and you didn't care what they did
but I've never known a woman
so averse to just opening up and having a good time sexually
and experimenting and trying things
and seeing where it might take you

No
only because I loved you so much
did I live with what I always thought was
a frustrating and unsatisfying sex life
for you as well as me, I'm sure,
that I only thought maybe, maybe one day
if you ever came to love me and trust me enough
you might overcome whatever trauma of the past
had made you this way
and if you never did
I loved you so much
that a great fuck was way way down the list of important things
to me about you
the biggest thing was always that I loved you completely and forever

I loved your brains and your sensibility
we were soul mates
we felt and thought the same things in the same ways
all the little subtle things in life felt the same to us
the same things were funny and stupid and heartbreaking
the same things were pretty
the same things were good to eat
we liked the same light in the sky in Provence
we liked the same roads
we liked the sounds of the cicadas
we liked the same room in the hotel

we felt the same about Nostradamus's house
and about the people who ran it
and about the little stone pool back away from the house
we liked the same things when you decorated the living room
we liked the same scenes in the same plays
ten thousand million little things held us together
like no one I've ever known
I wanted to be inside you
inside your love
inside your feelings
inside your thoughts and how you felt the world
I wanted to feel things as you felt them
I wanted to be in your heart
and so often I felt I was
I felt we were together in that way
and in that way
you were the greatest fuck I ever had
but not the great fuck in the hot little dress
the great fuck because of who you were in your heart
and how I loved you more than life itself

I remember
when we went to see the Greek play
"The Danaids"
in the abandoned marble quarry
and I thought:
We are connected to this human life
and to one another
for all eternity.

> [*They sit looking at one another while we hear the Handel "Sarabande from Suite No. 11 for Harpsichord."*
>
> Then **RICHARD** shoots **POLLY**. *She is shot in the head, and astonished. He shoots her again. She is open-mouthed with surprise and anguish and slips slowly to the floor. He shoots her again. She jerks involuntarily and lies still. He puts the pistol into his mouth and blows his brains out. Brain and blood splatter behind him.*]

RADIO TALK SHOW VOICE: Usually, in life,
we're so busy doing things,
we don't stop to look at each other anymore.

2ND VOICE: That's so true.

TALK SHOW VOICE: But you won't be here forever.

2ND VOICE: No.
Right.

TALK SHOW VOICE: You won't even be the same person tomorrow.
Things go by so fast,
and then they're gone.
Your children grow up
and get married
and you never took the time to look at them.

2ND VOICE: Like that couple in upstate New York.

TALK SHOW VOICE: Who's that?

[*While the radio talk continues, PHIL and JIM come in and pick up RICHARD and carry him out; SHIRLEY and BONNIE carry out POLLY. RED DICKS picks up the odd Coke can, bit of clothing, as the radio show continues.*]

2ND VOICE: You heard that: this man who shot his wife;
she was sleeping with their son,
near Utica.

TALK SHOW VOICE: Oh. Oh. Right.
Well, not their son.
His son. Her stepson.

2ND VOICE: That's the one.
He shot her
and then he shot himself.
And then it turned out they weren't married after all.

TALK SHOW VOICE: Right.

2ND VOICE: He died. But she lived.

TALK SHOW VOICE: I understood he lived, too.

2ND VOICE: He lived? I didn't know that.

TALK SHOW VOICE: Yeah, he lived.
I guess, you know, he sort of lobotomized himself
but he was still able to pump gas
so they gave him a job there
and I guess he does okay.
They say that he seems happy.

2ND VOICE: I didn't know that.
But I did know that she
even though he shot her a couple of times—
once in the head—
she lived;
and she recovered,
well not completely, I guess—
she had a little trouble with her memory,
but otherwise she was okay.

TALK SHOW VOICE: And she moved into a trailer
with the stepson.

2ND VOICE: Right.
In the trailer park off the old Route 32.
And they lived there together
raising pit bulls.
I heard they have thirteen pit bulls
living with them there in the trailer.
And the husband's in the trailer next to theirs.
I guess you could say
they lived happily ever after.

TALK SHOW VOICE: Right. Well.
That's a love story.

2ND VOICE: Yeah. That really is.

   [*Silence.*]

TALK SHOW VOICE: Okay!
Well,
here's some more music
a familiar old song.
This is Hank Snow singing "I Don't Hurt Anymore."

2ND VOICE: I like this song.

TALK SHOW VOICE: I've got to say,
I love this song.

   [*The garage band picks up the Hank Snow piece and drowns out the radio as*
   RED DICKS *straightens up, throwing things into the kiddie pool.*]

END OF PLAY

EURYDICE

SARAH RUHL

SARAH RUHL's plays include *The Clean House* (Susan Smith Blackburn Award, 2004), *Melancholy Play, Late: a cowboy song, Orlando,* and *Passion Play.* Upcoming productions of her work will be seen at Yale Repertory Theater, Woolly Mammoth Theatre, South Coast Repertory, and Berkeley Repertory Theater. Her work has been developed and produced across the U.S., as well as in London and Germany. She has received commissions from Playwrights Horizons, McCarter Theatre, and Arena Stage. She holds an M.F.A. from Brown University, and is originally from Chicago, where she has a long-standing association with Piven Theater Workshop. In 2003, she was the recipient of a Helen Merrill award and a Whiting Writers' award. She is a resident playwright of New Dramatists.

From the Writer
SARAH RUHL

Eurydice came to me in the form of an image. I kept imagining the moment when Orpheus turns around to face Eurydice; I kept thinking, what if she speaks his name, what if she startles him? What if language is in this story, along with music? What if Eurydice is accountable in some way for the loss of faith when Orpheus turns around? I began with that moment and then wrote backwards.

We don't know all that much about Orpheus and Eurydice through the first sources. We know from Ovid that Eurydice and the world-famous musician Orpheus got married one day. Eurydice is chased on the day of her wedding by an amorous shepherd; during the chase, she is bitten by a snake. She dies. Orpheus is so sad that he plays the most beautiful and sad music at the gates of hell to find her. Hades takes pity on Orpheus and lets him in—his music is so transformative that the stones weep. Orpheus strikes a bargain; he can have Eurydice back if he manages to lead her out of the underworld without speaking to her or looking at her. If he looks back at her, she dies twice. Most of us know how the story ends.

There have been many retellings of the Orpheus story—Cocteau, the operas, *Black Orpheus*. . . . We know a great deal about Orpheus's loss. But for some reason we never hear from Eurydice—she's always a cipher, someone who dies twice. I'm interested in her voice, a voice that hasn't been heard before. I'm interested in anyone who dies twice.

I'm interested in how personal stories can be articulated through mythic architecture. The architecture of myth—its structure, its bigness, its formal elegance—can frame stories that are smaller and more personal. I wrote Eurydice for my father, who died too young. The play is, in some ways, a desire on my part to experience more conversations with him. I think that theater can connect our personal mythologies to stories that are bigger than us—that connection between bigness and smallness brings me back to theater again and again.

This statement has been adapted by the author from an interview with dramaturg Lenora Brown for the Madison Repertory Theatre newsletter at the time of the play's premiere (2004).

THIS PLAY IS DEDICATED TO MY FATHER

PRODUCTION HISTORY

University of California-San Diego Department of Theater and Dance's production of *Eurydice*, directed by Daniel Fish. PHOTO: JASON H. THOMPSON

Eurydice received a workshop production at the Children's Theater Company in Minneapolis directed by Darron L. West and Rebecca Brown, September 2002. The play received its premiere at Madison Repertory Theatre, Wisconsin, in September 2003. It was directed by Richard Corley; the set design was by Narelle Sissons; the costume design was by Murell Horton; the lighting design was by Rand Ryan; the sound design was by Darron L. West. The cast was as follows:

EURYDICE. . . . . Laura Heisler
ORPHEUS . . . . David Andrew McMahon
FATHER . . . . John Lenartz
NASTY MAN. . . . . Scot Morton
LITTLE STONE. . . . . Polly Noonan
BIG STONE. . . . . Jody Reiss
LOUD STONE. . . . . Karlie Nurse

It was subsequently produced at University of California-San Diego Department of Theater and Dance, directed by Daniel Fish; at LAMDA in London, directed by Davis McCallum; at the Piven Theater Workshop in Evanston, directed by Joyce Piven; and at Berkeley Repertory Theater, directed by Les Waters.

SPECIAL THANKS to Paula Vogel, Mac Wellman, Polly Noonan, Joyce Piven, Rick Corley, Les Waters, Daniel Fish, Rebecca Brown, Darron L. West, Chuck Mee, Davis McCallum, Susannah Melone, Craig Watson, Christopher Steele-Nicholson, Kathy and Kate Ruhl, all the theaters who developed this play around the country, Andy Bragen, Jorge Ignacio Cortinas, Charlotte Meehan, Laura Zam, Stacia St. Owens, Caridad Svich, Joseph Pucci, David Konstan, 87 Hope Street where I wrote the play, and to my father.

CHARACTERS

EURYDICE
Her **FATHER**
ORPHEUS

A CHORUS OF STONES: BIG STONE, LITTLE STONE, LOUD STONE

These characters below should be double-cast:
a **NASTY INTERESTING MAN** (called **MAN**)
a **CHILD (LORD OF THE UNDERWORLD)**

EURYDICE's **GRANDMOTHER** (the **FATHER**'s mother)
OLD WOMAN (THE VORACIOUS MOTHER OF THE CHILD)

THE SET

contains a raining elevator, a water-pump, some rusty exposed pipes, an abstract River of Forgetfulness, an old-fashioned glow-in-the-dark globe.

NOTES

EURYDICE and **ORPHEUS** should be played as though they are a little too young and a little too in love. They should resist the temptation to be "classical."

The underworld should resemble the world of Alice in Wonderland more than it resembles Hades.

The **STONES** should be played as though they are nasty children at a birthday party. They might be played by children.

The play should be performed without an intermission.

FIRST MOVEMENT

SCENE 1

A young man—ORPHEUS—and a young woman—EURYDICE. They wear swimming outfits from the 1950s. ORPHEUS makes a sweeping gesture with his arm, indicating the sky.

EURYDICE: All those birds?

[*He nods. They make a quarter turn and he makes a sweeping gesture.*]

And—the sea! When?

[*ORPHEUS opens his hands.*]

Now? It's mine already?

[*ORPHEUS nods.*]

Wow.

[*They kiss. He indicates the sky.*]

Surely not—surely not the sky and the stars too.

[*ORPHEUS nods.*]

That's very generous.

[*ORPHEUS nods.*]

Perhaps too generous?

[*ORPHEUS shakes his head.*]

Thank you.
Now—walk over there. Don't look at me.

[*ORPHEUS walks away from her.*]

Now—stop!

[*He stops. She runs towards him and jumps in his arms.
He doesn't quite catch her and they fall down together.
She crawls on top of him and kisses his eyes.*]

What are you thinking about?

ORPHEUS: Music.

EURYDICE: How can you think about music? You either hear it or you don't.

ORPHEUS: I'm hearing it then.

EURYDICE: Oh.

[*Pause.*]

I read a book today.

ORPHEUS: Did you?

EURYDICE: Yes. It was very interesting.

ORPHEUS: That's good.

EURYDICE: Don't you want to know what it was about?

ORPHEUS: Of course.

EURYDICE: There were—stories—about people's lives—how some come out well—and others come out badly.

ORPHEUS: Do you love the book?

EURYDICE: Yes—I think so.

ORPHEUS: Why?

EURYDICE: It can be interesting to see if other people—like dead people who wrote books—agree or disagree with what you think.

ORPHEUS: Why?

EURYDICE: Because it makes you—a larger part of the human community. It had very interesting arguments.

ORPHEUS: Oh. And arguments that are interesting are good arguments?

EURYDICE: Well—yes.

ORPHEUS: I didn't know an argument should be interesting. I thought it should be right or wrong.

EURYDICE: Well, these particular arguments were very interesting.

ORPHEUS: Maybe you should make up your own thoughts. Instead of reading them in a book.

EURYDICE: I do. I do think up my own thoughts.

ORPHEUS: I know you do. I love how you love books. Don't be mad.

[*Pause.*]

I made up a song for you today.

EURYDICE: Did you!?

ORPHEUS: Yup. It's not *interesting* or *not*-interesting. It just—is.

EURYDICE: Will you sing it for me?

ORPHEUS: It has too many parts.

EURYDICE: Let's go in the water.

[*They start walking, arm in arm, on extensive unseen boardwalks, towards the water.*]

ORPHEUS: Wait—remember this melody.

[*He hums a bar of melody.*]

EURYDICE: I'm bad at remembering melodies. Why don't you remember it?

ORPHEUS: I have eleven other ones in my head, making for a total of twelve. You have it?

EURYDICE: Yes. I think so.

ORPHEUS: Let's hear it.

[*She sings the melody. She misses a few notes. She's not the best singer in the world.*]

Pretty good. The rhythm's a little off. Here—clap it out.

[*She claps. He claps the rhythmic sequence for her.
She tries to imitate. She is still off.*]

EURYDICE: Is that right?

ORPHEUS: We'll practice.

EURYDICE: I don't need to know about rhythm. I have my books.

ORPHEUS: Don't books have rhythm?

EURYDICE: Kind of. Let's go in the water.

ORPHEUS: Will you remember my melody under the water?

EURYDICE: Yes! I WILL ALWAYS REMEMBER YOUR MELODY! It will be imprinted on my heart like wax.

ORPHEUS: Thank you.

EURYDICE: You're welcome. When are you going to play me the whole song?

ORPHEUS: When I get twelve instruments.

EURYDICE: Where are you going to get twelve instruments?

ORPHEUS: I'm going to make each strand of your hair into an instrument. Your hair will stand on end as it plays my music and become a hair orchestra. It will fly you up into the sky.

EURYDICE: I don't know if I want to be an instrument.

ORPHEUS: Why?

EURYDICE: Won't I fall down when the song ends?

ORPHEUS: That's true. But the clouds will be so moved by your music that they will fill up with water until they become heavy and you'll sit on one and fall gently down to earth. How about that?

EURYDICE: Okay.

[*They stop walking for a moment. They gaze at each other.*]

ORPHEUS: It's settled then.

EURYDICE: What is?

ORPHEUS: Your hair will be my orchestra and—I love you.

[*Pause.*]

EURYDICE: I love you too.

ORPHEUS: How will you remember?

EURYDICE: That I love you?

ORPHEUS: Yes.

EURYDICE: That's easy. I can't help it.

ORPHEUS: You never know. I'd better tie a string around your finger to remind you.

EURYDICE: Is there string at the ocean?

ORPHEUS: I always have string. In case I come upon a broken instrument.

[*He takes out a string from his pocket. He takes her left hand.*]

ORPHEUS: This hand.

[*He wraps string deliberately around her fourth finger.*]

ORPHEUS: Is this too tight?

EURYDICE: No—it's fine.

ORPHEUS: There—now you'll remember.

EURYDICE: That's a very particular finger.

ORPHEUS: Yes.

EURYDICE: You're aware of that?

ORPHEUS: Yes.

EURYDICE: How aware?

ORPHEUS: Very aware.

EURYDICE: Orpheus—are we?

ORPHEUS: You tell me.

EURYDICE: Yes.
I think so.

ORPHEUS: You *think* so?

EURYDICE: I wasn't thinking.
I mean—Yes. Just: Yes.

ORPHEUS: Yes?

EURYDICE: Yes.

ORPHEUS: Yes!

EURYDICE: Yes!

ORPHEUS: May our lives be full of music!

[*Music. He picks her up and throws her into the sky.*]

EURYDICE: Maybe you could also get me another ring—a gold one—to put over the string one. You know?

ORPHEUS: Whatever makes you happy. Do you still have my melody?

EURYDICE: It's right here.

[*She points to her temple. They look at each other. A silence.*]

What are you thinking about?

ORPHEUS: Music.

[*A pause.*]

Just kidding. I was thinking about you. And music.

EURYDICE: Let's go in the water. I'll race you!

[*She puts on her swimming goggles.*]

ORPHEUS: I'll race *you*!

EURYDICE: I'll race *you*!

ORPHEUS: I'll race *you*!

[*They race towards the water.*]

SCENE 2

The FATHER, dressed in a grey suit, reads from a letter.

FATHER: Dear Eurydice,
    A letter for you on your wedding day.
    There is no choice of any importance in life but the choosing of a beloved. I haven't met Orpheus, but he seems like a serious young man. I understand he's a musician.
    If I were to give a speech at your wedding I would start with one or two funny jokes and then I might offer some words of advice. I would say:

Cultivate the arts of dancing and small talk.

Everything in moderation.

Court the companionship and respect of dogs.

Grilling a fish or toasting bread without burning requires singleness of purpose, vigilance and steadfast watching.

Keep quiet about politics, but vote for the right man.

Take care to change the light bulbs.

Continue to give yourself to others because that's the ultimate satisfaction in life—to love, accept, honor and help others.

As for me, this is what it's like being dead: The atmosphere smells.

And there are strange high-pitched noises—like a teakettle always boiling over. But it doesn't seem to bother anyone. And, for the most part, there is a pleasant atmosphere and you can work and socialize, much like at home. I'm working in the business world and it seems that, here, you can better see the far-reaching consequences of your actions.

Also, I am one of the few dead people who still remembers how to read and write. That's a secret. If anyone finds out, they might dip me in the River again.

I write you letters. I don't know how to get them to you.

Love,

Your father

[*He drops the letter as though into a mail-slot. It falls on the ground.*
Wedding music.
In the underworld, the **FATHER** *walks in a*
straight line as though he is walking his daughter down the aisle.
He is affectionate, then solemn, then glad, then solemn, then amused, then solemn.
He looks at his imaginary daughter; he looks straight ahead; he acknowledges the guests at the wedding; he gets choked up; he looks at his daughter and smiles an embarrassed smile for getting choked up.
He looks straight ahead, calm. He walks.
Suddenly, he checks his watch. He exits, in a hurry.]

SCENE 3

EURYDICE, by a water pump. The noise of a party, from far off.

EURYDICE: I hate parties.

And a wedding party is the biggest party of all.

All the guests arrived and Orpheus is taking a shower.

He's always taking a shower when the guests arrive so he doesn't have to greet them.

Then I have to greet them.

A wedding is for daughters and fathers. The mothers all dress up, trying to look like young women. But a wedding is for a father and a daughter. They stop being married to each other on that day.

I always thought there would be more interesting people at my wedding.

[*She drinks a cup of water from the water pump. A man wearing a trench coat appears.*]

MAN: Are you a homeless person?

EURYDICE: No.

MAN: Oh. I'm on my way to a party where there are really very interesting people. Would you like to join me?

EURYDICE: No. I just left my own party.

MAN: You were giving a party and you just—left?

EURYDICE: Well—yes.

MAN: You must be a very interesting person, to leave your own party like that.

EURYDICE: Thank you.

MAN: You mustn't care at all what other people think of you. I always say that's a mark of a really interesting person, don't you?

EURYDICE: I guess.

MAN: So would you like to accompany me to this interesting affair?

EURYDICE: No, thank you. I just got married, you see.

MAN: Oh—lots of people do that.

EURYDICE: That's true—lots of people do.

MAN: What's your name?

EURYDICE: Eurydice.

[*He looks at her, hungry.*]

MAN: Eurydice.

EURYDICE: Good-bye, then.

MAN: Good-bye.

[*She exits. He sits by the water pump. He notices a letter on the ground. He picks it up and reads it. To himself:*]

Dear Eurydice.

[*Musty dripping sounds.*]

SCENE 4

The FATHER tries to remember how to do the jitterbug in the underworld. He does the jitterbug with an imaginary partner. He has fun.

On the other side of the stage, ORPHEUS and EURYDICE dance together at their wedding. They are happy. They have had some champagne. They sing "Don't Sit Under the Apple Tree" together.

EURYDICE: I'm warm; are you warm?

ORPHEUS: Yes!

EURYDICE: I'm going to get a drink of water.

> [*On the other side of the stage, the FATHER checks his watch. He exits, in a hurry.*]

ORPHEUS: Don't go.

EURYDICE: I'll be right back.

ORPHEUS: Promise?

EURYDICE: Yes.

ORPHEUS: I can't stand to let you out of my sight today.

EURYDICE: Silly goose.

> [*They kiss.*]

SCENE 5

EURYDICE at the water pump, getting a glass of water. The NASTY INTERESTING MAN appears.

EURYDICE: Oh—you're still here.

MAN: Yes. I forgot to tell you something. I have a letter. Addressed to Eurydice—that's you—from your father.

EURYDICE: That's not possible.

MAN: He wrote down some thoughts—for your wedding day.

EURYDICE: Let me see.

MAN: I left it at home. It got delivered to my elegant high-rise apartment by mistake.

EURYDICE: Why didn't you say so before?

MAN: You left in such a hurry.

EURYDICE: From my father?

MAN: Yes.

EURYDICE: You're sure?

MAN: Yes.

EURYDICE: I knew he'd send something!

MAN: It'll just take a moment. I live around the block. What an interesting dress you're wearing.

EURYDICE: Thank you.

SCENE 6

ORPHEUS, from the water pump.

ORPHEUS: Eurydice?
Eurydice!

SCENE 7

The sound of a door closing. The Interesting Apartment—a giant loft space with no furniture. They enter, panting.

MAN: Voila.

EURYDICE: You're very high up.

MAN: Yes. I am.

EURYDICE: I feel a little faint.

MAN: It'll pass.

EURYDICE: Have you ever thought about installing an elevator?

MAN: No. I prefer stairs. I think architecture is so interesting, don't you?

EURYDICE: Oh, yes. So, where's the letter?

MAN: But isn't this an interesting building?

EURYDICE: It's so—high up.

MAN: Yes.

[*Pause.*]

EURYDICE: There's no one here. I thought you were having a party.

MAN: I like to celebrate things quietly. With a few other interesting people. Don't you?

[*She tilts her head to the side and stares at him.*]

MAN: Would you like some champagne?

EURYDICE: Maybe some water.

MAN: Water it is! Make yourself comfortable.

[*He gestures to the floor. He switches on Brazilian mood music. She looks around.*]

EURYDICE: I can't stay long!

[*She looks out the window. She is very high up.*]

EURYDICE: I can see my wedding from here!
The people are so small—they're dancing!
There's Orpheus!
He's not dancing.

MAN: [*Shouting from offstage.*] So, who's this guy you're marrying?

EURYDICE: [*Shouting.*] His name is Orpheus.

MAN: [*As he attempts to open the champagne, offstage.*] Orpheus. Not a very interesting name. I've heard it before.

EURYDICE: [*Shouting.*] Maybe you've heard of him. He's kind of famous. He plays the most beautiful music in the world, actually.

MAN: I can't hear you!

EURYDICE: [*Shouting.*] So the letter was delivered—here—today?

MAN: That's right.

EURYDICE: Through the post?

MAN: It was—mysterious.

[*The sound of champagne popping. He enters with one glass of champagne.*]
Voila.

[*He drinks the champagne.*]

So. Eurydice. Tell me one thing. Name me one person you find interesting.

EURYDICE: Why?

MAN: Just making conversation.

[*He sways a little, to the music.*]

EURYDICE: Right. Um—all the interesting people I know are dead or speak French.

MAN: Well, I don't speak French, Eurydice.

[*He takes one step toward her. She takes one step back.*]

EURYDICE: I'm sorry. I have to go. There's no letter, is there?

MAN: Of course there's a letter. It's right here.

[*He pats his breast pocket.*]

Eurydice. I'm not interesting, but I'm strong. You could teach me to be interesting. I would listen. Orpheus is too busy listening to his own thoughts. There's music in his head. Try to pluck the music out and it bites you. I'll bet you had an interesting thought today, for instance.

[*She tilts her head to the side, quizzical.*]

I bet you're always having them, the way you tilt your head to the side and stare . . .

[*She jerks her head back up.
Musty dripping sounds.*]

EURYDICE: I feel dizzy all of a sudden. I want my husband. I think I'd better go now.

MAN: You're free to go, whenever you like.

EURYDICE: I know.
I think I'll go now, in fact. I'll just take my letter first, if you don't mind.

[*She holds out her hand for the letter. He takes her hand.*]

MAN: Relax.

[*She takes her hand away.*]

EURYDICE: Good-bye.

[*She turns to exit. He blocks the doorway.*]

MAN: Wait. Eurydice. Don't go. I love you.

EURYDICE: Oh no.

MAN: You need to get yourself a real man. A man with broad shoulders like me. Orpheus has long fingers that would tremble to pet a bull or pluck a bee from a hive—

EURYDICE: How do you know about my husband's fingers?

MAN: A man who can put his big arm around your little shoulders as he leads you through the crowd, a man who answers the door at parties. . . . A man with big hands, with big stupid hands like potatoes, a man who can carry a cow in labor.

[*The MAN backs EURYDICE against the wall.*]

My lips were meant to kiss your eyelids, that's obvious!

EURYDICE: Close your eyes, then!

[*He closes his eyes, expecting a kiss. She takes the letter from his breast pocket. She slips under him and opens the door to the stairwell. He opens his eyes. She looks at the letter.*]

It's his handwriting!

MAN: Of course it is!

[*He reaches for her.*]

EURYDICE: Good-bye.

[*She runs for the stairs. She wavers, off-balance, at the top of the stairwell.*]

MAN: Don't do that, you'll trip!

EURYDICE: Orpheus!

[*From the water pump:*]

ORPHEUS: EURYDICE!

[*She runs, trips, and pitches down the stairs, holding her letter. She follows the letter down, down, down . . . Blackout. A clatter. Strange sounds—xylophones, brass bands, sounds of falling, sounds of vertigo. Sounds of breathing.*]

SECOND MOVEMENT

The underworld.
There is no set change.
Strange watery noises.
Drip, drip, drip.
The movement to the underworld is marked by the entrance of **THE STONES**.

SCENE 1

THE STONES: We are a chorus of stones.

LITTLE STONE: I'm a little stone.

BIG STONE: I'm a big stone.

LOUD STONE: I'm a loud stone.

THE STONES: We are all three stones.

LITTLE STONE: We live with the dead people in the land of the dead.

BIG STONE: Eurydice was a great musician. Orpheus was his wife.

LOUD STONE: [*Correcting* **BIG STONE**.] Orpheus was a great musician.
Eurydice was his wife. She died.

LITTLE STONE: Then he played the saddest music.
Even we—

THE STONES: the stones—

LITTLE STONE: cried when we heard it.

[*The sound of three drops of water hitting a pond.*]

LITTLE STONE: Oh, look,
she is coming into the land of the dead now.

BIG STONE: Oh!

LOUD STONE: Oh!

LITTLE STONE: Oh!
We might say—"Poor Eurydice"—

LOUD STONE: but stones don't feel bad for
dead people.

[*The sound of an elevator ding. An elevator door opens.*
Inside the elevator, it is raining. **EURYDICE** *gets rained on inside the elevator.*
She carries a suitcase and an umbrella.

295

*She is dressed in the kind of 1930s suit that women wore when they eloped.
She looks bewildered.*

*The sound of an elevator ding. EURYDICE steps out of the elevator.
The elevator door closes.*

*She walks towards the audience and opens her mouth, trying to speak.
There is a great humming noise.
She closes her mouth.
The humming noise stops.*

*She opens her mouth for the second time,
attempting to tell her story to the audience.
There is a great humming noise.
She closes her mouth—the humming noise stops.
She has a tantrum of despair.*]

THE STONES: Eurydice wants to speak to you.
But she can't speak your language anymore.
She talks in the language of dead people now.

LITTLE STONE: It's a very quiet language.

LOUD STONE: Like if the pores in your face
opened up and talked.

BIG STONE: Like potatoes sleeping in the dirt.

> [*THE STONES look at BIG STONE as though that were a dumb thing to
> say.*]

LITTLE STONE: Pretend that you understand her
or she'll be embarrassed.

BIG STONE: Yes—pretend for a moment
that you understand
the language of stones.

LOUD STONE: Listen to her the way you would listen to
your own daughter
if she died too young
and tried to speak to you
across long distances.

> [*EURYDICE shakes out her umbrella. She approaches the audience.
> This time, she can speak.*]

EURYDICE: There was a roar, and a coldness—
I think my husband was with me.
What was my husband's name?

> [*EURYDICE turns to THE STONES.*]

My husband's name? Do you know it?

[*THE STONES shrug their shoulders.*]

How strange. I don't remember.
It was horrible to see his face
when I died. His eyes were
two black birds
and they flew to me.

I said no—stay where you are—
he needs you in order to see!

When I got through the cold
they made me swim in a river
and I forgot his name.
I forgot all the names.
I know his name starts with my mouth
shaped like a ball of twine—
Oar—oar.
I forget.

They took me to a tiny boat.
I only just fit inside.
I looked at the oars
and I wanted to cry.
I tried to cry but I just drooled a little.

I'll try now.

[*She tries to cry and finds that she can't.*]

What happiness it would be to cry.

[*She takes a breath.*]

I was not lonely
only alone with myself
begging myself not to leave my own body
but I *was* leaving.

Good-bye, head—I said—
it inclined itself a little, as though to nod to me
in a solemn kind of way.

[*She turns to* **THE STONES**.]

How do you say good-bye to yourself?

[*They shake their heads.
A train whistle.*
EURYDICE *steps onto a platform, surveying a large crowd.*]

A train!

LITTLE STONE: The station is like a train but there is no train.

BIG STONE: The train has wheels that are not wheels.

LOUD STONE: There is the opposite of a wheel and the opposite of smoke and the opposite of a train.

[*A train pulls away.*]

EURYDICE: Oh! I'm waiting for someone to meet me, I think.

[*EURYDICE's FATHER approaches and takes her baggage.*]

FATHER: Eurydice.

EURYDICE: [*To THE STONES.*] At last, a porter to meet me!
[*To the FATHER.*] Do you happen to know where the bank is? I need money. I've just arrived. I need to exchange my money at the Bureau de Change. I didn't bring traveler's checks because I left in such a hurry. They didn't even let me pack my suitcase. There's nothing in it! That's funny, right? Funny—ha ha! I suppose I can buy new clothes here. I would *really* love a bath.

FATHER: Eurydice!

EURYDICE: What is that language you're speaking? It gives me tingles. Say it again.

FATHER: Eurydice!

EURYDICE: Oooh—it's like a fruit! Again!

FATHER: Eurydice—I'm your father!

EURYDICE: [*Strangely imitating.*] Eurydice—I'm your father. How funny! You remind me of something but I can't understand a word you're saying. Say it again!

FATHER: Your father.

THE STONES: [*To the FATHER.*] Shut up, shut up!
She doesn't understand you.
She's dead now, too.
You have to speak in the language of stones.

FATHER: You're dead now. I'm dead, too.

EURYDICE: Yes, that's right. I need a reservation. For the fancy hotel.

FATHER: When you were alive, I was your father.

EURYDICE: Yes, a hotel with potted palms sounds nice.

THE STONES: Father is not a word that dead people understand.
He is what we call subversive.

FATHER: When you were alive, I was your tree.

EURYDICE: My tree! Yes, the tall one in the backyard!
I used to sit all day in its shade!

[*She sits at the feet of her* **FATHER**.]

Ah—there—shade!

LITTLE STONE: There is a problem here.

EURYDICE: Is there any entertainment at the hotel? Any dancing ladies? Like with the great big fans?

FATHER: I named you Eurydice. Your mother named all the other children. But Eurydice I chose for you.

BIG STONE: Be careful, sir.

EURYDICE: The tree is talking in a language I don't understand.

FATHER: Eurydice. I wanted to remember your name. I asked the stones. They said: Forget the names—the names make you remember.

LOUD STONE: We told you how it works!

FATHER: One day it would not stop raining.

FATHER: I heard your name inside the rain—somewhere between the drops— I saw falling letters. Each letter of your name—I began to translate.

E—I remembered elephants. U—I remembered ulcers and under. R—I remembered reindeers. I saw them putting their black noses into snow. Y— youth and yellow. D—dog, dig, daughter, day. Time poured into my head. The days of the week. Hours, months . . .

EURYDICE: The tree talks so beautifully.

THE STONES: Don't listen!

EURYDICE: I feel suddenly hungry! Where is the porter who met me at the station?

FATHER: Here I am.

EURYDICE: I would like a continental breakfast, please. Maybe some rolls and butter. Oh—and jam. Please take my suitcase to my room, if you would.

FATHER: I'm sorry, Miss, but there are no rooms here.

EURYDICE: What? No rooms? Where do people sleep?

FATHER: People don't sleep here.

EURYDICE: I have to say I'm very disappointed. It's been such a tiring day. I've been traveling all day—first on a river, then on a train . . . I thought someone would meet me at the station . . .

[**EURYDICE** *is on the verge of tears.*]

THE STONES: Don't cry! Don't cry!

EURYDICE: I don't know where I am and there are all these stones and I hate them! They're horrible! I want a bath! I thought someone would meet me at the station!

FATHER: Don't be sad. I'll take your luggage to your room.

THE STONES: THERE ARE NO ROOMS!

[*He picks up her luggage. He gives* **THE STONES** *a dirty look.*
The sound of water in rusty pipes.]

SCENE 2

ORPHEUS *writes a letter to* **EURYDICE.**

ORPHEUS: Dear Eurydice,
   I miss you. No—that's not enough.

[*He crumples up the letter.*
He writes a new letter.
He thinks. He writes:]

ORPHEUS: Dear Eurydice,

[*A pause.*
Music.
He conducts.]

   Love, Orpheus

[*He drops the letter as though into a mail slot.*]

SCENE 3

The **FATHER** *creates a room out of string for* **EURYDICE.**

He makes four walls and a door out of string.
Time passes.
It takes time to build a room out of string.

EURYDICE *observes the underworld. There isn't much to observe.*
She plays hopscotch without chalk.

Every so often,
the **FATHER** *looks at her, happy to see her, while he makes her room out of string.*

She looks back at him, polite.

SCENE 4

The FATHER has completed the string room. He gestures for EURYDICE to enter. She enters.

EURYDICE: Thank you. That will do.

[*She nods to her FATHER. He doesn't leave.*]

Oh.
I suppose you want a tip.

[*He shakes his head.*]

Would you run a bath for me?

FATHER: Yes, Miss.

[*He exits the string room. EURYDICE opens and shuts her suitcase. She is surprised that nothing is inside. She sits down inside her suitcase.*]

SCENE 5

EURYDICE's GRANDMOTHER walks slowly in the background.
She looks refined, lost in thought.
She looks as though she is trying to remember a good joke.
She wears pearls and a stylish coat and hat from the 1930s.
No one notices her. She walks by.

SCENE 6

ORPHEUS writes his second letter.

ORPHEUS: Dear Eurydice,
I love you. I'm going to find you. I play the saddest music now that you're gone. You know I don't like writing letters. I'll give this letter to a worm. I hope he finds you.
Love,
Orpheus

SCENE 7

The FATHER enters the string room with a letter on a silver tray.

FATHER: There is a letter for you, Miss.

EURYDICE: A letter?

[*He nods.*]

FATHER: A letter.

[*He hands her the letter.*]

It's addressed to you.

EURYDICE: There's dirt on it.

> [*EURYDICE wipes the dirt off the letter. She opens it. She scrutinizes it.*
> *She does not know how to read it.*
> *She puts it on the ground, takes off her shoes,*
> *stands on the letter, and shuts her eyes.*
> *She thinks, without language for the thought,*
> *the melody: There's no place like home . . .*]

FATHER: Miss.

EURYDICE: What is it?

FATHER: Would you like me to *read* you the letter?

EURYDICE: "Read me the letter"?

[*Pause.*]

You mean with the raspberry jam?

[*The **FATHER** guides her off the letter, picks it up, and begins to read.*]

FATHER: It's addressed to Eurydice. That's you.

EURYDICE: That's you.

FATHER: You.
It says: I love you.

EURYDICE: I love you?

FATHER: It's like your tree.

EURYDICE: Tall?

[*The **FATHER** considers.*]

Green?

FATHER: It's like sitting in the shade.

EURYDICE: Oh.

FATHER: It's like sitting in the shade with no clothes on.

EURYDICE: Oh!—yes.

FATHER: [*Reading.*] I'm going to find you. I play the saddest music—

EURYDICE: Music?

[*He whistles a note.*]

FATHER: It's like that.

[*She smiles.*]

EURYDICE: Go on.

FATHER: You know I don't like writing letters. I'll give this letter to a worm.
  I hope he finds you.
    Love,
    Orpheus

[*ORPHEUS plucks one note on his guitar, tuning.*]

EURYDICE: Orpheus?

[*ORPHEUS plucks one note on his guitar, tuning.*]

FATHER: Orpheus.

[*A pause.*]

EURYDICE: That word!
It's like—I can't breathe.
Orpheus! My husband.

SCENE 8

EURYDICE's GRANDMOTHER walks slowly in the background.
She tries to remember how to do a dance step.
She wears pearls and a stylish coat and hat from the 1930s.
The stirrings of music from that era.
No one notices her. She walks by.

SCENE 9

EURYDICE and her FATHER in the string room.

FATHER: Did you get my letters?

EURYDICE: No! You wrote me letters?

FATHER: Every day.

EURYDICE: What did they say?

FATHER: Oh—nothing much. The usual stuff.

EURYDICE: Tell me the names of my mother and brothers and sisters.

FATHER: I don't think that's a good idea. It will make you sad.

EURYDICE: I don't care. I want to know.

FATHER: It's a long time to be sad.

EURYDICE: I'd rather be sad.

SCENE 10

ORPHEUS: Dear Eurydice,

Last night I dreamed that we climbed Mount Olympus and we started to make love and all the strands of your hair were little faucets and water was streaming out of your head and I said, why is water coming out of your hair? And you said, gravity is very compelling.

And then we jumped off Mount Olympus and flew through the clouds and you held your knee to your chest because you skinned it on a sharp cloud and then we fell into a salty lake. Then I woke up and the window frightened me and I thought: Eurydice is dead. Then I thought—who is Eurydice? Then the whole room started to float and I thought: what are people? Then my bed clothes smiled at me with a crooked green mouth and I thought: who am I? It scares me, Eurydice. Please come back.

Love,
Orpheus

SCENE 11

EURYDICE and her FATHER in the string room.

EURYDICE: Teach me another.

FATHER: Ostracize.

EURYDICE: What does it mean?

FATHER: To exclude. The Greeks decided who to banish. They wrote the name of the banished person on a white piece of pottery called ostrakon.

EURYDICE: Ostrakon.
Another.

FATHER: Peripatetic. From the Greek. It means to walk slowly, speaking of weighty matters, in bare feet.

EURYDICE: Peripatetic: a learned fruit, wandering through the snow.
Another.

FATHER: Defunct.

EURYDICE: Defunct.

FATHER: It means dead in a very abrupt way. Not the way I died, which was slowly. But all at once, in cowboy boots.

EURYDICE: Tell me a story of when you were little.

FATHER: Well, there was the time your uncle shot at me with a BB gun and I was mad at him so I swallowed a nail.

Then there was the time I went to a dude ranch and I was riding a horse and I lassoed a car. The lady driving the car got out and spanked me. And your grandmother spanked me too.

EURYDICE: Remember the Christmas when she gave me a doll and I said, "If I see one more doll I'm going to throw up"?

FATHER: I think Grammy was a little surprised when you said that.

EURYDICE: Tell me a story about your mother.

FATHER: The most vivid recollection I have of Mother was seeing her at parties and in the house playing piano. When she was younger she was extremely animated. She could really play the piano. She could play everything by ear. They called her Flaming Sally.

   [*EURYDICE's GRANDMOTHER walks by, in the distance.*]

EURYDICE: I never saw Grammy play the piano.

FATHER: She was never the same after my father died. My father was a very gentle man.

EURYDICE: Tell me a story about your father.

FATHER: My father and I used to duck hunt. He would call up old Frank the night before and ask, "Where are the ducks moving tonight?" Frank was a guide and a farmer. Old Frank, he could really call the ducks.

It was hard for me to kill the poor little ducks, but you get caught up in the fervor of it. You'd get as many as ten ducks.

If you went over the limit—there were only so many ducks per person—Father would throw the ducks to the side of the creek we were paddling on and make sure there was no game warden. If the warden was gone, he'd run back and get the extra ducks and throw them in the back of the car. My father was never a great conversationalist—but he loved to rhapsodize about hunting. He would always say, if I ever have to die, it's in a duck pond. And he did.

EURYDICE: There was something I always wanted to ask you. It was—how to do something—or—a story—or someone's name—I forget.

FATHER: Don't worry. You'll remember. There's plenty of time.

SCENE 12

ORPHEUS has a telephone on a silver tray.

ORPHEUS: For Eurydice—E, U, R, Y—that's right. No, there's no last name. It's not like that. What? No, I don't know the country. I don't know the city either. I don't know the street. I don't know—it probably starts with a vowel. Could you just—would you mind checking please—I would really appreciate it. You can't enter a name without a city? Why not? Well, thank you for trying. Wait—Miss—it's a special case. She's dead. Well, thank you for trying. You have a nice day too.

> [*He hangs up.*]

I'll find you. Don't move!

> [***ORPHEUS*** *touches an old-fashioned glow-in-the-dark globe.
> He passes his fingers along the lit up countries, looking for her.*]

SCENE 13

EURYDICE *and her* ***FATHER*** *in the string room.*

EURYDICE: Orpheus never liked words. He had his music. He would get a funny look on his face and I would say what are you thinking about and he would always be thinking about music.

If we were in a restaurant sometimes I would get embarrassed because Orpheus looked sullen and wouldn't talk to me and I thought people felt sorry for me. I should have realized that women envied me. Their husbands talked too much.

But I wanted to talk to him about my notions. I was working on a new philosophical system. It involved hats.

This is what it is to love an artist: The moon is always rising above your house. The houses of your neighbors look dull and lacking in moonlight. But he is always going away from you. Inside his head there is always something more beautiful.

Orpheus said the mind is a slide ruler. It can fit around anything. Words can mean anything. Show me your body, he said. It only means one thing. Or maybe two or three things. But only one thing at a time.

SCENE 14

*A big storm. The sound of rain on a roof. **ORPHEUS** in a rain slicker.*

ORPHEUS: [*Shouting above the storm.*] If a drop of water enters the soil
at a particular angle, with a particular pitch,
what's to say a man can't ride one note
into the earth like a fireman's pole?

> [*He puts a bucket on the ground to catch rain falling.*
> *He looks at the rain falling into the bucket.*
> *He tunes his guitar, trying to make the pitch of each note*
> *correspond with the pitch of each water drop.*
>
> ***ORPHEUS** wonders if one particular pitch*
> *might lead him to the underworld.*
> ***ORPHEUS** wonders if the pitch*
> *he is searching for might*
> *correspond to the pitch of a drop*
> *of rain, as it enters the soil.*
> *A pitch.*]

Eurydice—did you hear that?

> [*Another pitch.*]

Eurydice? That's the note. That one, right there.

SCENE 15

***EURYDICE** and her **FATHER** in the string room.*

EURYDICE: Tell me another story of when you were little.

FATHER: Let's see.

There was my first piano recital. I was playing "I Got Rhythm." I played the
first few chords and I couldn't remember the rest. I ran out of the room and
locked myself in the bathroom.

EURYDICE: Then what happened?

FATHER: Your grandmother pulled me out of the bathroom and made me
apologize to everyone in the auditorium. I never played piano after that. But I
still know the first four chords—let's see—

> [*He plays the chords in the air with his hands.*]

FATHER: Da Da *Dee* Da
Da Da *Dee* Da
Da Da *Dee* Da . . .

EURYDICE: What are the words?

FATHER: I can't remember.
Let's see . . .
Da da Dee Da
Da da Dee da . . .

[*They both start singing to the tune of "I Got Rhythm."*]

FATHER and EURYDICE: Da da Dee Da
Da da Dee Da
Da da Dee Da
Da dee da da doo dee dee da.

Da da Da da
Da da Da da
Da Da da Da
Da da da . . .

Da da Dee Da
Da da dee da . . .

THE STONES: WHAT IS THAT NOISE?

LITTLE STONE: Stop singing!

LOUD STONE: STOP SINGING!

BIG STONE: Neither of you can carry a tune.

LITTLE STONE: It's awful.

THE STONES: DEAD PEOPLE CAN'T SING!

EURYDICE: I'm not a very good singer.

FATHER: Neither am I.

[*EURYDICE's GRANDMOTHER walks by. EURYDICE sees her.*]

EURYDICE: Who is that?

FATHER: That's your grandmother.

THE STONES: Stop it!
Stop it!
Stop it!

EURYDICE: Why didn't you tell me?

FATHER: She can't remember you. She can't remember me either.

EURYDICE: So?

[*EURYDICE pulls her FATHER towards her GRANDMOTHER.*]

FATHER: I was going to tell you. There's plenty of time.

[*EURYDICE runs out of the string room towards her GRANDMOTHER.*]

Hello.

[*The GRANDMOTHER is silent.*]

This is Eurydice.
Your granddaughter.

EURYDICE: It's all right, you don't have to remember me. I don't mind.

GRANDMOTHER: Oh, I didn't like that. Because farming is hard work. When he opened a miniature golf course and two feed stores. To leave Iowa for Chicago. A doctor. In no hurry, oh boy was he taking his time. The last day of December—a little snow on the ground. All the way up the hill!

To the hospital. He was born with a subnormal temperature. Hurry up, hurry up! Oh, we thought we were the stuff. High on the hog. Care for a hump in the tulips? That's what John Berrymore said. Vera French was scandalized! Signed my copy of *Moby Dick*. Oh, and the piano. The piano! Every week. Through the mail. Matching blue chinchilla coats. Matching coats.

FATHER: I remember.

THE STONES: No you don't!
No you don't!
There were no coats!

GRANDMOTHER: No coats?

FATHER: Don't worry, Mother. There were coats.

[*EURYDICE's GRANDMOTHER looks at THE STONES.*]

GRANDMOTHER: Aren't they lovely children? No one looks after them, though. Well. I'm afraid I have to get to the lady's auxiliary meeting. Ring the back doorbell and I'll let you in to fix the furnace.

FATHER: Will do.

GRANDMOTHER: Good-bye, now.

FATHER: May I walk you to your meeting?

GRANDMOTHER: Oh, I don't know if that would be appropriate.

[*She looks at him. He seems respectable.*]

Well, all right. But no funny business.

FATHER: I promise.

EURYDICE: Good-bye.

[*EURYDICE hugs her GRANDMOTHER.*]

GRANDMOTHER: How funny! Like warm snow.

THE STONES: That is not allowed!

[*The FATHER and GRANDMOTHER walk off, arm in arm. They wave to EURYDICE. She waves back.*]

SCENE 16

EURYDICE walks into her string room.

The LORD OF THE UNDERWORLD enters on his red tricycle.
Music from a heavy metal band accompanies his entrance.
His clothes and his hat are too small for him.
He stops pedaling at the entrance to the string room.

CHILD: Knock, knock.

EURYDICE: Who's there?

CHILD: I am Lord of the Underworld.

EURYDICE: Very funny.

CHILD: I am.

EURYDICE: Prove it.

CHILD: I can do chin-ups inside your bones. Close your eyes.

[*She closes her eyes.*]

EURYDICE: Ow.

CHILD: See?

EURYDICE: What do you want?

CHILD: You're pretty.

EURYDICE: I'm dead.

CHILD: You're pretty.

EURYDICE: You're little.

CHILD: I grow downward. Like a turnip.

EURYDICE: What do you want?

CHILD: I wanted to see if you were comfortable.

EURYDICE: Comfortable?

CHILD: You're not itchy?

EURYDICE: No.

CHILD: That's good. Sometimes our residents get itchy. Then I scratch them.

EURYDICE: I'm not itchy.

CHILD: What's all this string?

EURYDICE: It's my room.

CHILD: Rooms are not allowed!
[*To THE STONES:*] Tell her.

THE STONES: Rooms are not allowed.

CHILD: I'll have your room removed.

EURYDICE: Please, don't.

CHILD: Oooh—say that again. It's nice.

EURYDICE: Please don't.

CHILD: Say it in my ear.

EURYDICE: [*Towards his ear.*] Please, don't.

CHILD: I like that.

   [*A seduction.*]

I'll huff and I'll puff and I'll blow your house down!

   [*He blows on her face.*]

I mean that in the nicest possible way.

EURYDICE: I have a husband.

CHILD: Husbands are for children. You need a lover. I'll be back.
[*To THE STONES:*] See that she's . . . comfortable.

THE STONES: We will!

CHILD: Good-bye.

EURYDICE: Good-bye.

THE STONES: Good-bye.

CHILD: I'm growing. Can you tell? I'm growing!

   [*He laughs his hysterical laugh and speeds away on his red tricycle.*]

SCENE 17

ORPHEUS writes a letter.

ORPHEUS: Dear Eurydice,
  I wonder if you miss reading books in the underworld.

  [*ORPHEUS holds the Collected Works of Shakespeare with a long string attached. He drops it slowly to the ground.*]

SCENE 18

EURYDICE holds the Collected Works of Shakespeare.

EURYDICE: What is this?

  [*She opens it. She doesn't understand it. She throws the book on the ground.*]

What are you?

  [*She is wary of it, as though it might bite her.
  She tries to understand the book.
  She tries to make the book do something.*]

[*To the book.*] What do you do?
What do you DO?!
I hate you!

  [*She stands on the book, trying to read it.*]

Damn you!

  [*She throws the book at **THE STONES**. They duck.*]

THE STONES: That's not allowed!

SCENE 19

*On his way to the string room,
the **FATHER** picks up the book.
He brushes it off. He looks at it.*

*Drops of water.
Time passes.
In the string room,
the **FATHER** teaches **EURYDICE** how to read.
She looks over his shoulder as he reads out loud.*

FATHER: We two alone will sing like birds I'th'cage.
When thou dost ask my blessing, I'll kneel down
And ask of thee forgiveness; so we'll live,
And pray and sing. . . .

SCENE 20

ORPHEUS: Eurydice!
Before I go down there, I won't practice my music. Some say practice. But practice is a word invented by cowards. The animals don't have a word for practice. A gazelle does not run for practice. He runs because he is scared or he is hungry. A bird doesn't sing for practice. She sings because she's happy or sad. So I say: store it up. The music sounds better in my head than it does in the world. When songs are pressing against my throat, then, only then, I will go down and sing for the devils and they will cry through their parched throats.
Eurydice, don't kiss a dead man. Their lips look red and tempting but put your tongue in their mouths and it tastes like oatmeal. I know how much you hate oatmeal.
I'm going the way of death.
Here is my plan: tonight, when I go to bed, I will turn off the light and put a straw in my mouth. When I fall asleep, I will crawl through the straw and my breath will push me like a great wind into the darkness and I will sing your name and I will arrive. I have consulted the almanacs, the footstools, and the architects, and everyone agrees. Wait for me.
Love,
Orpheus

SCENE 21

EURYDICE: I got a letter. From Orpheus.

FATHER: You sound serious. Nothing wrong I hope.

EURYDICE: No.

FATHER: What did he say?

EURYDICE: He says he's going to come find me.

FATHER: How?

EURYDICE: He's going to sing.

SCENE 22

Darkness.
*An unearthly light surrounds **ORPHEUS**.*
He holds a straw up to his lips in slow motion.

He blows into the straw.

The sound of breath.
He disappears.

SCENE 23

The sound of a knock.

LITTLE STONE: Someone is knocking!

BIG STONE: Who is it?

LOUD STONE: Who is it?

  [*The sound of three loud knocks, insistent.*]

THE STONES: NO ONE KNOCKS AT THE DOOR OF THE DEAD!

THIRD MOVEMENT

SCENE 1

ORPHEUS stands at the gates of hell.
He opens his mouth.

He looks like he's singing, but he's silent.
Music surrounds him.
The melody ORPHEUS hummed in the first scene,
repeated over and over again.

Raspberries, peaches, and plums drop from the ceiling into the River.
He keeps singing.

THE STONES weep.
They look at the tears, bewildered.
ORPHEUS keeps singing.

The LORD OF THE UNDERWORLD comes out of a trap door.

CHILD: Who are you?

ORPHEUS: I am Orpheus.

CHILD: I am Lord of the Underworld.

ORPHEUS: But you're so young!

CHILD: Don't be rude.

ORPHEUS: Sorry.

[*The CHILD picks up a plum from the ground and takes a bite.*]

CHILD: Pretty good!

ORPHEUS: Did you like my music?

CHILD: No. I prefer happy music with a nice beat.

ORPHEUS: Oh.

CHILD: You've come for Eurydice.

ORPHEUS: Yes!

CHILD: And you thought singing would get you through the gates of hell.

ORPHEUS: See here. I want my wife.

[*An OLD WOMAN comes out of a trap door. She is an unrefined master of the burlesque. She moves towards ORPHEUS in a lecherous way.*]

CHILD: [*To ORPHEUS.*] This is my mother.

ORPHEUS: Hello.

OLD WOMAN: [*To ORPHEUS.*] Lay your body down, my love,
Oh, lay your body down.
I'll love you hot and white and brown.
Oh, lay your body down.

I'll play your ribs a harp, my love,
your chest a violin.
I'll sound out all the air inside
the hollow place within.

   [*She mounts ORPHEUS.*]

I'll make your body sing, my sweet,
the praises due to love
until the wheeze of death
that blows in every lover's lungs.

That festive sad accordion,
goes wheezing up and down,
Oh lay your body down, my love,
Oh lay your body down.

CHILD: You'll have to excuse my mother. She gets this way. She has . . .
needs.

ORPHEUS: I want my wife. What do I have to do?

CHILD: You'll have to do more than sing. My mother has needs. Everyone
has needs. My mother liked your singing. She thought you had a real pretty
voice.

ORPHEUS: I'm not sure what you mean, sir.

CHILD: You scratch my mother's back, and I'll scratch yours, in common
parlance. When you're done, start walking home. Your wife just might be
on the road behind you. We make it real nice here. So people want to stick
around. As you walk, keep your eyes facing front. If you look back at her—
poof! She's gone. Do you understand me?

ORPHEUS: I look straight ahead. That's all?

CHILD: Yes.

ORPHEUS: That's easy.

OLD WOMAN: Good.

CHILD: Okay, then. I'll leave you two alone.

   [*The CHILD smiles. He exits. ORPHEUS and the OLD WOMAN are left
alone.
She moves towards him.*]

316

SCENE 2

EURYDICE and her FATHER.

EURYDICE: I hear him at the gates!
That's his music!
He's come to save me!

FATHER: Do you want to go with him?

EURYDICE: Yes, of course!

[*She sees that his face falls.*]

Oh—you'll be lonely, won't you?

FATHER: No, no. You should go to your husband. You should have grandchildren. You'll all come down and meet me one day.

EURYDICE: Are you sure?

FATHER: You should love your family until the grapes grow dust on their purple faces.
I'll take you to him.

EURYDICE: Now?

FATHER: It's for the best.

[*He takes her arm.*
They process, arm in arm, as at a wedding.
The sound of bells.
They are solemn and glad.
They walk.
They see **ORPHEUS** *up ahead.*]

Is that him?

EURYDICE: Yes—I think so—

FATHER: His shoulders aren't very broad. Can he take care of you?

[*EURYDICE nods.*]

Are you sure?

EURYDICE: Yes.

FATHER: There's one thing you need to know. If he turns around and sees you, you'll die a second death. Those are the rules. So step quietly. And don't cry out.

EURYDICE: I won't.

FATHER: Good-bye.

[*They embrace.*]

EURYDICE: I'll come back to you. I seem to keep dying.

FATHER: Don't let them dip you into the River too long, the second time. Hold your breath.

EURYDICE: I'll look for a tree.

FATHER: I'll write you letters.

EURYDICE: Where will I find them?

FATHER: I don't know yet. I'll think of something. Good-bye, Eurydice.

EURYDICE: Good-bye.

[*They move away.*
The **FATHER** *waves.*
She waves back,
as though on an old steamer ship.
The **FATHER** *exits.*

EURYDICE takes a deep breath. She takes a big step forward towards the audience, on an unseen gangplank.
She is brave.

She takes another step forward.
She hesitates.
She is all of a sudden not so brave.
She is afraid.

SHE LOOKS BACK.

She turns in the direction of her **FATHER,** *her back to the audience. He's out of sight.*]

Wait, come back!

LITTLE STONE: You can't go back now, Eurydice.

LOUD STONE: Face forward!

BIG STONE: Keep walking.

EURYDICE: I'm afraid!

LOUD STONE: Your husband is waiting for you, Eurydice.

EURYDICE: I don't recognize him! That's a stranger!

LITTLE STONE: Go on. It's him.

EURYDICE: I want to go home! I want my father!

LOUD STONE: You're all grown up now. You have a husband.

THE STONES: *TURN AROUND!*

EURYDICE: Why?

THE STONES: *BECAUSE!*

EURYDICE: That's a stupid reason.

LITTLE STONE: Orpheus braved the gates of hell
to find you.

LOUD STONE: He played the saddest music.

BIG STONE: Even we—

THE STONES: The stones—

LITTLE STONE: cried when we heard it.

[*She turns slowly, facing front.*]

EURYDICE: That's Orpheus?

THE STONES: Yes, that's him!

EURYDICE: Where's his music?

THE STONES: It's in your head.

[*ORPHEUS walks slowly, in a straight line, with the focus of a tightrope
walker.*

EURYDICE moves to follow him.
She follows him, several steps behind.

THEY WALK.

EURYDICE follows him with precision, one step for every step he takes.

She makes a decision.
She increases her pace.
She takes two steps for every step that ORPHEUS takes. She catches up to him.]

EURYDICE: Orpheus?

[*HE TURNS TOWARDS HER, STARTLED.*
ORPHEUS LOOKS AT EURYDICE.
EURYDICE LOOKS AT ORPHEUS.
THE WORLD FALLS AWAY.]

ORPHEUS: You startled me.

[*A small sound—ping.*
They turn away from each other, matter-of-fact, compelled.
The lights turn blue.
They walk away from each other
on extensive unseen boardwalks,
their figures long shadows.]

EURYDICE: I'm sorry.

[*They continue to walk on long lines away from each other, looking ahead.*]

ORPHEUS: Why?

EURYDICE: I don't know.

ORPHEUS: [*Syncopated.*]
You always clapped your hands
on the third beat
you couldn't wait for the fourth.
Remember—
I tried to teach you—
you were always one step ahead
of the music
your sense of rhythm—
it was—off—

EURYDICE:
I could never spell the word
rhythm—
it is such a difficult
word to spell—
r—y—no—there's an H in it—
somewhere—a breath—
rhy—rhy—

ORPHEUS: I would say clap on the downbeat—
no, the downbeat—
It's dangerous not
to have a sense of rhythm.
You LOSE things when you can't
keep a simple beat—
why'd you have to say my name—
Eurydice—

EURYDICE: I'm sorry.

ORPHEUS: I know we used to fight—
it seems so silly now—if—

EURYDICE: If ifs and ands were pots and pans
there'd be no need for tinkers—

ORPHEUS: Why?

EURYDICE: If ifs and ands were pots and pans
there'd be no need for tinkers—

ORPHEUS: Eurydice—

EURYDICE: I think I see the gates.
The stones—the boat—
it looks familiar—
the stones look happy to see me—

ORPHEUS: Don't look—

EURYDICE: Wow! That's the happiest I've ever seen them!

ORPHEUS: [*Syncopated.*]
Think of things we did:
we went ice skating—
I wore a red sweater—

EURYDICE:
Everything is so gray—
it looks familiar—
like home—
our house was—
gray—with a red door—
we had two cats
and two dogs
and two fish
that died—

ORPHEUS: Will you talk to me!

EURYDICE: The train looks like
the opposite of a train—

ORPHEUS: Eurydice!
WE'VE KNOWN EACH OTHER FOR CENTURIES!
I want to reminisce!

Remember when you wanted your name in a song
so I put your name in a song—
When I played my music
at the gates of hell
I was singing your name
over and over and over again.

Eurydice.

[*He grows quiet.*
They walk away from each other on extended lines until they are out of sight.]

SCENE 3

THE STONES: Finally.
Some peace.
And quiet.
Like the old days.
No music.
No conversation.
How about that.

[*A pause.*]

FATHER: With Eurydice gone it will be a second death for me.

LITTLE STONE: Oh, please, sir—

BIG STONE: We're tired.

FATHER: Do you understand the love a father has for his daughter?

LITTLE STONE: Love is a big, funny word.

BIG STONE: Dead people should be seen and not heard.

[*The FATHER looks at THE STONES.*
He looks at the string room.
He dismantles the string room, matter-of-fact. There's nothing else to do.
This can take time.
It takes time to dismantle a room made of string.
Music.
He sits down in what used to be the string room.]

FATHER: How does a person remember to forget.
It's difficult.

LOUD STONE: It's not difficult.

LITTLE STONE: We told you how it works.

LOUD STONE: Dip yourself in the river.

BIG STONE: Dip yourself in the river.

LITTLE STONE: Dip yourself in the river.

FATHER: I need directions.

LOUD STONE: That's ridiculous.

BIG STONE: There are no directions.

[*A pause. The FATHER thinks.*]

FATHER: I remember.
Take Tri-State South—294—
to Route 88 West.
Take Route 88 West to Route 80.
You'll go over a bridge.
Go three miles and you'll come
to the exit for Middle Road.
Proceed three to four miles.
Duck Creek Park will be on the right.
Take a left on Fernwood Avenue.

Continue straight on Fernwood past
two intersections.
Fernwood will curve to the right leading
you to Forest Road.
Take a left on Forest Road.
Go two blocks.
Pass the first entrance to the alley on the right.

Take the second entrance.
You'll go about one hundred yards.
A red brick house will
be on the right.

Look for Illinois license plates.
Go inside the house.
In the living room,
look out the window.
You'll see the lights on the Mississippi River.
Take off your shoes.
Walk down the hill.
You'll pass a tree good for climbing on the right.
Cross the road.
Watch for traffic.
Cross the train tracks.
Catfish are sleeping in the mud, on your left.
Roll up your jeans.
Count to ten.
Put your feet in the river
and swim.

[*He dips himself in the river.*
A small metallic sound of forgetfulness—ping.
The sound of water.
He lies down on the ground, curled up, asleep.

EURYDICE *returns and sees that her string room is gone.*]

EURYDICE: Where's my room?

[***THE STONES*** *are silent.*]

[*To* ***THE STONES.***] WHERE IS MY ROOM?
Answer me!

LITTLE STONE: It's none of our business.

LOUD STONE: What are you doing here?

BIG STONE: You should be with your husband.

LOUD STONE: Up there.

EURYDICE: Where's my father?

[***THE STONES*** *point to the* ***FATHER.***]

It's me! Orpheus looked! I've come back!
[*To* ***THE STONES.***] Why is he sleeping?

[***THE STONES*** *shrug their shoulders.*]

EURYDICE: I decided to come back!

LOUD STONE: He can't hear you.

LITTLE STONE: It's too late.

EURYDICE: What are you talking about?

BIG STONE: He dipped himself in the River.

EURYDICE: My father did not dip himself in the River.

THE STONES: He did!
We saw him!

LOUD STONE: He wanted some peace and quiet.

EURYDICE: [*To THE STONES.*] HE DID NOT!
[*To her FATHER.*] Listen. I'll teach you the words. Then we'll know each other again. Ready? We'll start with my name. Eurydice. E U R Y . . .

BIG STONE: He can't hear you.

LOUD STONE: He can't see you.

LITTLE STONE: He can't remember you.

EURYDICE: [*To THE STONES.*] I hate you! I've always hated you!
Shut up! Shut up! Shut up!
[*To her FATHER:*] Listen. I'll tell you a story.

LITTLE STONE: He can't hear you.

BIG STONE: He can't see you.

LOUD STONE: He can't remember you.

LITTLE STONE: Try speaking in the language of stones.

LOUD STONE: It's a very quiet language.
Like if the pores in your
face opened up and wanted to talk.

EURYDICE: Stone.
Rock.
Tree. Rock. Stone.

> [*It doesn't work.*
> *She holds her FATHER.*]

LOUD STONE: Didn't you already mourn for your father, young lady?

LITTLE STONE: Some things should be left well enough alone.

BIG STONE: To mourn twice is excessive.

LITTLE STONE: To mourn three times a sin.

LOUD STONE: Life is like a good meal.

BIG STONE: Only gluttons want more food when they finish their helping.

LITTLE STONE: Learn to be more moderate.

BIG STONE: It's weird for a dead person to be morbid.

LITTLE STONE: We don't like to watch it!

LOUD STONE: We don't like to see it!

BIG STONE: It makes me uncomfortable.

[*EURYDICE cries.*]

THE STONES: Don't cry!
Don't cry!

BIG STONE: Learn the art of keeping busy!

EURYDICE: IT'S HARD TO KEEP BUSY WHEN YOU'RE DEAD!

THE STONES: It is not hard!
We keep busy
and we like it
We're busy busy busy stones
Watch us work
Keeping still
Keeping quiet
It's hard work
to be a stone
No time for crying
No no no!

EURYDICE: I HATE YOU! I'VE ALWAYS HATED YOU!

[*She runs towards them and tries to hit them.*]

THE STONES: Go ahead.
Try to hit us.

LITTLE STONE: You'll hurt your fist.

BIG STONE: You'll break your hand.

THE STONES: Ha ha ha!

[*Enter the CHILD.*
He has grown. He is now at least ten feet tall.
He now resembles the NASTY INTERESTING MAN
more than he resembles the CHILD.]

CHILD: Is there a problem here?

THE STONES: No, sir.

CHILD: [*To EURYDICE.*] You chose to stay with us, huh? Good.

[*He looks her over.*]

Perhaps to be my bride?

EURYDICE: I told you. You're too young.

CHILD: I'll be the judge of that.
I've grown.

EURYDICE: Yes—I see that.

CHILD: I'm ready to be a man now. I'm ready—to be—a man.

EURYDICE: Please. Leave me alone.

CHILD: I'll have them start preparing the satins and silks. You can't refuse me. I've made my choice. My mother's needs have been satisfied. I'm ready to be a man now.

EURYDICE: Can I have a moment to prepare myself?

CHILD: Don't be long. The wedding songs are already being written. They're very quiet. Inaudible, you might say. A dirt-filled orchestra for my bride. Don't trouble the songs with your music, I say. A song is two dead bodies rubbing under the covers to keep warm.

[*He exits.*]

THE STONES: Well, well, well!

LITTLE STONE: You had better prepare yourself.

EURYDICE: There is nothing to prepare.

BIG STONE: You had better comb your hair.

LOUD STONE: You had better find a veil.

EURYDICE: I don't need a veil. I need a pen!

LITTLE STONE: Pens are forbidden here.

EURYDICE: I need a pencil then.

LOUD STONE: Pencils, too.

EURYDICE: Damn you! I'll push you in the water!

BIG STONE: Too late, too late!

EURYDICE: There must be a pen. There are. There must be.

[*She remembers the pen and paper in the breast pocket of her FATHER's coat.
She takes them out.
She holds the pen up to show the stones. She gloats.*]

EURYDICE: A pen.

[*She writes a letter.*]

EURYDICE: Dear Orpheus,
  I'm sorry. I don't know what came over me. I was afraid. I'm not
worthy of you. But I still love you, I think. Don't try to find me again.
You would be lonely for music. I want you to be happy. I want you to
marry again. I am going to write out instructions for your next wife.
  To my Husband's Next Wife:
  Be gentle.
  Be sure to comb his hair when it's wet.
  Do not fail to notice
that his face flushes pink
like a bride's
when you kiss him.
  Give him lots to eat.
He forgets to eat and he gets cranky.
  When he's sad,
kiss his forehead and I will thank you.
Because he is a young prince
and his robes are too heavy on him.
His crown falls down
around his ears.
  I'll give this letter to a worm. I hope he finds you.
  Love,
  Eurydice.

[*She puts the letter on the ground.*
She dips herself in the river.
A small metallic sound of forgetfulness—ping.
The sound of water.
She lies down next to her **FATHER,** *as though asleep.*

The sound of an elevator—ding.
ORPHEUS *appears in the elevator.*
He sees **EURYDICE.**
He is happy.
The elevator starts raining on **ORPHEUS.**
He forgets.
He steps out of the elevator.

He sees the letter on the ground.
He picks it up. He scrutinizes it.
He can't read it.
He stands on it.
He closes his eyes.

EURYDICE's GRANDMOTHER walks by slowly in the background.
Stirrings of music from the 1930s.
She looks refined, lost in thought.
She walks as though she is walking towards
something delightful—
she can't remember its name.
No one notices her.]

END OF PLAY

IPHIGENIA CRASH LAND FALLS ON THE NEON SHELL THAT WAS ONCE HER HEART

(A RAVE FABLE)

inspired by Euripides' *Iphigenia at Aulis*

CARIDAD SVICH

PHOTO: E. SVICH

CARIDAD SVICH is a playwright-songwriter-translator and editor of Cuban-Spanish, Argentine, and Croatian descent. She is the recipient of a 2002–2003 Harvard University Radcliffe Institute for Advanced Study Bunting Fellowship, and a TCG/Pew National Theatre Artist Grant. Recently premiered: her play *Antigone Arkhe* at The Women's Project in New York as part of *The Antigone Project* (originally commissioned by the theatre company Crossing Jamaica Avenue), and her multimedia collaboration (with Todd Cerveris and Nick Philippou) *The Booth Variations* at 59 East 59th Street Theatre, also in New York. Other credits include her play *Alchemy of Desire/Dead-Man's Blues, Any Place But Here, Fugitive Pieces,* and *Twelve Ophelias (a play with broken songs).* She is editor of *Trans-global Readings: Crossing Theatrical Boundaries,* a collection of conversations on media, culture, language, and performance (Manchester University Press/Palgrave). She is co-editor of *Conducting a Life: Reflections on the Theatre of Maria Irene Fornes* (Smith & Kraus), *Out of the Fringe: Contemporary Latina/o Theatre and Performance* (TCG), and *Theatre in Crisis? Performance Manifestos for a New Century* (Manchester University Press/Palgrave). Her translations of five plays and thirteen poems by Federico Garcia Lorca are published in *Impossible Theater* (Smith & Kraus). She holds an M.F.A. from UCSD, and is resident playwright of New Dramatists. She is on the advisory committee of *Contemporary Theatre Review* (Routledge/U.K.), and contributing editor of *TheatreForum.* She has been selected for inclusion in the *Oxford Encyclopedia of Latino History.*

From the Writer
CARIDAD SVICH

"We're all kids of E . . ."

This is a trance tale, of death and dying, of dancing and swaying, of divination, hypnosis, religion, and ecstasy. This is an "ambient translation" (to use musician/mixer Bill Laswell's phrase) of a story that has been translated from ancient Greek to French to Spanish to English and back again. In every version, the same impulse seems to arise: how to rescue Iphigenia? How can Iphigenia escape death? The impulse drives Iphigenia herself, who is a woman trapped inside a society which will not give her a voice, a body she can call her own unless she offers that voice, that body, to the state. Iphigenia is trapped by a notion of heroism that is not even hers, but which over time she has been made to believe is noble. This is a tale about cowardice, lies, celebrity, ambition, and sacrifice. And love. Above all, love. Deep, passionate, screwed-up love . . . .

ecstasy (from the Greek for "being placed outside): *a state of exaltation in which the self is transcended*

Iphigenia lives in the walls of culture and descends to find herself. She sets herself loose onto a world she doesn't quite understand, filled with the memory of knowing too well what awaits her in the unchanging pattern of fate, and wondering what she can do to wreck it now, if she can. Eleggua is a god in the Santeria pantheon, in the syncretized religion that was born in West Africa and Cuba and then made its way to Brazil, the U.S. and other countries. He stands at the crossroads with conch-shell eyes and an open brain. He watches her being split in two. If she prays to him, she will find her way. Iphigenia begins to pray.

The prayer is set against the unrelenting eye of the media, which haunts everyone. It is part of the camera's function to look, to fix the gaze. Cultures are built around its rapt stare, which entrances its citizens. The prayer gives way to a mistrust of faith. The nation becomes a cadaver as Iphigenia roams outside the socio-familial-political cage that has held her over time and centuries. The voice is made corporeal (through screams, through song). The blindfold is placed willingly—the body begs for relinquishment. It stumbles toward something which can only be found through its own desires. Iphigenia wishes to rediscover pleasure, and her body. The split persona longs for some kind of integration, but the state, which governs and censors bodies and dismantles them, makes it hard for her to do so.

Memory jars, as longed-for affection is recalled. A father much loved by his daughter will no longer touch his child because tears must be avoided, and a new face must be put forth to deny the old one. Guilt hides in Adolfo's cheek, and Iphigenia, who once again is faced with the specter of death, throws a veil over a traumatic mirror, a mysterious guide called Violeta Imperial, who recedes in the shadows, but will remember her.

A swirl of sounds mixes in the night air as the template of rave culture plays in the background, allowing for the consumerist totems of this culture—a drug called Ecstasy; designer clothes that elaborate on infantilism, kitsch, S & M, and retro hippie-ness to enact their own mad neo-mod game; a repetitive mix of loops and hard-driving beats that live somewhere between glam, disco, and Philip Glass—to spur feelings of departure. Listen up. It's Brian Eno and Kraftwerk time again. It's about letting the body rage in the in-between stage all night, and straight through morning. No doom and gloom here in this nocturnal wonderland. This is a new revolution that has been going on for more than thirty years.

Iphigenia departs her body in order to find it. The *fresa* girls, the ghosts of girls killed by the hundreds in border towns along the Americas, dream of Iphigenia caressing their wounded flesh. In the distance Achilles sings to no one and everyone, and smiles. Iphigenia listens, and sinks into his song. They meet as one, and so a lovers' duel of chance, fate, and betrayal is played out again on the empty stage of history.

I hold Iphigenia in my hands. She fits in my palm. Her breath moves through me. I look in the mirror. Is that her face . . . ?

Tremble. Blur.

I let her go.

This is the way.

A longer version of this essay, "Euripides' Children," was originally published in TheatreForum, No. 25, Summer/Fall 2004.

回回回

FOR MY PARENTS

回回回

PRODUCTION HISTORY

7 Stages' production of *Iphigenia Crash Land Falls* . . . , directed by Melissa Foulger. PHOTO: YVONNE BOYD AND 7 STAGES

Iphigenia Crash Land Falls on the Neon Shell That Was Once Her Heart (a rave fable) was originally created as a one-act in a lab session conducted by Charles L. Mee at ASK Theater Projects in Los Angeles in 1999. This version was developed by Actors Touring Company, England, and was presented at the Euripides Festival in Monodendri, Greece, sponsored by the National Theatre of Greece in July 2000 in a workshop directed by Nick Philippou. Subsequently, the piece was read at the Flea Theatre in New York City with musical arrangements and additional scoring by Michael Gladis.

The play received its world premiere at 7 Stages in Atlanta, Georgia (Del Hamilton, Artistic Director), on January 22, 2004. It was directed by Melissa Foulger; the set design was by Ashlee A. White; the costume, makeup, and tattoo design was by Emily Gill; the lighting design was by Rich Dunham; the sound and music design was by Brian Ginn; the video design was by Sabina Maja Angel; live action video design was by Heidi S. Howard; prop design was by Patrick Campbell; the dramaturg was Steven Yockey. The cast was as follows:

IPHIGENIA . . . . Heather Starkel
ACHILLES/FRESA GIRL 3 . . . . Adam Fristoe
ADOLFO/FRESA GIRL 1/VIRTUAL MC/SOLDIER X/
  GENERAL'S ASS . . . . Ismail Ibn Conner
CAMILA/VIOLETA IMPERIAL/HERMAPHRODITE PRINCE . . . Kristi Casey
ORESTES/FRESA GIRL 2/NEWS ANCHOR/VIRGIN PUTA. . . Justin Welborn

The play was subsequently produced at The LIDA Project in Denver in 2004 under Brian Freeland's direction.

SPECIAL THANKS to Maria Delgado, Erik Ehn, Melissa Foulger, Michael Gladis, Del Hamilton, DD Kugler, Todd London, Matthew Maguire, Charles L. Mee, Nick Philippou, Jose Rivera, Ted and Adele Shank, and Gary Winter.

CHARACTERS

IPHIGENIA, a spinning girl of privileged means, slightly feral, she's used to being in the public eye, she's breaking down.

ACHILLES, an androgynous rock star, beautiful and damaged (on video and live); also (may) play **FRESA GIRL 3, CHORUS***

ADOLFO, Iphigenia's father, a contained and ambitious general (on video and live); also plays **VIRTUAL MC,** an obscene, liquid, techno-trip-hop vision (on video); **GENERAL'S ASS,** a mask from the satyr play, part commedia role, part Burroughs-like dream; **SOLDIER X,** a mercenary, who has no passion left; and **FRESA GIRL 1, CHORUS**

CAMILA, Iphigenia's mother, a narcotized prop wife possessed of a fierce hauteur (on video and live); also plays **VIOLETA IMPERIAL,** an ageless apparition, a messenger and prophet, earthbound; and **HERMAPHRODITE PRINCE,** a mask from the satyr play, a little lost and seriously messed up

ORESTES, Iphigenia's baby brother, an addicted, spewing child with an adult voice (on video); also plays **NEWS ANCHOR,** a plastic icon on the TV (on video and live); **VIRGIN PUTA,** a mask from the satyr play, who is Iphigenia's other twin; **GLASS-EYED MAN** (on video), a specter; and **FRESA GIRL 2, CHORUS**

*The **FRESA GIRLS** should be played by men. If **ACHILLES** is not doubled, then **FRESA GIRL 3** should be played by an additional actor.

TIME

The present. An unnamed country in the Americas during a time of unrest.

SETTING

The frame of an aircraft hangar. Dust, dirt, and a stained party dress nailed to a battered wall. Oddly dyed carnations on the ground. The wall is jagged and impossibly high. A bank of surveillance cameras to one side: the silent, red eye.

NOTES

There are Spanish words and phrases incorporated in the text, which are either translated directly by a character or can be determined from context. No "Hispanic" accents should be used. Melodies to original songs may be obtained by contacting the author, or the lyrics may be reset by another composer.

CURTAIN SPEECH

*As the music lightens up, the voice of the **VIRTUAL MC** is heard.*

VIRTUAL MC: Listen up, children, or you will lose your way
    in this neo-psychedelic maze.
There are rules here, you see. Even in this grand party
    of electro-tragic proportions
We have to submit to authority. Are you willing to submit yourself to me?
Say you will, say you will, lovers and freaks,
Cause if you don't, you'll never please me, and I like to be pleased;
Don't we all like pleasure in this regulated state of supreme ecstasy?
Okay, okay, sluts, so this is what you do, this is what I need:
If you want to find your way out, there's the one you came in,
    and the way opposite,
Just like Orpheus and *pinche* Eurydice;
If you got a call waiting, a beep beep on your beep beep mobile
    ringing the latest tone from the acid police,
Shut that phone off, and shut it good. Vibrate in the boudoir of your dreams.
And if you like me, if you really, really give your head up
    for this baby border tragedy
then come on back, swing on by, tell your friends that the rave keeps spinning . . .
A little pseudo amyl nitrate and we're ripped fine to the bone
In this plastic synthetic hard-core fantasy we call a new century.
But hey, sluts, at the end of a crap-ass day
there's nothing sweeter than the feel of my virtual tongue
    on your scarred knees.

PROLOGUE

*In the distance is heard the chorus to Christoph Gluck's opera "Iphigenia in Aulis" (1774). It is remixed to a techno beat. In the background, an image is projected on screen: **IPHIGENIA**, in a pink Chanel outfit, sits next to **ADOLFO**, in a military coat. In the foreground, live, **ADOLFO** and **CAMILA** sit ready for a press photograph. **IPHIGENIA** is at their side. She wears a double of the pink Chanel outfit in the video image.*

ADOLFO: There was a young woman who lived in a small house by the sea, and the man who loved her.

> *[In the foreground, live, **ADOLFO** kisses **IPHIGENIA** on the lips.*
> *In the background, image on the screen: slowly, **IPHIGENIA**'s outfit begins to peel off her body and her skin begins to burn, while **ADOLFO** continues sitting, his body warm inside his coat.]*

He loved her so much that he would do anything for her.

> *[In the foreground, live, **ADOLFO** kisses **IPHIGENIA** on the lips again.]*

This man was her father. He was a general. He had lived with fame at his side all his life. He envied others. He even envied his daughter from time to time.

> *[In the background, image on the screen: A **GLASS-EYED MAN** with a cane in hand, a cane with a snake's head as its scepter, looks at **ADOLFO** and **IPHIGENIA** in flames.]*

The father could tell his daughter was not happy living in the small house, which held her day and night. He could see that the low ceiling hurt her head, and her feet couldn't move without touching the edge of the front door. He liked looking at her. He liked having her in the house for safekeeping.

> *[The cry of baby **ORESTES** is heard.]*

But he would catch her looking out. Out the window of the small house, and the garden, out toward the sea.

> *[In the foreground, live, **IPHIGENIA** looks out, away from her father, who holds her by the hand.]*

"Dear, sweet Iphigenia," the father would think.

> *[Title card on screen: "How much for her flesh?" Image on screen: The **GLASS-EYED MAN** looks at the burning woman who was once **IPHIGENIA**, and at the warm man who is **ADOLFO**. The **GLASS-EYED MAN**'s stare fills the screen. In the foreground, live, **IPHIGENIA**'s eyes are drawn to those of the **GLASS-EYED MAN** on the screen. Title card: "How much for her skin?"]*

The young woman suffered from vanity. But she never told her father.

[*In the background, image:* **IPHIGENIA**'s *face is reflected in the eyes of the* **GLASS-EYED MAN**.]

Iphigenia never told her father anything, despite his love for her. And her father thought of nothing, nothing at all.

[*In the foreground, live,* **ADOLFO, CAMILA,** *and* **IPHIGENIA** *are caught in the camera's flash, in tight, frozen smiles, as their photo is taken. In the background, image fills the screen: flames and a pink outfit made ash. In the distance, the chorus to Gluck's opera remixed to a techno beat fades. In the background, only the press photo captures the screen.*]

PART ONE

IPHIGENIA'S FLIGHT (FROM THE CITY)

*The voice of the **VIRTUAL MC** is heard calling out in the darkness:*

VIRTUAL MC: [*Voice-over.*] The next, the next sound that you hear . . . the next sound you hear will be . . .

[*Ambient trance music fades up. In the background on a screen, a TV NEWS ANCHOR sits behind a desk. He is "on the air."*]

NEWS ANCHOR: It is estimated that one thousand one hundred and ten people have dis dis disappeared today in this land of *guerrilleros* and other corporate revolutionaries. General Adolfo will not confirm the disappearances, but will say that all citizens must vote for him in this week's elections, which already threaten his current standing in office, as the opposition is starting to gain ground. The general will need a miracle to stay in office.

[*In the foreground, live, in a garden, **IPHIGENIA** is revealed in light: a blind-fold over her eyes, and a branch in her hand. She wears a designer dress. There is a piñata over her, dangling from the air. The piñata is of a large frog, with a long, relentless tongue.*]

But if some great personal tragedy were to befall him, it is possible the country would embrace him again. No one can resist the tug of the human heart. One senseless death, of a rich girl, and we will be united in grief, sorrow, and peace. Do you hear me, Iphigenia?

[*IPHIGENIA turns slightly toward the screen.*]

Do you hear me?

IPHIGENIA: Iphigenia was born centuries upon centuries ago.
I have watched her grow up, only to see her die over and over, story upon story.
I have lived inside her skin which has been rearranged so that she will always remain a young girl with delicate wrists and tender breasts.
And I have kept silent.
I have done my father's doing; I have honored my mother's way.
I have let myself be adored by the faraway gaze of a crowd who wants to get a look at the girl, a good look at the girl, whom fortune has blessed.
And now on this day of saints, all I want is to be free of Iphigenia, to be free of her certain fate.

[*The specter of **CAMILA**, **IPHIGENIA**'s mother, is glimpsed through the garden, and through the camera's surveillant eye. She shout-sings:*]

CAMILA: Iphigenia! Iphigenia! Where are you, daughter?

[*In the background, on the screen, the* **TV NEWS ANCHOR** *looks on. Behind him a blur of fragments of newscasts real and imagined swirls: a mix of atrocities and shiny products ready for mass consumption.*]

NEWS ANCHOR: In the city today, Iphigenia, the general's daughter, had a birthday. It was a private affair. Sources will not say what she was given, but it is estimated that there were a lot of presents, many of them from Cartier.

[*In the foreground,* **IPHIGENIA** *strikes the piñata. She takes off the blindfold. The piñata tips for a moment, then releases a shower of dead black birds and dried black petals. Freeze. Light splits* **IPHIGENIA** *into harsh angles.*]

Some say this will be Iphigenia's last birthday, although this could not be confirmed. Nothing can be confirmed these days. But one thing is certain: it will only be a matter of time before death will find our beloved girl. It's all a matter of time down here, in the "ass of the continent," called such by great military and diplomatic entities who have never lost the fever of their ambition, before death finds us all. Do you hear me, Iphigenia? Do you hear me?

[*The specter of* **CAMILA** *reappears through the garden.*]

CAMILA: Iphigenia! Iphigenia! Where are you going?

IPHIGENIA: I'm going to the northernmost point of the city.
I'm going to shake loose the bad luck piñata that has rained down on my head black birds and black wings. I'm going to dance in the safe of an aircraft hangar that's been turned into a ballroom.

[*In the near distance,* **ACHILLES** *is heard singing a vocal intro line from "The Deluge."*]

ACHILLES: [*Singing.*] War is over, the gods are over, everything, everything is over . . .

IPHIGENIA: And I'm going to let my body reign over the ragged people with their pale gleam.

[*Ambient trance music grows louder, as* **ACHILLES** *vocal line repeats and fades into the mix.*]

I'm going to ooh, and aah. I'm going to let my body be. And stop, stop being the general's daughter who lives in a walled-up garden by the light of the police.

[*The specter of* **CAMILA** *reappears. She is narcotized, half-asleep.*]

CAMILA: Iphigenia! Iphigenia! Where are you, daughter?

IPHIGENIA: Iphigenia is spun out onto a dark street. Fragments of words fall upon her as she tries to forget who she is . . . . Dear gods, let me be anyone but Iphigenia. Erase my memory, escape my death. Only let me spin, oh gods, let me spin, for what I seek is an angel's rest.

[*The specter of a heavily narcotized* **CAMILA** *fades through the surveillant eyes. She is a blurred image reduced to a tight close-up of soft teeth.*]

CAMILA: Iphigenia . . .

IPHIGENIA: Iphigenia sends herself into a phantasmagoric orbit: a wasteland of factories and blood-red tracks. She is nearing the northernmost edge of the continent.

[**CAMILA** *disappears through the distorted lens of the camera, as does the* **TV NEWS ANCHOR**'*s face from the screen. The red eye remains, occasionally blinking.*]

There is a cross painted on a factory wall, a large pink cross painted over a woman's scrawled name.

[*Light catches a pink cross that is painted on a factory wall's façade.*]

I look to it for comfort.

[**IPHIGENIA** *reads the name written on the wall. She sings:*]

Adina . . .

[**IPHIGENIA** *tries to touch the cross, which fades at her touch. Light catches another pink cross, another name. She sings:*]

Natacha . . .

[**IPHIGENIA** *tries to touch the cross. It fades.*]

Who are these girls?

[*Out of a pale neon strip,* **VIOLETA IMPERIAL** *appears. She is a prematurely aged woman. She pushes a small cart filled with half-cooked chicken pieces.*]

VIOLETA IMPERIAL: Girls in newly sewn dresses. I see them. Not like you. I can see you're different. That's a nice dress. You buy it? I make dresses. Cheap. You want me to make you a dress? I can make it right now. I got needle and thread. See? What kind of dress do you want, girl? With ruffles? Cut on the seam? Come. I make it for you.

IPHIGENIA: No.

VIOLETA IMPERIAL: Why not? You don't like Violeta? You don't like Violeta Imperial? Have a piece of chicken. I got legs and wings. For running, and flying, girl.

IPHIGENIA: I'm not hungry.

VIOLETA IMPERIAL: The aircraft hangar is a bit further on. You'll need your strength.

IPHIGENIA: How'd you know where I was headed?

VIOLETA IMPERIAL: You're all in shadow, girl. I can barely see you. . . . Hey, aren't you—?

IPHIGENIA: No.

VIOLETA IMPERIAL: Yes, you are. You've got the same face. You're the asshole's daughter.

IPHIGENIA: My father's not an ass—

VIOLETA IMPERIAL: Take a good look. Take a look at Violeta Imperial.

[*VIOLETA IMPERIAL* opens her jacket to reveal a map of scars on her body. The map of scars is also reflected in a photographic image on the screen.]

This is your father's doing.

IPHIGENIA: He wouldn't . . .

VIOLETA IMPERIAL: His men took me into a room and cut me open with a blade. You hear screams? In the dry streets convulsing with electric signs? Those are the screams of the innocent, the tortured, the disappeared that find themselves in a potter's field.

IPHIGENIA: You're not in a potter's field.

VIOLETA IMPERIAL: Some are left. We're reminders. A walking warning for others who might wish to speak up against anything, or simply live in peace.

IPHIGENIA: What did you do?

VIOLETA IMPERIAL: Nothing.

IPHIGENIA: What do you mean?

VIOLETA IMPERIAL: I was taken into a cold room of a quiet house made of loose cinder block and cut open for nothing. For kissing a girl. "*Pata*," they called me. "We'll give you *pata*," they said as they cut through my flesh. I prayed to *Eleggua*, the god who opens all doors, and leads all ways. The god who stands at the crossroads with his conch shell eyes staring in the light. You pray to him, girl?

IPHIGENIA: To *Eleggua*?

VIOLETA IMPERIAL: You should pray to him. I prayed.

"PRAYER TO ELEGGUA"

[*She sings.*] Mi Dios, mi salvador, mi Eleggua.
Tell me what to do. Tell me what to do.
And I will.
[*She speaks.*] And he said "Close your eyes." I fainted and let them cut me, as I dreamed about the girl I kissed, the sweet girl with brown eyes and a ruthless tongue who worked for the police, the sweet girl who betrayed me.

IPHIGENIA: I can have her reported. I can ask my father—

VIOLETA IMPERIAL: She's dead. I woke up in a field at the edge of the city with her body next to me. They had made a hole in her throat, and had pulled her tongue out through the hole.

She was to be my reminder.

I don't get much kissed now. Not with this body stitched up by an errant doctor's hands.

Needle, thread and a splash of violet water. That's what I got. Violeta Imperial, Royal Violet water. Hence my name. You want a piece of chicken? I got legs and wings.

IPHIGENIA: If my father knew—

VIOLETA IMPERIAL: We all love our fathers. It's a daughter's curse. But ask him what he's done. And what you do by carrying his name.

IPHIGENIA: I am not my father's daughter.

VIOLETA IMPERIAL: You're going to be a bastard now?

IPHIGENIA: Those men that took you and—they will be punished. I will see to it. I will do whatever I can—

VIOLETA IMPERIAL: What are you going to do, Iphigenia, with your midnight lipstick and designer sheen?

IPHIGENIA: I was kidnapped last year. I was taken from my bed, stuffed inside a sack, and tossed into a jeep. I remember my nose bleeding. There was the smell of honeysuckle in the air. I was taken out of the car and tossed onto a hard floor. I could feel the bruises forming themselves on my skin. I kept still in the darkness of the sack.

VIOLETA IMPERIAL: In stillness lies virtue.

IPHIGENIA: You believe that?

VIOLETA IMPERIAL: It's a saying.

IPHIGENIA: There were voices in another room. Loud voices, and boots. I could hear a song on the radio.

[*VIOLETA IMPERIAL begins to sing softly, underscoring.*]

"LA MORNA"

VIOLETA IMPERIAL: All the young girls
die in my arms
die like wounded birds
strangled by the palms.

IPHIGENIA: [*Continuing.*] A torch song, the kind of song my mother sings alone in her room at night with the trace of vodka on her lips. The door to the room opened. A young man's voice said "Wake up, *puta.*" When I opened my eyes, I felt strong hands poking at me. I screamed. The young man said, "Shh. Your father's sending the money." And he pulled from deep inside his pants pocket some twine, and tied my hands together, and he took a thin strip of cloth from inside another pocket, and he gagged me.

VIOLETA IMPERIAL: [*Singing softly.*] All the silent girls
scream in the night
letting their tongues fall
upon the broken moonlight.

IPHIGENIA: He pulled me into another room and flashed a camera in my eyes. "This is for the papers," he said. "They'll pay for a picture of you."

[*Shift to the screen:* TV NEWS ANCHOR *is standing against a backdrop of a field dotted with palms. Sporadic gunfire.*]

NEWS ANCHOR: General Adolfo is trying to negotiate with the drug cartel to end its operation Project Zero which is making all the rich flee the country in fear that their sons and daughters will be taken away and held for ransom. There is no greater fear than the fear of losing prominent investors in what would be the largest growth of the multinational dollar in this country's history, either that or having a loved one's ear sent in the mail. [*Through the screen.*] You hear that, Iphigenia?

IPHIGENIA: [*To the screen.*] What?

NEWS ANCHOR: Nobody misses you.

[*Fade on the screen. Back to . . .*]

IPHIGENIA: A car pulled up. My father's secretary was let in. He carried an envelope in his hands. It was stuffed with dollar bills. I was quickly untied. There were cuts on my arms and wrists from the twine, and piss down my legs. The young man took me by the arm and dragged me over to my father's secretary. "Don't worry. She's still a virgin, *cabron.*" The next day, my picture was in the papers—the photo the young man had taken of me sitting on the stool: tied, gagged, and hungry.

[*Front page news photo of tied-and-gagged* IPHIGENIA *is reflected on the screen.*]

My father refused to recognize me. "The papers will print anything," he said, "My daughter, my dear, sweet Iphigenia, never went through this." I looked at my father with the memory of the young man's hands on me. "Father, why won't you hold me?"

VIOLETA IMPERIAL: They might as well have killed you up there in the country.

[*Photo fades on the screen.*]

IPHIGENIA: What?

VIOLETA IMPERIAL: You can't do anything. You're at the mercy of your father. Like me. Like a piece of chicken. Want a taste?

IPHIGENIA: Here, and into the trash with you, remnant of the mutant underclass.

[*IPHIGENIA throws dollar bills at VIOLETA IMPERIAL and starts to walk away.*]

VIOLETA IMPERIAL: I'm only speaking the truth.

IPHIGENIA: Which truth is that? To think I almost believed you when you said all that about being cut up by my father's men . . .

VIOLETA IMPERIAL: I've the scars . . .

IPHIGENIA: Put there by someone else.

VIOLETA IMPERIAL: What are you saying—?

IPHIGENIA: I'm at no one's mercy, least of all my father.

VIOLETA IMPERIAL: You're blind, Iphigenia.

IPHIGENIA: I'd rather be blind than a walking corpse.

VIOLETA IMPERIAL: You're your father's daughter, after all.

IPHIGENIA: Shut up.

VIOLETA IMPERIAL: Cruelty is in your blood. Thanks to you this city will be smashed, and every soul will be uprooted from their homes.

IPHIGENIA: I gave you money. I don't want to hear anything else. I hear things all the time: voices, screams . . . I sit in my garden and cover my ears while my brother cries, because he needs his fix, he needs coca to keep him alive. He's not even a year old and he's already a junkie. Look at my tits. Go on. Touch. *Pata.*

VIOLETA IMPERIAL: Don't.

IPHIGENIA: I want you to. I want your hands on me. Squeeze them. Go on. Feel my tits.

VIOLETA IMPERIAL: You mock me.

IPHIGENIA: I mock myself. I breast-feed my own brother. . . . Keep your hands.

VIOLETA IMPERIAL: No.

IPHIGENIA: I disgust you?

VIOLETA IMPERIAL: There is no place for tenderness in my life.

IPHIGENIA: I don't know what tenderness is. I look for it. All the time. I close my eyes and pretend it exists. And then I think of those men, of how I was taken, of how my father . . .

VIOLETA IMPERIAL: Iphigenia, where are you going?

IPHIGENIA: To the northernmost edge.

VIOLETA IMPERIAL: It's better for young girls not to be seen. Come, Iphigenia.

IPHIGENIA: Take the money, Violeta. Devastate yourself for the promise of a blessed touch from this god-less girl . . .

VIOLETA IMPERIAL: The chicken is good, Iphigenia. Eat.

IPHIGENIA: Do not follow me.

[*VIOLETA IMPERIAL picks up the money, and recedes into the shadows. IPHIGENIA burns in the evening's acid glow.*]

IPHIGENIA: The aircraft hangar is minutes away. I can see it from here, from the dust and gravel road that ruins the soles of my Gucci shoes. I can hear the unrelenting pulse of music made to un-still the heart.

[*In the distance, ACHILLES is heard singing from the chorus of "The Deluge."*]

ACHILLES: [*Singing.*] And all the pretty girls
dance in the deluge.
All the pretty girls . . .

IPHIGENIA: Aah . . . the crimson lights and purple strobe will soothe me, will make this birthday more than just a creeping, convulsive treachery played on me by gods unwilling to grant me peace.

[*Light catches another pink cross, another name on a factory wall's façade.*]

Another pink cross, another name, and . . . I am bathed in the most heavenly . . . [*She sings.*] Yvonne . . .

[*THREE FRESA GIRLS emanate from the factory walls. On their foreheads, metallic crescents are painted. Their club dresses are slightly stained. They have "anime" eyes, and shiny red lips.*]

FRESA GIRL 1: [*Appearing.*] Yvonne? That's me.

IPHIGENIA: [*Singing.*] Dulce . . . Magaly . . . Luz . . .

FRESA GIRL 2: [*Appearing.*] Luz? I'm Luz.

IPHIGENIA: [*Singing.*] Aminta . . . Gladis . . . Yoli . . .

FRESA GIRL 3: [*Appearing.*] Hey. They finally spelled my name right. Yoli. With an "I" at the end, not a "y," like all the bastards think.

IPHIGENIA: Names upon names
Foreign to my tongue
I move them around in my mouth
As I run my hands across the smooth surface of these factory walls

FRESA GIRL 1: Is that where we are? I haven't been near the factory in a long time.

FRESA GIRL 2: The last thing I want is to be near a sewing machine.

FRESA GIRL 3: We're here because of her.

FRESA GIRL 1: Who?

FRESA GIRL 3: Iphigenia.

FRESA GIRL 2 and 1: That bitch.

FRESA GIRL 2: She's been nipped and tucked since the day she was born.

IPHIGENIA: [*Singing.*] Maria . . . Clotilde . . . Azul . . .

FRESA GIRL 1: Azul's gone, too?

IPHIGENIA: I feel these girls' hands on me. I feel myself pulled . . . Oh, their touch warms my skin . . .

FRESA GIRL 1: She must think we're living.

FRESA GIRL 3: With our throats cut?

FRESA GIRL 2: [*To IPHIGENIA.*] Hey girl, take a look at my jagged necklace.

FRESA GIRL 3: [*To IPHIGENIA.*] Take a good look, because your blood will be let soon.

IPHIGENIA: Everything is alive here. Everything I'd ever want . . .

FRESA GIRL 1: Oh. She doesn't know about us.

FRESA GIRL 2: What?

FRESA GIRL 1: The *fresa* girls.

FRESA GIRL 3: The ripe girls, like strawberries, who come from the deep country to work in the factories.

FRESA GIRL 2: Who spend twelve hours a day at a sewing machine.

FRESA GIRL 1: Come time to get paid

FRESA GIRL 3: Mere dollars a week

ALL FRESA GIRLS: We'd go out all night

FRESA GIRL 1: To remind ourselves

FRESA GIRL 3: What a bit of tenderness

FRESA GIRL 2: What a bit of
candy limbs and tainted love can . . .

ALL FRESA GIRLS: Do to wreck a body.

IPHIGENIA: I could be one of these girls. Who says I have to be Iphigenia?

FRESA GIRL 1: She really doesn't know about us.

FRESA GIRL 2: The shit girls.

FRESA GIRL 3: Who find themselves dead.

FRESA GIRL 2: Killed by anonymous hands.

FRESA GIRL 1: Outside the clubs, bodies violated and slashed on the dirt-gravel fields.

FRESA GIRL 3: And no one knows . . . anything. [*To* **IPHIGENIA**.] Because who is going to lift a hand to save a fresa girl?

IPHIGENIA: [*Singing.*] Nesha . . . Mora . . . Doris . . .

[*The stage becomes filled with pink crosses and scrawls of women's names floating in space in a montage which frames* **IPHIGENIA** *as she moves, transported.*]

FRESA GIRL 2: Let's scare her. Let's show her our wounds.

FRESA GIRL 1: No. She's too happy.

FRESA GIRL 2: Bitch. Look at that dress.

FRESA GIRL 3: Look at her swirl.

FRESA GIRL 2: It's a Chanel.

IPHIGENIA: The names of all these girls enter my brain.
I take them on, and undulate.
Oh. I am losing myself.

[**IPHIGENIA** *spins among the crosses.*]

FRESA GIRL 3: I remember dancing.

FRESA GIRL 1: Yeah?

FRESA GIRL 3: Like she's doing now.

FRESA GIRL 1: Remind me.

FRESA GIRL 3: I remember . . . hips, and torso . . .

FRESA GIRL 2: I remember arms. Lots of arms. And feet.

IPHIGENIA: I am losing every part of me,
and I'm all right.

FRESA GIRL 2: She's doing it all wrong.

FRESA GIRL 1: She doesn't know the moves. What can she know stuck in a garden all day?

FRESA GIRL 3: I like the way she dances.

FRESA GIRL 2: It's like she's stuck inside herself.

FRESA GIRL 3: Sexy-weird.

IPHIGENIA: I want to be just like you, girls.

FRESA GIRL 3: Like us?

IPHIGENIA: Names on a wall written by lovers who caress me.

FRESA GIRL 3: Caress us?

IPHIGENIA: You are beautiful girls.

FRESA GIRL 1: Hey, Iphigenia. Take us to the club, will you?

IPHIGENIA: To the club?

FRESA GIRL 1: You can get us in, can't you?

IPHIGENIA: I can get anyone in.

FRESA GIRL 1: Take us, then.

FRESA GIRL 3: And we will wear our hair in pillows.

FRESA GIRL 2: And our jackets square.

FRESA GIRL 1: And we'll go among the living again.

IPHIGENIA: Among the living?

FRESA GIRL 3: Take us dancing, Iphigenia.
Take us away from the walls of these factories where we left our skin.

IPHIGENIA: What?

FRESA GIRL 1 and 2: Take us.

ALL FRESA GIRLS and **IPHIGENIA:** Oohing and aahing into infinity.

[*ALL FRESA GIRLS freeze mid-dance. Burst of white noise as montage fades and music blares. IPHIGENIA is caught in the unending column of light of the aircraft hangar turned club. Her voice is amplified.*]

IPHIGENIA: The aircraft hangar opens an electric wound.
Somnambulant bodies throb under the crimson light.
Girls with cellophane chests
Put blue pacifiers in their tender mouths
While Diesel shirt boys twirl and hip-shake
To a subsonic bass line.

[*ALL FRESA GIRLS un-freeze, and move among the throbbing mass of shadows. FRESA GIRL 2 shouts over the club's noise.*]

FRESA GIRL 2: Hey. It's gotten faster.

FRESA GIRL 1: What?

FRESA GIRL 2: Everything. Look at the screen.

FRESA GIRL 3: What?

FRESA GIRL 2: The screen.

[*A rapid-fire succession of images pulsates on a large screen—innocent geometric shapes, atrocities, fragments of magazine ads, jumbles of letters.* **FRESA GIRL 1** *shouts:*]

FRESA GIRL 1: It's cool.

FRESA GIRL 2: What?

FRESA GIRL 3: Let's move.

[**FRESA GIRL 3** *writhes to the sound. The other* **FRESA GIRLS** *join her.*]

IPHIGENIA: A thousand factory girls move as the beat consumes
The everlasting promise of sundown.
Iphigenia feels her name escape through the pale insomnia
Of the fake Gucci, Prada, and Helmut Lang seething around her.
"Ooh, and aah," she lets herself cry

ALL FRESA GIRLS: Ooh, and aah . . .

IPHIGENIA: As the cobras hiss in the blue lounge to one side of the wide-open hangar.
I have become invisible in this flickering light.
Lick me.

[*IPHIGENIA joins the writhing* **FRESA GIRLS** *midst the throbbing shadows. On the screen, the images give sharp way to the digital image of the* **VIRTUAL MC,** *a floating face with an obscene mouth and liquid eyes, who speaks with the hollow, teasing sounds of a true lounge lizard cum DJ. He is the one who spins the music that keeps the writhing at maximum.*]

VIRTUAL MC: Lick her, cries the Virtual MC, and welcome to the end, *el fin,* finis!
Lick her face and rub up against the climactic wood of a planet about to go dust.
This is *el fin,* children. This is the end. Hold onto your *cojones.*
We got the sound to un-still your hearts blasting through tomorrow, *hasta mañana,* until the wee bleak trash-can Sinatra hours of a dim morning that will go on for days,
or until the next brutality brings us face-to-face.
Lick and moan, *cabrones.* Moan in the creep of this psychedelic light
Because here we do what the state says.

[*On a part of the screen, the video image of* **ACHILLES** *is found. He wears a close-fitting woman's tunic, fishnet stockings, boots, glitter lipstick, and black nails. He has a tattoo of a large tiger down one arm. His looped vocal line "War is over, the gods are over, everything, everything is over" is barely heard underneath the thumping bass.*]

Lift up your hands, guerrilla ballerinas showing off your Hello Kitty straps.
It's time to smash your heads, down those raspberry martinis, and dream of Mars,

Because "the war is over, the gods are over, everything . . ." *hijos* and *hijas de la gran puta*, is over.
So lick the scab off those valentine lips,

[*On the screen, **ACHILLES** offers his tongue to the **VIRTUAL MC**, who places a tab of E onto it. Simultaneously, live, **FRESA GIRL 2** places a tab of E on **IPHIGENIA**'s tongue, mid-dance.*]

and give your tits and dicks up for our very own war-bred pop myth with Day-Glo hips that move, oh yes.

IPHIGENIA: Who's he talking about?

FRESA GIRL 2: The boy with the body. See?

VIRTUAL MC: The boy with cherry crush, crazy love, hot pink, star red

[*The image of the **VIRTUAL MC** begins to disintegrate.*]

Lips.
Achilles.

[*A piercing sound. Large letters on the screen now read "Patria o Mierda." These letters bleed into smaller letters that read "Die for Your Country or You're Fucked." **ACHILLES** is on video on all the screens. Behind him mutated geometric shapes spin. He sings:*]

"THE DELUGE"

ACHILLES: Stoked up on the cocaine
Living with a migraine
Looking for an end to end all my days.
Strolling through the backwoods
Living on the wild glue
Taking what I can for what I pay.

Swimming with the *ratas*
Behind *la policia*
Cutting white snow on the hoods of *la migra*
Pulling small razors from inside *mi lengua*
Cutting young men *en carne viva*

And all the pretty girls
Dance in the deluge
All the pretty girls
Kiss . . .
Why don't you kiss me?

Killing for a bum rush
Off a lousy bum fuck
Putas in the corner
Begging for a blow job

Caught in *la tijera*
Of a road *sin pena*
Spinning my brain: oh what can I, what can I . . . ?

And all the pretty girls
Dance in the deluge
All the *fresa* girls Die . . .

> [*The FRESA GIRLS swoon to the image of ACHILLES on video on the screens. He continues singing:*]

Why don't you die . . . ?

> [*ACHILLES looks at IPHIGENIA through the screen, and sings:*]

Where is your father, girl?
Where is your father?
He's left you all alone in the world.
Tell me.

> [*IPHIGENIA is about to answer ACHILLES' image, but ACHILLES kisses the camera's eye, and sings:*]

And all the pretty girls
Dance in the deluge
All the pretty girls
Kiss . . .

> [*ACHILLES' image freezes on the video. Time shift. Pin spot on IPHIGENIA, still.*]

IPHIGENIA: Hold me. My limbs ache. I tremble. I blur. One hundred and twenty beats per minute: my heart goes.

> [*ACHILLES' video image fades.*]

The *fresa* girls surround me with their stained skirts, and metallic foreheads. I move, pulse, escape. The inside of my chest bursting. I tease myself into thinking no one can find me here. And then I see you standing beside me, Father, except you don't look like yourself. You wear a smart coat and tall hair, and you're smiling with razor teeth, Father.
You place your hand over my eyes, and whisper "Shh, angel."

> [*The FRESA GIRLS hiss.*]

ALL FRESA GIRLS: Shh.

IPHIGENIA: As a knife comes into my back and I feel myself fall a thousand feet down

ALL FRESA GIRLS: Shh.

IPHIGENIA: A thousand feet into darkness. And you don't say anything, Father. You don't even say

ALL FRESA GIRLS: Shh.

IPHIGENIA: You just smile. With white snow on your tongue.
I am laser-lit. Suspended. A hundred million particles of light. Iphigenia is dying. Hold me.

[*Time shift. Spot dims on* **IPHIGENIA** *and the* **FRESA GIRLS** *as they move in an ecstatic orgy. The* **VIRTUAL MC** *reappears on the large screen.* **ACHILLES'** *image is no longer on the screen. Only geometric shapes remain where his video face and body used to be.*]

VIRTUAL MC: Well, sluts, it looks like our kissing boy with the pretty chemise has "disappeared,"
as our dear general Adolfo likes to say. Isn't that right, Iphigenia?

IPHIGENIA: What?

VIRTUAL MC: Not to worry. Our blinking eyes may catch the lipstick trace of this divining angel in the not-too-distant time we have to say good-bye.
Every state has someone to absolve them of their debts, and well, we've got Achilles,
The glam messiah for the savagely tricked.
A little moving of those hips, and everyone swoons on the beat.
Plunge, my million and one disgraced ones, my sorry children who live day to day. Here's some ooh and aah to send you into *la mala noche* of my sad dreams.

[**VIRTUAL MC'***s face fades.*]

IPHIGENIA: Where did they take him? Where's Achilles?

FRESA GIRL 1: I don't know. Who knows anything around here?

FRESA GIRL 2: He's got *chulo* legs, eh?

FRESA GIRL 1: Yeah. And in that slip. You can see right up his . . .

FRESA GIRL 2: *"El chulo culo,"* that's what I used to call him.

IPHIGENIA: What?

FRESA GIRL 1: The ready ass.

IPHIGENIA: Where is he?

FRESA GIRL 3: You don't want him, girl. He's inside the screen. Stay here. We'll keep dancing.

IPHIGENIA: He couldn't have disappeared.

FRESA GIRL 1: You want to see Achilles? You want to kiss the twisted boy with the golden eyes?

IPHIGENIA: You know where he is?

FRESA GIRL 1: Give us the dress.

IPHIGENIA: I have to go.

FRESA GIRL 2: You're not going anywhere, Iphigenia.

[*The* **FRESA GIRLS** *attack* **IPHIGENIA**. *They tear off her dress, nylons, shoes, earrings. As they do so, they improvise a chant. Everything is captured by the camera's eye.*]

ALL FRESA GIRLS: In the land of the living, the dead will reign.

FRESA GIRL 1: Yvonne,

FRESA GIRL 2: Luz,

FRESA GIRL 3: Yoli . . .

FRESA GIRL 1: A litany of the dead,

FRESA GIRL 2: Of the forgotten and unforgiving
Who have been left to walk

FRESA GIRL 3: without graves.

[**IPHIGENIA** *is left wearing only a slip, as the* **FRESA GIRLS** *toss her clothes about and speak-sing their chant.*]

FRESA GIRL 3: Mmm. Gucci.

[**FRESA GIRL 3** *exits with* **IPHIGENIA**'*s shoes.*]

FRESA GIRL 2: Mmm. Dior.

FRESA GIRL 1: Mmm. Prada.
For her.

FRESA GIRL 2: For her

FRESA GIRL 1 and 2: Everything is for her . . .

[*The remaining* **FRESA GIRLS** *exit in the fading somnambulant beat. Silence.* **IPHIGENIA** *sings:*]

"PRAYER TO ELEGGUA (REPRISE)"

IPHIGENIA: Mi Dios, mi salvador, mi Eleggua . . .
Tell me what to do.
And I won't ask for anything anymore,
But your love.

[*A close-up of* **IPHIGENIA** *on the screen.* **ACHILLES** *is heard singing, live.*]

"THE DELUGE (REPRISE-VARIATION)"

ACHILLES: And all the pretty girls
dance in the deluge

All the pretty girls
Cry . . .

> [*ACHILLES appears in performance mode. He is wearing the same tunic, boots and makeup as in his video. A pacifier hangs from his neck. He sings:*]

All the pretty girls
Sing in the darkness
Letting their torsos fall
Upon the morning's light.

> [*ACHILLES sees* **IPHIGENIA**. *His face is captured on the screen in a still frame as he walks away.* **IPHIGENIA** *follows him.*]

PART TWO
IPHIGENIA IN BETWEEN

A field outside the aircraft hangar. Night. **IPHIGENIA** *and* **ACHILLES**, *both in their slips, are entwined. They are back-lit with neon, seen in silhouette.* **FRESA GIRL** *1 and 2 appear. They each wear a version of the Chanel dress they tore from* **IPHIGENIA.**

FRESA GIRL 1 and 2: Iphigenia moves through the killing fields unaware of the bones in her midst.

FRESA GIRL 2: She slums with the boy who glitters at the furthest edge of the city.

FRESA GIRL 1: Cherry crush, crazy love, hot pink, star red:

FRESA GIRL 1 and 2: their lips bleed.

FRESA GIRL 1: Tattoo me a cross, Iphigenia.

[*FRESA GIRL 1 disappears as FRESA GIRL 2 transforms into the TV NEWS ANCHOR, while a montage shows CAMILA and ADOLFO multiplied in the eyes of the surveillance cameras. The TV NEWS ANCHOR is outside the screen.*]

"(DARK TRANCE IN THE) HOUSE MIX"

NEWS ANCHOR: In Chalkis or Pylos or wherever else floods and famine . . . Hundreds of thousands are killed. There is no count. No numbers have been released in what is the most devastating disaster of the century which changes every minute. This is a long century and some people like to count the days. Though you won't find me, ladies and gentleman; I have been covering this story for so long I don't get to count. I just look for the airplane to get me the hell out. One more body dug up from a grave and I will shoot them all to splinters.
Put the magazine in and let me rip. You hear that, General? General Adolfo?

[*ADOLFO is inside the screen. The TV NEWS ANCHOR remains live outside the screen.*]

ADOLFO: I recommend a good plate of chicken broth with potatoes, and yams.

NEWS ANCHOR: Is that your official statement, General?

ADOLFO: I think it's safe to say that when we move on, there will not be a shred of evidence we were here.

NEWS ANCHOR: What about your daughter, General?

ADOLFO: My daughter?

NEWS ANCHOR: She's been missing for hours. Some say she's been kidnapped again. Some say you have engineered the kidnapping yourself to have her killed, and thus win your people's eternal sympathy, not to mention, the election.

ADOLFO: My daughter is at home, where she always is.

NEWS ANCHOR: Like when she was taken last year, General?

ADOLFO: No harm will ever come to my daughter. Not from my hands.

NEWS ANCHOR: Is that what your wife says, General?

[*CAMILA is inside the screen, an oversize cocktail glass in hand.*]

CAMILA: I hope they plaster her body all over the papers. Hang her up, boys. Get some bamboo and string up my Iphigenia. Screw her 'til sundown.

ADOLFO: A general has many burdens.

[*ORESTES can be heard crying from inside the box.*]

NEWS ANCHOR: Like your son, General?

ADOLFO: My son?

NEWS ANCHOR: Orestes.

ADOLFO: He's a baby. He doesn't know about such things.

NEWS ANCHOR: General?

ADOLFO: The name is Adolfo. Leave us in peace.

[*ADOLFO and CAMILA disappear inside the darkness of the screen. TV NEWS ANCHOR, not knowing what to do, stands for a moment, then decides to follow them into the screen. End of "House Mix" section. Neon rises. IPHIGENIA and ACHILLES are seen. The camera watches them.*]

ACHILLES: Slip me your dick.

IPHIGENIA: I don't have one.

ACHILLES: I thought the rich had everything.

IPHIGENIA: Don't be coarse.

ACHILLES: Does it offend you?

IPHIGENIA: Stop.

ACHILLES: You're in me. I can't.

IPHIGENIA: I like your skin.

ACHILLES: Taste it. Lick it. Do what you will. I am used to being devoured. Slip me your tongue.

IPHIGENIA: I don't . . .

ACHILLES: You want it all, girl. That's why you asked for the stars to come down and screw you.
You see this? This is my hand. I'm going to stick it—

IPHIGENIA: Stop.

ACHILLES: I'm crude. I'm what you want. Lick me. Suspend yourself in my cradle.
I am falling down like a mutant star hungry for skin.
You are the girl-boy-thing I need. This is another sex we're making, twin. Kiss me.

IPHIGENIA: . . . And my tongue moves through your open mouth sinking into saliva and teeth and all that makes you.
I watched you last night, my eyes were transfixed. I caught a glimmer of myself in them.
At first I didn't realize I was looking at my eyes, but then I looked again, and realized
they were my eyes transformed by yours, burned by your iris. My slip became yours, and our legs became one.

ACHILLES: There's death here.

IPHIGENIA: Where?

ACHILLES: All around. Bones. Bodies torn, buried in graves. Left by men hungry for money.
You know the kind I mean. Like those men that took you in the night . . .

IPHIGENIA: I don't want to think about that.

ACHILLES: Everyone knows the girl framed in the magazine: Buy her picture. She'll suffer for you as you sleep.

IPHIGENIA: Did you buy a picture of me?

ACHILLES: Pleasure comes in ways you can't even dream. The pursuit of it blasts us all.
Rip down the wall and you will see one hundred million atrocities
Perpetuated and executed in the name of pleasure.
I've been asked to be frozen, caught in an image on a screen.
"Just sing, convulsive angel. Sing that line over and over. Move those hips.
But don't make a sound, a true sound, because we will kill you."
So I spit poison in the night. I graffiti my skin. I fuck my own celebrity.

IPHIGENIA: There are better pictures of me than the one you bought. I can show you.

ACHILLES: Zig down my spine, twin. Let's make love on top of the dead bodies that have been lying beneath us for centuries. Because that's what you want—a touch of the obscene.

[*The tabloid photo of IPHIGENIA, bound and gagged, is projected onto ACHILLES' slip, his body.*]

IPHIGENIA: The fields disappear in a sting of light that bleeds colors foreign to the eyes.
Mouths eclipse each other. Consume me.

ACHILLES: Can you come straight through me? In a flash?

IPHIGENIA: I will burn you.

ACHILLES: Slow down.

IPHIGENIA: I want to kill the tabloid girl that envelops your skin. I want to bury her in your mouth and thighs . . .

ACHILLES: You move too fast, girl.

IPHIGENIA: You bought my picture when it was sold on the street. Did you make love to me then?
Did you press the picture of me against yourself and blush at the thought of me bound—?

ACHILLES: Sink to me.

IPHIGENIA: I will sink and get rid of every bit of me.

ACHILLES: What is your weakness? I will give it to you.

[*The tabloid photo engulfs them. FRESA GIRL 1 and 2 appear. They are in yet another version of the Chanel dress, which is becoming unrecognizable now— barely a trace of its origin.*]

FRESA GIRL 1: Iphigenia stirs inside the flesh of the boy with the glitter lips flaunting her sex for all to see.

FRESA GIRL 2: Where do you think you are, girl? You don't get anything here for free.

FRESA GIRL 1: A tabloid lover will find you on the debris river and sink you into the junk food wrappers
Stretched past greasy fingers and salty lids itching for sleep.

FRESA GIRL 2: Tattoo me a tiger, Iphigenia. Just like the one Achilles has down his arm. Give me its milk.

[*The FRESA GIRLS disappear. The tabloid photo fades in flickering black-and-white.*]

IPHIGENIA: You are the sorriest boy I ever met. What's that you got in your bloodstream: nicotine, caffeine, coke, glue?

ACHILLES: A Mars bar, some acid tabs, and E.

IPHIGENIA: All muscle. Didn't you used to be an archer, boy? A wing-footed archer with limbs traced in golden armor?

ACHILLES: I used to be everything.

IPHIGENIA: A regular dream.

ACHILLES: Curl around me.

IPHIGENIA: I don't want anything but your tongue.

ACHILLES: Coax it. It will sing for you. I am easily won.

IPHIGENIA: Scar.

ACHILLES: Feel nothing but my tongue.

IPHIGENIA: Right on the eyebrow. You were cut once.

ACHILLES: I cut myself with a blade when I was young. I wanted to brand myself before someone else would. I wanted a mark on me.
Everyone is branded here. Even those that pretend they are unmarked.
So, I cut. On the slant of my brow. Until blood ran into my eyes. Here. Look at it. Burn your candle on it. It says I am a boy and girl at once.
And what I do, who I am, is punishable by death, or worse: endless repetition.
[*He sings:*] War is over, the gods are over, everything, everything is over . . .
[*He speaks:*] The crowd trips and sways for a trick of my light. Take me into your bloodstream.

IPHIGENIA: Erase me.

[*She takes a tab of acid from his tongue with a kiss.*]

ACHILLES: We are night-crawling, girl.
Your heart is racing inside the soft part of my chest
Where you hide like a drop of rain
And never cry.

[*ACHILLES and IPHIGENIA are rapt in the night air. They are suspended in light, and sleep. Time shift. Light comes up on silver clouds and jagged trees. Three masks appear between the trees, as if this were a stage set: A VIRGIN PUTA, who sounds like IPHIGENIA, a HERMAPHRODITE PRINCE, who sounds like ACHILLES, and the GENERAL'S ASS, who sounds like ADOLFO. The GENERAL'S ASS carries a thin whip in his hand. This is played as a commedia piece for an imaginary audience. It is IPHIGENIA's nightmare hallucination.*]

VIRGIN PUTA: The Story of a Virgin Puta

HERMAPHRODITE PRINCE: The Hermaphrodite Prince

GENERAL'S ASS: And the Blessed General's Ass

VIRGIN PUTA, HERMAPHRODITE PRINCE, and GENERAL'S ASS: A satyr play.

[*The 'satyr play' begins.*]

VIRGIN PUTA: You should've seen the sky. It was beaming green. Pulse pulse . . . I was dancing.

GENERAL'S ASS: Slap.

VIRGIN PUTA: Oh, father, don't hurt me. I only wish to please.

GENERAL'S ASS: Don't you like my ass, daughter?

VIRGIN PUTA: I love it, but you can't walk around with it out in the open all night.

GENERAL'S ASS: Slap.

VIRGIN PUTA: Oh, Father, don't hurt me.

GENERAL'S ASS: You were made to be sacrificed, daughter. Open your legs.

VIRGIN PUTA: But how will I stand, Father?

GENERAL'S ASS: You will be bent.

VIRGIN PUTA: Is that the custom, Father?

GENERAL'S ASS: It is for all the virgin *putas.*

VIRGIN PUTA: How long will you stay in me, Father?

GENERAL'S ASS: Until you've learned the truth about me.

VIRGIN PUTA: I prefer lies, Father. They go down so much better.

GENERAL'S ASS: Slap.

VIRGIN PUTA: Do I offend, Father?

GENERAL'S ASS: You have been made meat.

VIRGIN PUTA: I am still your daughter. Love me.

GENERAL'S ASS: You must resist me.

VIRGIN PUTA: I will.

[*The* **HERMAPHRODITE PRINCE** *dances, lost in himself, while in real time* **ACHILLES** *slips away unnoticed from* **IPHIGENIA***'s side, and disappears past the edge of the field.*]

HERMAPHRODITE PRINCE: [*Singing.*] "Bathroom girl, oscillate those eyelids. Smuggle my gaze."

GENERAL'S ASS: Who sings? Tell me. Speak.

VIRGIN PUTA: It is a prince, Father.

GENERAL'S ASS: This bitch?

HERMAPHRODITE PRINCE: [*Singing.*] "Silver strands of moaning flesh will I be . . ."

GENERAL'S ASS: Do not dance for me.

HERMAPHRODITE PRINCE: Don't you want to watch me?

GENERAL'S ASS: What?

HERMAPHRODITE PRINCE: Make love to your daughter.

VIRGIN PUTA: Oh, Father, please.

HERMAPHRODITE PRINCE: I'll be any sex you want me to be.

GENERAL'S ASS: Scratch her with your fingernails. Suckle her, boy.

HERMAPHRODITE PRINCE: [*By rote.*] Whore. Bitch.

VIRGIN PUTA: More.

HERMAPHRODITE PRINCE: Iphigenia.

VIRGIN PUTA: Don't call me that.

HERMAPHRODITE PRINCE: Isn't that your name?

GENERAL'S ASS: There are no names here. Only bodies. Do as you are told.

[*The **GENERAL'S ASS** strikes the **HERMAPHRODITE PRINCE** on the ass with the whip.*]

HERMAPHRODITE PRINCE: I bleed.

GENERAL'S ASS: Hands on her throat. That's right.

VIRGIN PUTA: But, Father . . .

[*The **HERMAPHRODITE PRINCE** chokes the **VIRGIN PUTA**. She falls limp.*]

HERMAPHRODITE PRINCE: [*Singing.*] Iphigenia . . .

[*The **HERMAPHRODITE PRINCE** collapses.*]

GENERAL'S ASS: Her double. But you've done the trick, bitch. Now I will tell you how she should be killed:
Lead her into a quiet house off the main road. She will follow you if you tell her a lover waits for her. Then close the door, blind her, and pierce her with a knife.
She's not my daughter anymore. She has abandoned me.

IPHIGENIA: Father?

GENERAL'S ASS: I love you so much I will do anything for you. Anything.

IPHIGENIA: Father, hold me!

[*The mask of the **GENERAL'S ASS** spews black birds from its hole. **IPHIGENIA** screams. The **HERMAPHRODITE PRINCE**, the **VIRGIN PUTA**, and the **GENERAL'S ASS** drop their masks to reveal **VIOLETA IMPERIAL**, **FRESA GIRL 2**, and **FRESA GIRL 1**. End of 'Satyr play.'*]

Iphigenia comes back to me. Her story is fresh upon my skin. Destroy me.

FRESA GIRL 1: What's the matter, girl? Didn't you like our show?

IPHIGENIA: Scavenge me. Wreck my heart.

FRESA GIRL 2: Who are you talking to, girl?

IPHIGENIA: Money. Do you need money?

VIOLETA IMPERIAL: What are you saying, child?

IPHIGENIA: Under my bed. I have new bills that aren't even in circulation yet.

FRESA GIRL 1: We don't want anything.

IPHIGENIA: What do you mean? Everybody wants . . .

VIOLETA IMPERIAL: We don't need anything, child.

FRESA GIRL 2: We disappeared a long time ago. Nobody needs anything from us.

IPHIGENIA: What are you—? Your throat . . .

FRESA GIRL 2: Razor. Right on the breath.

IPHIGENIA: You're dead?

FRESA GIRL 1: We're all dead.

FRESA GIRL 2: Another pink cross, another name . . .

[*FRESA GIRL 1 and 2 start to walk away.*]

VIOLETA IMPERIAL: The country needs you, Iphigenia. We need a girl like you to give us hope.

IPHIGENIA: What?

[*VIOLETA IMPERIAL touches IPHIGENIA's forehead with the palm of her hand: a benediction.*]

VIOLETA IMPERIAL: You're dead.

[*VIOLETA IMPERIAL joins the FRESA GIRLS. They walk away, and disappear among the jagged trees. Time shift. IPHIGENIA is awake, trembling. ACHILLES emerges from a part of the field. He is in a state of delirium. He is high.*]

"LIQUID HAZE"

ACHILLES: [*Singing.*] Wake me at dawn pierced through feeling
Reinscribe the terror
Of the pulsing light.

IPHIGENIA: Achilles, did you know . . . ? Did you know we were being watched?

ACHILLES: [*Singing.*] No sign,
No sign of trembling.
I have left you dry.

IPHIGENIA: Did you know that we are surrounded by ghosts? You have tricked me.

ACHILLES: [*Singing.*] Trick and sway the boy twist.
He's got a gadget up his sleeve,
And he knows
How to use it.

IPHIGENIA: Look at me. Please.

ACHILLES: [*Singing.*] I got a blue tab.
Do you wanna split it with me?

IPHIGENIA: You have poisoned me. My teeth gnash, are made raw.

ACHILLES: [*Speaking.*] Where are you going?

IPHIGENIA: I want to hear the people scream.

ACHILLES: [*Speak-singing.*] Lacerate me.

IPHIGENIA: I've heard screams in my sleep. Blinding shots of electricity: into earlobes and soles of feet. And I have closed my eyes, and covered my ears. I have pretended I couldn't feel anything. I have been dreaming, Achilles: reckless in sleep.

ACHILLES: You're with me.

IPHIGENIA: I have been trying to erase every bit of me, so that I could make something else out of myself, so that I could feel something with this body that has been denied for so long.
But Iphigenia is still here, isn't she? She still owes her country.

ACHILLES: You don't owe anybody anything.

IPHIGENIA: Where are we?

ACHILLES: In the sky.

IPHIGENIA: Every muscle in my body is trembling.

ACHILLES: The sun will be up soon.

IPHIGENIA: Everything hurts.

ACHILLES: Shh.

[*FRESA GIRL 1 and 2 are heard hissing in the distance. Their hiss is amplified and electronically distorted.*]

FRESA GIRL 1 and **2:** [*Voice-over.*] Shh.

IPHIGENIA: The girls hiss.

ACHILLES: What?

IPHIGENIA: The dead girls from the factory, from the club . . .

ACHILLES: You're dreaming.

IPHIGENIA: Are you going to kill me?

ACHILLES: . . . I'm a coward, Iphigenia.

IPHIGENIA: You were raised by centaurs. You'll do anything.

ACHILLES: I don't know what centaurs you speak of.

IPHIGENIA: Achilles, son of the sea-nymph, raised by a glorious centaur, a deceiver of men.

ACHILLES: That's in the past, isn't it?

IPHIGENIA: Do you remember? I remember things that I haven't even lived.

ACHILLES: I have erased everything.

IPHIGENIA: With acid tabs and a Mars bar?

ACHILLES: I am completely remade.

IPHIGENIA: I think I am what the past has made me.

ACHILLES: You think too much.

IPHIGENIA: . . . You won't let me die, then?

ACHILLES: . . . Lean on me, twin.

[*They embrace.*]

IPHIGENIA: Look. Your tiger has tattooed itself on my skin.

ACHILLES: You'll forget me.

IPHIGENIA: No.

ACHILLES: You'll walk into the club one night, and you'll spit at me.

IPHIGENIA: Don't.

ACHILLES: You'll grab my legs and trip me out of the screen . . .

IPHIGENIA: I'll do anything. Watch me.

ACHILLES: And you'll beam your Novocain teeth, and pound me,

IPHIGENIA: I will destroy every bit of your celebrity.

ACHILLES: [*Continuing.*] as the virtual MC strings me up and floats me above your reach:
[*In the voice of the VIRTUAL MC.*] "Pull a limb off the dangling boy, girls. Shake his tree.
He won't feel anything. His blood is soaked in E."

IPHIGENIA: There will be no one left to adore but me.

ACHILLES: And you'll pull off my arms while I hang from the invisible hook attached to the ceiling. And you'll parade my limbs for all to see. Then another girl will take my legs
And you'll start to cut me. "Let's make a flower from his flesh," you'll say.
And my twitching eyes will watch you make a corpse of me.

IPHIGENIA: You curse me.

ACHILLES: Give me your body.

IPHIGENIA: My teeth are numb.

ACHILLES: Put this in your mouth.

[*ACHILLES puts a pacifier in her mouth, as he turns her body against him. Shift to baby ORESTES, who appears on the screen. He speaks in an adult voice, and is stoned.*]

ORESTES: Right in my sock mouth yeah, that's what I need, my sister dear, my sister be.
You are loud and right in my face.
Is that why you got me stoked up for? I got *coca* in my brain since the day I was born.
I don't need any more Coca-Cola, or any other *yanqui* dollar, get me?
I bounce without any help from the motorcycle slaves killing off girls on the side of the street.
You think I don't know anything? Pink cross on a factory wall. That's me.
I'm the painter, dear. Your brother Orestes.

[*IPHIGENIA spits out the pacifier.*]

IPHIGENIA: Orestes?

ACHILLES: There's no one here but me.

ORESTES: I'm the one marking the time, day, and the very *santo espiritu* moment.

[*ORESTES makes the sign of the cross with his tiny hands.*]

of the *fresa* girls meeting their death outside the rave. Rev, rev, rev on, sister.

[*A lid is placed over ORESTES' head by an anonymous hand. We see he is inside a designer shoebox labeled "Gucci." Night bleeds into morning.*]

IPHIGENIA: What have you done to me?

ACHILLES: Shh.

IPHIGENIA: I'm bleeding.

ACHILLES: I'm sorry.

IPHIGENIA: You wanted to split me.

ACHILLES: We're one, girl.

IPHIGENIA: You're a monster.

ACHILLES: I'll be dead soon.

IPHIGENIA: What?

ACHILLES: I've had AIDS for years. It's all a matter of time . . .

IPHIGENIA: You're lying.

ACHILLES: Why do you think they show me every night dancing in the
same image? They know I'll die soon.
"He'll be delirious in a beat. Watch him. Watch him lose his mind. He's our
original rock 'n' roll suicide." I feel it sometimes. Words get botched.
Everything goes slow.

IPHIGENIA: . . . Kiss me.

ACHILLES: You still want me?

IPHIGENIA: I want everything. I see myself in the sky, and I don't have this
weird film on my skin.
The whole earth has been irradiated, and I'm flying through the air looking
down on my house, except it's not there anymore. There's nothing, except
land and a few flowers made of human bones where my room used to be.
And my baby brother is swimming in this large pool shaped like a guitar,
like the one Elvis used to have. And he's happy. He's not drowning in *coca*
anymore. He's free. And I'm on the gulf where the sea is gray, and no one
wants a piece of me,
not the newspapers, not the boys in fatigues, not even my father . . .

[*She kisses him.*]

ACHILLES: You kiss without shame.

IPHIGENIA: Will you betray me?

ACHILLES: Will you forgive me?

IPHIGENIA: . . . Give me your hands.

ACHILLES: What?

IPHIGENIA: You have bewitched me.

[*Sun burns upon **ACHILLES** and **IPHIGENIA** as he gives her his hands.*]

PART THREE
IPHIGENIA'S RETURN: SEVEN CUTS FROM A DREAM

ONE

In the city's gleam, **IPHIGENIA** *is standing.*

IPHIGENIA: Back arched. The neck pivots on tired shoulders.
Iphigenia comes home from the dance.
The streets are empty. Dots of houses lie low against the horizon.
Iphigenia is headed home, but she takes her time.
She walks with the last trace of Achilles on her skin. Her father is far
  from her mind.

[*VIOLETA IMPERIAL appears. There is a dress over her arm.*]

VIOLETA IMPERIAL: You're going to need your strength.

IPHIGENIA: Get away from me.

VIOLETA IMPERIAL: You've a temper in the morning, eh? Come on. Try on
  this dress. I made it special with lace. You want to look good for Achilles,
  don't you, child?

IPHIGENIA: For Achilles? Yes.

[*IPHIGENIA lets VIOLETA IMPERIAL place the dress on her.*]

VIOLETA IMPERIAL: I made you this dress, Iphigenia. From Queen Anne's
  lace. These hands sewed night and day praying for your return, while
  another pink cross, another girl's name went up on the factory wall.

IPHIGENIA: Another girl was killed?

VIOLETA IMPERIAL: Where do you think I got the Queen Anne's lace?

IPHIGENIA: Take this off me.

VIOLETA IMPERIAL: It's all right, child. I washed it. This dress has been
  cleansed of all blood. You are safe.

IPHIGENIA: Hold me, Violeta. I'm scared.

VIOLETA IMPERIAL: I can't have anyone near me. You know that.

IPHIGENIA: No one will see.

VIOLETA IMPERIAL: You think because you're out here that no one can see?

IPHIGENIA: Hold me. Please. I can feel the dead girl's breath inside this
  dress. I feel all the dead through me.

VIOLETA IMPERIAL: Girls die every day here, and no one mourns them.

367

IPHIGENIA: I want to mourn them, Violeta. I want to free them of their pain. I want your scars on me.

VIOLETA IMPERIAL: Look around you, Iphigenia. There are eyes everywhere. They've seen everything.
Your death will help us make some sense of it all. Our grief will finally have a place.

IPHIGENIA: I'm not dead.

VIOLETA IMPERIAL: They're selling pictures on the street.

[*The screen flashes a thousand photos of* **IPHIGENIA***'s body splayed on the field outside the club. In each photo, her eyes are either ecstatically blank, or scratched out.*]

We need someone to mourn for, Iphigenia. We need a girl we can look up to.

[*The screen rests on a close shot of* **IPHIGENIA***, slightly bloodied, with the pacifier in her mouth.*]

This one's my favorite. Fifty dollars for a premium shot of Iphigenia sucking on her baby blue. Of course, I wouldn't sell it. I sell chicken. Legs and wings. For running, and flying, see?

[*The close shot of* **IPHIGENIA** *with blank eyes is magnified now. Image upon image. Eyes, mouth, nose. Cropped shots overlaid as* **VIOLETA IMPERIAL** *fades into the periphery.*]

IPHIGENIA: The dress of a dead girl sticks to her skin.
Iphigenia sees her father's eyes staring at her from behind the screen.
The centuries fade in ribbons. Father . . . ?

[**SOLDIER X***, a mercenary, appears.*]

SOLDIER X: Give us back your body, girl. It's never been yours to keep.

IPHIGENIA: She closes her eyes against the sky as it turns to day. Away from her dreams. Away.

TWO

SOLDIER X and IPHIGENIA stand a few feet apart from each other.

IPHIGENIA: When will you kill me?

SOLDIER X: I'm a mercenary, Iphigenia. I kill for money, not out of rage.

IPHIGENIA: Has my father paid you yet?

SOLDIER X: Let's not discuss such things.

IPHIGENIA: Make my father pay you. I want you to lead me into a quiet house off the main road, and tell me Achilles is waiting for me. I want you to close the door, and cover my eyes and when I ask "Why?" I want you to pierce me with a knife.

SOLDIER X: You're growing up too fast, girl.

IPHIGENIA: I never liked childhood.

THREE

IPHIGENIA talks to ORESTES, who is inside the designer shoebox. ORESTES' face is seen on the screen.

IPHIGENIA: I don't think you will ever grow up. You haven't grown an inch since I put you in here.
You're so thin, and your fingers are so . . . Your eyes are spinning, Orestes. Stop looking at me.

[*IPHIGENIA rocks the box. ORESTES' face contorts in restless, wide-eyed sleep on the screen. She sings:*]

"LULLABY FOR ORESTES"

Marry the winged messenger with a foot on the grave.
Here we do what my father says.
The *fresa* girls work in factories all day
Waiting for young men to kill them.

Dream, dream, Orestes.
Dream, dream, with blood on your mind.
Dream, dream, Orestes.
Dream my death
With your stoned eyes.

FOUR

CAMILA is combing her hair. IPHIGENIA watches her.

CAMILA: Iphigenia's the eldest. My first. I'm supposed to be proud of her. But when I look at her, I feel hatred. Inexplicable, for it was an easy childbirth I had with her. Her brother, on the other hand, was hard. They had to cut me open. But Iphigenia popped out in minutes, eager to be out in the world. She burns my fingers. She is the fruit of Adolfo's rape of me. Such glorious, poisonous fruit. He married me against my will. He smashed the head of a baby boy whose name is no longer remembered and stuck his cock inside me. For the good of the country. For the promise of a model wife at his side. "My dear, sweet Iphigenia," Adolfo would say. "She is the best of us."

I slap her. Across the face. I make her take care of her baby brother, because I know he cries all night, and she won't be able to sleep. I know what she wants. She wants to touch me. Like any daughter. Iphigenia. I will never love you.

FIVE

IPHIGENIA walks like a ghost through her own house, and out into the street, toward the light of the hangar, past everything.

IPHIGENIA: It is night. I see fragments.
My mother braids her hair in the moonlight.
My brother cries from inside the box that once held my Gucci shoes.
My father sleeps with his feet facing the window. I kiss him for the last time.
　　No tears, Father. Everything will be all right.

I move to the whispers of soldiers in neon out on the street, outside the house that holds me.
The *fresa* girls leave the factories with their party dresses on.
Hey, girls. Let's go dancing.
Pulse I go in the mirrorball. Pulse . . . Spin, spin a drop of magenta green in the open sky. Give me a kiss, fair Achilles, give me a deep, wet dizzy with E . . .

I am caught in my father's eyes. They stare out of every camera.

[*IPHIGENIA motions to SOLDIER X, who appears out of the shadows.*]

Lead me now, soldier. Be my blissful mercenary.

[*IPHIGENIA offers SOLDIER X her arm.*]

This is how I want to be remembered:
With E on my tongue, and the rush of love in my heart,
And the whole world spinning with my glory.
Pulse. Pulse. I go.

[*SOLDIER X takes her in a shiver of electric light.*]

SIX

The FRESA GIRLS at the club are on the TV screen.

FRESA GIRL 1: Yeah, I saw her. She had a Chanel on. She was looking for Achilles. You think I look good? I've been thinking about plastic surgery.

FRESA GIRL 2: Everybody was dancing. I couldn't see anything. Hey. Hey. Do you like Prodigy?

FRESA GIRL 1: I could make myself into her. With the right smile, the right teeth . . . I could be Iphigenia.

FRESA GIRL 3: Hey. Hey. Don't you want to talk to me? I saw everything. Yeah. Soldier X, the mercenary, came in through the back of the club. She waved to him.

ALL FRESA GIRLS: What?

FRESA GIRL 3: She was no saint. I saw her. You hear me? I saw him kill her. I saw everything. Like I had the eyes of God. Hey. What are you—?

[Sound and image out on the TV. TV NEWS ANCHOR's face fills the screen. He is "off-camera."]

NEWS ANCHOR: No, Walter. I do not know where the Knicks are playing tonight. Can't you goddamn look it up? This is the information age, for God's sake. Everything's at the touch of a . . . What? What?

[He is "on the air."]

In late news tonight, the general's daughter Iphigenia is said to be dead. I repeat, "This is a rumor," but sources tell us she was seen outside an aircraft hangar shortly before midnight escorted by a man yet to be identified, and she has not been seen since. Unlike other incidents involving the general's daughter, reports lead us to believe this is not a kidnapping. Blood has been seen on the ground at a short distance from the hangar in a house made of cinder block. And experts confirm it does match Iphigenia's blood type. I repeat "This is a rumor. This is a rumor. This is a rumor."

[TV NEWS ANCHOR fades as ADOLFO is seen, live. He wears pajamas.]

ADOLFO: She was very still. I made the sign of the cross with my hands. The man took out the knife. My daughter's cry was heard but once. When I lifted my eyes, she was gone.
There was blood everywhere. But no sign of my Iphigenia.

[In the background, ADOLFO is seen on video, dressed in a military coat, speaking to the nation.]

[On video:] God took her. I believe God's will has been done. We must pray that all the fighting will stop. We must remember Iphigenia, and everything she did for us. As your leader, I will do my best, in this time of great sorrow for our family, to live up to her precious memory. Iphigenia is a saint. *[Live:]* I will be re-elected. No one will throw a father who has just lost his daughter out of office.

[CAMILA appears, live.]

CAMILA: A saint?

ADOLFO: Listen, Camila. The people are praying. She escaped death. She'll save us all.

[*On video:*] In Iphigenia's name. I call for our nation to be united.

CAMILA: My dear Iphigenia, where have the gods taken you? Where are you, Iphigenia?

[*ADOLFO embraces CAMILA. The sound of baby ORESTES crying in the background. Fade on the scene. The VIRTUAL MC comes up on the screen, disembodied, and grinning in the light.*]

VIRTUAL MC: Well, my little sluts, it looks like our dancing daughter has taken flight.

Angels bring her rest while we change places on a wooden bench and take our crystal high.

If it's not one brutality, it's another, and the way we count the days is by the pulse of this light.

Skip on, crashers. Shine on. You get me, dolls?

This is about pigtails and ankle socks and setting yourself up for burying your heads between your knees. There is no tomorrow, children.

There is only the night. And we're going to live it through for eternity.

[*The VIRTUAL MC's grin escapes the image of ACHILLES, live, who nevertheless seems to be ghosting a corner of the ever-expanding space. He sings in performance mode:*]

"MY EYES TO YOUR EYES"

ACHILLES: Insomnia trace my skin to you.
My eyes to your eyes,
My eyes to your eyes.

[*Image projected on the screen: close-up of IPHIGENIA's face through a surveillance camera.*]

Save the hour, sweet angel,
And I will follow. Hold your breath, dear angel,
And I will follow. I will follow.

Peel off my scab, restart the wound.
I will follow.
I will follow . . .

[*ACHILLES disappears into the darkness.*]

SEVEN
IPHIGENIA IN EXTASIS

A view from the camera. **IPHIGENIA** *remains. She is both live, and on the screen.*

IPHIGENIA: Crash. I am not cut, but I am bleeding.
There is black sand on my feet, but no water.
Only the sound of waves rushing.
I am standing.
I have wings.
They grow out of my shoulder blades
Out of the veil of the TV screen.
I am not cut, but I am bleeding.

Crash.
I remember falling,
Kissing
Through the garden,
To the neon lights on the street,
Splitting me into threads of skin.
Wings lift me.
I am moving.
I am at the edge of the city.
I am atop the aircraft hangar and its beams of green.
Boys, girls and a million vacant eyes.
Look at me.
I stand on the metal ledge.
Black liquid sand slipping off my skin.
The story has been told again.
A wreath has been placed upon Iphigenia's head.

Crash.
Every part of me is breaking.
But I'm all right.
Give me your hands.
Give me your hands,
Cause you're wonderful.

END OF PLAY

PHAEDRA IN DELIRIUM

(A NEW VERSION INSPIRED BY VARIANTS OF THE MYTH)

SUSAN YANKOWITZ

PHOTO: DAN ROUS

SUSAN YANKOWITZ is a playwright, novelist, lyricist, and librettist. Among her plays are *The Revenge, Under the Skin, Terminal* and *1969 Terminal 1996,* both pieces collaborations with Joseph Chaikin's Open Theatre (Drama Desk Playwright's Award); *A Knife in the Heart* (O'Neill Conference winner; West Coast premiere October 2002 at Sledgehammer Theatre); and *Night Sky,* presented throughout the United States and internationally. Her plays have been translated into French, Japanese, Catalan, Dutch, and German; they have been widely published and anthologized. She is also the librettist/lyricist of *Slain in the Spirit,* a gospel-and-blues opera with music by Taj Mahal; *Cheri,* an opera/music theatre work with Michael Dellaira which will be seen in workshop at the Actors Studio; and bookwriter/lyricist of *True Romances,* a musical fantasia with Elmer Bernstein. In addition to her work for the stage, she has written a novel, *Silent Witness,* published by Knopf, as well as several films and television plays. Her work has been honored by grants from the Guggenheim Foundation, NEA, NYFA, TCG, Berilla Kerr, McKnight and Rockefeller Foundations, among others. She is a frequent fellow at Yaddo and MacDowell, and is a member of New Dramatists, PEN, the Dramatists Guild, and WGA.

From the Writer
SUSAN YANKOWITZ

What I like best about writing is the license to enter and inhabit other lives, other worlds. The characters that take shape in my imagination and persist there become, at least temporarily, welded to my own consciousness. For a period I speak (in my writing) with their voices, their rhythms and syntax; I experience (and try to communicate) their thoughts, passions, idiosyncrasies of reaction and mood—and because theatre involves physical life, my own body dictates certain movements and gestures, energies that are not my own but must lurk somewhere inside me, unexpressed in daily life. I am extremely glad that no one sees me, in my little study, jutting my chin or broadening my chest in front of the computer as I take on the identity of this one or that one—but if diverse and theoretically alien aspects of human nature were not accessible to me, if I couldn't lock my everyday self away and discover parts of my being that are suppressed in ordinary life (or that ordinary life does not elicit), I would be restricted to writing plays about white Jewish middle-class American females 'of a certain age.' What a prison!

The view that certain experiences are 'owned' by a given group and cannot be understood by anyone else—that writers must write only about what they literally know and are, using the most narrow definitions—irrevocably segregates us. Why incarcerate ourselves when, through a leap of empathy, the imagination can liberate us to climb inside the skin of someone altogether 'other': the murderer, the diva, the sheik, the sex slave, even the hyena?

Of course the League of Sex Slaves or of Hyenas might rise up in arms about this, as certain segments of the population do when a white person writes about blacks, or a heterosexual portrays gays, for instance, condemning such efforts as hubris, violations of identity or literary colonialism. But isn't 'pretending' the fanciful transformation of the self into another, at the very heart of all creative acts? And isn't it the very essence of 'play' (in all its meanings) and fantasy?

Phaedra in Delirium delves into the obsession of an older woman for a young man; the dangers inherent in extremes, whether of eroticism, or chastity; the horrible, irrevocable power of words; and the hairline split between masculinity and femininity. In my version, The Friend switch-hits: male with Hippolytus, female with Phaedra. But even more central to the themes of the drama, and to me personally, is the conception of Theseus and Hippolytus as twinned (not opposite) aspects of the same character, designed to be performed by one actor who plays the lusty womanizer of forty-five and his own virginal son at age twenty. For when Phaedra falls in love with Hippolytus, it is the young Theseus she sees in him, a man who purports to adore her but leaves her alone for weeks while he indulges himself.

THESEUS: Women women women. What do I love best about them?
The odors that waft from them, the odors of deserts and of seas, of wild-
flowers and of fish, odors that aren't odors only but personalities, each
one an invitation, a pure yes, a yes and no, a maybe, a husky no. What
does it matter if their skin is like silk or like sandpaper, if their thighs
are loose or tight as violin strings, there's music in all of them, in their
voices and in their hips, inside where the darkness hums. Women, with
their eyes opened like windows or narrowed to squeeze a man's breath
away, eyes that shut in self-defense when the fire burns too hot, eyes that
take you by the hand and lead you in, far inside, where it's always a
mystery, and if you take your time, the mystery doesn't disappear, it
deepens. And where are you when you're in there, in women,
surrounding yourself with them, sliding into darkness that is your own
darkness, too, a darkness that you can't find alone . . .

I believe I actually closed my eyes to write this monologue, to find its phallic thump and throb, the rhapsodic rhythms and metaphors that cluster and rush toward orgasmic fulfillment. The swaggering conqueror, the roué with a seductive smile and maybe a cigar is a familiar character, in life as in art. This made the portrayal particularly challenging, especially for me as a female writer: to get inside the desire of a man who desires to get inside a woman. In Greek plays, all violent passions, no matter what sort, lead to tragedy. Phaedra, of course, has to choke on hers (in halting, interrupted phrases) because society has ordained such desires shameful in women. It was therefore a delicious pleasure for me to create the rolling, sensuous abundance of Theseus's imagery and his unfettered freedom to articulate it.

Hippolytus is a different breed, an Ashley Wilkes to his father's Rhett Butler. Rigidly chaste and self-righteous, he speaks in a language that seesaws between a lyrical longing for his father's company and a clipped, emphatic resentment toward Phaedra for stealing it from him. Even within a single speech his cadences, the length of his sentences and his focus, so different from those of Theseus, shift back and forth.

HIPPOLYTUS: Relent, bend, curry favor. That's what men do when
they're dependent on others. I can't wait till my father gets back. If he
were here, this would still be our house, the fields our fields, and the
days would be filled with our steps and our horses racing side by side in
the mountains, and our talk at night. . . . Where is he now? Where has
he gone? Without him, I don't belong here. Since he married Phaedra,
everything's changed. When he's home, the door to his bedroom is locked,
I hear him laughing at night with her, he forgets me, he forgets I exist.
And when he's away, the house feels . . . contaminated; it reeks of
Phaedra's perfume. She's everywhere . . . an enormous slug, swallowing
all the oxygen, spilling over into every inch of space.

These days, Hippolytus's aversion to women might be interpreted as Oedipal fear or repressed homosexuality—but are any of us really so amoebic, so simple that we can be encapsulated within categories of gender, sexuality, race, religion, or class? What makes Hippolytus fascinating to me is how alien he is to contemporary definitions of manhood, how far from Theseus. The underwear and aromas that excite the father arouse revulsion in the son. Situating the libertine and the ascetic in the same play, in the same actor's body, in fact, doubled my trouble and my fun.

In life, after all, the computer nerd may yearn to wear high heels, the housewife to be a mechanic and lie beneath a car instead of her husband, the nurse to wield a gun rather than a thermometer, the soldier to give birth. As for me, writing about the infinite variety of others, transforming into men (and sometimes women), wearing their clothes, skin, or demonic smiles, is the only way I know of being Tiresias.

PRODUCTION HISTORY

Sledgehammer Theatre's production of *Phaedra in Delirium*, directed by Kirsten Brandt. PHOTO: KIRSTEN BRANDT.

Phaedra in Delirium had its first workshop at NYU, directed by Kristin Marting. An early draft was given a reading at Primary Stages in New York, with direction by Rhea Gaisner, and another at New Dramatists. Women's Project & Production and Classic Stage Company co-produced the original production at CSC from January 20–February 15, 1998. It was directed by Alison Summers with set design by Christine Jones, costume design by Teresa Snider-Stein, lighting design by Beverly Emmons, and sound design by Fabian Obispo. The cast was as follows:

PHAEDRA . . . . Kathleen Chalfant
HIPPOLYTUS/THESEUS . . . . Peter Jay Fernandez
FRIEND . . . . Sandra Shipley

In 2003, the play had its West Coast premiere at Sledgehammer Theatre in San Diego, directed by Kirsten Brandt and David Tierney.

SPECIAL THANKS to Kristin Marting, Rhea Gaisner, Julia Miles, David Esbjornson, Ted Weiss, Renee Weiss and Kirsten Brandt for their faith in this play—and to Herbert Leibowitz and Gabriel Sky-Leibowitz, *my* two men, for their faith in me.

CHARACTERS

PHAEDRA, a woman in her forties

The **FRIEND,** an androgynous person of either gender, aged thirty to thirty-five, who plays both Phaedra's female confidante and Hippolytus' male friend

THESEUS/HIPPOLYTUS, a single actor who plays a man of forty-five and his own son at twenty; or two actors who convey their physical similarities as father and son by using the same inflections, postures, and gestures at key moments in the play

SETTING

A large canopy bed and the wild outdoors outside, visible through a window or, more abstractly, a world of beds and mirrors, surrounded or invaded by lush, brutal nature

The FRIEND, an androgynous figure who appears more feminine in scenes with PHAEDRA, and masculine in those with HIPPOLYTUS, addresses the audience. Nearby is a four-poster bed with a canopy, surrounded by curtains. These now are closed.

FRIEND: Phaedra's sick. For weeks she's been in here, rooted to her bed. Sleeping. Not sleeping. Lady of leisure, or lady of lamentations: lady layabed. She needs me now—I know she does—and so I packed my bag and settled in to keep an eye on her. Not that it helps, not that she cares. She barely answers when I talk to her, doesn't drink, doesn't eat, doesn't really see me, and doesn't budge from that bed, as if she didn't know the difference between night and day, day and night. Sometimes I hear her tossing and turning, full of moans and sighs; and the rest of the time—

[*The FRIEND pulls open the curtains that conceal the bed. PHAEDRA sits there, supported by pillows, looking at herself in a mirror.*]

—she stares in that mirror, stares and stares, as if she's married to it. But she's not. She's married to Theseus, a wealthy man, a powerful man, Theseus who is away, frequently away, I hear, on business, he says, always on business—but what business can that be? He's almost newlywed, and he lets business seduce him from his home? [*Moving closer.*] That's what's eating her up, it must be. I'm a woman and her friend; I know these troubles. She feels abandoned, she longs for him, she worries that he regrets the marriage already, that in six months' time he's bored with her, lost himself in a strange woman's lap . . .

PHAEDRA: [*Delirious.*] It's so hot in here, I'm suffocating asleep   awake, my dreams are heavy with him, my tongue is parched, my lips can't open without his lips near   The mountains! I want to go with him to the mountains, to be with him in the air, with the wind on my skin and the rustle of leaves and the silence that has wildness in it, the sense that something could happen   anything could happen in the night   in the dark.

FRIEND: [*Touching her forehead.*] Shh. Shhh. The fever's making you talk like this. You're burning up.

PHAEDRA: Good. I'll be consumed, I'll turn to flame, to ash, I'll become pure . . . yes, pure spirit.

FRIEND: You're sick, that's all. People live through sickness and go on to love their lives. Let me call the doctor, get you some medicine.

PHAEDRA: There's no medicine for this.

FRIEND: It's been three days. You have to eat something.

PHAEDRA: I can't! I'll live on nothing—or better still, not live at all.

FRIEND: Now why are you so morbid!? The man adores you, worships you. Everyone knows that. So he's away for a while. So it's hard to be without your husband. But it's no tragedy.

PHAEDRA: You! What do you know of tragedy?!

FRIEND: [*Offended.*] And what do you know of me? I understand suffering, believe me. I'm not ignorant of life. So I never married. Haven't you ever suspected that sex might be better without a ring on your finger?

PHAEDRA: It has occurred to me.

FRIEND: I'm not exactly a virgin, you know. I'm just . . . discreet.

PHAEDRA: So that's your secret. That's why in all these years I've never once seen you possessed, taken over by a passion.

FRIEND: Would I compete with you? Thank God one of us is balanced. I know how to enjoy myself without going crazy. Without driving everyone else crazy! You may love your extremes; I prefer the middle ground.

PHAEDRA: How comforting for you.

FRIEND: You could be comfortable, too. But you won't let yourself. You give in to every feeling, you wallow in your misery as if it were pleasure. What's wrong? Tell me.

PHAEDRA: Please. Go away.

FRIEND: I won't. I'll wait right here until you tell me what's happened. Why else did I come to stay with you? I've been up all night, worrying, worrying; my nerves are shot. What awful news have you heard? [*Silence.*] Oh great suffering angel, great mum's-the-word, great martyr of the bleeding silence, talk to me! Is Theseus hurt? In danger of some kind? Speak up! Is he dead?

PHAEDRA: I've heard nothing about Theseus. Nothing at all.

FRIEND: Well, then, why all the fuss? Some women would be thrilled to have their husbands out of town for a while, then suddenly, excitingly, turn up one lonely night and slip between the sheets.

PHAEDRA: Some other woman, maybe. Some other sheets.

FRIEND: So he *is* with another woman. Don't deny it, I see it in your eyes, that green flame. What did you expect? We all know Theseus. That man never could resist a woman! So what? Who cares if he's having a fling? Look at the fabulous life you have! I've never seen such luxury: this beautiful house, the gardens, horses, a lake . . . [*Stroking the bed linens.*] In my entire life, I've never even touched sheets like these.

PHAEDRA: Trust me, you wouldn't want to lie in this bed.

FRIEND: Oh yes, I would. I'd delight in everything you have! Why can't you? You don't have cancer, your heart is strong; I can hear it pounding from here. You're too young for this 'sickness unto death.'

PHAEDRA: Too old, you mean, to suffer the petty griefs of love. Come here. Closer. Look. Gravity has her hands on me, she's pulling at my skin, pulling down down down, turning muscle soft and falling off the bone.

FRIEND: [*Touching her cheek.*] I like your skin.

PHAEDRA: My cheekbones are vanishing. And my hair is losing its color. Do you see? There's a stripe of gray right here.

FRIEND: That's not a disease. It's nature.

PHAEDRA: I hate nature! I hate what she does to us. You'll understand soon enough. Every woman who's reached my age knows what I mean. Suddenly, overnight, we become invisible. We could walk down the street naked and no one would notice. Oh, yes, we can celebrate our 'glorious, our liberating maturity'—but who burns for us now? Who pours out his heart in poetry and midnights? No one. Never. It's obvious: we're the fate that every woman is trying to escape.

FRIEND: You have great character in your face.

PHAEDRA: Thank you so much. That's what every woman wants to hear.

FRIEND: No one's ever said *I* have great character.

PHAEDRA: Maybe you don't.

FRIEND: I beg your pardon!

PHAEDRA: Why would anyone care about your character? You're still young enough to catch the eye. And pretty, too.

FRIEND: You think so?

PHAEDRA: Does it matter what *I* think? The world has its standards. You meet them.

FRIEND: You're very beautiful.

PHAEDRA: Beautiful, oh yes—for a woman my age. That's what people say and think they're being kind. 'How beautiful she is for a woman her age!' But I can't fool myself; I have eyes. Everywhere I go I see them, the girls with glowing skin, their faces and throats like unmarked paper, their stomachs little bowls turned inside out. That's where men go to fill themselves.

FRIEND: They'll get older, too, you know.

PHAEDRA: But they have time! They have time now, when they need it! Oh God, how fast it goes. Only yesterday I walked down the road, sending up clouds of musk. My breath was an invitation. No man would have refused me.

FRIEND: Who would refuse you now? No one, no one.

PHAEDRA: Really?

FRIEND: Is *that* what happened? You met a man and you wanted—?

PHAEDRA: Wanted?! Me? What could I possibly want?! I'm a wife, the wife of Theseus, a great figure in the world, an important man!

FRIEND: And he should be with you. I'm going to track him down. It shouldn't be too hard. He leaves a strong scent. Men who love women always do.

[*The FRIEND exits. PHAEDRA turns around on her bed to face the audience, her head bowed forward under the weight of an enormous mass of hair piled on top.*]

PHAEDRA: [*Tries to lift her head; she can't.*] This hair   I can barely lift up my head   so neat, so proper, no wisps flying   it weighs me down [*Occasionally she succeeds in raising her head but slaps herself down.*] Girl   run through the fields   hair flying   unbraid the braids   raise the sails   let the horses loose   slap!   grow up!   running   toes like worms, feet like birds   where are your shoes?   slap! slap! grow up!   can't see the stars the sun the skies the floor is gray and dirty, the ground hits my eyes   lift!   slap me down!   pins in my scalp a torture, pins like needles, needle in the haystack, jumping falling hay in my hair slap!   can't go wild, can't go child   stop! slap! sit still   grown up   heavy heavy heavy the head that   can't move can't dance can't throw back my head for song or love or   heavy   heavy   heavy

[*THESEUS has entered and watched her. He moves closer and grips her hair, pulls back her head, kisses her on the lips.*]

THESEUS: I love your hair, your eyes, your mouth, your lower lip, the way it quivers now, your throat, and how you offer it to me now. [*He kisses her strained throat.*] It was always you I wanted, not Ariadne. But Ariadne showed me the way, she kept me from death, I owed her my love; I did what was right. But you were the one I desired, it was you, Phaedra, behind my eyes while I gazed into hers, you I held in my arms at night, you, the sister. Time waited until I was free—and finally you belong to me, you share my bed, my breath. [*He kisses her lips though her head is still arched back.*] You wanted me, too, when I wasn't yours. And now, now that I'm here and in the flesh, tell me: is reality better than your dream? Tell me, darling. How do you feel now? [*Although he releases her, she is left with her head flung so far back that she can't lift it forward or speak. She makes a strangulated sound.*] You don't have to say a word. I know how you feel. Don't change. Stay the way you are. I'll hold this image of you in my heart. [*He kisses her again before leaving.*] I'll be home in a week.

[*PHAEDRA again can't lift up her head. After several attempts, she raises her hands and begins to pull the pins from her hair. One by one she plucks them out and drops them to the floor. Her long hair begins to hang loose. As the floor, perhaps the whole stage, becomes littered with pins, lights come up elsewhere on THESEUS in rhapsody.*]

Women women women. What do I love best about them? The odors that waft from them, the odors of deserts and of seas, of wildflowers and of fish, odors that aren't odors only but personalities, each one an invitation, a pure yes, a yes and no, a maybe, a husky no. What does it matter if their skin is like silk or like sandpaper, if their thighs are loose or tight as violin strings, there's music in all of them, in their voices and in their hips, inside where the darkness hums. Women, with their eyes opened like windows or narrowed to squeeze a man's breath away, eyes that shut in self-defense when the fire burns too hot, eyes that take you by the hand and lead you in, far inside, where it's always a mystery, and if you take your time, the mystery doesn't disappear, it deepens. And where are you when you're in there, in women, surrounding yourself with them, sliding into darkness that is your own darkness, too, a darkness that you can't find alone.

[*The last hairpin falls as THESEUS vanishes from view. Finally PHAEDRA can lift her head. She is facing the audience. She takes a deep breath, then swirls her hair around and around her with increasing freedom. She pulls down her nightgown so that her bare shoulders are exposed, and lets her hair move over them. Her eyes are closed, and she is smiling, standing in a field of hairpins.*]

PHAEDRA: This is how he saw me when he saw me first. This is how I felt, this is how it felt when he saw me first. [*She swirls her hair.*] This is how I want it to feel   like hands on me   like fingers playing on my skin. This is who I was when he saw me first. This is how I felt when—

[*Spotlit elsewhere,* **HIPPOLYTUS** *appears, dressed in a white linen suit.* **PHAEDRA** *turns in his direction. Slowly, as if against her will, she walks toward him. She stands directly in front of him.*]

So. You're Hippolytus.

[*He nods and stares at her awkwardly. Transfixed, she takes his hands in hers and holds them for a long time.*]

Hippolytus. You have your father's hands.

[**HIPPOLYTUS** *grabs back his hands and stares at her as she backs away from him, her eyes fixed on his, until she is once again ensconced in her canopied bed and pulls the curtains shut. During this, the Female* **FRIEND** *has entered with a broom to sweep up the hairpins.*]

HIPPOLYTUS: [*Staring at his hands.*] Why did she touch me?

[*The* **FRIEND** *turns around, in his Male aspect now,* **HIPPOLYTUS**'*s* **FRIEND**.]

Why did she touch me?

FRIEND: You know how it is with women.

HIPPOLYTUS: No, I don't. She sends me away on ridiculous errands; she makes sure we're never in the same room; she avoids talking to me, eating with me, even looking at me—but when we happen to meet, she puts her hands on me. She puts her hands on me.

FRIEND: So? She doesn't have leprosy.

HIPPOLYTUS: I don't like people touching me.

FRIEND: She's not 'people,' she's your mother.

HIPPOLYTUS: No, my stepmother, my father's wife. I'm no part of her. She doesn't want a son; she's been cold to me from the start. So why does she touch me?

FRIEND: Why? Put yourself in her place. She's probably lonely, scared. She's not used to being alone. And here she is, in a big house in the country, too much land, too few people, no neighbors, no visitors, no shops, even. Your father doesn't let her know where he is, how he is. I don't think she's heard one word from him. She's worried to death, I bet.

HIPPOLYTUS: My father's been around. He knows the world. What could happen to him?

FRIEND: Women. Women could happen to him. You know that. Women have always been his problem.

HIPPOLYTUS: When he was young. That's all over now.

FRIEND: You think so? A man like him? Come on, use your imagination. He's in a desert, right? It's hot. He's thirsty, looking for water. He's all alone. He sees a woman, any woman. Aha, an oasis! What does he do? He drinks!

HIPPOLYTUS: He's not in the desert. He's in Europe.

FRIEND: Oh. There are no women in Spain, on the beaches in Nice.

HIPPOLYTUS: He loves Phaedra.

FRIEND: Sure he does, sure. But love isn't the problem, it's sex, my friend, desire, that body itch, that lowdown cry, nothing to do with conjugal sheets. And when that rises up, when passion grabs hold of a man, it makes him forget everything else, it murders what you call love, it kills loyalty, it—

HIPPOLYTUS: Put it in jail, then.

FRIEND: You don't know what I'm talking about, do you?

HIPPOLYTUS: I have better things to do than study diseases of the heart.

FRIEND: Diseases, you call them. Well, Hippolytus, one thing's for sure: you are not your father's son.

HIPPOLYTUS: When it comes to women—I guess not. I think I'll take a ride.

FRIEND: Alone?

HIPPOLYTUS: No. I'll have my horse.

FRIEND: Oh. Great company, a horse. Much better than a human being.

HIPPOLYTUS: That's not it. I don't have anything against people. It's just that I like nature better.

FRIEND: Rocks don't try to touch you, huh? Trees don't expect you to share their troubles. The moon stays far above you, cool, distant and cool.

HIPPOLYTUS: You understand me perfectly.

FRIEND: What am I going to tell Phaedra when she finds out you're gone?

HIPPOLYTUS: The truth, what else? Her husband's son is staying in the mountains for a few days. She'll probably sleep better, knowing I'm away.

FRIEND: She doesn't sleep at all. Once or twice last night, and the one before, I heard her footsteps down the hall. They stopped outside your door.

HIPPOLYTUS: Why?

FRIEND: How should I know? Maybe she's afraid *you're* lonely now that Theseus is gone. Maybe she's listening for your tears or nightmares, ready to comfort her young charge.

HIPPOLYTUS: She'll have to find someone else to mother. I won't be here tonight.

FRIEND: You promised your father to look after her. Do it, then. Give her a few minutes of your attention. Bend a little. People admire a man who goes his own way—but they don't like him. Not really.

HIPPOLYTUS: I don't care.

FRIEND: Maybe you should learn to care. You're part of the race.

HIPPOLYTUS: A man can't change his nature.

FRIEND: But you aren't natural.

HIPPOLYTUS: Not natural? Me?

FRIEND: No. Look at that body of yours, all those muscles and economy. Beautiful, sure—but like a statue, chiseled, cold. And inside, I sometimes think, you're made of marble, too. You don't let anyone close. Tell me: who do you laugh with? Who holds you when it's dark at night? Who consoles you?

HIPPOLYTUS: I don't need consolation.

FRIEND: Come off it. Everyone needs consolation; everyone wants love.

HIPPOLYTUS: Everyone, everyone! I don't give a damn about everyone! Why should I pretend to be someone I'm not? If I were a dwarf, you wouldn't keep pushing me to grow another three feet. If I were blind, you wouldn't insist I see. I'm not going to twist myself out of shape. Not for you, or anyone. I am who I am and I'm happy that way.

FRIEND: People hate arrogance like yours. Take my word for it: set yourself above the rest of humanity and humanity will do everything it can to bring you down.

HIPPOLYTUS: But I don't feel better than other people; I just feel . . . separate. I want to be a man as powerful as my father but closer to sky than to earth, like air or light, cut loose from everything, from fevers and tomorrows, deserts and fish, sea and caves. Why should people hate me for that? It's what we all become at the end.

FRIEND: But why hurry there? This is the world, this is life, and we're not air. As for me, I like bodies . . . [*Tracing the line from HIPPOLYTUS's neck to shoulder.*] . . . how the neck flows so smoothly into the shoulder, and the shoulder curves into the arm. I think it's beautiful the way we're made. Don't you?

HIPPOLYTUS: [*Confused.*] You mean . . . aesthetically, right?

FRIEND: [*Embarrassed.*] Right. [*Moves away.*] I'll see you in a few days. But while you're gone, think about what I said. Go easy. Relent.

[*The **FRIEND** exits. **HIPPOLYTUS** remains on stage and addresses the audience.*]

HIPPOLYTUS: Relent, he says. Bend. What he really means is, curry favor. That's what men do when they're dependent on others. I can't wait till my father gets back. If he were here, this would still be our house, the fields our fields, and the days would be filled with our steps and our horses racing side by side in the mountains, and our talk at night. He'd smile at me, he'd grip my shoulders in his hands and study his face in mine, he'd tell me of the years before we met, when he was just a name to me, an image, a big man with a beard, like God. Where is he now? Where has he gone? Without him, I don't belong here. Since he married Phaedra, everything's changed. When he's home, the door to his bedroom is locked, I hear him laughing at night with her, he forgets me, he forgets I exist. And when he's away, the house feels . . . contaminated; it reeks of Phaedra's perfume. She's everywhere! In the sink, on the tiles, sometimes on the china, I see strands of her hair; her stockings are draped over the chairs; I find her slippers on the stairs I have to walk to reach my bed. She's like an enormous slug, swallowing all the oxygen, spilling over into every inch of space. It's disgusting.

[*Slowly, without his awareness, the curtains begin opening around **PHAEDRA**'s bed. Little by little, she can be seen listening to him, completely gripped by his presence, his words.*]

I have to get away, into the hills and the mountains behind the hills, the covering leaves and the surprise of flowers where there seemed only dirt, and the paths that seem made for my foot, or the hooves of my horse. We graze and gallop and never stumble. I'm strong in the hills, I know who I am and where I am, I never lose my way, I just keep mounting higher and higher till there's no sight of this house at all, not even of the smoke rising from the chimney. That's where I belong: above the swamps and marshes and the perfectly ploughed fields of farmers, the perfectly groomed lawns of perfect families, high up, alone, where the air has no perfume, no perfume at all . . .

PHAEDRA: [*Stepping out from her bed, startling him.*] Hippolytus!

HIPPOLYTUS: What?! What is it?

PHAEDRA: I heard you're going away.

HIPPOLYTUS: Yes.

PHAEDRA: Overnight?

HIPPOLYTUS: Maybe a few nights.

PHAEDRA: A few. Two? Three?

HIPPOLYTUS: I'm not sure yet.

PHAEDRA: Would you like something to eat before you go?

HIPPOLYTUS: No, no thank you. I'm fasting today.

PHAEDRA: Fasting. So am I. I haven't eaten in days.

HIPPOLYTUS: I heard. I'm sorry. You've been sick.

PHAEDRA: Running a fever. Burning up. Here. Just feel my forehead.

HIPPOLYTUS: [*Stepping back, nervous.*] I don't need to do that. I can see for myself. And you're doing right. It's better not to eat when you have a fever.

PHAEDRA: Oh, it is, it is. There are advantages to fasting, I've discovered, at least for me. I gained so much weight in the last few months. And now, well, as you can see, I'm quite a bit thinner. [*A silence.*] Don't you think so?

HIPPOLYTUS: I can't say. I don't think I noticed.

PHAEDRA: Does that mean you never thought I was overweight?

[*HIPPOLYTUS doesn't know what to say.*]

Or that you didn't look. In all this time, you never really looked at me. Is that what you mean?

HIPPOLYTUS: I'm sorry, I just don't know anything about women's . . . weight.

PHAEDRA: But there must be a *type* of woman you find attractive. Curvaceous ones, for instance. [*No response.*] Or slim boyish ones. Or motherly types with big bosoms and round arms. [*Still no response.*] Most men have a definite preference.

HIPPOLYTUS: I guess I'm not most men. [*A silence.*] I think I should go and pack.

PHAEDRA: Already? Why? What time is it?

HIPPOLYTUS: I'm not the kind of person who lives by the clock. I never notice the time.

PHAEDRA: But you can't escape it. Time passes. It passes like a dream. [*Almost to herself.*] It passes and leaves you behind. With everything broken.

HIPPOLYTUS: I won't break.

PHAEDRA: You're very strong, I know.

HIPPOLYTUS: [*Proudly.*] You can see that?

PHAEDRA: Anyone with eyes can see it. And to tell the truth, your body, your physique, I suppose I should say, makes me wonder if I . . . if maybe *I* could become stronger, too.

HIPPOLYTUS: I don't know about that.

PHAEDRA: But you could help me. The problem is I've gone all soft: my arms, my legs, even my neck. Sometimes I can't even lift up my head with all this hair on it! When I was growing up, girls didn't exercise; it wasn't feminine. But things are so much different now. Oh, I'd love to be a young girl today. I'd run, I'd swim, I'd ride horses, bareback—I could ride with you! in the mountains! with the manes of the horses wild in the wind! [*She lets her hair fall against her shoulders.*] I'd learn to keep my seat and hold on tight with my thighs, I'm sure I could do it! I could build up the right muscles. You could teach me everything. [*No response.*] Well, what do you think? Tell me. Is it too late?

HIPPOLYTUS: I don't know. Probably.

PHAEDRA: You mean I'm too old.

HIPPOLYTUS: If you've let your muscles get too weak . . .

PHAEDRA: I'm not sure they're *too* weak. [*She holds out her arms.*] Here. Feel.

HIPPOLYTUS: [*Backing away.*] I think you should talk to my father about this. He knows how a woman's arms should feel; I don't, I don't have any idea. Now please, excuse me. I have to go.

[*He wheels away and leaves, as PHAEDRA yearns after him, recapitulating her prior remarks.*]

PHAEDRA: Would you like something to eat?
　　　　I was very casual; my voice was relaxed, a mother
　　　　talking to a son.
Would you like something to eat?
　　　　Then on to the inevitable:
Am I too fat? Too thin? What kind of woman do you like best?
　　　　I embarrassed him. But he was polite; he tried to answer. And then
he tried to go. I wouldn't let him. What time is it? I asked. Time passes,
it passes like a dream.
　　　　He didn't know what I was talking about; he's young.　　So young.
I'm too soft, I said. But you could teach me, I could learn. When I was
growing up, girls didn't exercise; it wasn't feminine.
　　　　I think I smiled when I said that.
It wasn't feminine.
　　　　Then:
I could ride with you. Bareback.
　　　　Oh God, I didn't say that!
Ride bareback. With you. Do you think it's too late?
　　　　Probably, he said. Probably it's too late.

[*The Male FRIEND enters.*]

FRIEND: Excuse me. I'm looking for Hippolytus.

PHAEDRA: Looking here? Why? How should I know where he is?

FRIEND: I thought I heard his voice. If he needed my help, I was going to saddle his horse for him. I wasn't sure when he was leaving.

PHAEDRA: Immediately, I assure you, and without looking back! He was in a terrible hurry to get away.

FRIEND: That's Hippolytus. Can't wait to be alone, out of reach, out of touch, no embraces or good-byes. He's probably off already—

PHAEDRA: Probably.

FRIEND: —saddle or no saddle.

[*He goes to the window and looks out.*]

PHAEDRA: [*Overlapping.*] Saddle or no saddle. Bareback. Probably.

FRIEND: He's headstrong, stubborn, won't be reined in, just like his horse. I wish I had more influence on him—[*He turns around and transforms into the Female FRIEND.*]—and on you, sweetheart. Are you feeling better now? Have you eaten? Slept?

PHAEDRA: No. No. And no.

FRIEND: You can't keep this up, can't keep testing the edge; you'll fall over one of these dark nights.

PHAEDRA: Good. Then it will be finished.

FRIEND: For you. But what about me? What will happen to me?

PHAEDRA: Who knows? Maybe you'll marry. There are always new widowers popping up. Maybe you'll marry Theseus.

FRIEND: [*Touching PHAEDRA's forehead.*] You do have a fever! Lie down. You need to rest.

PHAEDRA: If I rest, I'll give in. I have to keep fighting.

FRIEND: Fighting what? Why? Tell me. Please. Maybe I can help.

PHAEDRA: No one can help. It's in my blood, I can't escape. You know my history. All the women in my family have been ruined by love: my grandmother, my mother, and my sister, my poor sister . . .

FRIEND: Why dredge that up? It happened years ago.

PHAEDRA: A lifetime ago. Theseus was young then. And so was I. Ariadne fell in love with him at first sight—and so did I. [*She moves into a separate light, lost in a repetition of obsessive memory. The FRIEND listens from the distance.*] But she was the one he chose. I was only fifteen years old. He seemed like a god to me, so tall and slim, his skin bronzed by the sun. Golden, that's how he looked, golden, walking toward us through the sand. I'll never forget. I kept praying he would change his mind and turn to me, I kept waiting, waiting for someday, for somehow, all my girlhood, waiting, in the daylight thinking of him, in the nighttime dreaming of him, wanting him, in my bed, in my white sheets, in my white nightgown, dreaming of white and waiting for it, and how it would feel, and love, and love-making, and love-words, to me, for me. But he made a pact with my sister. She helped him through the maze and in return he married her. He gave her a night or a week, made her pregnant with his child, and left her on an island all alone. And then what happened? What happened then? No one knows, no one was there, no one is certain how she died, in the agony of childbirth or by her own hand. No one was with her at the end.

FRIEND: [*Leading her out of her isolation.*] She was far away and you were just a girl yourself; it wasn't your fault.

PHAEDRA: It was a monstrous fate! And what did I do? Avenge her, murder him? Oh no. On the contrary. I took her place, I filled her absence, I married the man she married.

FRIEND: You wanted to be happy.

PHAEDRA: I believed I would be happy! And now the wheel turns to torture me.

FRIEND: I'll stop the wheel, I'll send the torturers away! [*Tenderly.*] Tell me now. Tell me everything.

PHAEDRA: [*Sorrowfully.*] What do you think love is?

FRIEND: Something sweet, something bitter.

PHAEDRA: It's only the bitterness I've known.

FRIEND: How can that be? Theseus would give you the world. He's a great man in this country and he's made you his wife.

PHAEDRA: Why do you keep jabbering about Theseus?!

FRIEND: What? [*Silence as she grasps it.*] You mean it's love—but not Theseus?

PHAEDRA: Finally. Light dawns.

FRIEND: Who is he?

PHAEDRA: I can't say.

FRIEND: Why not? Worse things have happened. Don't hold back now. Tell me who it is.

PHAEDRA: A boy.

FRIEND: A boy? . . . You mean someone young?

[*PHAEDRA nods.*]

Much younger than you?

[*PHAEDRA nods.*]

Well, that's lucky. Right in fashion, too.

PHAEDRA: I could *set* a fashion with this one.

FRIEND: Who is it?

PHAEDRA: A relation. But not a relation.

FRIEND: Don't tease me.

PHAEDRA: My husband has loved him longer than I. But there's no sin in that for him. No, not for him.

FRIEND: You don't mean—

PHAEDRA: He has a room in this house. At night I hear him breathing. What divides us? Walls.

FRIEND: Him!?

PHAEDRA: Walls of wood and plaster. Even with my own weak hand I could strike them down. Then he would be next to me. In the darkness. Then he would be in—

FRIEND: No.

PHAEDRA: —my arms and his lips would be on mine and I would whisper into his mouth his name.

FRIEND: Hippolytus!

PHAEDRA: You're the one who said it, not I. Not I.

FRIEND: And he, does he say he loves you, too?

PHAEDRA: How could he? He doesn't know how I feel. I'm so ashamed. Oh, what should I do? What?

FRIEND: You ask *me?* I have no husband, I have no son. How should I know?

PHAEDRA: Just imagine yourself in my place: you have years of experience doing that!

FRIEND: I don't think I have the imagination for this! Hippolytus? Oh, how could you do this to yourself! Don't even try to answer. Let me think. You can't put him out of your mind. No, it's gone too far; he's that fever in your body, in your heart. You can't give him up, and you can't give up your hopes either. Well, then, is there a chance he wants you?

PHAEDRA: How could I even guess? He's so shy, so proper, so virtuous.

FRIEND: There must be some way to find out.

PHAEDRA: It can't happen. It shouldn't happen! For God's sake, he's almost my son.

FRIEND: Almost. One little word that makes all the difference. There's a solution for everything. Let me see what I can see.

PHAEDRA: No. Please. Don't give me away.

FRIEND: [*Already hurrying out of the room.*] I won't say anything. I promise.

[*The FRIEND exits. PHAEDRA is left alone.*]

PHAEDRA: I never meant for it to happen. But it did. On the very day I stood beside the man who was to be my husband, on that same day, another man . . . possessed me. Not in body, no, I don't mean that, but my heart, that had been so cool, so still, went mad. In a minute I was changed, in a foreign land, heaven, hell, I don't know, but filled with knowledge, a new and terrifying knowledge. Theseus turned to slip the ring on my finger—

[*THESEUS reappears and puts the ring on her finger.*]

—but as I gave him my hand, I saw a young man, dressed in white linen, standing at the edge of the garden in the high grass so he seemed to grow out of it, his hair curling like vines, his face like marble. [*To THESEUS.*] Who is that boy?

THESEUS: Him? I told you about him. That's my son, Hippolytus.

PHAEDRA: [*Echoing.*] Your son, Hippolytus. I should have guessed. I see your face in his.

THESEUS: Good-looking, isn't he?

PHAEDRA: Beautiful.

THESEUS: But stiff. Tight. Life hasn't shaken him up. . . . He has my eyes, doesn't he?

PHAEDRA: Your eyes. Yes. But clearer.

THESEUS: Colder. There's ice in his blood.

PHAEDRA: Is there?

THESEUS: Nothing melts him. Not yet anyway. By the time I was his age, I'd had a dozen women in as many cities, I'd risked my life for a chance at immortality. You remember. You were there. But this boy! This boy still drinks milk.

PHAEDRA: He looks the way you did the first time I saw you. When Ariadne and I saw you. You had no beard then, you were thin, and your shoulders looked like knives, knives or wings, yes, you looked like an angel; I thought I was hallucinating. Am I? Am I?

THESEUS: What's the matter? You're trembling.

PHAEDRA: I've never felt like this before.

THESEUS: You've never been married before. What woman wouldn't feel nervous? Come closer, darling. Lean on me. Use my strength.

[*He takes her in his arms.*]

PHAEDRA: He's watching us.

THESEUS: [*Irritated.*] You wouldn't know if you weren't watching *him*.

PHAEDRA: You're right, I'm sorry.

THESEUS: Almost everyone's gone. He'll leave, too.

[*He starts to kiss her; she pulls away.*]

PHAEDRA: He hasn't moved. Ask him to leave.

THESEUS: I don't know why it's so important to you.

PHAEDRA: It's my wedding day. I want to be with you now, only with you, alone with you. Please. Send him away.

THESEUS: [*Gesturing for HIPPOLYTUS to go.*] There. He's off and running. Happy now?

PHAEDRA: He has such long legs . . . Who was his mother?

THESEUS: It doesn't matter. The past is past.

PHAEDRA: I want to know.

THESEUS: Well, I am consecrated to satisfy you. But you will not be satisfied, I'm sure; there's so little to tell. I barely knew his mother. She was a woman I slept with one night because we were both in the mood. Oh, maybe it was two nights. Or five. She was hot-blooded and so was I. Sometimes, you know, no force on earth is as strong as human passion.

PHAEDRA: Nothing on earth. Oh yes. I know.

THESEUS: The affair meant nothing.

PHAEDRA: How can love mean nothing?

THESEUS: But it wasn't love. Not for me or for her. She didn't care a damn for men, only the pleasures they gave her. She had no feeling for me—and less for Hippolytus. She couldn't wait to give him up.

PHAEDRA: He must have been hurt by that.

THESEUS: Hippolytus? I don't think so. He's a stoic, that boy, always was, from the day she sent him to me when he was twelve. I took him in, that scrawny thing. What else could I do? But as time went on, he grew on me. We spent days together, sometimes weeks.

PHAEDRA: [*Echoing.*] Days together, weeks together.

THESEUS: Now don't tell me you're jealous!

PHAEDRA: I won't tell you anything. [*She kisses him. Then:*] I think he has your mouth, too.

[*THESEUS pulls PHAEDRA down on the bed and draws the curtains. There is the sound of the bedsprings moving rhythmically, and thick breathing. These sounds continue—even after PHAEDRA slips out from the curtains and talks to the audience.*]

And whenever I kissed my husband after that, I felt the son's mouth on mine, and whenever I wrapped my arms around him, or my legs, it was the younger body I enclosed. From the first moment I saw him, I was incurable. I did what I could, sent him away, and when he was near, avoided the sight of him, the sound of his voice, the casual touch in the hallway, but then in secret I hid so I could watch him lifting weights in his room, naked, his muscles tensing and relaxing, opening and closing, and all the while I held my breath, terrified of being caught. But he never saw me, so intent was he upon his discipline, that severe young man, that beautiful boy. And every night I tried to drown myself in Theseus's love. Then he left, on business, he said, urgent, essential. He shouldn't have gone. He shouldn't have left me here with this dreadful feast on my table, tempting me, forbidding me—fatal! fatal! To put on the plate of a starving woman the only food she craves, and the only one that will poison her—fatal!

[*THESEUS emerges from the bed, rumpled, and embraces her.*]

THESEUS: I'll be home as soon as I can.

PHAEDRA: Don't go. Stay here. Please.

THESEUS: Before you start missing me, I'll be back.

PHAEDRA: I'm frightened. I won't feel safe.

THESEUS: Don't be absurd. There's nothing to be afraid of here. Anyway, Hippolytus will be around. He'll look after you.

PHAEDRA: Hippolytus? No. No. That's not the answer. No.

THESEUS: I imagine he seems young to you but he's very strong. Really. He can take charge. Don't worry. [*He kisses her.*] I'll talk to him now. He'll be proud to be the man of the house in my absence. There's nothing he wants more than to prove himself to me. It's really very touching, don't you think?

PHAEDRA: I don't want to be touched! I won't be able to sleep. Don't go. I beg you! [*But THESEUS has gone.*] Take me with you. Or take him. Oh, God, don't let me drown in this terrible sea! Why won't you understand what I'm saying?

[*It's already too late. HIPPOLYTUS appears, beardless, awkward, a youthful version of his father.*]

HIPPOLYTUS: Excuse me, but my father just asked me to make sure that—

PHAEDRA: [*Drawing herself up haughtily.*] Your father was mistaken. I don't need anything from you. [*She starts to turn away, then stops. She brushes her hand against his cheek, almost a caress.*]

HIPPOLYTUS: [*Jumping back.*] What are you doing?

PHAEDRA: I thought   I think   there was a mosquito on your cheek

HIPPOLYTUS: [*Incredulously.*] A mosquito? In November?

[*He backs away from her and exits.*]

PHAEDRA: [*Staring after him.*] On the edge   swaying on the edge   in the country, on the mountains and the cliffs   don't push me! tempted by the edge   cold sweat, thunder heart, brain on fire   where are you? day dawns   wake up   empty pillow   where are you?! no one home   door creaks, wind howls, racing pulse, fever high   stay with me!

[*Lights up dimly on* **THESEUS** *taking off his clothes in candlelight.*]

You cast your shadow over my life   I was lost in it   lost . . .

[***PHAEDRA** watches as he speaks to someone unseen.*]

THESEUS: I swore to be a faithful husband. I thought I would lose myself in happiness with her, and I did, I did. For a week, a month, maybe more. But life is cruel: it makes us bored with the passion we know best. It doesn't kill the appetite, though. No, it just leaves you craving a different taste, a new delicacy. The older I get, the hungrier I am. I like a full meal at breakfast, a bite at lunch and a nibble at dinner, with a wide variety of specialties on the side, and then a nightcap, always a nightcap.

[***PHAEDRA** watches with anger and disgust as he takes off his trousers.*]

PHAEDRA: Theseus's hair is turning gray. He doesn't see it, or maybe he thinks it looks distinguished. His waist has thickened, like mine, veins braid his legs, gravity has a grip on him, too, his skin is loosening, as flabby as mine, he has age spots on his cheeks and hands, and soon he'll have a turkey neck, like mine—but that doesn't stop him from gobbling!

THESEUS: So I'll break a promise. Why should I fight it? Lie down. Yes, lie down here. [*Naked, he bends over someone not seen.*] I want your taste on my tongue, making my dinner sweet. I want to be in your arms, between your thighs, in the deeps of your belly. [*He straddles the other.*] Stay open for me. Yes. Like that. We'll pull the night over us, we'll make the darkness sing. A man can't be a saint. [*Seductively.*] Anyway, women don't want saints, do they? [*He begins a sexual rhythm.*] No, no, they don't want saints; they want men. Race with me, darling. Rage with me. We'll get there together.

[***PHAEDRA** steps into the near darkness and picks up the candle, carries it toward her bed.*]

PHAEDRA: Why should I be different? I love the heights and the deep places, too. I know the song and I want to sing it, now, now, before my candle goes out, before I forget that I was beautiful once, before I forget my name, before time goes out with the candle and I forget my dreams, forget that night follows day and shades into day again, forget what a button is for—[*She begins to unbutton the neck of her robe.*]—and what's underneath the clothing, and underneath the skin where the blood runs fierce and my spirit shows its pulse, before the darkness steals in and I forget my face that loves his face, my face that might grow young in the light of his eyes before it becomes a stranger, even to myself.

[*She picks up the mirror again and studies herself intensely. The* **FRIEND** *enters, watches, then breaks the silence.*]

FRIEND: Can't keep away from yourself, can you?

PHAEDRA: It's written on my face: my life as a woman is over. But Theseus, Theseus is in his prime!

FRIEND: [*Gently taking the mirror away from her.*] I love those little laugh lines at your eyes.

PHAEDRA: Crow's feet.

FRIEND: You call them that because you don't laugh anymore. Because you don't even remember you laughed. I remember.

PHAEDRA: Write it on my gravestone. "She laughed, once."

FRIEND: Oh stop! You can't push time back, you can only disguise its mischief. Women have always used artifice. Cleopatra did, Nefertiti did; there's an entire history of art devoted to these tricks. Henna for the hair and cheeks. Kohl for the eyes. Sand. Mud. The sting of bees on the lips.

PHAEDRA: Thank you. I'll forgo the bees.

FRIEND: You can make age an illusion, too. It's a grand tradition. Why shouldn't you take your place in it?

PHAEDRA: I need a miracle, not some fiction in a bottle.

FRIEND: I'll cover up those little flaws you hate so much. Tilt your head back, sweetheart, yes, good. [*She takes out* **PHAEDRA**'*s cosmetics and starts to work.*] We can conceal these shadows under your eyes; they look like graves, for pity's sake. Of course if you slept at night . . . ! And I can hide a few of those crinkles you detest, too.

PHAEDRA: I don't think he's ever been with a woman.

FRIEND: [*Applying mascara.*] There's a first time for everything. Keep your eyes open. The mascara will give you a more open, vulnerable look. [*She looks at her handiwork.*] Yes, yes, it does. You look like a virgin. [*She takes a hairbrush and brushes.*] Let's fluff out your hair, make it full and soft around your face. There. Like a halo. He'll like that. [*She employs rouge and lipstick.*] Now for some color, a sense of excitement in the flesh. A warm radiance on the cheeks. And on your mouth, a deep rose or burgundy— yes, burgundy is better; it suggests wine, intoxication. I'll put a little gloss, right here in the middle of your lower lip, a hint of petulance—excellent! because petulance reminds us of sulking and sulking reminds us of adolescence. And adolescence, as we know, adolescence reminds us of sex. [*She can't help herself and kisses* **PHAEDRA** *on the mouth.*]

PHAEDRA: What?!

FRIEND: Just testing. Making sure you get the response you want.

PHAEDRA: You mean now I'm . . . irresistible?

FRIEND: That was the idea, wasn't it?

PHAEDRA: You have my burgundy on your mouth.

FRIEND: Does it make me irresistible, too?

PHAEDRA: It makes you a stranger. [*She hands a tissue to the FRIEND.*] I liked you better the way you were.

FRIEND: [*Wipes lipstick off her mouth in a tense silence.*] All right, sweetheart. Listen to me. Here's what I've been thinking. Everyone lives for love, right? And what good is love if it kills? Or if it dies, strangled in its own cord? If you put your ear to the wind, you hear, in all corners of the world, in all its mountains and valleys, in mansions and in slums, women sighing, men wailing—and for what? The glorious pains of love.

PHAEDRA: Not glorious to me.

FRIEND: Only because unsatisfied.

PHAEDRA: Satisfaction! As if that were everything! We're human, not animals. I feel what I feel, I can't help it, but I can hold myself back, I can rise above my passions, and I will, I swear I will—or die!

FRIEND: Better to lie beneath Hippolytus and live!

PHAEDRA: You? You tell me that? You who almost collapsed when you heard my confession?

FRIEND: I was upset, it's true, but I've had second thoughts. I want your happiness above everything.

PHAEDRA: Above morality. Above law. Above natural law.

FRIEND: Love and desire, that's what's natural.

PHAEDRA: My only desire is *not* to desire.

FRIEND: And what would *I* do, then?

PHAEDRA: You could get your own life.

FRIEND: But I prefer yours. It gets so boring walking back and forth on the middle ground. Besides, I'm terribly fond of that little softening under your chin. [*She touches her there.*]

PHAEDRA: Don't! It's repulsive.

FRIEND: No: human. Everything changes, everything life touches. Even this mattress. [*She moves near to it.*] It isn't straight or firm anymore, as it was the first night you slept here. It's taken the shape of your body—where you lie, where you roll, how your weight distributes. It's a little lumpy now, uneven; not a perfect model, but one that bears your imprint, right for *you.*

PHAEDRA: And for Theseus? If I lay here with his son, would that be right for him?

FRIEND: Who knows? Maybe Theseus will do what thousands of husbands do: see and not see at the same time.

PHAEDRA: Love may be blind. Theseus isn't.

FRIEND: Of all people, Theseus knows that it's natural to sin. Tell Hippolytus. Tell him and be rid of your obsession.

PHAEDRA: You must be insane.

FRIEND: No: selfish. I don't want to go through another week like the last one. I couldn't find him when I searched. I ran here and there for hours. Why would he come to me, anyway? He can't guess what's in your heart.

PHAEDRA: And in his? He trains horses; he breaks them, makes stallions obedient to the bit in their mouths—but with me, he's afraid. His voice cracks like a boy's at puberty; he looks everywhere but into my eyes.

FRIEND: If wild animals can be tamed, so can he. Criminals and saints, both extremes have surrendered to love. Why not Hippolytus? Take the chance. Tell him, I say.

PHAEDRA: My tongue would go dead in my mouth.

FRIEND: Use my tongue, then.

PHAEDRA: You'd speak for me?

FRIEND: I would.

PHAEDRA: No! Go and find your own love! Then you won't have to worry so much about mine.

FRIEND: [Stung.] All right. If that's how you feel. I'll pack my bags. Believe me, the last thing I want is to interfere. Sleep well.

PHAEDRA: I'll never sleep again.

FRIEND: There you go again, so melodramatic! Don't you know by now that only death is forever, nothing else—not even this anguish you suffer today? Or my anguish. [She turns to leave.] Good-bye.

PHAEDRA: No. Don't leave me.

FRIEND: Make up your mind.

PHAEDRA: My mind is torn.

FRIEND: Well, get it together then. Fast. Hippolytus is coming.

PHAEDRA: You hear him?

[The FRIEND nods.]

What will I do?! I can't see him; I'm too weak. Send him away. Tell him to get his saddle, mount his horse and ride, ride far away. Tell him I'm deathly sick, and all because of him. No, no, don't say that.

FRIEND: Let me feel him out. Trust me.

PHAEDRA: But once you put my feelings into words . . .

FRIEND: I won't. I swear. I'll talk around it. I'll lead him on and see how he follows. But he can't know you're here. Hide. Hurry. Hurry!

[PHAEDRA runs to her bed. The FRIEND quickly draws the curtains, just as HIPPOLYTUS appears.]

HIPPOLYTUS: What are you doing?

FRIEND: Oh, nothing. Straightening up. Phaedra left her bed such a mess. She's really been sick, poor thing.

HIPPOLYTUS: She's not here?

FRIEND: You don't see her, do you?

HIPPOLYTUS: It's just as well. Tell her that I came to say good-bye.

PHAEDRA: [In a whisper.] Good-bye?

FRIEND: [Overlapping.] Good-bye? But where are you going?

HIPPOLYTUS: I have to find my father. Something's happened to him, I'm sure of it.

FRIEND: Really? What makes you think so?

HIPPOLYTUS: My dreams. They wake me at night, show me blood on the waves, foaming on the mouth of my horse, show me black wings swooping low. If I don't go for him now, I'm afraid the worst will happen. [*He tries to leave, but the* **FRIEND** *detains him.*]

FRIEND: But Phaedra's on the case. She's sent messages everywhere, across every sea, to track him down. Her devotion will turn the tide. Wait a little.

HIPPOLYTUS: I can't. He's never been gone this long before. I have to help him! A man is contemptible if he doesn't take action when his family is in danger.

FRIEND: But you promised your father you'd stay with Phaedra. He'll be furious if you leave home.

HIPPOLYTUS: It isn't my home now; it's hers. I can't stand it anymore. Anyway, she has you to care for her. [*He starts to leave.*]

FRIEND: [*Restraining him.*] She'll fall apart if you go. Don't you understand? The man who possesses her heart seems indifferent to her. Other women might lose themselves in drink or drug themselves to sleep: not Phaedra. At night her eyes don't close, and on the screen that darkness brings, she sees her lover's face. She cries out for him, she reaches out her arms, she's wild with love and longing.

HIPPOLYTUS: I never doubted the depths of her love.

FRIEND: But have you understood its true nature?

HIPPOLYTUS: Why ask me that? I'm no authority on women, or on love.

FRIEND: Exactly. And there is the crux of the problem. You don't know the power you exert on her.

HIPPOLYTUS: I?

FRIEND: Yes, you. You, the son.

HIPPOLYTUS: Oh.

FRIEND: Your father's son. Here, in this house, while he's away.

HIPPOLYTUS: Oh. Oh. I see.

FRIEND: Do you?

HIPPOLYTUS: Yes, yes, I do. How stupid of me! No wonder she can't bear to have me around, gets flustered when our paths cross.

FRIEND: Yes? Yes?

HIPPOLYTUS: My presence, my very existence, reminds her of him. But I'm here—and he isn't.

FRIEND: Yes, that's right.

HIPPOLYTUS: And I never suspected! It never occurred to me that I brought her pain! Well, she'll soon be free of all the grief I've caused. When you see her, tell her I've gone to search for him, and I won't rest, won't sleep, until I have him safe at home and back where he belongs, in her arms. [*He turns to go. The* **FRIEND** *grabs his arm.*]

FRIEND: You still don't understand. Nothing will please her if you leave now.

HIPPOLYTUS: You make no sense! Please! Take your hand off my arm.

FRIEND: Oh, why won't you listen?!

PHAEDRA: [*Drawing the curtains and stepping out.*] Yes, please, listen.

FRIEND: Phaedra, wait. Don't—

PHAEDRA: It's too late. I have to. Leave me with him. [*As the **FRIEND** hesitates:*] Do as I ask. Go.

[*The **FRIEND** exits. To **HIPPOLYTUS**:*]

What she said is true. I do miss your father, terribly, not as he is now, with his great swagger and pride, but as he once was, a young man, brave and gentle, even a little shy, and handsome—as handsome as you are now.

HIPPOLYTUS: As I am? What do I have to do with it?

PHAEDRA: He had your eyes, the curve of your lips, the smooth marble of your skin, shadowed then with its first beard. Everywhere he went, women threw themselves into his arms. Who could blame them? My own sister deceived her family and taught him how to cheat death with a thread so he would take her for his wife. I wanted him for myself but held my hopes in check, was patient, made another life. But I would have abandoned all my scruples, if it had been you; I would have stolen her place and stood by your side all the way to the end—

HIPPOLYTUS: What?

PHAEDRA: —facing death with your hand in mine; and if we'd died then, together, I would have been happier than living a thousand years with someone else.

HIPPOLYTUS: You don't mean what you say. You're feverish; you're sick.

PHAEDRA: Sick with love, yes, yes, I am. I've put myself into your hands; do what you want with me.

HIPPOLYTUS: What I want? [*He pushes her away.*] What I want is never to have heard the words you've spoken today, never to have laid my eyes on you—no, no!—had your eyes fall on me.

PHAEDRA: But if the food is tempting, why shouldn't I taste it? Why shouldn't you?

HIPPOLYTUS: Tempting? It's disgusting—for you to come to me like this, your body half-uncovered, shameless, shameful! Your 'love,' as you call it, is horrible to me! Get back! The sight of you, the smell of your perfume, even your breath on my face, make me feel dirty.

PHAEDRA: Shhh. Shhh! You're shouting.

HIPPOLYTUS: After these confessions, do you expect me to be calm? Get away from me. Don't infect me with your corruption! God, I hate you.

PHAEDRA: I fought it, I did, I swear I did!

HIPPOLYTUS: What am I going to say to my father when I see him?

PHAEDRA: . . . You'll tell him?

HIPPOLYTUS: I won't have to. Don't you think he can see the difference between a clear glass of water and a polluted one?

[*He exits. **PHAEDRA** stands in shocked silence, then walks to her bed and opens the curtains. The disarray of her bed confronts her. She begins pulling off the* *bedclothes and folding them in neat little piles. The FRIEND enters and watches in silence, increasingly worried.*]

FRIEND: What did he say? [*No response.*] What are you doing? [*No response.*] Stop that folding, stop it, please!

[*PHAEDRA rebuffs her.*]

Please, sweetheart, tell me what happened. You're making me afraid.

PHAEDRA: [*Coldly.*] You? Why should you be afraid?

FRIEND: Don't keep secrets from me now. Please. What did he say? What happened?

PHAEDRA: [*Mimicking.*] 'What happened? Tell me what happened.' You have to know everything, don't you? Be involved with everything! You, with your insatiable curiosity! You'd ask a corpse to describe the guillotine that cut off her head.

FRIEND: No. It can't be that bad. Maybe he was shocked—

PHAEDRA: [*Handing her a pile of bed linens.*] Burn these sheets.

FRIEND: What are you going to do?

PHAEDRA: You've done everything else I asked—even what I didn't ask. Burn them, I said!

[*The FRIEND doesn't move, distraught.*]

Why do you stand there paralyzed? My faithful and loving friend! You couldn't wait to 'help' me before. Why won't you help me now?

FRIEND: You make my heart stop, you look so cold.

PHAEDRA: It's good to be cold. [*She continues folding.*]

FRIEND: All right, I must have misjudged him, I see, I must have failed, but it was all for you! For love of you! If he had run to you and taken you in his arms, then you would call me your best, your only, your one true friend. You're not angry because I did something wrong; it's because I didn't succeed.

PHAEDRA: Finally, a moment of truth.

FRIEND: I'm sorry, so so sorry.

PHAEDRA: I'm sure you are.

FRIEND: I never meant to hurt you, I swear it.

PHAEDRA: I believe you. So?

FRIEND: So? So? . . . I have something else to tell you.

PHAEDRA: What else can there be? I have nothing now, not my self-respect or *his* respect, not my pride or the little flame of hope that lit my darkness. And *you* were the one who tempted me; *you* sang of the glories of love and I listened. If not for you, would I have spoken at all? You've destroyed me. Cry, yes, cry.

FRIEND: It's not for myself I'm crying. Theseus is back.

PHAEDRA: What?!

FRIEND: He arrived last night; he means to surprise you, I heard. He could be here at any minute.

PHAEDRA: What will I do, what will I do? Where are your solutions now, my friend!

FRIEND: Stay calm, you must be calm.

PHAEDRA: Do you think Hippolytus will be calm? No, no. My words will pour from his lips and then, and then—Theseus will break me between his hands; my life will be over. Because of you. Because you pushed me to this.

FRIEND: I wanted what you wanted; I moved your desire forward. For you, for your happiness. I was sure you'd overcome his impossible pride, his fear.

PHAEDRA: Fear? Loathing, you mean! It was insane to think I could seduce him from his chastity, me, with these furrows on my forehead and my body stinking of desperation!

FRIEND: Use your head. Be clever. Go to Theseus the minute he arrives and—

PHAEDRA: And what? What brilliant plan have you hatched now?

FRIEND: Accuse Hippolytus.

PHAEDRA: Place my crime in his mouth?

FRIEND: What choice do you have?

PHAEDRA: Accuse Hippolytus?

FRIEND: You woke last night to find him leaning over you. Terrified, you cried for help and I, hearing your voice, went to you just in time to see the monster running from your room.

PHAEDRA: I'd cut out my tongue before I add lying to my sins.

FRIEND: If you're afraid to speak, write it down. Send Theseus a letter before he meets his son or God knows what will happen! You know his temper!

PHAEDRA: I know my crime.

FRIEND: But Theseus doesn't. He'd never suspect. He, with his stupendous ego. [She brings pen and paper.] Here. Write. There's not much time.

PHAEDRA: I can't.

FRIEND: Hurry, or Hippolytus will betray you first. He'd denounce you in a minute to keep his father's love.

PHAEDRA: Haven't you done enough harm?

FRIEND: I want to make it up. Why should you let Hippolytus get the best of you twice? Didn't he laugh at your confession? Humiliate you? To hell with him. Save yourself.

PHAEDRA: Don't you understand yet? I can't be saved.

FRIEND: You want to sacrifice your life for Hippolytus? What good will come of that? Think it over. [As she exits:] I'll keep Theseus at the door to give you time. But don't delay. Write the letter!

PHAEDRA: [Alone; sits, stands, paces.] He stared at me with such contempt. There's no time, no time! How can I? Time, time is running out! [She begins to write.] "My dearest Theseus, If only I could greet you with open arms and open heart but I barely have the strength to tell you what has happened or to name the guilty one." [She pauses; stops writing.] And whose name do I write? Whose? [She begins to write again. THESEUS enters, unseen, a stack of gift-wrapped boxes in his arms, and listens.] "All the ties of blood could not hold him back from me. When he first accosted me in the garden I ran from him in horror. For days I resisted his pleas. I took to my bed, feverish. The household worried for me, believing I was sick. To insure my safety, I sent for my friend and had her sleep in the next room." [*She pauses, then writes.*] "Ask *her* what happened on that fateful night, in the hour just before dawn, when she heard my screams and, running to my bed, saw the intruder bending over me, his naked body glowing in the moonlight, that body you, his father, created, that beautiful boy you trusted and—"

[*THESEUS has dropped his packages, startling PHAEDRA, and now runs in to grab the letter.*]

THESEUS: Hippolytus? It's my son who has done this?

[*PHAEDRA stands mute, paralyzed.*]

Answer me!

PHAEDRA: I can't, I can't!
THESEUS: So that's it. That's why he didn't run to meet me. Oh God, it's unbelievable. My own son.

[*PHAEDRA collapses. THESEUS kneels beside her.*]

Dearest. Darling.

PHAEDRA: Don't touch me.
THESEUS: Let me carry you to your bed.
PHAEDRA: No! You mustn't touch me. No. Not now.
THESEUS: Are you taking his sin upon yourself?
PHAEDRA: No. Yes. Please. Please forgive me.
THESEUS: Forgive you? You? This is intolerable! No, my darling, no, my sweet, you mustn't blame yourself.
PHAEDRA: I didn't want you to go away, I begged you!
THESEUS: Now I see! How blind I was! He never looked at women because he was obsessed with *you*! And you knew it. You were afraid, all along, you were afraid of him. And I was too slow to understand. [*He draws himself up.*] I won't be slow now.
PHAEDRA: What do you mean?
THESEUS: I will be swift to justice. How dare he put his hands on you!
PHAEDRA: He's young. He didn't know what he was doing.
THESEUS: You would plead for him? I won't hear of it! [*Thundering.*] Where is my son?!
PHAEDRA: He's not here, he left the house to search for you.
THESEUS: So you'd imagine you were safe and he could steal back at night. Oh, I could do murder!
PHAEDRA: No. Please. Don't hurt him.
THESEUS: How could I have stayed away so long? If I'd been here, nothing would have happened. [*He embraces her.*] I'll never leave you again. [*He lifts her up and carries her to the bed.*] You can sleep now. And when you wake, my son will not be here to cast his shadow over you.
PHAEDRA: You'll send him away?

THESEUS: You will never have to see him again. And he will never lay his eyes on you. [*He leaves* PHAEDRA *on the bed and moves behind it. The rear canopy conceals him. Only* PHAEDRA, *reacting to every moment of the following scene, can be seen.*] Hippolytus!

HIPPOLYTUS: I'm here, Father. I'm so happy and relieved you're safe. I told Phaedra—

THESEUS: Phaedra! How dare you mention her name?

HIPPOLYTUS: What?

THESEUS: Hypocrite! Even snakes shed their skins in the open air but you, you hide in the grass and blend with it, and call it nature! Well, I see your nature now!

HIPPOLYTUS: You're talking in circles.

THESEUS: Then you should understand me. You're used to double-talk, to the twisted tongue, the crooked road. If a traveler used you for a star, he'd wind up in a bottomless pit—

HIPPOLYTUS: Father!

THESEUS: —or in his mother's bed!

HIPPOLYTUS: What? Who told you this lie?

THESEUS: Do you accuse your mother of lies?

HIPPOLYTUS: My mother? . . . No. I accuse no one. But remember who I am. I never wanted any woman; you thought it was a fault. Other boys took their girls into the bushes. I rode into the mountains alone to find my raptures and meet my Gods face-to-face. My Gods, not yours, Father.

THESEUS: Get out of my sight. Leave my home this instant!

HIPPOLYTUS: How can you believe—?

THESEUS: [*Thundering.*] Go! And never let my eyes light on you again!

HIPPOLYTUS: I'm your son, Father. I'll do as you say. And I forgive you. [*He crosses in front of* PHAEDRA *and pauses.*] Even a pig, wallowing in its own shit, is cleaner than you. [*He exits.*]

PHAEDRA: He would never have spoken, never betrayed me. As I betrayed him. [*She steps down from her bed and shouts:*] Theseus!

THESEUS: [*Entering.*] How amazing that guilt can sound so much like innocence! Oh Lord, what could be worse than a father cursing his own child? [*Moving toward* PHAEDRA.] Here, come into my arms. [*He folds her against him.*] I have been your revenge and now I will be your refuge.

PHAEDRA: There will be no refuge for either of us. Call him back. Quickly. Quickly!

THESEUS: You're burning up.

PHAEDRA: Yes. Burning as I burned when you were gone. Not in fear as I told you but—Quick! Call him back before it's too late.

THESEUS: But you're safe now. Your enemy is gone, and gone forever.

PHAEDRA: No, no, the enemy is here, *here*—[*She strikes her breast.*]—in me.

THESEUS: You were the victim, you were helpless against him.

PHAEDRA: *He* is the victim, he, your son! Go after him, I beg you. He's taken his horse; I hear the hooves in a gallop. They'll head for the cliffs. I know the path he favors. Hurry. He'll kill himself to prove his innocence.

THESEUS: Innocence?

PHAEDRA: Call him back, call him back before it's too late.

THESEUS: [*Shaking her roughly.*] What possesses you?

PHAEDRA: *He!* He possesses me! Not through any act or wish of his but . . . but I . . . I wanted him. He never touched me. That's the truth, I swear it.

THESEUS: He never touched you?

PHAEDRA: Never.

THESEUS: But your letter . . . ?

PHAEDRA: Lies.

THESEUS: He never came to your bed?

PHAEDRA: Only in my dreams.

THESEUS: You say that to me?! Better die than dream such dreams! [*He strikes her.*] You filthy thing! You animal!

PHAEDRA: Don't.

THESEUS: To lust for your own son!

PHAEDRA: *Your* son, yours! It was you I loved, your youth, mine. I don't blame Hippolytus for despising me. But you—you with your married women and little girls!—you have no right to hit me.

THESEUS: I have every right! Since time began and women were false, men have taken law into their own hands—taken their wives' throats into their own hands! [*He starts to choke* PHAEDRA.]

PHAEDRA: Nothing happened, don't you understand? Only words, only desire.

THESEUS: I'll tell the world what you desired. Wherever you go, people will point their fingers at the woman who forgot to look in the mirror, who tried to seduce a boy, her husband's son. Yes, the world will laugh at your ridiculous "love." [*He slaps her.*] Slut!

PHAEDRA: Oh yes. Only the great man is entitled to a great passion, fury or love, it doesn't matter which. It's natural to have animal emotions when that bludgeon, that staff, that *scepter!* swings between your thighs!

THESEUS: You're proud of what you've done?

PHAEDRA: The stars in my heaven have all gone out.

[*HIPPOLYTUS's FRIEND enters.*]

THESEUS: Have you found him?

FRIEND: Yes.

THESEUS: Thank heaven. Where is he? Well? Well? Won't he come to me?

[*The FRIEND shakes his head.*]

Never mind then. I'll go to him.

FRIEND: It's too late for that.

PHAEDRA: Too late? Already?

THESEUS: That's impossible. He knows my rages, how I lash out. I was wrong, I'll admit it. I'll go down on my knees, I'll beg him to come home.

FRIEND: You may beg for the rest of your life but he won't hear.

THESEUS: What terrible thing are you trying to say? Tell me!

FRIEND: Your voice was still thundering as he jumped on his horse. He was crying, he couldn't see for the tears. I was afraid for him; I got my horse and followed, shouting warnings against the wind. But Hippolytus was hell-bent. His hand cracked the whip and together they climbed the cliffs higher and higher, galloping so fast that the trees disappeared. In no time there was nothing but icy air and bare rock. The clouds lowered themselves onto his head and made a kind of wreath for him. At least that's how it looked to me.

THESEUS: So that's where he is? On the peak?

FRIEND: Not anymore. Suddenly a snake darted out from under a rock, its forked tongue hissing, and the horse reared back. Hippolytus fell, and got tangled in the reins.

PHAEDRA: My doing. My undoing.

FRIEND: The horse bolted and charged forward, dragging the helpless rider over the stony ground, and on they raced as if they were a single creature, the poor boy hanging upside down, his head crashing against rocks and turning them bloody, the skin tearing from his body in strips.

THESEUS: Enough! My son, my son . . . I gave in to my anger, I condemned him on Phaedra's word.

PHAEDRA: I could rip my tongue out by the root.

THESEUS: If only I'd held back!

FRIEND: Hippolytus, too: the way he leaped on that horse.

THESEUS: Quiet! How dare you speak ill of him now?!

FRIEND: I loved him as much as you. But his virtue destroyed him.

THESEUS: Show me where he is. I want to hold him one last time.

PHAEDRA: Let me go with you.

[*She freezes at* THESEUS's *expression. He turns away and exits with the* FRIEND. PHAEDRA *begins to pin up her hair.*]

You fear it—and it comes to pass. You try to escape—and it comes to pass. You weep and you struggle and you bargain with your Gods—and still it comes to pass. Lost. Everything. Lost.

[*In a moment, the* FRIEND *returns in her female aspect.*]

FRIEND: If only I could go back in time, undo what I've done.

PHAEDRA: No more words now. Please.

FRIEND: I was too eager to make you happy. I let my reason find excuses.

PHAEDRA: Can't you be quiet even now? Hippolytus is dead; and it was I who killed him. My love that killed him.

FRIEND: I should have known. One deceit always leads to another, and then we're trapped for good.

PHAEDRA: You're not trapped.

FRIEND: Won't you forgive me?

PHAEDRA: Yes. But who will forgive me? [*Her hair is tightly pinned up now. She begins to knot a sheet.*]

FRIEND: What are you doing with that sheet? [*No response.*] Phaedra, what are you doing?

PHAEDRA: Theseus will have his freedom; it's what he loves most, you know. I can give him that, at least. Now that I've thrown everything away. [*She ties the last knot in the sheet.*] I'm almost finished. You should be relieved: I'll be able to sleep again.

FRIEND: But you can't! No. You can't do that.

PHAEDRA: Quiet. I've had enough of your advice. [*She throws the sheet over the canopy frame, and tightens it.*] It's better for you to leave now.

FRIEND: No.

PHAEDRA: All right, stay. Be with me to the end. [*She makes a noose.*]

FRIEND: I *do* have a heart, you know.

PHAEDRA: Come here. A kiss will keep me warmer than words. [*She kisses the FRIEND.*] Thank you.

FRIEND: Isn't there another way?

PHAEDRA: No. [*She takes off shoes and steps on the bed; smiles.*] So. *This* is how I'll escape old age.

[*Blackout.*]

END OF PLAY

TOWARDS A VERTICAL THEATRE (AN AFTERWORD)

[*Colin Teevan was born in Dublin in 1968. Apart from original works for stage and radio, his dramatic work includes adaptation, translation, and reinterpretations that relocate ancient stories and forms, most often from classical Greece, in the modern context. His translations and adaptations include: Euripides'* Bacchai,[4] *commissioned by and premiered at The National Theatre, London, and Epidaurus, Greece, in 2002, directed by Peter Hall and scored by Harrison Birtwistle;* Iph . . . ,[5] *Lyric Theatre, Belfast, 1999, and subsequently performed in mise-en-espace National Theatre, London, 2002. This piece draws from a longer interview with Colin Teevan conducted by scholar Madeline Dewhurst in London in 2004.*]

Like Shakespearean drama, Greek drama offers us the chance to confront diffi-cult issues, such as ingrained prejudice and bias, in an imagined world that appears other and hence, perhaps, safe. We must remember that even the trage-dians of fifth-century Athens set their plays in the distant and mythological past.[6] A play like the *Bacchai*, for example, is like a prism through which the light of any moment is refracted into its constituent beams.

There are many other things that attract me as a writer to, and that I have drawn from, Greek texts. The first is the engagement with the very beginnings of drama. These first principles of storytelling do not change from one genre to another or from one period to another. While Aristotle is perhaps often seen as the "how-to" guide for writing plays and film, he simply reflects on why good Greek dramas work. The principles he derives from these observations in the *Poetics*, such as what makes a plot work, the concepts of beginnings, middles, and ends, reversals, catharsis, and recognition, survive almost in these forms to the present day.

What's so interesting about the Greeks is that we get a chance to see the dramatic form that has become the template for film, TV, and drama, in its most pristine state. For this reason, the principles of storytelling are explicit rather than implicit. This is crucial dramatic storytelling which is still exploring the potential of the new medium. Compared to this, consider the restrictiveness the predominant contemporary social realist form in British and I believe American theatre at least, where a premium has been put on authenticity, authenticity meaning how exactly speech, décor, and acting, can imitate the real world.

This is the second way in which I engage with the Greeks. I see social realism as a self-conscious attempt to pretend that we, the practitioners and the audience, are not engaged in the acts of pretense that we patently are engaged in. Social realism is so literal, so reductive, that it trivializes theatre; it makes the concerns of theatre social and material issues, not the big philosophical and political questions. In this way I look to the Greeks for inspiration, the scale of the philosophical and political issues they confronted, and I derive aesthetic energy from them. It is articulation on a wholly different scale. It is vertical, a complaint made from the earth with the face turned out and upwards towards the audience and the heavens.

And that is my third point of engagement, the democracy of the form. The articulation of ancient Greek drama is not character-to-character with a pretense that the audience is not there. Some people have described the contemporary monologue, as seen in much recent British and especially Irish dramatic writing, as Greek. I think this is a complete misunderstanding of the function of the monologue in Greek drama. In Greek drama the audience is a character, the audience is the people of Thebes in the *Bacchai,* the gathered armies in *Iphigenia in Aulis,* the plague-ridden people of Thebes in *Oedipus* and therefore the audience is part of the drama, the audience has a stake in the drama. We are being asked to consider the arguments by protagonist and antagonist, arguments that are crucial to our society, whereas in the contemporary monologue we have characters walking outside the drama and telling us about the story they as individuals have experienced somewhere else. For these reasons I see Greek theatre as an extraordinarily political form, not a retrograde form. It exposes the issues of power and philosophy and debates them in front of the people.

My final point of engagement with the Greeks is that, because we can re-translate it, Greek drama can be classical and completely up-to-date in its rhythms, patterns and delivery. For example, in my version of the *Bacchai* I wrote in iambic pentameter but nevertheless used wholly contemporary language and syntax.

It is important to remember that Greek drama was perhaps the most popular form of drama ever. Their theatres held 15,000 to 20,000 people and this in cities whose population were rarely over 100,000 people. The modern theatre has discovered that plays such as those of Euripides were actually oppositional and democratic dramas; they weren't the instruments of Empire and property of the elite that they became in the nineteenth and early twentieth century. Once again, it is the prismatic nature of these great works. They enable each age and society to articulate their debates through them. As W. H. Auden said, each society invents an ancient Greece in its own image.

Colin Teevan
Literary Fellow
Newcastle and Durham Universities, England

SELECT BIBLIOGRAPHY

Anouilh, Jean. *Five Plays Vol. 1.* New York: Hill & Wang, 1958.

Barthes, Roland. *On Racine,* trans. Richard Howard. New York: Hill & Wang, 1983.

Barker, Howard. *The Ecstatic Bible.* London: Oberon, 2004.

Barton, John. *Tantalus: Ten New Plays.* London: Oberon, 2001.

Burton, R.W. B. *The Chorus in Sophocles' Tragedies.* Oxford: Clarendon Press, 1980.

Bushnell, Rebecca W. *Prophesying Tragedy: A Sign and Voice in Sophocles' Theban Plays.* Ithaca, NY: Cornell University Press, 1988.

Cook, Elizabeth. *Achilles.* London: Methuen, 2001.

Crimp, Martin. *Cruel and Tender.* London: Faber & Faber, 2004.

Derrida, Jacques. *Archive Fever,* trans. Eric Prenowitz. Chicago & London: University of Chicago Press, 1995.

Easterling, Pat (ed.), *The Cambridge Companion to Greek Tragedy.* Cambridge: Cambridge University Press, 1987.

Euripides. *Iphigenia at Aulis,* trans. W.S. Merwin and George E. Dimock, Jr. New York: Oxford University Press, 1978.

Euripides. *Iphigenia at Aulis,* trans. Don Taylor. London: Methuen, 2004.

Euripides. *Medea and Other Plays,* trans. James Morwood. Oxford & New York: Oxford University Press,1997.

Euripides. *Orestes and Other Plays,* trans. Philip Vellacott. New York: Penguin, 1972.

Hughes, Ted. *Tales from Ovid.* London: Faber & Faber, 1997.

James, Vanessa. *The Genealogy of Greek Mythology.* New York: Melcher Media, 2003.

Kalb, Jonathan. *The Theater of Heiner Muller.* New York: Limelight, 2001.

Kane, Sarah. *Blasted & Phaedra's Love.* London: Methuen, 1996.

Kott, Jan. *The Eating of the Gods,* trans. Boleslaw Taborski and Edward J. Czerwinski. New York: Random House, 1970.

Laurens, Joanna. *The Three Birds (after Sophocles).* London: Oberon, 2000.

Maraini, Dacia. *Only Prostitutes Marry in May (Four Plays),* ed. Rhoda Helfman Kaufman. Canada: Guernica, 1994.

McLeish, Ken. *Orpheus.* London: Oberon, 1997.

Moraga, Cherrie. *The Hungry Woman (A Mexican Medea)*, in *Out of the Fringe: Contemporary Latino/a Theatre and Performance*, eds. Maria Teresa Marrero and Caridad Svich. New York: TCG, 2000.

Muller, Heiner. *A Heiner Muller Reader: Plays, Poetry and Prose*, trans. Carl Weber. New York: PAJ Books, 2003.

Racine, Jean. *Phaedra and other Plays*, trans. John Cairncross. Baltimore, MD: Penguin, 1963.

Rosenmeyer, Thomas G. *The Masks of Tragedy*. Austin: University of Texas Press, 1963.

Saunders, Graham. *'Love me or kill me': Sarah Kane and the theatre of extremes*. Manchester: Manchester University Press, 2002

Sierz, Aleks. *In-Yer-Face Theatre: British Drama Today*. London: Faber & Faber, 2001.

Maguire, Matthew. *The Tower*. Los Angeles: Sun & Moon Press, 1993.

Teevan, Colin. *Bacchai: After the Bacchai of Euripides*. London: Oberon, 2002.

Teevan, Colin. *Iph . . . .* London: Oberon, 2002.

Tuan, Alice. *Ajax (por nobody)*, in *Play: A Journal of Plays*, eds. Sally Oswald and Jordan Harrison. New York and Minneapolis, 2004.

Vickers, Brian. *Towards Greek Tragedy*. London: Longman, 1973.

Weiss, Allen S. *Breathless: Sound Recording, Disembodiment and The Transformation of Lyrical Nostalgia*. Middletown, CT: Wesleyan University Press, 2002.

Wilson, Edmund. *The Wound and the Bow*. Boston: Houghton Mifflin, 1941.

CONTACTS AND REPRESENTATIONS

Troy Women copyright © 1997 and 2004 by Karen Hartman.
  For performance rights and direct script enquiries, please contact:
  Karen Hartman
  c/o Bruce Ostler, Bret Adams, Ltd.
  448 West 44th St.
  New York, NY 10036
  (212) 765-5030
  E-mail: lit.bal@verizon.net

Philoktetes copyright © 1993 by John Jesurun, previously published in English by Yale School of Drama/Yale Repertory Theatre's *Theater* Magazine, Volume 25:2, 1994; in Spanish by Ediciones El Milagro/Mexico in Teatro Norteamericano Contemporaneo II, 2003 in a translation by John Jesurun, Erwin Veytia, Martín Acosta.
  Contact: John Jesurun c/o shatterhand1@earthlink.net

Phaedra copyright © 1995 by Matthew Maguire, previously published by Sun & Moon Press.
  Contact: Matthew Maguire
  c/o Clinton Fisher at Hanly & Conroy LLP
  415 Madison Avenue
  New York, NY 10017-1111
  (212) 401-7557

The Elektra Fugues copyright © 1996 by Ruth E. Margraff.
  Contact: Ruth Margraff
  c/o Morgan Jenness, Abrams Artists Associates
  275 Seventh Ave, 26th Fl.
  New York, NY 10001
  (646) 436-8600 x223
  or contact New Dramatists, (212) 757-6960

True Love was written in 2001 by Charles L. Mee.
  Contact: Charles L. Mee
  c/o Libby Edwards at ICM
  40 West 57th Street
  New York, NY 10019
  (212)556-5600
  E-mail: asst._kooij@icmtalent.com

NOTES

[1] Margo Jefferson, "Revisions: As Melville Told Marlene, the Muse Leads the Music," *The New York Times* (September 18, 2000).

[2] Peter Stein, "Interview," *In Contact with the Gods? Directors Talk Theatre*, eds. Maria Delgado and Paul Heritage (Manchester & New York: Manchester University Press, 1996), p. 245.

[3] Laura Mulvey, "Phantasmagoria" in Rosalind Krauss's *Cindy Sherman 1975–1993* (New York: Rizzoli International Publications, 1993), p. 143.

[4] Euripides, *Bacchai*, tr. Colin Teevan (London: Oberon Books, 2002).

[5] Teevan, Colin, *Iph . . .* (London: Oberon Books, 2002).

[6] If the action of *Bacchai* has any historical reality, it is around 1500 B.C., soon after the founding of Thebes, which is a thousand years before Euripides was writing.

Printed in the United States
109704LV00003B/42/A